NIETZSCHE,

"the Last
Antipolitical German"

PETER BERGMANN

NIETZSCHE,

"the Last

Antipolitical German"

INDIANA

UNIVERSITY

PRESS

Bloomington and Indianapolis

Library of Congress Cataloging-in-Publication Data
Bergmann, Peter, 1942–
    Nietzsche, "the last antipolitical German."
    Bibliography: p.
    Includes index.
    1. Nietzsche, Friedrich Wilhelm, 1844–1900.
2. Philosophers—Germany—Biography.   I. Title.
B3316.B45   1986   320'.01'0924   85-46031
ISBN 0-253-34061-6
1 2 3 4 5 90 89 88 87

To Hans Rosenberg

CONTENTS

ACKNOWLEDGMENTS

For having first stimulated my interest in the problems of the emergent German nation-state, I remain indebted to my teachers, Wolfgang Sauer and Hans Rosenberg. The latter introduced me to the study of the Bismarckian era as an undergraduate and actively shaped my graduate training. His incisive judgments and demanding standards remain a formidable model for me. This project germinated in the former's seminar on German cosmopolitanism, and his penetrating criticisms guided the work throughout its lengthy travail. I owe a special debt to Alice Freifeld who for several years put aside her own project to improve this one. I am thankful to William B. Slottman for his sympathetic and generous encouragement, and to Leo Lowenthal and Martin Jay for their critical reading of the manuscript.

The University of California at Berkeley generously awarded me fellowships to pursue this project at its inception, while an International Research Exchanges Board (IREX) grant made it possible to examine the Nietzsche papers in the Goethe-Schiller Archiv in Weimar. Richard Bergmann, Richard Gringeri, Jonathan Knudsen, and H. Jurgen Meyer-Wendt read versions along the way, offering suggestions and incentive. The manuscript also benefited from the rigorous scrutiny of Roberta Diehl, Janet Rabinowitch, and the press's anonymous reader, although, alas, the responsibility for any remaining errors or deficiencies is solely my own.

σοφια maxima

NIETZSCHE,
"the Last
Antipolitical German"

The Anti-Motif

IN HIS AUTOBIOGRAPHY of 1888 Nietzsche claimed to be "the last antipolitical German,"[1] thereby underscoring his antagonistic relation to the political. As he characterized his stance rarely, this ambiguous phrase is well known, and all agree that its ambiguity was consistent with his rhetorical strategy and intellectual purpose. But this is as far as either his accusers or defenders have gone; both have simply chosen to employ the term antipolitical as a terminus of inquiry.[2] For the apologists it has been a sign of his quietistic removal from politics, while for his accusers it has been an indication of his irrational destruction of politics. If there is to be an understanding of Nietzsche's relation to the events of the 1930s and 40s, explication of the term antipolitical must be a starting point of study, for it is the key to the present stalemate in Nietzsche criticism.

Walter Kaufmann, his major existentialist defender, saw "the leitmotif of Nietzsche's life and thought" as "the anti-political individual who seeks self-perfection far from the modern world."[3] But concurrent with this quietistic interpretation Kaufmann referred often to political conflicts between Nietzsche and Wagner, to Nietzsche's opposition to German Imperialism and anti-Semitism. Thus he implicitly demonstrated Nietzsche's involvement in the issues of his time. Unfortunately, this approach acknowledges only those aspects of Nietzsche's political life which appeal to the apologist's own values and politics. They fail to consider Nietzsche's politics as a whole, and thus never enter into real dialogue with the antifascists.

George Lichtheim, one of Nietzsche's most dismissive critics, linked the posthumous Nietzsche directly to the fascist course taken by the German nation-state. He declared: "It is not too much to say that but for Nietzsche the SS—Hitler's shock troops and the core of the whole movement—would have lacked the inspiration to carry out their programme of mass murder in

Eastern Europe."[4] But this very realization of Nietzsche's influence on the politics of subsequent generations seems to have incapacitated the antifascist critics. They have used history to judge Nietzsche's relation to the events of the Nazi era, but they do not seriously study Nietzsche's interaction with the political events of his own time. Lichtheim dismissed Nietzsche as a political thinker. He warned against "the investigation of a non-existent theme: Nietzsche's political thought."[5] Thus, his accusers have placed him outside his time, while his defenders have placed him above his time. It is important now to begin treating Nietzsche as a participant in his time—the four decades following 1848.

Nietzsche was not one to deny the responsibility of thinkers for subsequent events; he insisted on understanding Socrates in terms of the later collapse of Athens.[6] Nietzsche similarly bears some responsibility for the coming German catastrophe: in his twenties he not only witnessed but participated in the formation of the German nation-state; he then vigorously championed Wagnerian cultural nationalism, only to spend the later part of his career in grim speculation about the future of Europe. Nietzsche's relation to politics was subject to dramatic reversals. He espoused what can be called the "anti-motif," which eventually brought him into collision with the political realities of the Second Reich. To situate Nietzsche within his political environment is to grapple with this use of the anti-motif: how it governed his reactions to changing political events, precluded withdrawal, drew politics into his thought, and politicized his prose. The anti-motif provides the key to the understanding of Nietzsche's relation to politics and his ambiguous and charged legacy which proved to be a touchstone for the Left and Right.

Before the Renaissance the only words utilizing the anti-construction were antichrist, the adjective antichristian, and its analogue antipope. Antipolitical is a modern word. The term antipolitical emerged during the religious wars, when the Politiques defended the new notion of the secular commonwealth by labeling antipolitical all those who insisted on a theocratic conception of politics. Thomas Paine in the eighteenth century would denounce Edmund Burke's defense of church and state as "anti-political."[7] In the late nineteenth century the term was adopted by political scientists similarly seeking to protect the political from new threats to its autonomy.

In 1878 Julius Froebel attacked the Wagnerian movement (and thereby Nietzsche, its publicist) for interjecting "decidedly antipolitical" attitudes into the political arena.[8] By turning the opera into the new educational institution of the young, Froebel saw Wagner projecting the inner world of passions onto an external political stage, and doing so through an ultra-modern aesthetic linked to anti-modern political values. It was, he feared, ideological subversion, a depoliticized flight into aesthetic-religious intellectualism that could undermine the polity. In *Die Gesichtspunkt und Aufgabe der Politik* (The viewpoint and task of politics), he assessed the new "political religion" emanating from Bayreuth as the most serious challenge facing the German empire.[9] After the first Bayreuth festival in 1876, Nietzsche also came to oppose the Wagnerian movement. But although Nietzsche implicitly accepted much of Froebel's critique, he did not turn on the Wagnerians in the name of Froebel's conception of politics. Froebel's liberal notion of politics perceived the political as contained within a small sphere of life defined by a set of political institutions that were both vulnerable and in need of protection from encroachment by the passions of society. This positivist definition of politics as virtually synonymous with parliamentary activities and diplomatic relations was far too static and benign for Nietzsche. Froebel had dedicated his political science treatise to the "parties"; but to Nietzsche politicization seemed an aggressive force of modernization intent on subsuming all aspects of social life.

The liberal relation of state and culture which Matthew Arnold developed complemented that of the political scientist. Arnold posited "culture and anarchy" as the key dichotomy of modern life, and looked to the state as the protector of threatened cultural traditions from the effects of social chaos. "Culture," he argued, "is the most resolute enemy of anarchy, because of the great hopes and designs for the State which culture teaches us to nourish."[10] As a German, Nietzsche had a far more menacing image of the state than Arnold needed to have, and his conception of politicization foresaw the state's ability to absorb and manipulate the cultural life of the nation. So while for Arnold it was the political which was needed to redress the balance between culture and society, for Nietzsche politicization was the very thing to be opposed and resisted as a threat to culture.

Nietzsche attacked Wagner for compromising culture when he made his peace with the new Germany, the Bismarckian state. In Nietzsche's eyes, Wagner's great error lay in believing that culture and state could be reconciled, that increased political power might regenerate culture. Having earlier shared these hopes, Nietzsche's position was that of a renegade attacking previously held positions. In *Twilight of the Idols* he would write:

> Culture and state—one should not deceive oneself over this—are antagonists: the *Kulturstaat* is merely a modern idea. The one lives off the other, the one thrives at the expense of the other. All great cultural epochs are epochs of political decline: that which has been great in the cultural sense has been unpolitical, even *antipolitical*. . . .[11]

This polarity turned politics into a seductive force, a temptation which needed to be denounced in the harshest terms. It was "the prostitution of the spirit," a "fever," "necessarily dirty," a "sacrifice" of talent.[12] He repeatedly returned to his central theme: "the political growth of a nation almost necessarily entails an intellectual impoverishment," that "culture is indebted most of all to politically weakened periods."[13]

Nietzsche resisted politicization as an all-enveloping force which threatened to engulf both the religious and the cultural. In its previous usages the term antipolitical had been invoked in defense of the political, to ward off the encroaching religious sphere. Nietzsche was convinced that with politicization had come secularization and as a consequence the three "historical potencies" outlined by Burckhardt—state, religion, and culture[14]—were being reduced to a polarity between culture and state. It was in Nietzsche's time that the full implications of secularization were being realized. Now with the church only a shadow of its former importance, the cultural sphere was being subsumed too by the state—the secular state now truly appeared to be the unchecked Leviathan. Nietzsche reversed the Politique's use of the term antipolitical to isolate and confine the new danger, the secular state, in the name of culture.

Nietzsche would proclaim himself "antipolitical," embracing the very word Froebel had used against him a decade earlier, becoming, I believe, the first to give an affirmative meaning to the previously pejorative term. In reviving the rare term and posing the stark dichotomy, Nietzsche had launched a new cultural critique of the political. His attack on the political was rooted in resistance not in indifference; hence it is misleading to confuse the word "antipolitical" with "unpolitical," to mistakenly call Nietzsche the "last unpolitical German" as some have done.[15] Of all Nietzsche's contemporaries, Nietzsche's position most closely resembled that of the anarchists who have been called "anti-political and political."[16] The anarchists also conceived of a contest between culture and politics, and although they were moved to dismiss Nietzsche as "a slave to bourgeois prejudice," and he, in turn, to dismiss them "as the mouthpiece of *declining* strata of society," the tension in their thought was similar.[17]

Nietzsche's rejection of the political first took the form of constant jibes and asides that politicized his prose. His thought was dialectical, with conflict its central principle. Unlike the dialecticians of German Idealism, Nietzsche did not seek to harmonize but rather to deepen conflict.[18] The emphasis Hegel placed on synthesis as the instrument of progressive order was displaced in Nietzsche's thought by a concern for the creative energy of antithesis. In his philological studies Nietzsche concentrated on the agon (the contest): he explicated the fable of the poetic agon between Hesiod and Homer; deduced the agon to be the central principle in Hellenic life; and in *The Birth of Tragedy* placed the Dionysian and Apollonian principles in contest with each other. These two forces in conflict propelled creativity, he claimed, producing a flowering of culture. The fruits of the Dionysian-

Apollonian dialectic could be seen in Greek tragedy, where a kind of unity was achieved on the theater stage. Nietzsche later criticized his early treatment of the Dionysian-Apollonian conflict for reflecting an urge toward unity, toward synthesis, something which "smells offensively of Hegel."[19]

His combative style projected Nietzsche into the world of his contemporaries by pitting him against a series of self-selected antipodes: he called himself variously the Anti-Strauss, Anti-Darwin, Anti-Wagner, and Antichrist. Nietzsche propelled his thought by creating antagonists in his contemporary world. As Paul Valéry noted, the distinguishing feature of Nietzsche's prose was the "emphasis on others, on polemic."[20] But Nietzsche's problem was to be that he lacked a powerful contemporary opponent, and he would come to speak of his "spiritualization of enmity. It consists in profoundly grasping the value of having enemies; in brief, in acting and thinking in the reverse of the way in which one formerly acted and thought."[21] When he launched his career as "the Anti-Strauss," his initial polemic caused a minor sensation, but German intellectuals chose thereafter to give him a wide berth. They responded to his later works with silence. When he became disillusioned with Wagner, liberals noted this with satisfaction, but did not concern themselves further with his views, and joined the Wagnerians in dismissing him. It was only after a decade of isolation that Nietzsche again had a public to address. He would then call himself the "Anti-Wagner."[22] "It is so pleasant, so distinguishing, to possess one's own antipodes,"[23] Nietzsche would reflect at the end of his career.

While isolated, he withdrew into himself and was drawn into a quarrel with himself. "Under peaceful conditions," Nietzsche wrote, "the warlike man sets upon himself."[24] Nietzsche's works have appropriately been read as a lifelong effort to fashion an "anti-self," one that would free him from the claims of the initial self.[25] Existentialists, concentrating on the struggles of the self, embraced what they perceived as Nietzsche's flight from the political. Consequently they can define culture in Nietzsche as the form that politics takes when the realm of politics is the self.

Weber would have Nietzsche and Nietzscheanism in mind when he characterized the "carriers of special antipolitical religions" as those intellectuals who sought doctrines of philosophical salvation rather than political influence.[26] While Buddhism with its "intellectualist attitude that was utterly antipolitical, pacifistic, and world-rejecting" had created a world religion, Weber believed the contemporary attempts of Tolstoy, Nietzsche and their followers to be a futile anachronism. He thought such antipolitical philosophies were produced and propagated by those "who had lost interest in politics, who were without influence in politics, or who had become disgusted by politics."[27] More recently Sheldon Wolin, in his history of political theory, analyzes the general nineteenth century intellectual "attack on the political" as the manifestation of a triumphant antipoliticism.[28] So pervasive was the call for the abolition of the political that it spanned the political spectrum and was as marked in Marx as in Durkheim or Nietzsche; "At bottom the century desperately sought to transcend the political."[29] The resulting decline of political philosophy, Wolin concludes, ill-prepared theorists for the new organizational settings of politics in the twentieth century. Thus Wolin sees the "last ditch efforts" of Kierkegaard, Nietzsche, and Sorel "to secure some place for unorganized individual action" to be "the last gasps of a romanticism doomed to expire before the age of streamlined organizations and rationally efficient bureaucracies."[30]

Unlike Kierkegaard, who remained antipolitical in the initial meaning of the term, i.e., disputing the secular, Nietzsche introduced an activistic and mythic element to his rejection of the political; but he never went as far as Sorel, who sought to organize and mobilize the political vanguard through a collective myth. Nietzsche stood between: a politicized figure—no longer apolitical, but not yet a political man. Nietzsche's solitary Superman was still individualistic but posed as a collective goal. It reflected his desire to find affirmations in his negations, a "yes" in his "no." The anti-motif was thus sometimes linked with a rhetoric of heightening, of overcoming (*überwinden*) which counterbalanced to some degree the language of negation, but joined with it in intensifying Nietzsche's prose. His anti-motif was in this way complemented by another rhetorical strategy, one utilizing the prefix *über* with its connotations of above, supra- and super- as in super-species (*Über-Art*), superman or superhuman (*Übermensch*) and supra-historical (*Überhistorisch*). The *über*-motif elevated the conflict of the genius against the Philistine into a struggle of the *Übermensch* with the ultimate mass man, *"der letzte Mensch."* In other places the two motifs were linked, as when he sought to promote the "supra-German" by writing books which he termed "anti-German."[31] But even when Nietzsche toyed with an evolutionary metaphysic he continued to assert the primacy of the anti-motif in a doctrine of eternal recurrence, one which postulated the perpetual·return to the same set of conflicts and antagonisms. He would argue, "with every growth of man his other side must grow too; that the highest man, if such a concept be allowed, would be the man who represented the antithetical character of existence most strongly, as its glory and justification."[32]

In his final months of sanity, Nietzsche would cast himself as the "last" German to resist politicization and the "first" to prophesy the coming age of *grosse Politik*. He warned of the cultural penalties of a country pursuing the illusion of *grosse Politik* in 1878.[33] In 1881 *grosse Politik* became the dangerous mobilization of the masses behind imperialist policies,[34] and by 1884 Nietzsche had internalized *grosse Politik*. It had become his "bird's-eye view" of European politics.[35] In his final year, the traumatic *Drei-Kaiser-Jahr* of 1888, *grosse Politik* interjected itself into the prophetic revelation of himself as a "man of calamity."[36] "It is only with me that the world knows *grosse Politik*," Nietzsche would proclaim. [37]

After years of obscurity and neglect, Nietzsche correctly sensed that he was soon to be discovered by the international avant-garde. This last period was marked by feverish activity; he wrote four books in four months. He defiantly courted the charge of *lèse majesté*, determined to create a literary scandal in *The Case of Wagner*, and to rally a counter-movement to Bayreuth in *Nietzsche Contra Wagner*. In its preface he warned the Italians not to make a misalliance with the Reich.

Sensing that his time was running out, he no longer was content in being the witness; Nietzsche craved and claimed real influence—to wield an ultimate veto, one held by the philosopher over his age. In his second and only other use of the term, Nietzsche embraced the activistic meaning of antipolitical. In *Ecce Homo* he wrote:

> Even by virtue of my descent I am granted an eye beyond all merely local, merely national conditioned perspectives; it is not difficult for me to be a "good European." On the other hand, I am perhaps more German than present day Germans, mere citizens of the German Reich could possibly be—I, the last *antipolitical* German. And yet my ancestors were Polish noblemen: I have many racial instincts from this source—who knows? In the end perhaps even the *liberum veto*.[38]

By December the line between political polemics and incipient megalomania was blurred. He sought to exercise a veto as if in the Polish Diet by declaring: "I disapprove." He pronounced "war to the Death against the House of Hohenzollern."[39] He issued epistles for the Polish nation to rise, a war council against the Reich, and execution of anti-Semites. His madness took political form.

The pathological conclusion of Nietzsche's antipolitics did nothing to impede his growing popularity. In adopting Nietzsche's new antipolitical style, the European avant-garde of the turn of the century would discover that Nietzsche's manner of saying no to the political could either be a formula of protest or defeat. The apolitical and the hyper-political could meet in Nietzsche's stance, with the result that the first Nietzscheans typically oscillated between moods of impassioned engagement and disdainful indifference. Nietzscheanism could produce either counter-statements and counter-strategies aimed at overturning the existing polity or it could lead out of the political. Helmut Kreuzer concluded in his study of the *Boheme* that it was precisely the "anarchist- and/or Nietzschean-influenced intellectuals" who repudiated the political while remaining actively involved in politics.[40] Nietzsche's antipolitics would consequently not only be open to activistic and quietistic interpretations but would also inspire extreme positions on the left and right. The *Aktivismus* of the Left Nietzscheans during World War I would be followed by the *Decisionismus* of the Right Nietzscheans during the crisis of the Weimar Republic.[41] The political history of Nietzscheanism in Germany exposes the contradictory and volatile features of Nietzsche's antipolitical stance.

Thus the attempt to understand Nietzsche through Nietzscheanism only leads one back to the contradictions apparent in Nietzsche's political biography. It is in relation to his times that his antipolitics must be studied to be understood. Nietzsche sought to be "untimely" by writing against his age, not outside his age. In the 1880 aphorism, "Auch den Gegensatz zu schmecken wissen" ("On also having a taste for the opposite"), Nietzsche gives a hint of how his relation to contemporary politics might be studied:

—Um ein Werk der Vergangenheit so zu geniessen, wie es seine Zeitgenossen empfanden, muss man den damals herrschende Geschmack, gegen den es sich *abhob* auf der Zunge haben.

—In order to enjoy a work of the past as its contemporaries experienced it, one must have the ruling taste against which it contrasted itself on one's tongue.[42]

CHAPTER TWO

The Clerical Son

NIETZSCHE WAS BORN an insider. As a clerical son from Luther's native region, as a grandnephew of Herder's clerical successor, as a Prussian from Prussianized Saxon Thuringia, he was expected to infuse in himself the values of Wittenberg, Weimar, and Potsdam, to integrate religion, culture, and politics into one. He was a particularly dutiful boy, fully participating in his family's Pietist religiosity and sharing in their enthusiasm for the Prussian royal house. It was this initial acceptance, this complete inculcation into the provincial world of the mid-century small town that would charge his later critique, and it was to be in revolt against the religious antipolitics of his youth that Nietzsche would come to define his own version of antipolitics.

His father, Pastor Karl Ludwig Nietzsche (1813–1849), delivered sermons with much emotion in the spirit of his theological mentor, Tholuck, who had believed that it was necessary "to descend into the deep horrors of one's own breast" for "we are truly all very evil."[1] Although his clerical supervisor may have thought Ludwig's pathos "a little too much," he still amply praised Ludwig as an "amiable man" and as "a talented teacher and preacher," "dedicated to his office."[2] Ludwig's style of preaching was entirely in keeping with that of the neo-Pietist "Awakening" to which he attached himself while studying at the Prussian university in Halle.

This Romantic movement, with its emotional commitment to the rejuvenation of the Evangelical church, also implied a political allegiance. Since the late 1820s the then Crown Prince Friedrich Wilhelm had personally supervised the recruitment of a Prussian Pietist clergy that could form one Evangelical state church, uniting Prussian Lutherans and Calvinists. Since Pietism was a religious movement motivated by no vital theological doctrine, but rather by the simple desire to reanimate Christian life, neo-Pietism could establish itself as the cement of the church union in the post-Napoleonic era. In the universities and in the countryside, Pietist theologians and country parsons became the vigilant censors of thought and behavior. Ludwig enthusiastically greeted Friedrich Wilhem IV's accession and his proclamation of the Christian state. Since he came from the only recently Prussianized province of Saxony, Ludwig's acceptance had in it the zeal of a convert. Among Prussia's six thousand Protestant clergymen, Ludwig would be one of the king's most ardent supporters, always believing in the bond between religion and politics.[3]

The great event in Ludwig's life was his meeting with Friedrich Wilhelm IV at the Thuringian court of Altenburg where Ludwig was tutoring the three princesses. Impressed by the young pastor, the king subsequently interceded on Ludwig's behalf, granting him a rural pastorate in the Saale river valley. From that point onward the family cherished the belief that Ludwig had an important career ahead of him and that eventually he might even become the court preacher in Berlin. Filled with optimism, Ludwig married and settled into his new post at the parsonage of Röcken with his bride, Franziska Oehler (1826–1897), his widowed mother, and two unmarried sisters. The young wife of only seventeen had to come to terms with his urbane mother and a "nervous," intellectual sister-in-law, Rosalie.[4] Franziska was a simpler rural type, daughter of a prosperous Saxon country pastor. As the sixth of eleven children, she had received only a minimal education, with but a dash of table-talk French. Franziska had been attracted to the studied manners, elegant attire, and earnest piety of the promising young pastor, while Ludwig found in her an admiring, attractive companion. They fully shared each other's pietistic enthusiasm. Franziska's strict, simple piety would remain undisturbed throughout her life, with her letters of the 1890s still breathing the emotive and by then anachronistic Pietist language of mid-century. Religion would always remain her central concern. She never developed either an interest in politics or indeed in anything outside her provincial, clerical milieu. Years later one of Nietzsche's friends characterized her as having a "harmless bird-like nature (*Vogelnatur*)."[5]

Franziska conformed to the traditional attitude of eighteenth century Pietists, the *Stillen im Lande*, whose religiosity was private and personal. Pietism, originally a quietistic response to the failure of militant, theocratic Protestantism in the seventeenth century, differed from Puritanism in its submissive stance toward political authority. It sought instead to create a popularly based Christian culture through missionary zeal, active philanthropy, and a lively pious literature, sharing with Quakerism an ethic of simplicity and with Methodism a revivalist eloquence. Within Pietist circles, the community of believers practiced a highly personalized, verbal religiosity.[6]

While Pietism fostered a kind of mystical separatism, the Pietist emphasis on awakening and conscience also engendered a missionary, quasi-chiliastic zeal. Alternately condemning the world and seeking to reform it, Pietists judged political, social, and economic developments in terms of good and evil. The rebirth of the individual was often followed by an effort to effect the rebirth of the national society. Thus although Pietism had lost the austere militancy and revolutionary impulse of the radical Reformation, it could retain a popular and reformist outlook, and it did so particularly in the German southwest and the Calvinist regions of the Rhine. But the very elasticity of the movement also permitted it to ally itself with absolutist tendencies as in Prussianized northern Thuringia where the Nietzsche family lived. Here the alliance between Pietism and the Calvinist house of Hohenzollern would blend statist and populist elements.[7]

By mobilizing religion Friedrich Wilhelm IV hoped to revitalize the bureaucratic absolutism he had inherited. His chief confidant, Ludwig von Gerlach, proclaimed, "We must give our consciousness of God a political form."[8] Religious politics was enjoying a final ascendancy. Throughout the 1840s religious debate and controversy became a substitute political forum. One of Metternich's aides observed that "religion is once again and will in the immediate future be even more the axis around which the world and its politics will revolve."[9] Ludwig was able to make the leap in this period from a quietistic to a politically attuned religiosity. He identified both his religious values and his own welfare with the ascendancy of the Hohenzollern monarch. A passionate supporter of the pious king, he was obviously moved by the coincidence of birth, October 15, 1844, which connected his first born to that of his king, and happily linked the identity of his son with that of his benefactor. "My son, Friedrich Wilhelm, so are you to be named on earth, in memory of my royal benefactor, on whose birthday you were born," Ludwig wrote in his emotional statement on Nietzsche's baptismal certificate.[10]

On both the left and the right the distinction between the religious and political spheres had become blurred. As Pietists identified the preservation of religion with the preservation of the monarchy, the radical intellectual opposition saw in atheism and the Hegelian inspired historical-critical method a means of undermining the existing order. Leading the opposition was a group of young Pietist renegades (e.g., David Friedrich Strauss, Bruno Bauer, and Friedrich Engels) who rallied to Ludwig Feuerbach's cry: "Politics must become our religion."[11]

The revolution of 1848 would bring this era of religious politics to an abrupt end. Nietzsche's earliest recorded memories were of peasants near his village celebrating the outbreak of the revolution with red flags.[12] The revolution had come as a profound shock to Ludwig Nietzsche. "The events of 1848 grieved him beyond all measure," his son would recall.[13] When

Ludwig read that his royal benefactor had sported the revolutionary cockade before the Berlin crowds, he abruptly left the room to weep in his study.[14] Never again would the Hohenzollern dynasty seek legitimacy in religious terms. The Protestant churches, it seemed, had lost their institutional hold over the populace, and in its stead the army had to secure monarchic authority.

The despair felt by Ludwig Nietzsche at the outbreak of the revolution was at its conclusion also shared by the radical literati. The revolutionaries proved equally incapable of marshaling the masses behind a coherent political program. The outcome of the revolution would discredit both the clerical and the radical intellectuals, for both had failed, canceling out each other's positions. Neither the revivalists nor the revolutionary idealism of the 1840s would carry over into the post-revolutionary period, leaving Nietzsche's age group to enter history as undertakers disposing of a parental legacy. Nietzsche's short-hand formula for this was "1830 into 1850," i.e., the transformation of the Romantic hopes of the July Revolution into the bleak pessimism of revolutionary defeat.[15]

Nietzsche would recall the revolution as one would a great natural disaster, intertwined with traumatic personal loss. While the revolution triumphed and failed, his father became ill and died, apparently deranged, on July 30, 1849. In his autobiography, Nietzsche would describe his father as "delicate, kind, and morbid, a being that is destined merely to pass by."[16] Six months later another family tragedy compounded the pain. Nietzsche dreamt he heard funeral music, and then:

> Suddenly a grave opened and my father arose out of it in funeral attire. He hurried into the church returning shortly with a child in his arms. The coffin opened, he entered, and its lid closed again. At that moment the organ music ceased, and I awoke.—The following day, little Joseph [Nietzsche's one-year old brother] suddenly became ill, was seized with cramps, and died within a few hours. Our sorrow was enormous. My dream had been completely fulfilled. The small corpse was then placed in the arms of the father.[17]

The father's and baby's deaths left the family disoriented. "Suddenly fear and tension displaced the golden joyous peace of familial happiness," he would write.[18] The death of her husband was a blow from which Franziska never really recovered. Although only twenty-three and attractive, she would never remarry, living out her life in the dark attire of a widowed Frau Pastor, making due with a most meager clerical pension. She accentuated the household's already reverential tone toward the dead Ludwig, and Nietzsche followed suit, cultivating an unusually pious remembrance of his father: "the complete picture of the rural cleric. Gifted with all the virtues of the Christian, he lived the peaceful, simple life and was admired and loved by all who knew him."[19] In turn, the mother and grandmother transferred many of the hopes placed in the father onto the son.

Grandmother Erdmuthe Nietzsche (1778–1856), and Aunts Rosalie and Auguste moved to the nearby town of Naumburg; Franziska and her two remaining children followed. Nietzsche now felt himself "without father, without home."[20] From the alley behind his new house Nietzsche sometimes thought he heard his father's ghost call warningly to him.[21] Nietzsche, his sister Elisabeth, and his mother would occupy the cramped back quarters of his grandmother's residence for the next six years. In this trying setting the grandmother dominated the household. Franziska generally acceded to the wishes of the older woman, even when Franziska's rustic Pietism was at odds with the older woman's rationalist orthodoxy. In later life Nietzsche would undoubtedly have Erdmuthe in mind when he stressed the role of grandparents in molding personality, reasoning that parents were not yet formed at the time of their children's birth.

The move back to Naumburg after her son's death was a natural one for the seventy-two-year-old Erdmuthe. She had first gone to Naumburg as a young woman to run the household of her brother, then cathedral preacher. Naumburg became her touchstone in adult life. In her first marriage, to Kotzebue's cousin, Erdmuthe was a fringe member of Weimar's cultural life, but she returned to Naumburg after the death of her husband and only child. It was also in Naumburg that she met her second husband, Friedrich August Ludwig Nietzsche, the *Superintendent* (Presiding Minister) of the nearby town of Eilenburg.[22] Two of her seven stepchildren lived in Naumburg, and she maintained some of the associations she had made there, particularly to the widowed Frau Privy Councillor Pinder, the matriarch of one of Naumburg's leading families. Naumburg was also an especially suitable place for widows of clergymen. Pensioners formed a sizable subculture within the clerical and the legal bureaucracy, the two dominant communities in this town of about 13,500. But for Nietzsche, sister, and mother, coming to the nearby town required a massive readjustment. "After living so long in the country, it was terrible to live in the town," Nietzsche wrote; "we avoided the dusty streets and sought the open air as a bird seeks to flee his cage. . . . After the quiet village where everyone knew everybody else, I was amazed to discover that the people often did not even know each other."[23]

Naumburg had become one of the three new Prussian judicial centers in the province. This new legal community came to dominate the town, with Ludwig von Gerlach, the ideologue of the "Christian state," setting the town's conservative, religious tone in the 1820s.[24] An undercurrent of opposition would come to the fore in the late 1840s. The Naumburg town council defied the king in 1846. In 1848 Naumburg briefly became a revolutionary center in the province. On March 24 a large revolutionary festival was held in which the revolutionary colors were displayed, Friedrich Ludwig Jahn, "the father of gymnastics," greeted the throng with tears in his eyes, and Frau Pinder's son delivered the commemorative speech honoring the martyrs of the March barricades. Eight new newspapers suddenly appeared and demands were made for the complete secularization of cathedral property. The electorate sent a radical young lawyer to the Frankfurt Parliament where he joined the extreme anti-Prussian left. Naumburg's revolutionary mood lasted until September when a sharpshooter's festival led to a violent anti-Prussian demonstration. But order was restored by Prussian troops, and after twenty-six arrests and one execution the six-month flirtation with revolution ended and Naumburg retreated into lethargy. By the time the Nietzsche family settled there in 1850 all traces of revolutionary sentiment had disappeared.[25]

Chastened and humbled, Naumburg had reverted back to the compliant conservatism of a town that had irrevocably lost its political role.[26] Frau Pinder's son now concerned himself with beautifying the city and furthering Pietist missionary activites. Indeed the only function Naumburg seemed to have in this period was as a stronghold of the Pietist missionary organization, the Gustav Adolphus Society, and as the site of an annual Bible festival. While such a climate of torpor was endemic to the German provincial towns in the aftermath of revolutionary defeat, the stagnation was particularly acute in Naumburg. It had ceased to grow. Between 1846 and 1855 the population rose by eight, six of whom can be accounted for by the arrival of the Nietzsche family. Dwarfed by Leipzig thirty miles to the southeast, an increasingly conservative Naumburg was also losing ground in its own electoral district to the industrializing towns of Weissenfels and Zeitz. Naumburg had become a quaint walled town, with its five gates still closing nightly between ten and dawn during Nietzsche's childhood. The townscape remained visually defined by the four sixteenth and seventeenth century Lutheran churches flanking the great twelfth century cathedral, the most eastern Romanesque structure built in Europe. The annual Cherry Festival captured the stagnant town's attempt to emphasize tradition and medieval glory. The absent crowd reappeared in a ritual reenactment of the appeasement of the Hussite army of 1432. Naumburg would be rediscovered in Nietzsche's lifetime as a tourist attraction of a sentimental cultural Protestantism.[27]

Naumburg had played a leading role in the Reformation. The burghers of the medieval bishopric broke with its clerical authorities at the outbreak of the Reformation. They were soon disappointed, however, to find that they had exchanged nominal clerical rule for princely rule by the new Saxon territorial state. An attempt to institute a more radical Reformation in 1587 failed and the citizenry was disarmed. The crucial battle of the Thirty Years War was fought within the pastorate of Ludwig Nietzsche, and Nietzsche would write a Scandinavian critic: "I was born . . . on the battlefield of Lützen. The first name I heard was Gustav Adolphus."[28] The Naumburg funeral of Gustav Adolphus ceremoniously ended the dream that Protestant armies might undo the Counter-Reformation, and the city seemed to memorialize this moment in time by retaining its seventeenth century façade and by never outgrowing the dimensions of that world. Already by the late sixteenth century Leipzig had siphoned off the once vibrant economic position of Naumburg, while cultural life gravitated toward the capital city of Dresden. Naumburg remained simply a pietistic religious center, but even here she was overshadowed by the nearby Prussian university town of Halle which became the intellectual center of the Pietist movement.[29]

Naumburg thus blended in with the other closely knit Saxon-Thuringian towns where German town life and German high culture were most highly developed. Saxony-Thuringia, Nietzsche would later write, was the country's "most dangerous region" for "here, for good or ill, one is dealing with Germany's intellectual drill sergeants and their mentors."[30] Luther had taught in Wittenberg, while Bach, Schütz, Buxtehude, and Handel had emerged from this region, giving it the reputation as the nurturing ground of German music.[31] And in the eighteenth century nearby Weimar would become the crucial center of German "classical" culture. The close proximity of such administrative and religious centers as Merseburg and Naumburg to the court towns of Weimar, Coburg, Altenburg, and Meinigen, as well as to the university towns of Jena, Halle, Erfurt, and Wittenberg had encouraged an elevated cultural level. A lively exchange existed between the residents of Naumburg and the other towns of the region, particularly Weimar. Erdmuthe was an example, marrying a Weimar lawyer, and her brother went from Naumburg to Weimar, succeeding Herder in the post of *Generalsuperintendent*.

Weimar high culture displayed an unusual integration of the religious and the secular. Herder, the critic, could also be court preacher; Goethe, the writer, could also be a state official, and both could coexist, each stimulating the other. It was in Weimar that for the first time in almost two hundred years secular literature sought to attain and surpass the high level previously maintained by the clergy. The French revolution stripped culture more definitely of its religious component, the intelligentsia became increasingly hostile to religion, and the clergy within the intelligentsia were driven further into a defensive posture. Nietzsche's grandfather, Superintendent Nietzsche, gained a certain reputation in this period as an author of theological tracts denouncing the irreligion emanating from Paris.[32] Similarly the conservative Kotzebue, after attending Erdmuthe's first wedding in Naumburg, used the town as the setting for his historical drama *Die Hussiten vor Naumburg im Jahre 1432* (1803), with its foreboding message of an imminent struggle with foreign invaders. The new heresy was not only a threat to religious sentiments, but to the very existence of traditional German town culture, he warned. Naumburg was indeed overwhelmed and overtaken by Napoleon's armies in 1805. The decisive battle for Germany was decided at nearby Jena. Erdmuthe suffered great personal loss as well, for her husband and child both died from disease that followed the battle.

Despite all this Erdmuthe entertained Nietzsche with stories of Napoleon and the Napoleonic era, and Nietzsche remembered her "as a Saxon" to be "a great admirer of Napoleon."[33] The new Saxon alliance with Napoleon was generally popular throughout the region with Privy Councillor Pinder negotiating Naumburg's surrender and welcoming Napoleon into his home. The area had long been exposed to Prussian incursions from the north, while under the Napoleonic system it served as a vital strategic link connecting the new kingdoms of Westphalia and Saxony, boxing a hostile Prussia onto the Baltic littoral.

After Napoleon's defeat Prussia had desired the complete annexation of Saxony, but Metternich, fearful of a powerful east German state on his borders, deflected the annexations to the Rhineland, conceding only Nietzsche's province of Saxony. Like most of the inhabitants, Nietzsche's paternal grandparents disliked the annexation. But in contrast to the Catholic Rhineland, the Prussianization of the province proceeded smoothly with its young generally developing loyalties to the new state. Ludwig Nietzsche's fervent commitment to the Prussian king was one striking example. Nevertheless a certain detachment toward Prussia did linger even into the second and third generations.[34]

The one famous institution in the vicinity was the royal academy of Schulpforta, housed in the twelfth century Cistercian monastery of St. Mary's Pforta, where Naumburg's clerical rulers had once lived. Founded in 1543, Schulpforta had become the most celebrated of the Saxon Latin schools, with Klopstock, Fichte, and Ranke among its graduates. After Prussianization Schulpforta retained its eminence and became a showcase of the Prussian educational ideal. Naumburg was allotted one scholarship to Pforta. Nietzsche would be told, "If you work hard it will not be long before you are an alumnus of Pforta, then a student, then a candidate, and finally a Herr Pastor."[35]

But believing that Nietzsche should first mix with boys of other social classes, Erdmuthe enrolled Nietzsche in the local grammar school, where he acquired the apt nickname of "little pastor." Nietzsche, his family, and schoolmates simply assumed that Nietzsche would follow in his father's footsteps. Nietzsche was accordingly super-correct. "As a child I never stole fruit from the surrounding orchards, as a man I never crossed an open field—I worshiped property to a ludicrous degree."[36] The children at the grammar school teased him for his seriousness, and Nietzsche for his part found this mingling with the other social classes unnerving. "I had seen much sorrow and grief in my young life and therefore was not as merry and wild as children tend to be," he recalled as an adolescent.[37]

After one year Erdmuthe pulled him out of the grammar school, arranging instead for a tutorial with two other boys, Wilhelm Pinder (1844–1928) and Gustav Krug (1843–1902), the grandsons of Erdmuthe's close friend, the widowed Frau Privy Councillor Pinder. Frau Pinder lived with her daughter's family, the Krugs, in a patrician home on the market square. Frederick the Great and Napoleon had both stayed in this green house standing directly across from the Renaissance city hall. It was here that Nietzsche was first introduced to music, the great passion of Gustav Krug's conservative father, an important musical patron in the town and a friend of Mendelssohn. His son Gustav, a robust child, became Nietzsche's enthusiastic guide to the "music of the future" heralded by Liszt and Wagner, while Wilhelm Pinder, a more delicate, withdrawn boy, shared Nietzsche's discovery of Goethe and the other luminaries of Weimar culture. Pinder's father sparked their enthusiasm and especially enjoyed staging family theatricals with the children.

For three years the boys were tutored privately by a theological candidate and under his relaxed genial supervision they became fast friends. All three boys were similarly well behaved, good students and preparing for professional careers—Pinder and Krug for law and Nietzsche for the church. "Fritz remains true to his purpose of becoming a cleric," Franziska could proudly write her brother Ernst in 1856. He "is setting psalms to music and also writing little theater pieces."[38] Nietzsche's unusual literary gifts, early evident to his friends and teachers, seemed particularly in keeping with his calling; the patricians like the Pinders strove to be cultivated, but it was the clergy that was expected to actively mold and promote culture.

As Nietzsche would later explain it, the preacher alone had kept alive the standard for public discourse, he "alone had a conscience in his ear," and so he would conclude, "the masterpiece of German prose is therefore fairly enough the masterpiece of its greatest preacher; the Bible has so far been the best German book."[39] With Luther as the model, the parsonage became the nursery school of German culture, providing one-fourth of all significant German poets between 1525 and 1900.[40] In lieu of an aristocratic culture writing in German, the Protestant clergy had assumed the guardianship of the vernacular. As Nietzsche would understand it, since "[North]

German culture originated not with a nobility as did the French, but with teachers [professors, organists, etc.] and preachers," submission to authority was coupled to a mental reservation, to the assumption that there remained "something higher" than the sovereign—one could always "take revenge in ideas."[41]

The boys moved from their private tutorial to the cathedral school during the Crimean war. From 1854 until its conclusion two years later, Pinder, Krug, and Nietzsche followed every detail of the war, feeding each other's fascination. Nietzsche immersed himself in military textbooks, compiled a little military dictionary, and even created a game of chance—the roll of the dice could determine, for example, whether Napoleon III would die or withdraw the following year. When Sebastopol fell, the three boys, having taken a pro-Russian position, were terribly disappointed.[42]

Nietzsche also tried to amuse himself and his sister by latching onto a family legend of an aristocratic Polish forebear, a "von Nietzky," who had supposedly fled the Counter-Reformation as a pro-Saxon, Protestant conspirator. The Nietzsche family name, however, was in all likelihood a medieval derivative of Nicholas. Both sides of his family had lived for centuries as artisans in the area of Saxony adjoining Thuringia, and the most significant members of the Nietzsche family were the most recent, revolving around Erdmuthe, her marriages, and her brother. Nietzsche and his sister preferred their conjured romantic version.[43]

In these years Nietzsche's most important identification was with his regal namesake, Friedrich Wilhelm IV. He loved the fact that his birthday was not only a family festivity but also included a military band display in the morning and a special celebration at the cathedral school in the afternoon. Family and friends fostered the connection. In regular birthday letters an older friend of his late father, Pastor Osswald, urged the boy "with the king's name and the king's birthday" to become "as pious and good a Christian as our dear king."[44] And on his birthday Nietzsche made it a habit to pretend that what was said of the king in the special church service that day was applicable to himself.[45] He signed his name Friedrich Wilhelm and waited three hours in the rain to see the *Landesvater* visit Naumburg in 1856— hence the traumatic effect of the news of the king's mental collapse in 1857 He was acutely aware of the embarrassment felt by the populace on his thirteenth birthday. It was a sad day. Aunt Rosalie set the tone by solemnly toasting the king's and Nietzsche's health. What had been an untroubled day of mutual celebration would now become a subdued day centering on "the illness of our dear king."[46]

Nietzsche entered Schulpforta the day before Friedrich Wilhelm IV fell from power. No newspapers were allowed within the walls, thus once he entered Pforta he found himself cut off from everyday politics. News of the proclamation of the regency on October 7, 1858, reached him only as a rumor. He wrote home for further information. On the 9th Nietzsche sadly reported home that observance of the king's birthday had been canceled at the school. While in his Pietist home the king's madness seemed a blow to the ideal of the "Christian state," within Prussia the fall of Friedrich Wilhelm IV was widely heralded as the beginning of a "New Era," allowing stifled discontent to rise freely to the surface.[47] There was a sense of liberation in the universities and Gymnasiums, such as Schulpforta, which had felt the brunt of post-revolutionary reaction.

Schulpforta's Rector and guiding spirit, Carl Peter, supported the revival of liberalism. He embraced the combined ideal of *Bildung* and cultural nationalism as formulated by Herder. Herder's classic definition of *Bildung*—a personalized striving for inner growth, a secularized form of grace—adapted the English Augustan notion of "self-breeding" and brought to the secular many of the essential thrusts of Pietism. After being trained as a Pietist theologian, Peter had himself turned to the study of ancient history and as an educator promoted the study of the classics within a historical context, believing in what he called "historical *Bildung*." The word *Bildung* by this time had acquired a much extended significance. In its social meaning the cultivated, the *Gebildeten*, were distinguished from the *Ungebildeten*, the uneducated and uncultivated. Peter concurred with the widely accepted belief that a self-perpetuating *Bildungsbürgertum*, comprised of those who had acquired certain educational qualifications, was qualified and destined to lead the nation.[48]

Nietzsche's teachers were "classical liberals" in its double meaning: they identified themselves with the traditions of Weimar classicism and also epitomized mid-century Prussian liberalism. Their views were shaped by such influential journals as the *Preussische Jahrbücher* and the *Grenzboten* in which such literary and academic notables as David Friedrich Strauss, the critic Rudolf Haym, and the novelist Gustav Freytag pamphleteered for a constitutional regime in Germany under Prussian auspices.[49]

The Gymnasium seemed in these years to provide the model for European education, and Matthew Arnold during his educational tour of German schools would be especially charmed by Schulpforta. Schulpforta seemed an ideal Gymnasium. "No school in Prussia, or indeed Germany," he wrote, "can compare with Schulpforta, which by its antiquity, its beauty, its wealth, its celebrity, is entitled to vie with the most renowned English schools."[50] He praised the strenuous classical training, the Latin grace sung at dinner, and the weekly day set aside for private study. He was taken by the setting: the spacious gardens, the large athletic field, the proximity of the Saale river, and "by the pleasant country of Prussian Saxony," but most especially by "the venerable pile of buildings rising among its meadows, hills and woods."[51]

The motto borne on the arms of the old abbey read, "This is none other than the house of God, and this is the gate!" It was only after passing through the gate in silent prayer that "a deep peace came over me," Nietzsche would write Pinder of his arrival.[52] No longer the promising small-town boy seemingly destined to enter the intellectual elite, Nietzsche now was one of the some 150 scholarship boys in an elite student body of 200. When he first approached the cloistered walls of Schulpforta, he feared he was entering a "prison."[53] The "military-like coercion" practiced in the school would indeed require a massive readjustment.[54]

Like his friend, classmate, and fellow clerical son, Paul Deussen (1844–1919), Nietzsche was unprepared for the disciplined life. But Deussen, a Rhinelander, was somewhat able to maintain a detachment toward what he considered Prussian customs, at least better than Nietzsche who had grown up in the shadow of the school. Nietzsche came to accept "the uniform discipline of a structured school" that provided a "surrogate paternal education" as a corrective to his previous upbringing. Lacking a father, he had been deprived "of the strict and superior guidance of a male intellect."[55] The school prided itself in being, in the words of the 1843 Rector, "an enclosed school-state subsuming all aspects of the individual."[56] Despite the infusion of liberal faculty and a move toward a liberal-nationalist political tone since the appointment of Peter as Rector in 1856, the school routine continued to adhere to the old traditions. The school day began at dawn with prayer, followed by more prayer in the Gothic chapel, then classes from eight to four with a two-hour lunch break, and finally two hours of study in the evening.

The school year ended with carnival festivity and graduation pageantry "of which Naumburg could have no conception," Nietzsche boasted.[57] At the graduation ceremony that spring Peter gave a solemn speech in which he made warning allusions to imminent war. News of French and Piedmontese armies battling the Austrians would greatly excite German national feeling. Even the future socialist leader, August Bebel, tried to leave his apprenticeship to volunteer on Austria's behalf. Nietzsche was as caught up in the excitement as anyone. He wrote his mother for more news "about the latest political events," saying, "I am so very curious and would like so much to hear something about it."[58] And his mother, after visiting the annual school festival in May, wrote her family that the boys marched about in formation, just as in a "military academy."[59] When the Habsburg armies suffered decisive defeats in June, Schulpforta's graduating class was ordered to Naumburg to await induction in the expected war on the Rhine.

When news of the armistice came during the summer vacation, Nietzsche reacted negatively; "There was no real joy in peace," he noted; "one feared that the lion was only withdrawing to gain strength for another charge."[60] Nationalist feelings generally ran high. Spending that summer in Jena as guest of the mayor, a distant relative, Nietzsche approached this university town as a cultural shrine wherein "the leaders of the nation" had lived and studied.[61] He attended a meeting of the Teutonia, the first student *Burschenschaften* to organize resistance to Napoleon. When he returned to school in the fall his own nationalistic and gloomy position was given credence by one of his teachers, Karl Steinhardt, a Plato scholar, who solemnly informed Nietzsche's class that "those of our circle" should expect war to interrupt their careers.[62]

In Schulpforta, as elsewhere, the faculty thought itself preparing the new generation for the coming conflicts. But once the immediate war scare passed, these impending struggles were increasingly posed in cultural rather than in military terms. The celebration of the Schiller Centennial in November released all the pent-up energy generated in the months of war preparation. One chronicler reported that everywhere, everyone was caught up in the excitement of torchlight parades, impassioned orations, provocative displays of the revolutionary colors—"except, of course, the strict Catholic party and the supporters of the Pietists."[63] At Schulpforta the Schiller festival was celebrated with a particular seriousness; the school felt it was also honoring its own period of greatness, when Schulpforta disseminated the new classical pedagogy throughout Central Europe.

Cultural nationalism could be congenial to Nietzsche, Deussen, and other clerical sons because the secular quest for national unity retained the idea of awakening and personal mission which had been so important to evangelical Christianity. Thus Nietzsche and Deussen easily converted to a belief in *Bildung* and quickly dispelled the Pietist suspicion of secular festivity. Of all nineteenth century celebrations of genius, the Schiller Centennial came closest to a secular form of worship. On its eve, David Friedrich Strauss called upon the intelligentsia to usher in new forms of popular festivity that could compensate for the failing hold of religious festivity and would involve the people anew in the communal drama of national unity. His expectations seemed fully met as the countless commemorative gatherings held throughout the German cultural world assumed the character of a great revival meeting of the Schiller cult of yesteryear, ritually reenacting the canonization of Schiller as the national saint.

During the 1840s Schiller had served as the unifying symbol of the opposition, one capable of drawing together the federalists of the right, the nationalists of the center, and the revolutionaries of the left. At the dedication of the first Schiller statue in 1839 the King of Württemberg was forced to celebrate with the "people" in the face of the ostentatious boycott of the realm's clergy and nobility.[64] Robert Blum then emerged from Leipzig's theater world to transform the Schiller Societies into organs of agitation; Schiller's birth and death became semi-annual celebrations of the dramatist of freedom and subversion. It was the pathos of Schiller's *Don Carlos*, the royal revolutionary, which radicals most frequently invoked on these occasions. Wagner, Froebel, and other leftists from the middle-sized states would greet the revolution in this spirit, appealing to their respective sovereigns to side with the people in the creation of a "social kingdom." As Blum became the principal martyr of 1848, radicals interpreted the revival of the Schiller cult in 1859 as a revival of a former militancy. Lassalle and his associate, von Schweitzer, endeavored to repoliticize the theater through political dramas, while Engels would eventually become active in the Schiller Institute of Manchester.

Already several weeks before the Schiller festival, Nietzsche proclaimed that he was being consumed by a new passion for "universal *Bildung*."[65] "No other writer has awakened such universal interest as Schiller. And not only among the educated, no, also among the lower strata of the people was there lively participation in the national festival," Nietzsche wrote in his private account of the celebration. The climax of the event in Nietzsche's mind was the "excellent speech" by Wilhelm Koberstein, the school's distinguished Goethe scholar—an imposing but charming and somewhat theatrical figure. Koberstein told the boys, "This national festival is a vital sign of reawakened German national feeling. This celebration presages beautiful hopes for the future."[66]

The success of the November commemoration in tapping and spiritualizing the war scare of the summer of 1859 made it something far more than a revival of the "Hurrah for Schiller" enthusiasm of the older generation or the induction of a new generation into the cult of genius, freedom, and unity. The Schiller festival was a new starting point in German politics. As in 1840, the threat of imminent war with France suddenly galvanized the German speaking world. Before this momentary mood fully passed, the Schiller festivities channeled sentiment into a new form of festive politics. The classical liberals inaugurated an "era of festivals"—a series of commemorative anniversaries, celebrations, and demonstrations that lasted until Nietzsche's graduation in 1864. These memorials became occasions of patriotic display intended to impress upon the public, often student in nature, the imminence of the national awakening. The "era of festivals" was anti-climactic, it is true. None of the events which followed even approached the significance and scope of the Centennial. One may even argue that the some one million participants in all the festivals, demonstrations, and assemblies of the first half of the 1860s represent only a fraction of the forty million finally brought into the German nation-state. Yet even if it is conceded that the agitation primarily concerned Nietzsche's own stratum of the *Bildungsbürgertum*, it is clear that the new festive politics did succeed in completely deflating the counter-festivity of the dynastic state.

Karl Steinhardt, so ready to prepare the students for war at Schulpforta, also took charge of these political festivities. Steinhardt had fought to preserve a nationalist celebration of the 1813 battle of Leipzig during the reaction and now used the occasion to deliver festal orations calling for German unification. Nietzsche became quite engaged in the event, even entering two poems for the school competition. Thus if Nietzsche's birthday had ceased to be a festive day, only three days later, Schulpforta would with ever greater fanfare embrace the legend of the "war of liberation" against Napoleon, celebrating its own Prussianization—while conveniently ignoring the school's enthusiasm for Napoleon in 1813.[67] Nietzsche became increasingly uncomfortable with his childhood association to the ailing king and began to drop his middle name and initial. "Think occasionally of your brother in name and birth, the poor king in Sans-souci!" Pinder exhorted Nietzsche on his sixteenth birthday.[68] But Nietzsche chose instead to concern himself with Steinhardt's festive oration on Freiherr von Stein, the hero of the "war of liberation."[69]

A Prussian-sponsored unification now seemed to be on the agenda, and through these festivals the *Bildungsbürgertum* wished to lay claim to its future role within the nation. This group's standing seemed unimpaired by the setback of 1848, for the accumulated prestige of the German educational system then at its zenith was on its side, and it retained the support of the commercial and industrial bourgeoisie. Festival politics became the politics of optimism—the politics of a segment of the population yet outside power but seemingly destined to power.

In contrast the neo-Pietist movement entered a process of dissolution. The king's madness had seriously embarrassed the supporters of the "Christian state"; their emotional religiosity now seemed out of place. When the Pietist leader Moritz August von Bethmann-Hollweg became Prussian Minister of Culture in 1858, a friend warned him that "the country is filled with a disgust for Pietism that borders on contempt."[70] The school's easygoing senior cleric, Karl Niese, who had pamphleteered against the rationalists in the forties and championed the "Christian Gymnasium" in the fifties, had become disillusioned with Pietist religiosity, preferring philosophical discussions with his colleagues. Very often conspicuously absent from the dawn religious service, he had become a thorn in the eye of the bureaucracy, who labeled him a "weak, dependent character, more concerned with securing a comfortable living for his family" than with providing religious guidance to the students at Pforta. Repeated attempts were made to transfer him.[71]

Only the personal, apolitical Pietism of the school's junior cleric, Pastor Buddensieg, still commanded general admiration. Even Nietzsche's irreverent friend Guido Meyer could extol him as "one of the few, so very few, honest, childlike, believing Christians."[72] Buddensieg was particularly important to Nietzsche; he was his tutor, he was kindly toward him, sought to console him during his recurrent bouts of homesickness, and had made a point of befriending Franziska and the other clerical members of the family. When Nietzsche's grandfather Oehler died in December 1859, Nietzsche had a strong reaction and became ill. Buddensieg sought to comfort and help him by reawakening Nietzsche's piety. Concentrating on Nietzsche's interest in music, the tutor encouraged his pupil's ambitious plan to compose a Christmas oratorio. Buddensieg would guide Nietzsche into and through his confirmation year.

As the time for his confirmation approached he began to consider the significance of the ceremony which marked the entrance into the world of "adult Christians." In congratulating Pinder on his confirmation in March 1860 Nietzsche wrote, "You live in the serious time of preparation when all ideas and sentiments are directed to that which is most important, when the most holy decisions and aims are established for the rest of one's life."[73] Two days after Pinder's confirmation Nietzsche made the symbolic gesture of giving alms to a "blind mathematician."[74] Having lost half a year by transferring to Schulpforta, Nietzsche still had his confirmation class before him. The family decided to send Nietzsche to the new parsonage of his young uncle, Pastor Edmund Oehler, in the Thuringian forest for the summer since his grandfather's old parsonage was now closed to him. Nietzsche kept a lengthy travelogue: a dining companion denounced the clergy as leeches; a traveling companion had boasted of an acquaintance with the Pietist leader Bethmann Hollweg, and his uncle's sermon on the theme of reconciliation succeeded in resolving a feud between two villagers. Nietzsche became moved with a similar desire to reconcile his cultural and religious interests. That summer the three old friends, Nietzsche, Pinder, and Krug, founded the Germania Society, each pledging to exchange monthly aesthetic communications. But while these took a secular form for his friends, Nietzsche devoted himself to the composition of religious music. He even riled Krug by suggesting that the oratorio represented a higher, more sublime and universal art form than the new grand opera of Berlioz and Wagner.[75]

Nietzsche began his confirmation class in the fall of 1860 in an earnest spirit. Most schoolboys rather dreaded the whole experience, recalled the

Swiss poet Carl Spitteler, who was confirmed in the same year as Nietzsche. One felt overburdened, faced "with biblical studies in addition to school work"; worse still was "the denial of all pleasure during the whole winter, never laughing, never joyful, nothing but eternally reflecting on one's own sinfulness."[76] Nietzsche's confirmation winter was to be particularly bleak. Death and mourning were poignantly felt: there was the sudden death of his uncle, Pastor Knielung, in the spring; during the annual Festival of the Dead in late November, he thought mournfully of his grandfather's death a year before. The death of Friedrich Wilhelm IV on January 2, 1861, just compounded the feeling.

Buddensieg's memorial service for the dead king was unusually emotional. He recounted how as a young man he had stood despondently before the palace in Berlin during the revolutionary days of 1848. The vision of the king's piety among his unfaithful people had moved him to tears and filled him with pride that nowhere in the world was there a king to equal the Prussian sovereign. Not that Friedrich Wilhelm was a saint, Buddensieg hastened to add, rather a poor but pious sinner who bore his cross and rejected the temptation to become German Kaiser; in his last years, his mind gone, he maintained his sweet disposition, bearing his heavy burden, a royal sufferer patiently awaiting the call of the Lord. The king's career, hailed at the outset, became a martyrdom. He was denounced as a reactionary, a bigot, a secret Catholic, a drunkard, a bloodhound—a man hated by the "world." The pastor called upon his listeners to ask the Lord's forgiveness for what "we and the fatherland have sinned against our blessed king."[77]

Nietzsche came down with rheumatic fever in late January, and after spending eighteen days in sick bay he was sent home to recover; he returned to find the school in the grip of a measles epidemic that would kill a fellow student. Death and illness intensified the foreboding, brooding, and melancholy of the otherwise difficult confirmation period.[78]

With his confirmation, Nietzsche was inundated with congratulatory family letters. His guardian, the lawyer Bernhard Daechsel, told him to keep his father's "example before you and I do not doubt that you will come to resemble him," while a grand-aunt wrote Nietzsche that "you are the image of your father, and he was a good, understanding, lovable man whom you will certainly want to resemble ever more."[79] But despite Nietzsche's pious replies, he became unwilling to make the type of religious commitment his family hoped and expected from him. He quarreled with his mother during the Easter vacation. And in an autobiography which Nietzsche wrote as a school assignment in May, Ludwig Nietzsche appeared as a distant, nebulous figure, most remarkable for succumbing "to an inflammation of the brain whose symptoms have an unusual similarity to the disease of the late king."[80]

Deussen recalled that he and Nietzsche had approached their confirmation with some pious elation, especially in the weeks preceding the March ceremony, but that their faith, so important to them when they entered Schulpforta, was no longer secure. It had been "undermined" by "the historical-critical method with which the ancients had been taught, which had, as matter of course, been carried over to biblical studies."[81] The Schulpforta classicists took special pride in instilling the historical critical method, believing that this "scientific" textual criticism had brought Germany primacy in western scholarship. Pupils were encouraged to trace the genealogy of sources, to dismantle and dissect in the quest for contradictions, interpolations, and misreadings. In the month of his confirmation, Nietzsche became fascinated with the legends surrounding the East Gothic King Ermanaric. That summer he presented the Germania with a historical sketch of his hoary protagonist committing suicide in the face of internal dissension and the imminent invasion of his kingdom by Attila the Hun; a year thereafter he declaimed his poem "Ermanaric's Death" at the school's Fichte Festival; and finally his lengthy essay, "The Development of the Saga of the East Gothic King Ermanaric to the Twelfth Century," would establish his academic reputation at the school. Nietzsche found that what was applicable to Germanic mythology was easily extended to the Christian faith. Religion, Nietzsche now reasoned, was the product of the "childhood of peoples."[82]

The school was taken to task by the Ministry of Culture in an official review of July 1861, for not maintaining a proper religious atmosphere. The faculty was chastised for a lack of commitment, especially for avoiding the early morning service. The report claimed that although the faculty seemed supportive of tradition, they had distanced themselves from the religious content of that tradition.[83] In August Nietzsche was rescoring parts of his Christmas oratorio to Kerner's melancholy poem, *"Schmerz ist der Grundton der Natur,"* when Pastor Buddensieg suddenly died of a cholera epidemic sweeping the area. The death of his religious mentor hastened Nietzsche's inner break with Pietism, and he plunged into the study of the "life of Jesus literature" which had turned Christianity into a subject of historical analysis. In November he precipitated a family quarrel by suggesting that Elisabeth's Christmas gift be a church history and a life of Jesus by the theologian Karl Hase, "the brilliant champion of an idealistic rationalism."[84]

But it was one thing to distance oneself from a Pietist movement that seemed increasingly anachronistic and quite another to break altogether with the church. As a clerical son, not to accept this professional calling was to defy both family tradition and a calling from God, as the profession was perceived in his spiritualized household. Nietzsche learned to keep the full extent of his doubts to himself, for not to follow in his father's footsteps seemed to be a denial of the sanctity of his father's memory. He was painfully aware that the last four generations of Nietzsches had been clerics and that as the last male of the line he would be breaking a clerical chain that stretched back over a hundred and fifty years. Thus Nietzsche continued to go through the motions of preparing for a theological career. He became the assistant to Buddensieg's youthful successor, Pastor Kletschke, who encouraged Nietzsche's interest in the "mediating theology," a middle course between Pietist orthodoxy and liberal rationalism. Nietzsche proved an indifferent student in Hebrew class, and when his family pressured him to join his cousin, Oscar Oehler, in the study of theology at his father's alma mater of Halle he balked, announcing that he was willing to go "anywhere but Halle."[85]

Eventually Nietzsche and Deussen presented their families with a compromise, agreeing to study both theology and philology at the university in Bonn. The pragmatic Deussen privately decided that if he continued to excel in the classics, he would study philology, and if he did not, he would study theology.[86] Once in Bonn Nietzsche would balance his membership in the *Burschenschaften* Franconia with that in the Gustav Adolphus Society. Two months after his arrival he wrote his family about a speech he planned to deliver to this religious organization: "The Religious Situation of the Germans in North America." But in the same breath he also announced that he planned to abandon his theological studies at the end of the semester. The speech he gave was uninspired, derivative, and managed basically to ignore the religious issues by focusing instead on the cultural milieu of the minority German population.

Nietzsche and Deussen were preoccupied instead with the Young Hegelian critique of Christianity. In his memoir of these years, Deussen recalled that while Nietzsche found Feuerbach "shallow," they both immersed themselves in the new popular edition of Strauss's main work, *The Life of Jesus for the German People* (1864). When Deussen expressed agreement with it, Nietzsche warned him that the issue had a serious consequence: "If you give up Christ, you will have to give up God."[87]

When Nietzsche went home for Easter vacation in 1865, he took the Strauss volume with him, ostensibly to show it to his sister. It was as if he had waved a red flag before his Pietist household. A major family scene ensued with Nietzsche refusing to attend Easter service. Aunt Rosalie consoled a tearful Franziska by assuring her that all truly religious men experienced periods of doubt. But his sister found her brother's arguments persuasive. Disturbed by this threat to "the most holy, at least most believable" aspect of her faith, Elisabeth fled to her clerical uncle's for fortification of her piety, for a "reconversion" to the "correct" path. A few weeks later she would write Nietzsche a chatty letter on behalf of the family. But in it she also told him how upset she was that he "had brought the unhappy Strauss with [him] during the vacation," that he had told her so much about it, "for that is the first step toward a new belief or unbelief." If one once permits such a basic aspect of faith to be questioned, she feared, "a solid, protective wall would fall, and he would stand before a large, planless, confused, murky wasteland where nothing would be certain, where our poor, wretched, and so oft erring intellect would be our sole guide."[88]

Within the household the son's antagonism toward religion was also easily confused with a rejection of the family. Thus his mother could wound him terribly during a family quarrel in 1883 by accusing him of bringing "disgrace upon my father's grave."[89] "My mother at one point so forgot herself," he told Overbeck, "as to say one thing which made me pack my bags and leave early the next day." "In brief," he reflected, "I have 'the virtues of Naumburg' against me."[90]

In the sixties Pietism was in retreat on all fronts. Within the church an ascendant neo-Orthodox theology was determined to uproot the Pietist influence. The leading theologian of the younger generation, Albrecht Ritschl, would devote a decade to his scathing *History of Pietism*. What positive feelings remained were largely a certain defensive nostalgia over the passing of pastoral Pietism as in Wilhelm Raabe's early novel, *Der Hungerpastor* (1863). And even here Raabe could bring to life his sentimental portrait of a maudlin pastor "hungering" for spirituality only by contrasting it to the most negative stereotype available of a hapless, provincial Jewish confidence man.

In this mood to be a critic of Pietism carried no special luster nor a particularly focused critique of society. Nietzsche, like the other mid-century renegades raised within the Pietist tradition such as Van Gogh and Strindberg, found it especially difficult to define their break with religion. The inner struggle of those breaking with Pietism after mid-century necessarily could not fit the heroic mold of those in the preceding generation who rejected Pietism when it had seemed a formidable power in culture and society. By challenging Pietism in the 1830s David Friedrich Strauss had appeared as "the critical hero of the century" to the young Rudolf Haym.[91] Friedrich Engels could similarly embrace communism as a radical response to the stifling Pietism of his native Barmen.[92] But the rebels of the 1860s, coming when Pietism was no longer in command, would flounder in an ambiguous position, partly reviving or maintaining in their attacks that which was already disappearing. Nietzsche's Basel intimate, the church historian Franz Overbeck (1837–1905), would consider his own Pietist ordination the result of a "youthful misunderstanding"—an attraction "to the shallowest philanthropic ideal of the pastor" popular at mid-century. "I can well say that Christianity has cost me my life, insofar as I never possessed it," Overbeck reflected, "and my life has been used up trying to become completely free of it."[93]

Björnsterne Björnson assessed Strindberg in 1894 as having been "a Pietist in the past, and in spite of having got over it many times, a Pietist is what he still is."[94] Nietzsche would similarly find himself drawn into a lifelong struggle with what he would come to label as "the virtues of Naumburg." Herein, Michael Hamburger has observed, lies the origin of Nietzsche's "anti-self."[95] By never resolving his relation to Naumburg, by keeping the conflict alive within himself, Nietzsche kept the dilemma of the clerical son before him throughout his life.

The revival and failure of religious politics would make secularization the critical issue facing Nietzsche's generation. They had first witnessed the collapse of clerical authority in 1848 and would come of age in a period of rapid de-Christianization among Protestants. Among no group was this tension more deeply felt than that of the clerical sons. Secularization threatened to leave them displaced and rootless, yet enticed them forward with the alternative of a post-religious identity as the first of the "new men." At the turn of the century, Nietzsche's contemporary, the philosopher Friedrich Paulsen, could write, to our "parental generation a life without the church would have been unthinkable, while the generation now growing up would hardly be conscious of any great gap in their lives if the church were suddenly to disappear."[96] Nietzsche's generation would experience this transition. As they entered adulthood, they were simultaneously secularized and politicized.

CHAPTER THREE

The Generation of 1866

Stone, bronze, stone, steel, stone, oakleaves, horses' heels
Over the paving.
And the flags. And the trumpets. And so many eagles.

                                              T. S. Eliot, "Coriolan"

NIETZSCHE WAS SEVENTEEN when Bismarck came to power and went insane a year before the Iron Chancellor was dismissed from office. Nietzsche's time is the Bismarckian era. It was during Bismarck's rise to power and through the climactic events of the 1860s that Nietzsche and his generation came of age politically. During the wars of unification Nietzsche was one of those college students who affirmed the German nation-state, and who thereby concurred in the legitimation of the political reality that would govern German political life from 1866 to 1945. Just as Nietzsche stressed that Socrates shared responsibility for the subsequent collapse of the Athenian polis, so too the German catastrophe has to be studied first in the generation of 1866, and cannot then be detached from that generation's most significant thinker. A dialogue between Nietzsche and Bismarck, if one is to be reconstructed, is not simply one of contrasting, parallel greatness, but also of generational tension, fear, and conflict.[1]

In hindsight, one can reestablish a connection that was not there in the eyes of contemporaries. As the longtime cultural critic of the *Pester Lloyd* put it in 1895, German public life and culture suddenly seemed to have become rigid and stuck in the 1880s. What was new was imported. France had its Zola, Russia its Tolstoy, Scandinavia its Ibsen; only Germany, the land of thinkers, was silent and dependent on its neighbors.

And yet, [Silberstein continued], it was not so, for the most original of the original, the deepest among the deep, was once again a German. It was a lonely thinker, now languishing in an insane asylum, Friedrich Nietzsche, who was not known to the world of contemporaries, who is only now becoming known, and of whom posterity will say this idolater of energy and worldly joy could only have appeared in the iron age among the Germans, as the literary double of the great Chancellor.[2]

Nietzsche would launch his career as a spokesman for his generation. The events of the 1860s would both initiate this age group into politics and reawaken in them the generational idea absent in the 1850s. Few age groups entered politics with such high expectations for themselves. They thought they possessed a new youthful collective identity that promised a life of political importance, that they were at the threshold of a new cultural flowering. But what was done under the elderly king proved permanent, and the appointment of the unpopular Chancellor in the 1860s was not the temporary, stop-gap measure it had seemed. The generation of 1866 would never develop a strong voice and nothing innovative or truly brilliant was done in their name. The Crown Prince would never emerge from the shadow cast by the elderly king, and Nietzsche, too, would remain obscure in his lifetime—only to be discovered in a youthful avant-garde explosion against the stolidness of his age group. Nietzsche's later political eccentricity can be understood as an aspect of his anti-motif, as his attempt to reverse his initial commitment made on behalf of his generation of students, and to reject what he saw was their subsequent Philistinism.

From Nietzsche's confirmation just prior to Easter 1861 to his graduation in the fall of 1864, a mood of calamity pervaded Prussia and infiltrated the courtyards of Schulpforta. The bureaucracy placed increasing pressure on the school in these years to "accentuate the [Prussian] patriotic element in history teaching."[3] The constitutional crisis in Prussia, which Bismarck was able to manipulate and then master, had begun during the Regency and reached a boiling point at the time of the formal accession of Wilhelm I. The formal accession of the Regent would not in itself have been particularly upsetting either to Nietzsche, for whom the entire issue of Friedrich Wilhelm IV's madness and death was problematic, or to the nation, for whom the rule of Wilhelm I was already a given. Yet the date chosen made it particularly unpleasant to Nietzsche: October 18, only three days after his and the late king's birthday. While on his birthday Nietzsche was filled with melancholy reflections on the passing of Friedrich Wilhelm IV, three days later he had to attend coronation festivities at Schulpforta. "On October 18," he wrote his mother, "I wanted more than ever to spend a comfortable afternoon in your presence, and I felt very uncomfortable in Pforta. The gymnastic display was terribly boring," he complained, "the fireworks on the hill and the bonfire only a little less so, and then the whole evening. It was ghastly."[4]

The coronation of the sixty-one-year-old king highlighted the disparities within the nation. He seemed to have turned his back on the new Prussia, on Berlin, when he had himself crowned in the old city of Königsberg in a ceremony unused in Prussia since 1711, amidst the entire panoply of the "old Prussia." Instead of underscoring the principle of monarchical authority he touched off a succession crisis. The iciness of the king's reception on the streets was matched by growing demonstrations on behalf of the Crown Prince. The day chosen for the coronation was laden with its own significance, for it was also the birthday of the liberal Crown Prince, the future Friedrich III (1831–1888), whose imminent succession the father dangled before the government and army as his ultimate threat. October 18 was also a holiday in its own right, the anniversary of the battle of Leipzig. This commemoration evoked the legend of the crusade against Napoleon, of the heroism and dynamism of a young generation willing to enlist to fight for their national identity. Nietzsche's generation had been primed to identify themselves with the students of 1813 and their struggle against Napoleon. Thus while this holiday could be viewed as a nationalistic event encompassing all of Prussia, and Wilhelm I could feel himself rightly connected to it, the day had become identified with the liberal ideology and the younger generation.

Soon after the coronation the Progressive Party won an electoral triumph which brought the political crisis to a collision point. The new king preferred abdication to a constitutional regime. Wilhelm I, a lifelong soldier, refused to compromise over army reorganization, the length of conscripted military service, and the dismantling of the militia system, while the liberals were unable to surrender the principle of a constitutional army and unwilling to compromise the future of the militia. This constitutional impasse seemingly brought Prussia to the verge of civil war. At no other time between 1848 and 1914 did the choice between a constitutional breakthrough and a *coup d'état* seem so imminent as in the eighteen months between the death of Friedrich Wilhelm IV and the appointment of Bismarck as Minister President. The atmosphere in December 1861 discharged a flood of radical, subversive ideas, at least for the moment. Even Nietzsche in the days just preceding the convening of the oppositional parliament began to read a work of political sociology, *Geschichte der Gesellschaft* by Theodor Mundt. While written by a neo-conservative thinker, a one-time Young German, it tried to consider leftist thought and its implications. Nietzsche read the book carefully, writing an elaborate précis. But in his summary of Mundt's argument on the social question, it is obvious that Nietzsche had little empathy for the values of leftist social theory. He concurred with Mundt's view that the communist attack on private property might destroy "the essential essence of the human personality."[5] And a few months later Nietzsche wrote: "all socialist and communist ideas suffer from the error" of wanting to impress "stereotypes" upon state and society.[6]

Nietzsche remained tied to a royalist position and recoiled at the prospect of the opposition's ascendancy, declaring that "the future is bleak and anxious."[7] A religious royalist vocabulary reasserted itself in his dialogue with his family. His birthday letter to Aunt Rosalie in January 1862, for instance, infused the expected Pietist metaphors with political concern: "as the welfare of the individual is conditioned by the welfare of the state, so we must include in our prayers pleas on behalf of the king and country as well as for peace among nations."[8]

While the crisis gave more credence to radical thought, it also focused more attention on leadership or the lack of leadership. Nietzsche's royalism and his classical liberal education had similarly fostered a respect and fascination with the heroes of history, the nation, and the classics. Nietzsche, it is true, made unusual choices of heroes, reflecting a personally troubled mood which the ongoing political crisis only seemed to confirm. After having exhausted the theme of Ermanaric's suicide amid the collapse of his vast Germanic empire, Nietzsche discovered the melancholy and revolutionary lyricism of Hölderlin and was even able to convince the reluctant Germania Society to acquire the work of the then unpopular poet.

On the day following the coronation, Nietzsche wrote a school essay championing Hölderlin for hating "in the German the mere expert, the Philistine," and in it he defended the poet's "sharp and cutting words against German 'barbarism.' This distaste for reality," Nietzsche would argue, was "compatible with the greatest love of fatherland which Hölderlin also possessed to a high degree."[9] Nietzsche's definition of patriotism differed from the one in general use. And not surprisingly, such a defense of the "mad poet" of German classicism, coming at a time when memory of the death of the mad king was still fresh in everyone's mind, prompted a critical response from his teacher, Koberstein, the school's guardian of the pedagogic cult of genius. In the margin of Nietzsche's essay Koberstein scrawled that Nietzsche should avail himself of a "healthier, clearer, and more German model in the future."[10] But Nietzsche persisted in taking the liberal cult of genius the logical next step, idealizing the most audacious and creative poets of youthful rebellion. He discovered Byron and Petöfi, moving from the classical genius to the political rebels of poetry, and then transferring the concept of the artistic genius to politics.

By January 1862 Nietzsche could write, "A genius is dependent upon laws higher than and different from those governing the average person." He argued that "These laws often appear to violate the general principle of morality and law, but are one and the same with them when viewed from a higher standpoint."[11] This pronouncement began the paper "Napoleon III as President" which Nietzsche prepared for the Germania Society. It was greeted with some consternation by his friends. Pinder's liberal sensibilities were troubled; he wrote a rejoinder in February. Schulpforta's Rector had in the annual Schulpforta magazine the year before already confronted the attractions of the new Caesarism in a critical review of Mommsen's new history of Rome.[12] The stern and gaunt Peter remained true to his Hellenism and to his liberal principles of 1848. But Nietzsche would not be alone in his indifference to the rhetorical liberalism of the "era of the festivals." For the "younger generation out of the thirties," Wilhelm Dilthey would recall, "the ever growing democratic Caesarism of Napoleon III" had become an obsession; "one cannot imagine today how this mysterious Caesar and his growing political power preoccupied us."[13] Napoleon III, seizing power through plebiscites and a *coup d'état,* touting aggression while maintaining order, seemingly underscored the possibility, perhaps even the inevitability of major political and social change. Already in 1854 a former radical, August Ludwig von Rochau, deduced that in Germany too a Caesarist policy—this time under Prussian leadership—could and would unify Germany. To distinguish the new politics, he coined the term *Realpolitik.*[14]

The hero worship fostered in the preceding decade became the link between liberal ideology and the *Realpolitik* that would supplant it. Realism became the ultimate justification for every political stance, and in the name of such realism extra-constitutional acts by the "great man" could be justified. Nietzsche defended Louis Napoleon's *coup d'état* on the basis of such realism. He concluded an admiring sketch of Louis Napoleon's tactics between 1848 and 1850 with the judgment that, "the splendid result, an electoral majority of six million, fully justified him in allowing himself to be proclaimed Emperor on the fateful Second of December."[15] "It is not blameworthy," he wrote, "to seize power from unworthy hands in order to effect a people's well being if one has the guarantee of political genius."[16] "It is in success that one recognizes the genius," Nietzsche added.[17]

It did not occur to Nietzsche—or anyone else—that Bismarck might be such a political genius. Nor did Nietzsche take particular note of Bismarck's arrival on the scene. On September 22, 1862, the day of Bismarck's fateful interview with the king, Nietzsche happened to chronicle the activities of the Germania Society for the preceding six months. Here he attributed the "dissipation, disruption, and apathy" that were threatening to ruin the Germania Society to "political excitement," and jokingly utilized the polit-ical metaphor of a "constitutional crisis in which inviolable statutes had been violated so that the Germania almost perished."[18]

Bismarck arrived in power announcing that he was opposing the politics of "speeches and resolutions" with a policy of "iron and blood." The new minister proceeded by proclaiming a constitutional loophole that allowed him to break the rules without actually canceling the political game as it was then being played. By transforming the conflict into a legalistic controversy, he took the sting out of the immediate confrontation. The mood of the polity relaxed. Nietzsche's Naumburg friends busied themselves with their final examinations and the Germania Society collapsed. In the following six months, Nietzsche assumed a new irreverent tone, he became a less serious student and turned his back on politics. He became part of a faster crowd at school, escaping with them to the neighboring village taverns to play billiards and drink. Nietzsche and the rebellious Guido Meyer now scorned the industrious "Papa" Deussen, refusing to talk to him for a six-week period. An incredulous Krug wrote Nietzsche in October, "I could hardly believe my ears when I heard that the solid Nietzsche was drinking at Riege's with some friends from Pforte."[19] In November Nietzsche was punished for appending some humorous, offhand comments to his report as weekly inspector. The school warned that he was jeopardizing his standing as *Primus*, his mother complained of the "error of vanity," and his Uncle Edmund urged him to remain firm in his faith.[20] In February Guido Meyer was apprehended returning from an unauthorized flight from the school and expelled. His departure was for Nietzsche "the saddest day that I have experienced in Pforta."[21] Six weeks later Nietzsche and another boy were caught staggering back to Schulpforta after each had consumed four pints of beer in a single hour. He felt painfully embarrassed at his fall as *Primus*, and was forced to contritely ask the young Pastor Kletschke's forgiveness.[22]

Having completed his confirmation and having assumed the religious role of an adult, Nietzsche's late adolescent rebellion reflected itself not only in drinking and in the writing of erotic Gothic tales, but also in questioning his faith. The authority figures and attachments of his child-hood—his grandfather, Pastor David Oehler, his namesake, Friedrich Wilhelm IV, and his religious tutor, Pastor Buddensieg—were dead and had lost their hold over him. The school itself was in a rebellious and defensive mood against the new educational policies of Bismarck's Minister of Culture, Heinrich von Mühler. The orthodox Mühler was convinced that the emphasis on the classics and the historical-critical method had succeeded in eroding the faith of the young. The Minister declared the liberal conception of *Bildung* false, offering instead his own bureaucratic version of "Christian *Bildung*."[23] This drew Schulpforta, as the leading examplar of classical pedagogy, into a deepening ideological struggle with the conservative Berlin bureaucracy. The school chose to demonstrate its dissension in May 1863 at its gala ten-year reunion, attended by several hundred illustrious alumni and other dignitaries. The bureaucracy was particularly affronted by an address on Lessing delivered by one of Nietzsche's friends.[24] The principal guest speaker was Hermann Schulze-Delitzsch, a leader of the parliamentary opposition, whom Wilhelm I considered the "chief scoundrel" of the opposition. In defending its cherished ideal of *Bildung*, the school presented itself as a beleaguered cultural aristocracy which mingled the best of aristocratic and academic sensibilities. They juxtaposed to this the parvenu, the Philistine, and the *Ungebildet*. When placed in such an opposition to Philistinism on the march, Nietzsche could wholeheartedly identify with his allegedly skeptical, subversive training.[25] At the time of the Schulpforta reunion Nietzsche wrote an essay on *Julius Caesar* in which he praised Cassius, extolling once again the rebel, but in this case the aristocratic rebel who dared to strike at Caesar.[26]

Festival politics seemed to be reaching its climax in the summer of 1863. Freytag rallied the opposition by invoking the memory of armed festivity of the late medieval peasant militias, and Treitschke emerged from the national festival of gymnasts as the tribune of the young. But this revival of the memory of the Wartburg festival of 1817 proved to be of no avail. Meanwhile, Lassalle in 1863 launched his own separate festive agitation by declaring that the liberals had become the fools of festivity, celebrating victory in defeat. The cult of genius had produced in Lassalle a man of genius or, at least, a man willing to play out the role of genius. Through leaflets, pamphlets, impassioned orations, and courtroom speeches, Lassalle single-handedly revived the spirit of the revolutionary Hambach festival of 1832. For a time he even distracted attention from the coming war with Denmark. In his fearful festival of incipient insurrection, Lassalle rallied the people, now defined as the proletariat, by rekindling the spirit of revolutionary community. Although he shared Marx's disappointment in the organizational results of the agitation, the Lassallean rally did succeed in transporting the participant to a realm where revolution seemed possible and probable. As Nietzsche discovered when he joined a throng of 10,000 at one such rally in 1866, the vast majority was moved to acclaim the Lassallean candidate as their own without, however, having this enthusiasm translate into votes at the ballot box. When the Danish war came, Lassalle's hand was in any event played out; his death soon thereafter only marked its formal conclusion. Of all the events of the "era of festivals" only Lassalle's day of death was memorialized, becoming the first holiday of the German socialist movement.

Idealism aside, festival politics shared many of the central assumptions of *Realpolitik*. It, too, had before it the example of the Italian war of unification; it, too, celebrated the hero-epic popularized by a resurgent Bonapartism; and it, too, sought to tap the spirit of war enthusiasm, albeit for a different purpose. Bismarck brilliantly diverted national passions by making the overriding issue of national unity focus on confrontations with external forces—in this case against the Danish liberals seeking to assimilate the predominantly German duchies of Schleswig-Holstein. Bismarck dampened the internal opposition and turned what had been a controversial issue of strengthening the army into an item of national pride. Establishing the primacy of external over internal politics proved to be Bismarck's master stroke and the Achilles heel of constitutional liberalism. Under Friedrich Wilhelm IV the army had served as an instrument of the counter-revolution, externally pursuing a conciliatory or neutral policy; the army would now become an aggressive instrument of national unity.

Nietzsche was obliged to register for the draft in the weeks just preceding the federal occupation of the duchies. He did so in the knowledge that he had until October 1 of his twenty-third year (1867) to begin service as a one-year volunteer. Despite his poor eyesight he was judged fit, and Nietzsche accordingly followed the course of the Danish conflict with particular excitement. Nietzsche's idealization of the aristocratic rebel was sometimes expressed as anti-Caesarism, but at other times was employed against middle class pacifism, as when he would champion the "free warrior caste" over "the boring narrow-minded Philistines" in a school assignment on *Wallenstein*.[27] He prepared himself for the coming war, anticipating that he might spend the following Christmas in "a winter campaign for Schleswig-Holstein." "To avoid [military service] would be difficult," he wrote his family, "moreover, I have little desire to do so."[28]

The Danish war contained one heroic episode—the storming of the fortifications at Düppel, an event duly and ecstatically celebrated at Schulpforta—but it ended by clouding the symbolic issues involved. A war which had modeled itself on the Italian expulsion of the foreigner concluded in a squalid struggle between Prussia and Austria over the spoils. In the disillusionment which followed, festival politics was granted a final lease on life. The news of the Prussian seizure of the Danish fort at Düppel had an extraordinary effect upon German public opinion. When Deussen recited his patriotic Latin poem celebrating the Prussian victory at the school festival in May, Steinhardt was so overcome with emotion that at its conclusion he rushed up and kissed the embarrassed Deussen on the mouth.[29] Nietzsche also took special pleasure praising "the fatherland's army for its glorious deeds."[30] But the victory also seemed to beg a conflict with Austria over the division of the spoils. One autobiography recalled the "unforgettable hour" when a teacher, hitherto a pacifist, told a hushed class that war with Austria was now inevitable.[31] And at Schulpforta, Wilhelm Corrsen, Nietzsche's Latin and history teacher, declared that "Germany's future can only be built on Austria's ruins," a sentiment which Nietzsche remembered as daring and "quite red."[32]

Indifferent, even suspicious of Bismarck, Nietzsche remained fascinated by the type he seemed to represent. In Nietzsche's valedictory essay on Theogonis of Megara, he likened the Hellenic poet to a "well educated, ruined Junker with Junker-like passions," one that embodied "the aristocracy in the eyes of the popular revolution." This Junker-like Theogonis was a figure "who always saw his special privileges threatened and who was as passionately fighting for the existence of his class as for his own existence." While criticizing Theogonis's reactionary elitism, he also saw in him an expression of the Hellenic dichotomy between the "good" (the artistocratic, the wealthy, and the cultivated) and the "bad" (the poor, the embittered, and the uneducated).[33]

With the term over, Nietzsche produced a farewell address obediently expressing his gratitude to the king, country, and his "honored teachers," and left Schulpforta.[34] The Danish war past, he felt no compunction to begin his military year, and set out for Bonn. The university town of Bonn still believed itself to be a tiny Prussian island surrounded by what Nietzsche would complain was a "bigoted Catholic population."[35] The actual Catholic presence in Bonn was minor, but, aware of the antagonism just outside, Nietzsche detected "Jesuit influences" everywhere and joined the Gustav Adolphus Society as a "counter-force."[36] The university had been founded with the Prussian annexation fifty years before and was still largely boycotted by the Rhenish population surrounding it. The university was instead a small, liberal Protestant option to the neighboring Catholic university of Cologne and drew its eight hundred students primarily from the Prussian east and the German southwest. Alienated from its surroundings, the Bonn university turned in on itself, producing a hothouse atmosphere in which any political or academic controversy was exacerbated.

In his first week in Bonn, Nietzsche and his Schulpforta friends scouted the various fraternities. Bonn student life was divided between the aristocratic, conservative Corps and the middle-class, nationalist fraternities. Very few students remained outside them, and rivalries within the student body were played out between these groups. "The student who wishes to know his time and place must become a fraternity man," Nietzsche wrote his aristocratic Schulpforta friend Carl Gersdorff (1844–1904), "for these associations and their opinions present the next generation's type in boldest relief."[37] Nietzsche, Deussen, and five other former classmates joined the Franconia, the oldest of the Bonn fraternities, noted for its elegance and its particularly high representation of philologists.

The Franconia also had a long tradition of activism. Under the leadership of Carl Schurz it had spearheaded the town's revolutionary movement in 1848. This was not a fact that Nietzsche chose to relay to his family, preferring instead to inform them that the novelist Friedrich Spielhagen and the historian Heinrich von Treitschke had been Franconians in the 1850s. He was especially proud of the association with Treitschke, who seemed at that moment the elder statesman of the resurgent student movement. "All eyes were focused on Treitschke because of his style, his partisanship, the originality of his great will, and the manner in which it was expressed. He was like a flame that irresistibly rose upwards," Dilthey would write.[38]

Students saw themselves finally realizing the aspirations of the students of 1813, and doing so through the vehicle of the fraternity. "The fraternity stands as a pioneer of progress vis-à-vis the pathetic mass sunk in political indifference, who hamper the good cause more than that little group of open reactionaries," proclaimed a pamphlet Nietzsche acquired.[39] Students were, however, uncertain as to what could or should actually be done. All they had "was a hazy notion that the fraternities stood for Germany's unity and greatness," Paulsen would recall.[40] The philosopher Rudolf Eucken wrote in his memoirs of a "great warmth of moral feeling, especially in the shape of the conviction that educated youth was called upon to bring about a free and united Germany."[41] In the winter 1864/65 student leaders were busy creating a national organization that could mobilize the scattered student movement into a cohesive moral authority.[42] Thus despite Bismarck's successes, the student movement persisted in believing that unification could not be engendered by the conservative regime, but rather required a national consensus to which the efforts of the student movement were pivotal.

Nietzsche became part of that faction in the fraternity which sought to bring this "higher tone" to fraternity life. He helped initiate "scientific evenings" where "works or lectures with political content were presented and debated in parliamentary form."[43] These were to replace one evening of drinking a week; Nietzsche was offended by the otherwise boisterous, beer-drinking conviviality of the Franconia, while many of his fraternity brothers apparently held a similar ambivalent attitude toward the somewhat aloof "musician" who remained in the foyer playing the piano during his first visit to a bordello in Cologne. Nietzsche never accustomed himself to the more democratic, liberal attitudes swirling around him in the fraternity. He remained resistant to populist attitudes which students from the more democratic German southwest were seeking to introduce into Bonn student politics.[44]

Nietzsche grumbled about his taxing social schedule which included fraternity activities, attendance of frequent concerts, and membership in the Bonn choral society and the religious Gustav Adolphus Society. Nevertheless, he went through the motions of a fraternity man, even fighting a friendly duel with an equally awkward acquaintance from a rival fraternity, inflicting a little scar on his opponent. In the humorous skit he presented to display his wit to his fraternity brothers, his political jibes were limited to mocking the old bogey, Minister von Mühler.[45] And when speaking seriously about the "Political Poets" of the 1840s he was critical of what he termed their illusions about the value of political poetry and their possible role in reforming society.[46] When he mentioned the revolution of 1848 in a talk to the Gustav Adolphus Society he did not counter the prevailing opinion "that the years 1848 and 49" were "years of great and beautiful hopes," but he dismissed the exiles who had fled to America as "the most unworthy representatives of the German name"—a stance he would have felt he had to modify in the fraternity setting.[47] When the Eisenacher League of Fraternities decreed that its affiliates should work for "the unification of Germany on a democratic basis," Nietzsche recoiled. He unsuccessfully fought the Franconia's decision that "a democratic association must have democratic colors" and that it should thus replace its white-red-gold colors with the revolutionary colors, black-red-gold.[48] Nietzsche reluctantly wore the new colors and even enjoyed parading around with his fellows, but in his letters he began to mock the pretensions of a fraternity that thought itself to be "the future of Germany, the seedbed of German parliaments."[49]

He found the new "national liberalism" of Heinrich von Sybel more congenial. He singled out Sybel's lectures, which attracted two to three hundred students and were full of "political allusions" and import, as the high point of his first semester at Bonn.[50] Sybel, a prominent historian and politician, had just resigned his seat in the Prussian Assembly so as to be in a better position to speak out on behalf of a new conciliatory liberalism. His lecture course, entitled simply "Politics," was given at this juncture to underscore the need to compromise with Bismarck. He had offered this course once before—in 1847/48—but he did so now as a defector from the liberal opposition, warning of the dangers of universal suffrage, parliamentarism, and the illusions of 1848.[51]

Nietzsche also came under the immediate sway of his philological instructors, who impressed him, motivated him in his studies, and helped him finalize his break with his clerical calling. He considered "Ritschl, who discussed philology and theology with me," and "Otto Jahn, who like myself, pursues philology and music without rendering the one secondary to the other" to be "heroes of scholarship."[52] Their presence had given Bonn the leading reputation in classical scholarship in Germany. But a dispute between Ritschl and Jahn over the hiring of a third philologist suddenly mushroomed into a major controversy. In the spring of 1865 Nietzsche found himself in the middle of what was soon dubbed the "Bonn philological war." The university was bitterly divided: students staged torchlight parades, some professors published angry pamphlets, only to have the Cultural Ministry exacerbate the whole controversy by dismissing one of Ritschl's most outspoken partisans.[53]

The Bonn philological war crisscrossed political lines. When the liberal opposition sought to embarrass the government by supporting the conservative Ritschl in parliament, supporters of the liberal Jahn helped Minister von Mühler fend off these attacks.[54] Sybel, in particular, championed Jahn as the herald of the new field of archaeology that promised a more modern, realistic, and thereby politically more relevant study of antiquity.[55] Archaeology seemed, at least to Sybel, to present a new bridge between the classicists in the university and the educated bourgeoisie. At a time when the middle class was in the process of raising monuments, past monuments offered a more graspable, more "realistic" avenue to antiquity. In contrast Ritschl represented the more traditional, aristocratic, and literary approach. He had trained the most prominent philologists of the past quarter century and viewed with alarm any attempt to dismantle the predominance of the classics over university curriculum. Nietzsche found himself forced to make a choice betwen Jahn, whom he had always thought the more sympathetic figure, and in this instance the more unduly injured one, and Ritschl, whose austere grammatical-critical methodology he saw as a necessary corrective to his own tendency toward belles-lettres. Nietzsche's interest in the classics was its literature and its thought; he was not caught up in the cult of Pompeii; and he would remain completely indifferent to Schliemann's discovery of Troy. Archaeology would never interest him. Thus when Ritschl announced that he was leaving for Leipzig, and it became clear that Bonn would lose its preeminence in the classics, Nietzsche also decided to leave Bonn.

Nietzsche would later melodramatically see himself having fled Bonn "as a refugee in the night."[56] But in the last weeks before he actually left, he availed himself of the festive occasions of the month of June and end of term. As Cologne was obliged to celebrate the fiftieth anniversary of the annexation of the Rhineland, accompanying festivity was staged to complement and counter that unpopular commemoration. Nietzsche sang in the mammoth three-day Lower Rhenish Music Festival, later remembered as the last of the great open-air music festivals. He attended the International Agricultural Exhibition held to display the city's new Zoological Gardens and to give expression to the new festivity of liberal capitalism. This exhibition marks the height of the "exhibition fever" in Germany as Bismarck would show himself implacably opposed to such displays, blocking, for example, all future plans for a German World's Fair. But the symbolic end of festival politics came when the liberal opposition announced a counter-festival of deputies to be held in Cologne. Prussian authorities banned the meeting, arrested the local organizer, used police detachments to prevent the seventy deputies who arrived from assembling. At Bonn's Arndt festival, two weeks later, Nietzsche shared the widespread indignation at this action.

Unlike the official anniversary festivities attended by the Prussian court and government, the Arndt Festival seemed to him to have a genuine festive air. The jubilation of the crowd which the newspapers had dutifully reported for the Cologne ceremonies he thought in truth to exist at this predominantly fraternity celebration highlighted by Sybel's nationalistic speech.[57] Caught up in the spirit of this event and the celebration of Franconia's twenty-year anniversary, Nietzsche even made vacation plans to attend the national festival of fraternities in Jena which commemorated the fifty-year existence of the student movement. But what Nietzsche termed a painful "rheumatism" attack, which some later scholars have conjectured was venereal disease, took him directly home instead.[58]

Once back at his mother's home for the vacation, he became concerned about his expenses and his scholarly future and was filled with remorse over what he now decided was his wasted year in Bonn. Disillusioned with fraternity life, it pained him to have to extend unfelt familiarity to some fraternity brothers he chanced to meet during a brief visit to Berlin. Among his first acts when he arrived in Leipzig was to write a curt, patronizing letter to the Franconia announcing his resignation. Happy to be free of the "black-red-gold *Jünglinge,*" he told a friend that "I find their political ability to be slight, involving only a few. I find their public presence to be plebian and repulsive."[59] Nietzsche had initially joined the Franconia swept up in the enthusiasm of his Schulpforta friends and had then sought to balance his displeasure with everyday fraternity life by a commitment to the lofty ideals of the fraternity movement. Nietzsche rejected fraternity life without repudiating the values he had championed as a fraternity man. Even in his condescending public letter of resignation, he wrote, "I do not cease to highly esteem the fraternity idea."[60] He remained too drawn to some of its basic tenets and had been too half-hearted a member for the anti-motif to become operative in his disaffection. Instead he would feel embarrassed about the way he had broken with the fraternity, about having publicized his personal dislikes, admitting two years later that he had been "unjust" in his criticisms.[61] Indeed, in other forms he would himself later champion some of the underlying principles which had been important in the fraternity movement such as its festivity, its generational idea, and its desire to create a morally cohesive socio-cultural community. His rejection was not motivated by a criticism of the central values of the student movement but rather of the social life he had been expected to lead. At the time he was just happy to be free of his associates and to exchange their intimacy for a more anonymous city atmosphere.

Leipzig's "high towered houses, lively side streets, and constant bustle" thrust Nietzsche into an urban environment for the first time.[62] Walking the streets, trudging up and down staircases in search for a lodging quickly exposed him to the odors and the seamier aspects of city life; he was relieved when he finally rented a room from a used book dealer in a crowded, garden courtyard. Like most of his two thousand fellow students, Nietzsche took his meals out and spent his free time in Leipzig's various cafés. Here town and gown were not segregated, fraternities played only a minor role. Although Wilhelm Roscher's lectures on "The Fundamentals of a Practical Politics" were tiresome in comparison with Sybel's lively polemics, Nietzsche was relieved that politics in Leipzig did not emanate from the university as it had in Bonn.[63] Flourishing trade and growing industry gave politics within Leipzig a more concrete character. It was the natural center of Saxon national liberalism but also of alienated radicalism. But after the hectic socializing of the preceding year, Nietzsche savored the isolation and anonymity which the new urban setting permitted.

Leipzig stood in a certain opposition to the old cultural and political capital of Dresden as Saxony's mercantile city, as the center of Germany's publishing industry, and as the last of the great European market places. Three times a year, during the New Year, Easter, and Fall fairs, the city of 85,000 (1864) would balloon in size and would take on the character of a true metropolis. Like many of his fellow students, Nietzsche affected disdain for the *Messezeit* and particularly for the Jews, the most conspicuous among the many outsiders who flooded into the city.[64] Nietzsche did enjoy participation in the Riedel choral society that was active during the fair season, but he had found a new all-absorbing interest.

He chanced upon a used copy of Arthur Schopenhauer's *The World as Will and Idea* and swallowed it whole. In the flush of discovery he imposed upon himself an ascetic regime which allowed him only four hours of sleep a night for two weeks. "Every line proclaimed renunciation, denial, resignation; here I found a mirror in which the world, life, and one's own nature was reflected in terrible majesty."[65] Such Schopenhauerian pessimism proved a boon to Nietzsche's new sense of scholarly commitment and made his scorn and rejection of the beer-drinking, social life of the fraternities all the more final. Believing he had stumbled upon a forgotten, neglected thinker, Nietzsche formed a little Schopenhauerian study group with two Schulpforta friends, Carl von Gersdorff and the philology student Hermann Maschacke. To these new devotees, Schopenhauer's philosophical antipolitics seemed to reduce politics to the realm of an unchanging and absurd war of wills, while also confirming the violence of the underlying political reality. They felt they were embracing a new realism that offered dispensation from the constant politicizing of the preceding years. Nietzsche and his friends devoted themselves to their studies, to their friendship with one another, and to Schopenhauer. When his friends left Leipzig a few months later, he wrote Gersdorff that he found consolation in three things: "Schopenhauer, Schumann, and lonely walks."[66]

Ironically, however, Nietzsche would now become even more a part of a group, and for the first and perhaps only time in his life he was popular and socially important among a group of peers whose values were no longer defined by fraternity sociability but by those academic standards in which he excelled. When Ritschl entered the packed auditorium to deliver his inaugural lecture, he flattered Nietzsche by singling him out in the audience, calling out as he passed, "Hey, Herr Nietzsche is also here!"[67] Ritschl would be so cordial to Nietzsche that although Nietzsche had only planned to stay one semester, he could not imagine himself returning to a Prussian university. Nietzsche would become ever more committed to Ritschl and consequently increasingly alienated from his Prussian opponents in philology. He felt at home in Leipzig. He was impressed when even King Johann of Saxony, himself a translator of Dante, came to hear Ritschl lecture, and would praise the monarch for being above the manner "of a non-commissioned officer" so characteristic "of other kings."[68]

Six weeks after their arrival, Ritschl invited Nietzsche and a few other students who had come from Bonn to his home and after dinner urged them to establish a student philological society that could help make Leipzig the new center of classical studies in Germany. Nietzsche and three others took up the suggestion, with Nietzsche clearly becoming "the soul of the organization."[69] His lectures dazzled and intimidated his fellows. "I work hard, but I am stolid," worried the future folklorist Wilhelm Wisser. "It is a terrible torment to be an ambitious but dumb person. When I think of people like N[ietzsche]—for him everything happens as in a dream. He achieves more in a day than I in a month." Wisser was crushed when Nietzsche pronounced his doctoral work unmethodological and was scarcely consoled when another told him that his topic was far too difficult and never should have been chosen as it was so problematic that "perhaps even Nietzsche would have failed." Nietzsche had been a more stern and uncompromising judge, however, than his teacher Ritschl, who told Wisser the work was "rigorous, methodological, and logical."[70]

Ritschl's arrival spotlighted philology at Leipzig. The number of students jumped from forty to a hundred and forty, and Nietzsche and his friends enjoyed the rapid success of their society, which was able to maintain itself long after their departure, if in a weakened form.[71] Nietzsche also searched for fellow students with whom he could share his interest in Schopenhauer, and Gersdorff urged him to pioneer a new Schopenhauerian conception of antiquity. In the philological society Nietzsche found the future folklorist Ernst Windisch and Hellenist Erwin Rohde (1845–1898), who agreed that a

Schopenhauerian perspective could generate a new interpretation of classical antiquity. Rohde, in particular, would come to share Nietzsche's conviction that the new pessimism provided the key to the understanding of ancient Greece, a point he would elaborate in his main work, *Psyche* (1894).[72] Their little group expanded quickly to include not only Rohde and Windisch but Rudolf Kleinpaul and Heinrich Romundt, who were neo-Kantian philosophy students, and Franz Hueffer, a Wagnerian aesthete and later member of the Pre-Raphaelite circle.[73] By the end of Nietzsche's first Leipzig semester, this group had become a lively circle which met regularly at the Kintschy café. These new Schopenhauer enthusiasts scoured the book stores and journals for anything on the philosopher. They were infuriated when they found Rudolf Haym's lengthy essay of 1864 which simply dismissed Schopenhauer as the "bizarre saint" of a new "nihilism."[74] The group saw this polemic by a leading liberal critic as further evidence of a growing rift between themselves and the older generation.

The young Schopenhauerians of Nietzsche's Leipzig circle perceived the Schopenhauerian system as a philosophy of youth. Indeed, Nietzsche would later understand Schopenhauer as a philosopher *only* of youth in his aphorism, "Every philosophy is a philosophy of an age of life." Schopenhauer's system was fashioned between his twenty-sixth and thirtieth year as a "mirror image of his passionate youth."[75] Schopenhauer took special pride in thereafter only producing addenda to his *magnum opus*. Embracing a philosophy so rooted in youthful attitudes now gave the Nietzsche group a sense of cohesion, excitement, and motivation, but it was, as Nietzsche later observed, to fail them in later life. Nietzsche's essay *Schopenhauer as Educator* (1874) attempted to characterize the experience of becoming a Schopenhauerian in the 1860s. Nietzsche rightly understood this experience as a generational one, for by the late sixties Schopenhauer would become the new interest of the intellectual young. Most of Schopenhauer's predominantly middle-class admirers would be drawn to the "realism" and/or the apoliticism of the new pessimism. They included such figures as the young Eduard von Hartmann who would become famous in 1869 for presenting his "philosophy of the unconscious" in the context of a Darwinian political realism, or a youthful Ernst Mach who would seek to fuse positivism with the Buddhist ethics he had found in Schopenhauer. It was Julian Schmidt's article "The New Generation," which this critic published at the beginning of the Hegel Centennial of 1870, that would formally announce what by then was an open secret: the young had found a new philosopher and were turning their backs on the Hegelian tradition.[76]

The new pessimism was more than simply a rejection of the optimism of Hegelian thought. It stimulated this generation's aesthetic interests, encouraged psychological introspection, and its doctrine of the will provided individualism with a new atheistic mysticism. In a less dramatic way its apoliticism and quietism freed the Nietzsche group from the political pathos of the "era of festivals." Nietzsche was especially happy to put the world of everyday politics behind him, attending only one political meeting in his first Leipzig winter. He and his friends submerged themselves in Schopenhauerian aesthetics and metaphysics and felt themselves pursuing a higher calling. But Nietzsche's initial encounter with Schopenhauer would illustrate how unstable this affected quietism was and how quickly it could turn into activism. Try as Nietzsche and his fellow Schopenhauerians might to throw off the political, the politicization of their world only created a boomerang effect, bringing them back into the political world as politicized men.

Schopenhauer formulated his thought during the collapse of the Napoleonic system. "My pessimism was worked out between 1814 and 1818 (at which date it was published in its final form)—that is, after Germany's liberation, the time of her greatest hopes."[77] As the son of Hanseatic patricians who had fled the Prussian seizure of Danzig, Schopenhauer did not share these hopes and stood in opposition to the general enthusiasm. When Fichte, his one-time teacher, called for student participation in the war of 1813, Schopenhauer retired to a Thuringian hideaway to philosophize. He countered Fichte's activism by idealizing disinterestedness, searching for confirmation of his political quietism in Buddhist and Brahman thought. Nietzsche and his friends had discovered Schopenhauer at a parallel but quite different moment, when Germany's "highest hopes" were again in the process of being realized but this time with seeming permanence. This propelled Nietzsche's circle in a direction very different from that initially envisaged by Schopenhauer's philosophy.

In the spring of 1866 he and his friends were suddenly pulled back into the vortex of political events. Bismarck had lulled public opinion into in-attention, and the crisis caught Nietzsche, like most Germans, by surprise. Some of his friends attended anti-war, anti-Prussian rallies, and Nietzsche's first thought was to support the liberal call for a reconvened German parliament that might avert war. He remained skeptical of Bismarck's policy, believing that "the dangers which surround Prussia are extremely grave, that it is quite impossible for this policy to succeed in complete victory. It is an audacity on Bismark's [sic] part to create a united Germany in this manner. He may have courage and consistency, but he underestimates the moral forces within the people."[78]

But once the war started he was a Prussian patriot: "The moment the war began all secondary considerations faded. I am as much an impassioned Prussian, as, for example, my cousins are impassioned Saxons."[79] This war did not unleash fundamental passions as war would in 1870 and 1914, but it did evoke the particularist loyalties of most Germans. Behind enemy lines Nietzsche felt his Prussianism all the more acutely. He was convinced that "the day is very near when I will be drafted," that it was "dishonorable to sit at home when the fatherland is beginning a struggle for life and death," signing one letter, "One who is ready to fight."[80]

He decided that "since Schopenhauer has taken the blindfold of optimism from our eyes, one sees more clearly. Life is more interesting, even if more hateful."[81] As Prussia swept from one victory to the next, Nietzsche felt that "One can learn much in such times. The earth, which appeared so solid and unmovable, quakes. Masks slip from faces, selfishness flaunts itself. Above all, one notices how weak are the power of ideas."[82] His only hesitation was that the political "drama might turn into a tragedy" by committing the new Schopenhauerians too deeply to the "role of statists."[83] But the next day when it appeared that Napoleon III might intervene on Austria's behalf, Nietzsche wrote Gersdorff, now an officer, that the time had come to overthrow the Napoleonic system. As long as Paris remained Europe's unofficial capital, everything would remain the same. "Our national struggle will not be spared the overturning of European conditions, or, at least, the attempt to overthrow them. If we fail, hopefully we will both have the honor of being struck down on the battlefield by a French bullet."[84]

The threat of French intervention soon passed, the Habsburg and south German armies had been crushed at Sadowa, and Nietzsche found himself in the anomalous situation of being a Prussian in occupied Leipzig. Anxious to represent the triumphant cause, Nietzsche identified with the small local band of Bismarckian liberals led by the novelist Gustav Freytag and the historian Karl Biedermann, supporting their call for the annexation of Saxony by Prussia. The intellectual leader of this annexationist agitation was Heinrich von Treitschke whose locally confiscated pamphlet *Die Zukunft der norddeutschen Mittelstaaten* (The future of the North German middle states, July 1866) Nietzsche read with enthusiasm. Treitschke applauded Bismarck's "revolution from above" for discharging the storm clouds which had hung over Germany for half a century, finally resolving the dualism between Prussia and Austria and allowing a new centralized Germany to emerge. This tract created a scandal in Saxony as Treitschke had dared demand what his father, a Saxon general, and his brother, a wounded Saxon officer, had fought to resist. The father publicly rebuked the son, and this family conflict became a central topic of debate in a Leipzig student world now divided socially between pro- and anti-Prussian cafés.[85]

At this critical juncture Nietzsche and Treitschke agreed on their positions toward the German nation-state, the role of Prussia in Germany, and their desire to break with the ideals of their fathers and with the old traditions of the various regions of Germany. Treitschke would be for the coming generation the ultimate Prussian. Yet since he came from outside, from a Saxon military family, the mythology of Prussia and the new Germany which he fostered was not prompted by a rootedness in the "old Prussia." He was never inhibited by its conservative religious traditions, and unlike Nietzsche he had neither to critique nor to integrate the "antipolitical" traditions of Prussian Pietism. When Nietzsche rallied to Bismarck, he was quite conscious that Prussian Pietists denounced this new war-born Germany, with Ludwig von Gerlach, their spokesman, declaring the "revolution from above" to be the negation of the "Christian state." Nietzsche took special pleasure in the discomfort of "Gerlach and other Westphalian Borneos."[86] What seemed particularly "revolutionary" to Nietzsche was Bismarck's apparent scorn for the moral claims on the political. So while Treitschke welcomed the disintegration of the Saxon army, Nietzsche watched with satisfaction the eclipse of the political world of his father.

Nietzsche was little concerned with the fate of the liberal opposition decimated in the Prussian wartime election, declaring that "basically every party which accepts the goals of [Bismarck's] policy is liberal."[87] With the old distinctions between conservatives and liberals breaking down, Nietzsche saw "in the conservative block in the Assembly only a new shade of liberalism." "It does no harm," he concluded, "when the name 'conservative' is retained for our form of government. For the insightful it is a label, for the cautious a kind of hiding place, and for our excellent king a kind of camouflage."[88]

Yet Nietzsche's mood of postwar euphoria was marred by the collapse of the local Bismarckian party. The Saxon National Liberals had seemed the politically ascendant force in late summer when Nietzsche left Leipzig to escape the cholera epidemic invading the city. But the political climate was very different when he returned in late October. The city, Nietzsche complained, was bedecked with both the green-white colors of Saxony and the democratic colors, black-red-gold. Strict censorship imposed during the Prussian military occupation had been relaxed and the ban on political demonstrations had been lifted. In this charged atmosphere the local election for the constituent Reichstag of the North German Confederation became a plebiscite on the new Bismarckian state. For the first and last time in his life, Nietzsche became caught up in a political campaign. The National Liberals ran an inoffensive candidate, Vice-Mayor Stephani, fearing that their leader Karl Biedermann was too controversial a figure. Stephani was able to present a respectable showing in a field of four; Nietzsche became his partisan. But Stephani was then completely swamped in the run-off election in which the local "patriots" of the left and right united against the pro-Prussian "traitors." Worse still, in Saxony as a whole, National Liberalism was able to muster only 10,000 votes out of the 303,000 cast.[89] The debacle soured Nietzsche on the political ability of his *"Gesinnungsgenossen"* (comrades in arms). Treitschke, a spokesman of the new national liberalism, emerged from the war declaring that he "did not despair for the future of liberalism, even though it cannot and will not rule in the immediate future."[90]

The events of 1866 took on an air of finality for the very old, and they quickly assumed a self-evident, inevitable quality in the eyes of the very young. For those just entering the Gymnasia, the expulsion of Austria from Germany, the founding of the North German Confederation, even the introduction of universal male suffrage on the federal level would only be overshadowed four years later by the defeat of France, the founding of the Reich and the onset of the *Kulturkampf.* But for university students and their teachers, 1866 remained a pivotal moment; for the latter it foreshadowed inevitable compromise, the scaling down of earlier hopes, for the former it began a new epoch, their political starting point. If the older liberal generation made the political compromise with Bismarck at war's end, aware all the while that it was a compromise, the young perceived it simply as the new reality. Thus although the two generations arrived at the same point, 1866 demarked the beginning of a rift between the age-groups.[91]

Nietzsche's Bismarckianism, for instance, was increasingly expressed in an aloof disdain for party politics, a growing belief that a parliamentary regime in Prussia had been shown to be unnecessary, even harmful, and a growing contempt for his initial educators—"the whole white race of liberals." He grew ever more disdainful of the two liberal leaders of Leipzig to whom he had rallied in the summer of 1866, Gustav Freytag and Karl Biedermann. In Freytag, the literary pope of the Leipzig scene, he came to see a special intellectual opponent. Freytag attempted to hail German unification as the culmination of the efforts of "nineteen generations," as the special achievement of the older liberal generation. It was "the elder generation," he thought, who "felt most this joy, having suffered so severely the deep pain and humiliation in an earlier time,"[92] while to Nietzsche and his friends the preceding half century, from 1815 to 1866, had become a closed chapter in which 1848 took on a farcical aspect as the *"tolle Jahr"* (mad year). Freytag became increasingly troubled by this youthful disdain for the traditions of 1848, publishing in 1869 a biography of Karl Mäthy, a Badenese politician active in the revolution, in order to "remind youthful contemporaries that we do not owe everything to the year 1866 and the action of one decisive man and that the liberals did not work in vain on behalf of the fatherland."[93]

In the aftermath of 1866, Nietzsche read Schopenhauer in a new spirit. He no longer felt himself to be an isolated devotee of a forgotten philosophy but in the vanguard of an intellectual movement that stood poised on the threshold of a new cultural epoch. "Schopenhauer is the philosopher of a regenerated Germany," Nietzsche would write in 1868.[94] It seemed axiomatic to him as to many other young intellectuals that the new political epoch inaugurated in 1866 would necessarily engender its cultural analogue. The political task which the older generation had set itself had now seemingly been largely completed; Gervinus's famous exhortation of 1839, that Germans should accept the passing of her great cultural epoch and embrace politics instead, no longer seemed relevant. Intellectuals, it seemed, could now return to their intellectual calling with a clear conscience. Bismarck's political solution had made possible, so Nietzsche thought, a cultural blossoming under the aegis of Schopenhauer.

Schopenhauerian philosophy seemed the new intellectual starting point—in Nietzsche's word, the "educator" of the new generation. He wrote Deussen urging him to join "the representatives of the philology of the future (i.e., the next generation after Ritschl . . .)" who were assembling in Leipzig.[95] When Deussen proved recalcitrant and took up his theological studies in earnest, Nietzsche bombarded him with letters describing the growing Schopenhauerian community and his own proselytizing exploits, notably the conversion of Pastor Wenkel of Naumburg to Schopenhauer. And when Deussen praised the biblical criticism of David Friedrich Strauss, Nietzsche scornfully dismissed such philologists as mere "factory workers" toiling blindly "on behalf of some philosophical demigod (the greatest of whom in the last millennium is Schopenhauer)."[96] After three years of such badgering, Deussen suddenly announced that Schopenhauer had become "for me almost a holy name." He thanked Nietzsche "for having preached to me the only gospel of salvation, the Messiah of the coming centuries— Schopenhauer the resurrected."[97] The last of his friends to convert would prove the most committed. Deussen would be the first to present a lecture course on Schopenhauer in a German university; one reviewer of *Die Elemente der Metaphysik* (1877) would see him acclaiming the philosopher as an *"Übermensch"*; and his main works, *The Philosophy of the Upanishads* and *The System of the Vedanta,* would seek to realize Schopenhauer's claim that "Indian thought streams back to Europe, and will produce a fundamental change in our knowledge and thought."[98] In 1913 Deussen would found the Schopenhauer Society.

Conscious of Schopenhauer's growing influence, Nietzsche dreamed of repeating the success of the Young Hegelians. He envisaged the founding of a Schopenhauerian journal "run by talented young men," which would become the gathering place of the like-minded—"our Freemansonry," "our community of heretics."[99] Above all he wanted to accentuate the differences between his circle and the semi-official Hegelian philosophers dominant within the university. He was infuriated when Kleinpaul's dissertation on Schopenhauer was rejected, but when another friend's dissertation linking Kant and Schopenhauer was accepted a year later, Nietzsche began making plans to switch fields and write a philosophy dissertation on "the concept of the organism since Kant."[100] But since Nietzsche had already launched a seemingly brilliant philological career (he was soon to be called to a position in Basel), he gravitated back to his initial goal of showing that "Schopenhauer is the philosopher of a reawakened classicism, a Germanic Hellenism."

What Hegel had been to the student generation of 1830, Schopenhauer would be for the generation of 1866. Schopenhauer, Wilhelm Wundt declared in 1877, had become "the head of Non-Academic philosophy in Germany."[101] Neo-Kantianism might have been the respectable means of protesting the predominance of a stale historicism, but it was in and through Schopenhauer that the radical break with the past was made. In 1854 Jacob Burckhardt could write a young correspondent, "Hegel is a drug on the market. Let him lie where he is."[102] Fifteen years later such a warning was unnecessary. Hegelianism seemed only an obstacle, an impediment to a true philosophy and particularly to the new interest in the science of psychology. The curriculum of philosophy departments seemed clogged with tiresome histories of philosophy and the semi-official boycott of Schopenhauer only increased youthful disdain for the last representatives of the Hegelian tradition. Lassalle, the last Young Hegelian, would discover with anger that his right-hand man and eventual successor, Johann Baptiste von Schweitzer, was a Schopenhauerian who had published a book reconciling Schopenhauer's voluntarism with a Rousseauian socialism.[103] A decade later Marx complained that Hegel was being treated like a "dead dog," but even Marx's belated praise of Hegel had little immediate effect.[104] Engels began his 1888 study of Feuerbach by declaring that Feuerbach's philosophy, conceived only one generation before, seemed as distant to the present generation as if it had been written a century before.[105] In the 1880s when Nietzsche reflected upon Schopenhauer's effect upon his generation, he wrote that Schopenhauer's "unintelligent wrath against Hegel has succeeded in wrenching the entire last generation of Germans out of the context of German culture...."[106]

Despite his later opposition to Schopenhauerian pessimism, Nietzsche's relation to Hegel remained representative of his age group. In championing Schopenhauer, he had dismissed Hegel in scorn. There is no evidence that Nietzsche ever seriously read a single work by Hegel. There were no Hegel volumes in his library, no records of his ever having withdrawn books on or by Hegel from the Basel library, and neither his letters nor his notebooks give any indication of any serious study of Hegelian philosophy. Those scattered quotations from Hegel that do appear in his work are apparently drawn from histories of philosophy. Of course, it was impossible to grow up in mid-century without encountering Hegelian categories and concepts at every turn. Nietzsche was, after all, trained in the historical-critical method which drew its sustenance from Hegelian thought. Nevertheless, Hegelianism was an exhausted movement by 1860. The Young Hegelians were no more: Kierkegaard and Stirner were dead, Feuerbach and Bauer were forgotten celebrities, Marx and Engels had transformed their youthful Hegelianism into an economic "science," and Strauss remained in the public eye only by playing the role of the fashionable, post-Hegelian cultural critic.[107]

In Bonn Nietzsche had still been fascinated by the intellectual life of the 1840s, and in a letter to a friend he could wonder "if we came into the world twenty, thirty years too late."[108] But by 1868 such thoughts were far from his mind. When Nietzsche rented a room in Biedermann's home, he was able to dismiss him as an archetype of the older generation. Nietzsche was aware of Biedermann's colorful past, his youthful connection to Hegelian philosophy, his leading role in 1848 and subsequent exile, but now Nietzsche saw in Biedermann only *"ein bieder Mann"*—dull, conscientious, and limited.[109] Nietzsche prided himself in his indifference to politics and to the social concerns which moved Biedermann. Biedermann had founded the Leipzig Workers' Educational Society in the early sixties, and with the help of his protégé, August Bebel, had turned it into the largest and most effective organization of its kind in Germany.[110] Its high-minded purpose of bridging the gap between urban classes had appealed to students as a way to break out of their social isolation and make contact with the "people."[111] When one of Nietzsche's philological friends, the son of the revolutionary poet Gottfried Kinkel, started lecturing at the Workers' Educational Society, Nietzsche complained that the younger Kinkel was "still caught up in the political principles of his father."[112] After one of their recurring arguments, Nietzsche noted with satisfaction that he had apparently convinced Kinkel that their dedication to the "selfless dignity of the science" of philology required them to maintain an outwardly apolitical stance.[113] True to his earlier attitudes, Nietzsche would oppose the attempt to uplift the workers through *Bildung,* which he would argue only exposed the lower classes to the hollowness of the existing *Bildungsprinzip.*

Biedermann's liberal social program, in any case, was proving ineffective. He was losing control of his organization to the Marxists who had their own critique of the *Bildungsprinzip.* The 1865 typesetters' strike demonstrated the emergence of a class-conscious proletariat, and the arrival of Marx's apostle, Wilhelm Liebknecht, recently expelled from Prussia, intensified local working class militancy. The issue was decided when Bebel threw his support to the radical socialists.

While liberalism was a known quantity which he and his friends had to push aside with a varying degree of social qualms, radicalism was a foreign curiosity for Nietzsche. Nietzsche's circle came in indirect contact with the new radicalism when the veteran revolutionary Bernhard Becker rented a room adjoining that of one of Nietzsche's friends in the winter of 1866/67.[114] They developed enough curiosity to attend an election rally of the Lassallean candidate that drew a crowd of at least 10,000, but Nietzsche was impressed neither with the speaker nor his program. His "powerful words," he said, were used to promote the "most impotent and unreal things, as for example, a European workers' state."[115] Subsequently Nietzsche read and recommended to Gersdorff a book that shed light on Lassalle's "irrational greatness."[116] This book presented Lassalle as a pivotal figure in recent German political history but it did so primarily to critique liberalism. Its author, Edmund Jörg, was an embittered Catholic conservative who delighted in presenting what Lassalle called his *Kulturkampf* against liberalism. The book's content was enough to satisfy Nietzsche's needs, although he did complain of the book's "sour aftertaste of reaction."[117] After grasping Lassalle's attack on Schulze-Delitzsch and the liberal *Bildungsprinzip,* Nietzsche showed little further interest in Lassalle or his successors.

Radicalism was too foreign to his background and seemed too irrelevant to his aesthetic concerns. Instead what he and so many of his fellow students gained from radical thought was a confirmation of their rejection of the liberalism of the older generation. Bernhard Becker in 1870 sensed such disaffection with liberalism was widespread among the young; he said the liberal movement was "destined to sink into the grave at the very latest with the present generation."[118] In the 1880 aphorism, "Criticism of our fathers," Nietzsche reflected upon the generational conflict of his youth:

> There is now always a new generation which feels itself in contradiction to the past and enjoys in this criticism the first fruits of its sense of power. In former times the new generation, on the contrary, wished to base itself on the old and began to feel conscious of its power, not only in accepting the opinions of its ancestors but, if possible, taking them even more seriously. To criticize ancestral authority was in former times a vice; but at the present time our idealists begin by making it their starting point.[119]

At a time when the rise of Schopenhauerian philosophy and the crisis of liberalism were widely interpreted in generational terms, it is not surprising that the consciousness of a generational mission grew ever stronger in Nietzsche. Generational conflict, of course, is a perennial in the human comedy, and the notion of generations is traceable back to the origin of thought. The oldest of the Pre-Socratic fragments is the Orphic injunction, "In the sixth generation cease the ordered arrangement of your song"; the myth of the prophetic "tenth generation" played an important role in the ancient Near East, and biblical prophecy concluded with the millenarian expectation of the "final" generation. Nevertheless, the concept of a distinct generation moving through time in opposition to the preceding generation, making its own future and thus possessing its own historical identity, is a product and aspect of modernity.[120]

In Germany the generational idea first emerged in the literary revolt of the *Jünglinge* during the *Sturm und Drang* era. Forty years later Friedrich Schlegel could discuss all subsequent literary movements in terms of literary generations. Yet it was only in the aftermath of the July Revolution, when the Parisian avant-garde called itself the "generation of 1830" and Mazzini's vision of "Young Europe" was imitated everywhere, that explicit generational ideologies were enunciated. But the distinction in this initial formulation was not so much between age groups, between the "old" and the "young," as between epochs, between the "new" and the "old." The Young Germans and Young Hegelians politicized the concept of youth, but included in the young all those who accepted the new; the young were simply those who acutely felt with Marx that "the tradition of all the dead generations weighs like a nightmare on the brain of the living."[121] Or in Kierkegaard's dispensation each new generation faced the test of Abraham, not Isaac.

It is only when the initial bearers of a generational ideology confronted their successors that the full implications of the generational theme became apparent. Thus, the earlier optimistic historicism was displaced after mid-century with morbid reflections on biology, nihilism, and the crisis of the family. Turgenev began the literary debate by contrasting the romantic idealism of "the men of the forties" with the "nihilism" of the new "men of the sixties" in *Fathers and Sons*; Dostoevsky responded in *The Possessed,* a work which would influence the mature Nietzsche's sense of himself and his age group.[122] Positivist scholars took up the precise measurement of generations; Dilthey made the concept an integral part of his historical writing. And Nietzsche would say of his *Untimely Meditations* (1872–1876) that they were written "as a young man for other young men."[123] In the first of these essays, referred to as "the anti-Strauss" among his friends, Nietzsche attempted to "assassinate" the leading exemplar of the older generation of liberal intellectuals, David Friedrich Strauss. Nietzsche concluded the second, *The Use and Abuse of History,* with an appeal to the younger generation to arise and create "the kingdom of youth." The last two essays were intended to exalt the new culture heroes of the young, Schopenhauer and Wagner.

By the late seventies, Nietzsche, too, had tired of his role, had become disillusioned with his initial ideals, and began to mordantly mock those who had placed so much faith in "the famous German *Jüngling.*"[124] But having himself utilized the generational idea to propel his entrance onto the public stage, placing before himself the image of an ideal audience and community, Nietzsche would find it impossible to fully relinquish his claims to a leadership role on behalf of his generation. Even in isolation and opposition, his ideas would circle back in opposition to the initial formulations he had made as a generational spokesman. He sought to undo the championship of his youthful culture heroes, such as Wagner and Schopenhauer. But once he had abandoned the notion of generations, he found no other public; it was only after his career came to an end that his works became an arsenal for the young during the revival of generational ideologies in the 1890s.

Precisely because Nietzsche has so often been annexed into the intellectual world of the preceding or succeeding generation—by those who have followed Karl Löwith in presenting Nietzsche as the last Young Hegelian or by those who confuse Nietzsche with Nietzscheanism—his own place within the ranks of his coevals needs to be emphasized.[125] It is only within the drama of his own age group that Nietzsche's antipolitics can be understood.

Those contemporaries who shared Nietzsche's cycle of life are recalled today as great-grandfathers of the present, as the men of the day before yesterday, familiarly perhaps but no longer vividly. Compounding the problem is the portrait of the late nineteenth century as an intellectual wasteland representing, as Whitehead put it, "the dullest stretch of thought since the time of the First Crusade."[126] Not surprisingly, Nietzsche criticism had tended to place Nietzsche above his age or disassociated him from it.

Nevertheless, Nietzsche intimately shared the dilemma of an age group which was destined to be overshadowed in its youth and overtaken in its prime. Like the students of 1813 upon whom Nietzsche's generation modeled themselves, the dramatic events of their youth would be followed by decades of relative political calm. As Leipzig and Waterloo brought a warlike period to a close, so did Sadowa and Sedan; both age groups experienced lives of peace and continuity, troubled by severe political crisis only at the end. Nietzsche's failure as a generational spokesman was largely due to the inability of his contemporaries to emerge from the shadow of "the type of 1830," and thus his savage attacks on Wagner as the ultimate representative of this "type."[127]

Nietzsche's age group characteristically failed to generate a name of its own. The suggestion of Hans Vaihinger in the mid-seventies that those who came of age during the epoch of Bismarck's wars be called the "Youngest Germany" not only failed to stick but was adopted in the following decade by a younger age group of writers and poets.[128] To call Nietzsche's student generation "the generation of 1866" seems justified since they were the first post-unification age group. Coming of age at this moment, they perceived 1866 as a turning point, building their expectations around it. The generational idea reemerged and flourished in the immediate postwar years; even if other groups shared their enthusiasm for the event, indeed orchestrated it, only the prospects of these young adults seemed to hinge on it. The significance of 1866—like the age group it represents—was purposefully obscured by the subsequent ideologists of the *Reich*. Given the subjective character of generational identity and community, no precise demarcation of the boundaries between age groups can be made. Yet a pattern in which the generational idea was introduced, elaborated, dropped, forgotten, and then rediscovered clearly began in the 1830s, 1860s, and 1890s.[129]

The following overview of the generation of 1866 is Nietzsche-centric, with the birth years of the two Hohenzollerns closest to Nietzsche providing the lines of demarcation. In 1866 German politics revolved around the fate of a single ruling family for the first time in centuries. Elevated to imperial status five years later, the Hohenzollerns came to dominate the imagination of their countrymen with the various age groups naturally associating themselves with the Hohenzollern closest in age. Nietzsche expressed no sense of generational solidarity with anyone older that Friedrich III, tending to associate those born in the 1820s with the "type of 1830." On the other hand, those born in the 1850s were young enough to be his students. He adopted a formal relationship with Jacob Burckhardt (1818–1896) and maintained a certain distance from his student Heinrich Köselitz (Peter Gast, 1854–1918). The birth years of his intimate friends ranged from the mid-1830s through the late 1840s, and it is this group which Nietzsche seemed to have in mind when he addressed his own generation. As inadequate and incomplete as is any such list, it should, nevertheless, provide a glimpse of the most important political and cultural figures remembered, if not by all, at least by some.

Birth
Year

1831	Friedrich III; Raabe; Caprivi
1832	Wundt; Busch; Waldersee
1833	Brahms; Dilthey; Dühring; Schweitzer; Schlieffen
1834	Treitschke; Haeckel

	1835	Stöcker; Sacher-Masoch; Yorck zu Wartenburg
	1836	Lenbach; Stumm-Halberg
	1837	Holstein; Marées
	1838	Schmoller; Mach; F. Brentano; Richter
	1839	Anzengruber; Hans Thoma
	1840	Bebel; Makart
	1841	Karl May; Gierke
	1842	v. Hartmann; Brandes; Cohen
	1843	Avenarius; Rosegger; v. Suttner
NIETZSCHE	1844	Leibl; Liliencron; L. Brentano; Riehl
	1845	Ludwig II; Spitteler; Wildenbruch
	1846	Mehring; Eucken; Most; M. G. Conrad; Paulsen
	1847	Hindenburg; Liebermann
	1848	Frege; Windelband; Stumpf; H. Delbrück
	1849	v. Bülow; Herbert Bismarck
	1850	Bernstein
	1851	Harnack
	1852	Vaihinger
	1853	
	1854	
	1855	
	1856	Freud
	1857	
	1858	
	1859	Wilhelm II

When taken as a whole, this list is lacking in truly great names. One need only consider that Wagner, Hebbel, Büchner, and Kierkegaard were born in 1813, the year of Nietzsche's father's birth, to realize how few significant figures are represented in this list. Even such an eminent composer as Brahms achieved fame by continuing and bringing the romantic tradition of German music to a final fruition rather than attempting to strike out in a new direction. In a cultural epoch known primarily for the Russian novel, Scandinavian drama, and French poetry and painting, the German contribution was embarrassingly slight. Even the few innovators, such as the painters Leibl and Marées, pale in comparison with their foreign rivals.

Nowhere was this more apparent than in the political sphere. The Socialists (e.g., Bebel, Bernstein, Mehring, Most, Schweitzer) remained in the shadow of *die Alten,* Marx and Engels. Moltke would similarly dwarf the generals; only Hindenburg was to achieve political importance as the grandfather from the Bismarckian era. Bismarck most clearly overshadowed all the political leaders of this age group. None of the Imperial Chancellors who followed (Caprivi, Bülow, Michaelis) could successfully fill or transform the Bismarckian legacy. Between the Bismarckian and

Wilhelmian era there was to be no Frederickian age. Friedrich III's tragic ninety-nine-day reign is perhaps the most appropriate symbol for this generation.

However one wishes to assess achievement, Nietzsche was the most striking and original figure among his contemporaries. He is the only figure to enter the realm of *Weltliteratur,* whereas such writers as Raabe, May, Sacher-Masoch, such poets as Liliencron, Busch, and Spitteler, as well as the little-remembered dramatists Anzengruber and Wildenbruch, remained enclosed within the province of German culture. Nietzsche and to a lesser extent Dilthey are the only philosophers who have maintained a substantial audience; Mach, Frege, and Franz Brentano do continue to demand critical attention, while the others are little read or recalled collectively as neo-Kantians (Avenarius, Cohen, Eucken, Riehl, Stumpf, Vaihinger, Windelband, Yorck). The long row of eminent scholars (e.g., Lujo Brentano, Hans Delbrück, Gierke, Harnack, Schmoller, Treitschke, Wilamowitz, Wundt) sustained the proud standing of the German universities without any of them achieving a contribution in thought that can be compared to that of Freud or Weber. Nietzsche is clearly the only great "genius" of his generation's creative elite. German culture would ironically gain its greatest international prestige precisely in this period of cultural stagnation. But such a cultural afterglow of preceding greatness soon dimmed, leaving this generation in a historical twilight.

CHAPTER FOUR

The Spectacle of Greatness

Now they go up to the temple. Then the sacrifice.
Now come the virgins bearing urns, urns containing
Dust
Dust
Dust of dust, and now
Stone, bronze, stone, steel, stone, oakleaves, horses' heels
Over the paving

T.S. Eliot, "Coriolan"

IN VICTORY, "the revolution from above" swept away the accumulated political symbolism of the preceding half century only to find itself facing a festive vacuum in its hour of triumph. For having fragmented the opposition, circumvented mass participation, and minimized collective sacrifice through brief wars lasting weeks or months, the rulers of the new German nation-state could not then easily orchestrate popular festive affirmation of their creation. And failing at this, an air of illegitimacy continued to cling to the substance of the Bismarckian state; a built-in vulnerability was exposed: the symbols of power lay open to attack. Hence that susceptibility to subversion by "antipolitical" ideas which Julius Froebel foresaw when he declared in the aftermath of the Bayreuth festival of 1876 that the Wagnerian movement presented the greatest single ideological threat to the future stability of the German nation-state.

Bismarck made no move to exploit the symbolic possibilities in victory. His immediate objective was to gain Prussian control over the military apparatus of the defeated middle states, and he was wary of any victory celebrations that might stiffen regional resistance to his plans. Bismarck was, moveover, too much a tactician, too involved in balancing and playing off various groups against each other, to concern himself with the festive façade of the new nation-state. Wilhelm I had an equally modest view of his cultural role. The regime did stage victory parades, but little else was forthcoming. The North German Confederation with its Prussian "President" neither satisfied the triumphant nationalists nor mollified the defeated federalists. Bismarck had allowed the Kaiser option to fall, and he would admit in the spring of 1870 when he again took up the idea of crowning the Prussian King Emperor that he had "underestimated the importance which externals have in the opinion of my countrymen."[1]

The defeated were thus curiously able to dictate the festive aftermath of war. The blind Hannoverian king arming his Guelph Legion in exile, the ostentatious demonstrations of local loyalties, the Frankfurt mayor's suicide in protest at the occupation, in short, the public drama of legitimism and regionalism, succeeded in crowding out the mood of celebration. Only the Luxemburg war scare in the spring of 1867 brought nationalists relief from the anticlimactic doldrums of the preceding months. Nietzsche and Gersdorff eagerly anticipated the possible war with France, for as before, a new, larger and more decisive war seemed to be the surest way of securing the needed symbolic unity of the nation.[2] To Nietzsche's disappointment war was avoided, and in fact, for Nietzsche as for most Germans, the fleeting Francophobia of the spring gave way to a greater renewed admiration of French culture then being displayed to the world in the Paris Exhibition of 1867. At this point Nietzsche planned a stay in Paris.

Nietzsche's festival ideal took form in these months. Nietzsche had been stimulated to explore and idealize the role of festivity in Hellenic life. In April he wrote Gersdorff that the Greeks had been "the people of harmony," being neither "scholars" nor "mindless gymnasts," and speculated that Christianity had effected "a cleavage in human nature" by forcing a choice between the two.[3] Pursuing this thought in his investigations of Diogenes Laertius's lives of the Pre-Socratic philosophers, Nietzsche stumbled upon the fable of the poetic contest between Homer and Hesiod. In this tale Homer won the favor of the crowd but the judge remained unconvinced and called for a second, final round of competition; Homer then sang of war and battle, Hesiod of peace and agriculture. To the dismay of the audience Hesiod was declared the victor, and the legend concluded by contrasting Hesiod's subsequent murder with Homer's growing fame. The story, whether based on fact or not, demonstrated, Nietzsche argued, the vital importance of the festive contest in the Pre-Socratic world. He established that this fable was not an invention of the second century A.D., as previously argued; rather, its author was Alcadamas, a pupil of Socrates Sophist rival Gorgias. And in his July lecture, "The Poets' Contest at Euboea," Nietzsche set himself the task of investigating "the concept and the history of the whole notion of the contest idea in Greek life."[4]

The agonal principle originated, Nietzsche would argue, in Hesiod's distinction between good and bad *eris*—strife and/or envy—which Nietzsche later redefined as the contrast between envy and resentment. Greek art became inconceivable "without the contest; Hesiod's good *eris*, ambition, gave its genius wings." What Hesiod championed in art, Heraclitus defined as the vital, essential Hellenic trait. He became for Nietzsche the ultimate Greek:

> Only a Greek was capable of finding such an idea to be the fundament of a cosmology; it is Hesiod's good *eris* transformed into a cosmic principle; it is the contest-idea of the Greek individual and the Greek state taken from the gymnasia and the palaestra, from the artist's agon, from the contest between political parties and between cities—all transformed into universal application so that now the wheels of the cosmos turn on it.[5]

Nietzsche's own thought would now revolve around one central theme, the analysis, elaboration, and celebration of the Hellenic contest motif, the agon. In presenting the public contest as "the fundamental idea" of the Greeks, Nietzsche found a focus for his philological career and a means of confronting what he now believed to be the critical problem of his time, that of "war and culture."[6] By isolating the agon as the mainspring of Hellenic culture, Nietzsche proceeded to evoke a festival ideal upon which his generation could build a new culture. The festive contest was for Nietzsche both the reflection of the underlying reality of life and the mechanism by which the worst aspects of that reality might be sublimated and discharged.

Nietzsche's agonism preceded his Wagnerianism and made possible his eventual break with it, for the agon placed conflict and competition at the center of his thought. By praising the competitive process itself rather than the creative resolution of competition, he struck out in a direction that ran counter to the harmonizing tenets of German Idealism. German thinkers had hitherto dealt with conflict either by preaching resignation as did Schopenhauer or by extolling the progressive movement of dialectical conflict as did Hegel. Through the agonal concept, however, Nietzsche came to espouse what might be called the tragic dialectic, and it was in this notion that his anti-motif first assumed a philosophical dimension. By rethinking Schopenhauer's voluntarism in a Hellenic setting, he moved away from Schopenhauer's view of culture as a refuge from the political. Nietzsche instead became intent on recreating a "heroic pessimism" in which culture contested the claims of the political.

This agonal ideal emerged during a series of storybook wars which had spread from the Crimea to Italy and Germany before finally concluding in France. Such conflicts brought little sense of devastation or loss. The ferocious bloodletting of the American Civil War was recognized by few Europeans to be a harbinger of future wars. Instead, "militarism," a neologism of the 1860s, connoted a relatively benign view of war and awakened a fascination with the "great men" tested in limited wars. Nietzsche joined many leading critics of the time in celebrating and aestheticizing war. John Ruskin, for instance, in *The Crown of Wild Olive* (1866) adopted the contest as the central metaphor of public life. "All the pure and noble arts of peace are founded in war; no great art ever rose on earth, but among a nation of soldiers," Ruskin declared, adding in his appendix, "Notes on the Political Economy of Prussia": "I know certainly that the most beautiful characters yet developed among men have been formed in war;—that all great nations have been warrior nations, and that the only kinds of peace we are likely to get in the present age are ruinous alike to the intellect, and the heart."[7]

Such aesthetic militarism became the creed of the late nineteenth century art revival. In muted form it reappeared in Walter Pater's 1894 essay, "The Age of Athletic Prizemen." "The athletic age" between the Persian and the Peloponnesian Wars represented for Pater (as for Nietzsche) the idealized "active phase of art" dedicated to "peaceful combat as a fine art." By engaging in "solemn contests" which "began and ended in prayer and sacrifice," athlete became priest, directing "the worship of the body" and instilling in the faithful the virtues "of abstinence, of rule, and the keeping under of one's self."[8] Germans were particularly prominent in drawing attention to the agonal age. Theodor Curtius called for a revival of the Olympic Games at the time of the Schiller festival, and obtained the Crown Prince's sponsorship of his landmark excavations of Olympia despite Bismarck's resistance.[9] Nietzsche's originality lay less in his exploration of the subject matter of the contest motif than in the results of his inner struggle to overcome the quietism of Schopenhauerian pessimism through the activism of his agonal ideal. In this regard, Nietzsche's melancholy friend Erwin Rohde proved the better Schopenhauerian; his classic study *Psyche* (1894) would thus trace agonism back to its origins in the Hellenic cult of the dead.[10] Nietzsche, however, was determined to imbue his agonism with concrete, contemporary meaning, becoming in time the prophet of the Wagnerian movement.

Schopenhauer had mocked the heroic qualities of war. "Never," J. P. Stern observes, "has the Hobbesian notion of universal war, of endless, fruitless, meaningless bloody conflict been taken up with greater gusto" than by Schopenhauer.[11] His view of war developed out of a quarter century of continuous, devastating war; he interpreted Napoleon's career as an illustration of the futility of even a powerful personality seeking to impose his will upon the political world. Nietzsche would later call Schopenhauer's pessimism "a reaction to the Napoleonic era" and the philosopher "anti-Napoleonic."[12] Tolstoy, after his disillusioning experiences in the Crimean War, would for that reason find in Schopenhauer a mirror image of his own portrait of Napoleon, exclaiming as he finished *War and Peace* (1869): "I do not know whether I shall ever change my opinion, but now I am convinced that Schopenhauer is the greatest genius of mankind."[13] But such Schopenhauerian inspired pacifism found little resonance in Nietzsche.

Nietzsche at first camouflaged his own break with Schopenhauer by perceiving his quest of the "Hellenic will" to be his extension of the philosophy of pessimism. Outwardly his enthusiasm for the philosopher seemed to have reached new heights. He prided himself on his proselytizing exploits and sought to interest his friends in an aesthetic pilgrimage to Paris where his "Schopenhauer club" might be rejuvenated by a new "literary mission."[14] But he was troubled by the suicide of a young Schulpforta teacher soon after a discussion with Nietzsche on Schopenhauer's view of suicide, and he remained too committed to the Greeks to ever surrender to the Schopenhauerian vision of India.[15] Unlike his friends Deussen and Windisch, he never pursued the connection between India and Greece.[16] Even as he celebrated the Schopenhauerian idea of genius, his own agonal conception of genius was increasingly moving away from that of Schopenhauer. The Schopenhauerian genius found himself in detachment and disengagement, while for the Greeks and for Nietzsche as well, genius was only realized in the act of displaying oneself in the public arena. Whereas Schopenhauer sanctified the ivory tower, Nietzsche thrust the genius into an activistic role, one that stimulated him to ever-greater creative achievements through the contest system. Not the extinction but rather the distinction of the will became the object of Nietzsche's thought.

In the spirit of his agonal ideal, Nietzsche tried developing a more active, virile persona. He took up riding with his new friend Erwin Rohde, and the two would appear at seminar meetings in riding dress, crop in hand. All this was partial compensation for the shortsightedness which he believed would disqualify him from military service. He paid no attention to his fast-approaching October 1, 1867, deadline for entering the army. Meanwhile the Prussian army, as part of its rapid buildup in the aftermath of the Luxemburg crisis, tightened restrictions, and Nietzsche suddenly found himself with but a week to enter the army as a one-year volunteer. He made a quick trip to Berlin to try to enlist in one of the royal guard regiments; after failing at that, he settled for the local Naumburg detachment of the mounted artillery.[17] The Prussian army enjoyed unparalleled popularity at the moment when Nietzsche entered. Few students would have dreamed of volunteering for the royal guards—the hated *Soldestka* of the counter-revolution—ten years before. But now the Prussian army had proven itself, having won one contest with Austria, and it was gearing up for another with France.

Nietzsche grumbled about having been wrenched from his studies but soon found that his riding experience was of great advantage, and he bragged to Rohde that he was considered the best rider among the thirty new recruits.[18] He began studying and preparing himself to qualify as an officer candidate. He wrote Gersdorff that he had become fascinated with "Bismark" [sic], reading "his speeches as if I were drinking a strong wine," slowly, savoring every drop. Even as he continued to philosophize about the agon, he was forced to concede that "now is not the time to philosophize" because "politics is presently the organ of all thought."[19] But everything abruptly changed for Nietzsche in March 1868 when he was injured in a riding accident. Two chest muscles were torn, bringing his active military service to a sudden end. He spent the last six months of his military year convalescing in Naumburg.

Nietzsche now turned his complete attention to developing his new dramatistic philosophy. He began outlining a dissertation, "Homero Hesio-dique aequalibus," presenting the poets as generational rivals. He saw thereby a means of restoring Homer's individuality, which he complained had been etherealized by Romantic notions of the "folk soul" and reduced by Hegelian conceptions to merely a reflex of the *Zeitgeist.* He also planned a more ambitious literary history that would trace the contest motif from the initial rivalry between the heroic Homeric and the didactic Hesiodic tendencies of the epic, following this through the flowering of the agonal idea in Pre-Socratic thought and city-state life to its final culmination in Greek tragedy. Once the agon elevated the theater to the determining institution of cultural life, Nietzsche argued, the decline of Greek tragedy would become synonymous with the decline of the agonal instinct and Greek culture in general.

The Ritschl school with which Nietzsche was associated was particularly concerned with the theater of antiquity. Ritschl's most notable studies concerned Plautus and the Roman theater. Not surprisingly, members of his school took a keen interest in the future of the contemporary German theater. While some earlier Ritschl students, such as Otto Ribbeck, came to the regretful conclusion that a revival was no longer possible—the German theater had had its "day"—Nietzsche remained an enthusiast, his theater-mania then reaching its heights.[20] At Schulpforta he had already toyed with playwrighting, and on his way to Bonn he had delighted in shocking "an old very pietistic lady" of Elberfeld with an impassioned defense of the theater.[21] In Cologne he found the theater exhilarating, and after a stopover, praised the theater of Berlin. In Leipzig he became an avid reader of the theater reviews in the *Leipziger Tageblatt,* marveled at Devrient's performances of Kleist and Shakespeare, and wrote a love-sick fan letter to a touring actress.[22]

Leipzig was, moreover, in the midst of its own theater revival. During Nietzsche's three-and-a-half-year connection to the city, he became caught up in the then burning question of what to do with the soon-to-be completed second theater.[23] A lengthy campaign began to oust the theater director, a jovial Hannoverian aristocrat, whose concentration on operetta and light comedy appealed to the audiences of the fairs but frustrated proponents of a new era in the Leipzig theater. The reformers eventually won the day by enticing Heinrich Laube to leave Vienna where he had established himself as the leading theater director in the German-speaking world.

Nietzsche became receptive to Wagner's theater plans during his first Leipzig winter. Although he had earlier experimented with the musical idiom of *Tristan* and included the photographs of Liszt and Wagner among his 1861 list of Christmas wishes, Nietzsche had gone to Bonn a partisan of Schumann, laying a wreath on the composer's grave and befriending Hermann Dieters, a fellow Schumann enthusiast and future biographer of Brahms.[24] His association with Otto Jahn, a noted mordant critic of Wagner, strengthened his resistance to the "music of the future." He even read Eduard Hanslick, the leading anti-Wagnerian, who was seeking to defend music from the literary claims of the theater. But once in Leipzig, he found himself ill prepared to deal with the impassioned arguments of that future Wagnerian music critic, Franz Hueffer.[25]

Frederick Love has observed that "Wagner's music remained for Nietzsche an unsolved problem from first to last, a problem that was temporarily suppressed during the period of closest association with the composer, and perhaps for reasons having little to do with music as such."[26] Whatever reservations Nietzsche might continue to harbor about Wagner's music in Leipzig, he could no longer deny that the composer was the one original force in the German theater of the day.

Of all the erstwhile Young Germans, Wagner was the most obsessed with realizing the high aesthetic and moral mission Schiller had bestowed upon the theater. As one born into the impoverished theater bohème of the 1810s, Wagner harbored a deep resentment toward a society that proclaimed the cultural value of the theater while stigmatizing the theatrical demimonde that spawned it. Although German culture had regained its voice in the theater of the 1770s, Wagner was disappointed in the failure of Weimar's golden age to engender the promised national theater. Wagner made the revitalization of the German theater his lifelong ambition.

Unlike his rivals who were destined to play the role of epigones, reviving something greater than themselves, Wagner struggled out of the shadow of Goethe and Beethoven. The example of Auber's *La Muette,* touching off the Brussels insurrection of 1830, suggested the dramatic potential of grand opera. The budding composer had joined the Leipzig student riots of that year as a "berserker."[27] At twenty-one he announced his intention to breathe life into German opera, left stillborn by the failure of the "national drama." Wagner believed that the theater had become merely "the bad conscience" of modern culture, because the initial unity of the arts found in the Greeks had been lost and forgotten. The "Greek *Gesamtkunstwerk*"—that harmonious balance of drama, poetry, and music—was to be "born anew" in the "German opera" of the future. By redressing the balance of music and the word, by presenting a cast of delineated characters, and by submerging the orchestra and otherwise heightening the visual aspect of operatic performances, Wagner did conjure up a distinctly original form of "music drama."[28] But what eluded him in his youth and thoughout his life was the creation of that ideal public that could properly respond.

At first Wagner sought simply to revive Hellenic theater festivity.[29] He visualized the promised national theater as a temple of art astride a hilltop, visible from afar, to which pilgrims would stream to free performances. This half-utopian vision was put aside at the outbreak of the revolution for more practical schemes. The composer busied himself with manifestos to the Saxon government proposing a national theater, and to the Viennese revolution urging reorganization of its theater.[30] Although the ensuing turbulence hardly proved conducive to these plans, and 1848 concluded as had previous revolutions in impoverishing most theater companies, it did at the outset place the theater at the center of revolutionary activity. The theater became the meeting place and rallying ground of revolutionaries, the site of benefit performances for revolutionary martyrs and the occasion of ecstatic performances.[31] As music director of the Royal Dresden opera, Wagner was in the thick of events. During the last stand of the Dresden revolution, he fell under the spell of Bakunin's apocalyptic anarchism, writing Liszt that he was now practicing "artistic terrorism" by becoming "as red as possible."[32]

Wagner arrived in his Swiss exile defiantly predicting that he would return to stage "a great dramatic festival" on the banks of the Rhine.[33] But revolutionary defeat transformed him. He scrambled to ingratiate himself in the eyes of the powerful who "at first sight recognize in me only the political revolutionary, and forgets the artistic revolutionary whom at bottom it has learned to love."[34] He gave public vent to his anti-Semitism.

At the same time he was impressed by the improvisational character of Swiss festivity, which had been given a great boost in the consolidation of the Swiss nation-state in 1848. These elaborate historical pageants, processions, and masquerades held throughout the Confederacy have been called "the one truly popular *Gesamtkunstwerk* of the nineteenth century," involving thousands and attracting tens of thousands.[35] The idea of temporary festival theaters in large open spaces began to fascinate Wagner.

But it was in the composer's twenty-five-year struggle to complete his *Ring* cycle that his festival ideal finally crystallized. Like so many German artists of the time, Wagner sought to reestablish the old Germanic sagas in the German imagination. His rivals largely failed; neither the flowery language of the late Romantic poets nor the dramatic realism of Hebbel's *Die Nibelungen* (1862) proved adequate to the task. But the suggestive power of Wagnerian music would succeed in making the old myths vivid, all too vivid, in the minds of the following generations. From Feuerbach Wagner had learned to view mythology as the projections of a people's psyche, and even when he exchanged the optimism of Feuerbach for the pessimism of Schopenhauer he continued to hold the great artist to be not only the herald of the future but also the therapeutic mystagogue guiding the inner life of the "people." His theory of the *Gesamtkunstwerk* consequently came to emphasize the origin of the theater in Hellenic religious ritual; his own *Ring* cycle, he decided, could only be staged within the recreated atmosphere of a religious festival.

In the 1850s this festival concept was but a recurring thought, which could be put aside for more practical pursuits. In 1859, for example, Wagner stormed the art capital of Paris, attempted to recruit Baudelaire and other Frenchmen into the cause his music had become. Wagner was in a rare cosmopolitan mood, unconcerned with the Schiller festival. But his Parisian campaign failed, and he became an embittered Francophobe. Rebuffed in Paris and then in Vienna, his influence seemed to have reached its lowest ebb at the close of the "era of festivals." Then the composer was suddenly and quite unexpectedly made royal favorite by the eighteen-year-old Ludwig II, the newly crowned king of Bavaria.

Ludwig discovered Wagnerian music at the same time as Nietzsche and Gustav Krug, in 1861. Krug, an amateur musician, was quick to embrace Wagner the musical revolutionary; Nietzsche, after long resisting the "music of the future," eventually seized on Wagnerian cultural politics as the means of launching the generational movement he dreamt of leading; but Ludwig saw himself immediately implementing the "new style," the "new era" in German art, through his patronage of Wagner.[36] Ludwig was the one member of Nietzsche's age group able to directly affect the symbolic politics of the "era of festivals." An aesthetic dreamer, Ludwig lived for the theater; he memorized Schiller plays and was inspired by the playwright to attempt his own "revolutionary" drama on a generational motif.[37]

Wagner was intent on steering Ludwig toward an ambitious renewal of festival politics. Instead of "those foolish festive gatherings with their theatrical processions, their silly speeches, and the cheerless empty songs wherewith one tries to make the German *Volk* imagine it is something special,"[38] Wagner envisaged a new set of permanent aesthetic institutions, engendering a higher phase of popular festivity which would serve to "nobly front the whole civilized world," present "a pattern for its purpose," and bequeath "a monument of the German Art-Spirit."[39] In his excitement about the new undertaking, the composer set aside the *Ring* for *The Meistersingers,* an opera which similarly sought to evoke a new mythic unity for Germans, but this time within the concrete, urban world of the Renaissance burgher. Wagner also aligned himself with the publicist of a greater German populism, Julius Froebel, then orchestrating Austria's propaganda campaign against Prussia.

When Ludwig installed Wagner in the Hotel Jochum and announced plans for a grandiose festival-theater in the heart of Munich, it was at first tolerated by the Bavarian public as preferable to the liberal cultural politics of his father, who had hoped to provide an aesthetic dimension to the political emergence of the third Germany by making Munich a new liberal Weimar. But with the polarization of German power politics, his policy of importing north German talent seemed only to lead to the sacrifice of Bavaria's aesthetic identity. Through Ludwig's neo-Gothic flamboyance and idiosyncratic personality, it was at first hoped that what was being lost in the political could be regained in the aesthetic realm. Ludwig's conception of politics was the opposite of that of Bismarck. Whereas the latter scorned the "externals" of power, Ludwig lived only for the outer manifestations of his power. He aestheticized the role of kingship, thereby appearing to such artists as Verlaine to be *"le seul vrai roi de ce siècle."*[40]

Although Ludwig tended to gaze at the ceiling and whistle softly to himself whenever the composer broached political topics, the monarch was given to understand that he was in danger of losing his throne as had his grandfather in the Lola Montez scandal of 1848. Ludwig was eventually forced to terminate a series of Wagner articles in the *Süddeutsche Zeitung,* a journal run jointly by Froebel and Wagner, when the composer's enthusiasm for the earlier youth movement spilled over into a defense of the assassination of Kotzebue by the student terrorist Karl Sand. But the last straw was the composer's scandalous affair with Cosima von Bülow, Liszt's daughter and the wife of Wagner's protégé, then conductor of the Munich symphony. The royal favorite was exiled in early 1866, although the money kept flowing. The impracticality and the direction of Wagner's thought were demonstrated when he urged Ludwig at the outbreak of the war of 1866 to abandon Munich in favor of Nuremberg and there declare himself at the head of the national movement.[41]

The whole character of German politics was fundamentally transformed by the dynastic civil war of 1866. Wagner's comet-like appearance faded beyond the horizon with the general revulsion against the tone and style of the "era of festivals." Liberals were particularly contrite; for example, in his "self-critique" Baumgarten bluntly told his fellow liberals that they had earned the world's scorn for losing themselves in "speeches and drinking" amidst "the boisterous festive jubilation of countless cities" during what should have been "the bitter seriousness of a great struggle."[42] Treitschke, who had been created by festival politics and whose constituency never grew beyond that which he had won in those years, became the leading apologist of *Realpolitik,* totally ignoring the role of symbolic politics in the lecture series, *Politics,* which he was to deliver to students in the coming decades. Compromise with Bismarck was justified on the grounds that liberals could never again allow themselves to be absent from the centers of power, even if they were forced to play a subsidiary role. Cultural politics, they decided, would have to be held in abeyance until the awaited accession of the Crown Prince.

But whereas liberals were contrite when faced with the success of *Realpolitik,* Nietzsche had assumed that the triumph of *Realpolitik* made possible a new round of cultural politics. His "philology of the future" seemed to him to be in perfect convergence with the "music of the future." After attending a summer 1867 music festival organized by Liszt and Hans von Bülow, Nietzsche noted with satisfaction that "this school has now passionately thrown itself upon Schopenhauer." He admitted, however, that he found the music of Bülow's "Nirvana" highly displeasing.[43] But he avidly followed the Munich premier of *Die Meistersinger* in the music press, obtained the score and was able to play "The Prize Song" for Sophie Ritschl during a visit to Leipzig in the summer of 1868. Jahn's assessment of Wagner, he now decided, was that of a mere *"Grenzboten* hero," irredeemably committed to a "healthy," safe *Bildung* acceptable to the readers of this liberal journal.[44] If Wagner's turbulent musical world was necessarily closed to Jahn, Nietzsche no longer wanted it impenetrable to him, declaring that he was no longer able to take a "critically cool" attitude toward Wagner's music.[45] His only qualm was that Jahn was probably correct in seeing Wagner as "a representative of that modern dilettantism that sucks up and ingests all cultural tendencies."[46] Still Nietzsche hoped to gain personal access to Wagner's world by cultivating Windisch's connections to Wagner's sister, the wife of Sanskrit professor Hermann Brockhaus.

When Nietzsche returned to Leipzig in October 1868, the city was anticipating the long-delayed arrival of Heinrich Laube. Nietzsche obtained press credentials and attended the theater in the company of the bright young critics of Leipzig.[47] But he was greatly disappointed in Laube's *Graf Essex* performed on the eve of the director's installation.[48] Although Nietzsche would subsequently frequent Laube's salon, it was already clear to him that this one-time Young German war-horse was not to be the promised *Reformator* of the German stage.[49] It had ceased to matter, however, as Nietzsche had finally met Richard Wagner.

In late October Wagner stopped over in Leipzig during one of his frequent incognito trips through Germany. After playing "The Prize Song" for the Brockhaus circle, Wagner was surprised to have Sophie Ritschl tell him that she was already familiar with the piece. Wagner thereupon expressed an interest in meeting Nietzsche, and Windisch hastily arranged it. Nietzsche impressed Wagner with his discourse on Schopenhauer as the one philosopher who understood the nature of music, and the composer extended the young philologist an open invitation to visit him in Switzerland to "pursue music and philosophy."[50] Nietzsche was ecstatic. He had met the one living "illustration of that which Schopenhauer calls a genius"; he now listened to Wagnerian music as "an exulting intuition, as an astonished self-discovery."[51] He urged Rohde immediately to read the new edition of Wagner's essay "Opera and Drama," which spelled out the theory of the *Gesamtkunstwerk,* so in tune with their own conceptions of Greek festive drama.[52]

Nietzsche might have remained but a distant admirer of Wagner had it not been for his sudden and unexpected appointment to the faculty of the university of Basel in the spring of 1869. The position had become vacant when Adolf Kiessling, a Ritschl student from Naumburg, transferred to a German university, and Wilhelm Vischer, the Hellenist in charge of the new appointment, wrote Ritschl in the hope that he might again recommend a similar candidate.[53] Vischer was eager to avoid appointing a Basel classicist who was drumming up local support, and when Ritschl replied that in thirty years of teaching he had never encountered as promising a student as Nietzsche, Vischer was relieved and elated. Nietzsche's reputation as the guiding spirit of the Leipzig Philological Society was another favorable sign, and the fact that he had graduated from Schulpforta only five years before actually worked in his favor, as half his time was to be spent teaching at the Pedagogium, a preparatory school which had long modeled itself on Schulpforta. The only complication was that the Basel university had been embarrassed by Kiessling's Prussian military eligibility during the war of 1866 and wished to avoid a similar incident in the future.

Nietzsche's military status was unclear. His commanding officer had told him at the end of his military year that he could still qualify as a reserve officer if he served an additional month of training in the spring. Nietzsche made plans to do so "since war is inevitable sooner or later, and as there is no prospect of being completely delivered from military bondage, an advancement to *Landwehr* lieutenant is of the utmost value."[54] Wisser gives us a glimpse of Nietzsche "in training" soon after his convalescence: "A rider galloped past me" in the Rosenthal, with its flooded frozen meadows and many children. "All the people stared at him. I thought it was a drunk. Suddenly a hat fell from his head. All the young started yelling. A man gave the rider back his hat, and the rider turned around. He sat so strangely stiff on his horse, like a Sunday rider. I stared at him—Nietzsche. He appeared to be embarrassed, therefore I did not make myself noticeable to him, and let him trot by. The old rented steed appeared to be responsible, for Nietzsche is a very good rider."[55]

But to satisfy Basel Nietzsche decided to take the drastic step of renouncing his Prussian citizenship, writing Vischer that he did so because he was certain that he would be called up in a future war and that he considered it irresponsible to make his teaching at the university "dependent on war and peace."[56] Although this was a symbolically drastic step, it did not carry the same finality as it would later. Citizenship in the 1860s could still be dropped and regained with little difficulty. With this problem thus resolved, the other stumbling blocks were quickly removed. Nietzsche had not yet written a dissertation so the Leipzig faculty hastily awarded him a doctorate on the basis of his two previously published seminar papers. A professorship at the age of twenty-four, even in the buoyant academic market of the 1860s, was quite a prize and seemed to verify Nietzsche's charmed life. Nietzsche's rather intemperate inaugural lecture, "Homer and Classical Philology," was also well received despite its polemical nature. Instead of being offended, the Basel audience warmed to Nietzsche's scathing dismissal of liberal classicism which singled out for special ridicule Freytag's theory of the Homeric epics as "national poems" embodying "the soul of the people."[57] Nor did the tactlessness of Nietzsche's partisan attack on Jahn, then critically ill, offend, for Basel's classicists were pleased to hear the Prussian school of philology attacked.

Nietzsche's first impression of Basel was negative, however. He missed Leipzig's lively theatrical and musical life, found Basel's Pietist atmosphere unpleasantly familiar, and felt uncomfortable in a stiff, partician world. Basel, he wrote Ritschl, was a place where "one could be cured of republicanism."[58] He worried that he lacked his predecessor's gregariousness, had trouble fitting in, and associated primarily with other newly arrived German academics. As the university had long served as a revolving door for aspiring young Germans, Nietzsche arrived with no commitment to an extended or permanent stay. It was only at the end of his second year that Nietzsche began to feel at home and identify with Basel. He was, however, fortunate in quickly establishing rapport with Burckhardt, twenty-six years his senior. In Burckhardt Nietzsche met the leading historian of festivity who was then turning his attention to the study of Greek cultural history. It is hard to imagine a more propitious moment for their meeting. Burckhardt was gratified to discover in Nietzsche another adherent of "the Philosopher"—as Burckhardt referred to Schopenhauer—and the two soon engaged in long walks and conversations.[59]

Switzerland was the European country with the strongest living tradition of political festivity, and Burckhardt became convinced of the crucial integrative role of political festivity as a young journalist covering the Swiss Sharpshooters' Festival of 1844.[60] During the Schiller Festival, he reminded his fellow German Swiss of their common Germanness and lauded Schiller's *Wilhelm Tell* as Germany's greatest gift to Switzerland.[61] In *The Civilization of the Renaissance in Italy,* published soon after the Schiller centennial, Burckhardt emerged as the historian and guardian of the festival idea. He implicitly lauded the Swiss as the bearers of Renaissance festivity, cultivating the urban festival during those centuries when festal display had shifted from the city square to the Baroque court. True popular festivity was made possible, Burckhardt argued, by "a free intercourse of all classes" guided by "the existence of an educated class as we now understand the word" and by "an art and culture common to the whole nation."[62] In Burckhardt's conception festivity was "a higher phase in the life of the people in which its religious, moral, and political ideas took visible shape"; it was "the point of transition from real life into the world of art."[63]

Nietzsche would introduce Burckhardt's ideas on festivity to Wagner's circle just as the composer was developing his plans for a *Festspiel.* What Nietzsche appreciated most about Basel was that his newly discovered culture hero, Richard Wagner, lived only a half-day's journey away. When Nietzsche first timidly appeared at the Triebschen villa on the lake of Lucerne, he discovered that he had come at a most opportune moment. Wagner was still smarting from his forced expulsion from Munich and remained isolated by the cloud of scandal surrounding his liaison with Cosima von Bülow. The composer saw in the morally upright young Basel professor a symbol of that respectability then denied the unmarried couple. Cosima was also impressed, noting in her diary that the new guest "thoroughly knows Richard's works and even quotes from 'Opera and Drama' in his lectures."[64] The friendship was cemented three weeks later when Nietzsche returned and happened to be present at the birth of the couple's son, Siegfried. Nietzsche was named godfather; he began to go on outings with the Wagner ménage; they became involved in his personal life and he in their daily routine. In August he accompanied the couple to a Singers' Festival in Lucerne, in September he aroused Wagner's wrath by sticking to a vegetarian diet after the composer denounced it as unhealthy, and by the end of the year Nietzsche was helping Cosima with the Christmas shopping. Nietzsche had become an informal member of the family, making some twenty-two visits between 1869 and 1872, usually for several days at a time.[65]

Nietzsche was entrusted with the confidential task of proofreading Wagner's secret autobiography, becoming privy to the composer's life history. But he did not become equally intimate with Wagner's music. In these years he saw only three performances of Wagner's works: *Die Meister-*

singer in January 1869; a concert Wagner personally conducted in December 1871; and *Tristan* in June 1872. He was forced to rely on piano scores and occasional impromptu Triebschen concerts. It was not so much Wagner the musician, nor even Wagner the artist, that dazzled Nietzsche as it was Wagner the herald of a new religion of art. Nietzsche felt the whole horizon of European culture expanding out before him and his own provincial background melting away behind him. He saw himself in the aesthetic vanguard of a new era. He had arrived just as Wagner was on the verge of his most ambitious plan for theater reform. Where resolution and royal patronage had failed, Wagner began making plans to create his own personal theater by appealing directly to the public. Wagner sensed that his great opportunity lay in the enthusiasm of a new generation. As Ludwig had rescued him financially, so the composer perceived Nietzsche to be the Hellenist destined to rejuvenate and propagandize the Greek festival ideal which motivated his future plans.

Wagner quietly revived his festival program at a moment when disillusionment with Bismarckian unification was deepening and growing within Germany. The preceding two and a half years, Rochau, the theorist of *Realpolitik*, sourly observed, demonstrated that German unity was "purely a business matter," involving taxes, military obligations, and jealously guarded local rights. The nationalist pathos of the "era of festivals" now seemed to Rochau a grand "self-deception"; so weak was true national feeling, he bitterly added, that if the principle of self-determination had been consistently pursued it was unlikely that one of the three hundred former Imperial territories would ever have disappeared from the map of Germany.[66] Nietzsche's relatively untroubled abandonment of his citizenship was another indication of how little this symbolic attachment had come to mean in 1869. Political disappointment and apathy were matched by a heightened sense of aesthetic inferiority. The international painters' exhibition in Munich, highlighted by the presence of the leading French Impressionists, had made public the backward and stagnant state of German painting.[67] As liberal historicism seemed to have reached a dead end, the ground was set for another resurgence of the "new German" quest for a "music of the future." Liberals had, moreover, grown weary of their long polemic with the composer; the campaign of Clara Schumann and Brahms to head off the popularity of the "new German" school had clearly boomeranged; but in 1869 most liberals preferred to console themselves with the view of one of their leading critics that "no one any longer expects a revolution in the arts" from Wagner.[68]

Meanwhile Nietzsche was acting as a cultural liaison between Triebschen and Basel, preparing a series of public lectures expounding Wagner's theories for the Basel public. He also became aware that he had arrived in perhaps the most critical year of Basel's nineteenth-century history. Ever since the traumatic civil war of 1831–33 which divided Basel into two half cantons, Basel-City had functioned as a veritable city-state, a condition zealously guarded and exalted by the city's intellectual and political elite. The rapid development and boom of the textile industry had prevented the city from shriveling up into itself; instead Basel enjoyed a cultural flowering not seen in the city since the days of Erasmus, Holbein, and Paracelsus. But the economic repercussions of the American Civil War burst the prosperity and well-being of the preceding quarter century. The most patrician of cities suddenly faced the most militant and the largest urban proletariat in all Switzerland. Almost overnight the International claimed over 1,000 members out of a factory work force of some 12,000; a strike wave ensued culminating in a December 1868 demonstration that seemed to authorities to teeter on the brink of insurrection. They responded with lockouts, the formation of a civil guard, and the conciliatory promise of a future factory law.

Basel captured the attention of the European left during 1869. The relative freedom and strength of the city's working class movement made it appear to be the test case for future developments. It became the cause célèbre for the fledgling International. In January Bebel launched a fundraising campaign on behalf of Basel's locked-out workers in twenty-two German cities.[69] Although the actual agitation started to wane shortly before Nietzsche's arrival, the preparations for the fourth Congress of the International planned for Basel in September kept the city in a high state of excitability and tension. Approximately seventy delegates from twenty countries arrived. Ostentatious parades were held up and down Basel's main streets, and conservatives such as J. J. Bachofen could only growl that this congress of "thieves" were "prating doctrines which a short time earlier would have landed them in jail."[70] Marx, in turn, declared in his written address to the congress that "Basel is a place that has retained to the present day many of the features of the medieval city with its local traditions, its narrow prejudices, its stockmarket-proud patriciate, and its patriarchal relations between employers and employees." For this reason "the economic revolt of Basel's workers represented a new epoch in Swiss social history." The city, he said, was in a "state of siege."[71]

Nietzsche, like most others in the Basel academic community, maintained a horrified distance from the congress which has since been remembered in the history of European socialism as the arena for the first open clash between the followers of Marx and Bakunin. Liebknecht, representing German Marxists at their first international gathering, propounded Marx's "scientific" position. But it was the colorful and exotic personality of Bakunin that dominated local perceptions of the congress. The explosive but transitory revolutionary mood of Basel's working class movement identified most readily with the anarchistic program of the Geneva-based Bakunin. The legendary Russian revolutionary also sentimentally embodied the internationalism so strongly rooted in a Basel work force comprised primarily of immigrants from Baden, Alsace, and the rural Catholic Swiss hinterland.[72] Nietzsche, aware of Wagner's association with the agitator in 1849, would attribute to Bakunin in the coming years the most sinister and far-reaching influence. Two weeks after the congress, Nietzsche announced to Gersdorff that he was abandoning his vegetarianism because it smacked of that "optimism" that made the world susceptible "to all kinds of socialism."[73]

In Wagnerian populism Nietzsche found an alternative and rival outlet for what he perceived as his own radicalism. By the end of 1869 he was drawn into Wagner's cult of the Dionysian. The composer had been long fascinated with this phenomenon; among his most treasured possessions was Bonaventura Genelli's painting "Bacchus among the Muses," which he had obtained from the fiery German painter after their meeting in Munich.[74] Now before this prominently displayed picture, Wagner and Nietzsche speculated about the impact of the enigmatic god on Greek culture. As befitting Wagner's populist ethic, Nietzsche stressed the communitarian and populist aspects of the Dionysian festivals. "The most beautiful brotherhood" had arisen in such festivity where "all the distinctions of caste established by deprivation and arbitrary power vanished; the slave is a free man, the aristocrat and the lowborn unite in the same Bacchic chorus." He lauded the Dionysian movement as "a social process of regeneration" espousing "the philosophy of the People." Dionysus, Nietzsche proclaimed, was the bearer of a "great revolution."[75]

In keeping with his agonal principle, Nietzsche soon postulated a new polarity between the turbulent creativity of the Dionysian and the countervailing force of balance and measure, the Apollonian. In Nietzsche's view, the Dionysian, previously the cause of terrible "Asiatic" upheaval, was checked in its invasion of Greece by the opposing power of the Apollonian. The foresight of the Delphic Oracle brought the competing divinities together in agonal festivity; in the archetypal agon which followed "both gods emerged from the contest as victors: a reconciliation on the field of battle."[76] Out of the ritual enactment of this mythic event, Nietzsche argued, tragedy could be born. All the dichotomies of his Leipzig years, as between Homer and Hesiod or Aeschylus and Euripides, were now incorporated in this master duality. Nietzsche was hardly the first to employ the Apollonian/ Dionysian polarity. Wilhelm Heinse had raised it during the *Sturm und Drang* era, Schelling and Friedrich Schlegel at the height of the Romantic era. Even two of Nietzsche's teachers, Ritschl and Jacob Bernays of Bonn, had concerned themselves with it. In addition, J. J. Bachofen in whose Basel villa Nietzsche frequently socialized was proceeding on similar lines.[77] But Nietzsche was the first to pose an agonal contest between the two gods—such a conception, it should be noted, was foreign to the Greeks themselves.

He gave the whole issue a new topicality by linking it to theater reform. In his January 1870 lecture, "Greek Music Drama," Nietzsche set out to show that the greatness of Greek theater lay in its roots in agonal festivity, that such dramatic spectacles engendered a "higher community," involving as many as twenty thousand at a single peformance and that the whole had been sanctified by religious festivity.[78] Without this grounding in an aesthetically oriented religiosity, Nietzsche argued, the tragic impulse withered and public involvement fell away; the tentative revival of drama in medieval Christian festivity proved fleeting, and the subsequent history of the theater from Shakespeare through Schiller to the present was but a failed "experiment" to breathe life into an aesthetic medium that had lost its roots.[79] "The ideal of the present *Kunstreformator*," however, offered hope of a rebirth of the theater in a new dynamic religion of art. And such a product of faith, Nietzsche believed, could be reawakened: "what we hope for in the future was once a reality—in more than two thousand years past."[80] He heralded Triebschen for having "allowed the artwork of the future to be resurrected through the past."

The next lecture, "Socrates and Tragedy," in February, was more controversial. As Nietzsche was of the opinion that "the whole liberal world is opposed to the spirit of music and its philosophical explication," he set out to demonstrate that Socrates was the gravedigger of ancient tragedy and that his modern liberal counterpart was the principle opponent of its rebirth.[81] Socrates, he later wrote, "fascinated because he touched on the agonal impulse of the Hellenes," but the "new kind of agon" which he introduced denuded the old, leaving a sterile intellectualism that became a force "against the agonal instinct."[82] The Socratic schools which followed worked actively toward the demise of the agon with Pyrrho, "a Buddhist for Greece," finally arriving at a perspective in which "the contradictions are overcome; no contest; no will for eminence: the denying of Greek instincts."[83] This was his mature formulation, but in 1870 his agonism turned not against "Buddhism" but solely against the optimism of cultural liberalism. And to make his critique all the more pointed he even planned to conclude the lecture by declaring, "this Socratism is the Jewish press; I need say no more." This was deleted when Cosima warned, "Do not name the Jews and particularly not *en passant*," urging him instead to take up this "terrible struggle" only after he had established himself professionally.[84]

Nietzsche's youthful prejudice toward Jews, nurtured by his reading of Schopenhauer, blossomed in Wagner's presence. To be sure, such feelings were standard fare back home in Naumburg, but since Jews were about as rare there as Catholics, they remained principally the butt of patriotic humor. For example, during a pilgrimage to Nuremberg in 1861 Nietzsche copied down the anti-Jewish stanza, "Throw Itzig out!" from a popular song.[85] (The same song would be sung by Prussian troops as they entered Frankfurt-am-Main in 1866.)[86] But it was only when Nietzsche began associating with a fellow Schopenhauerian philology student, Hermann Muschacke, that his prejudices became pronounced. In Leipzig he railed against the Jewish merchants of the fair season, but was also embarrassed when Hueffer unknowingly offended Sophie Ritschl, the first person of Jewish origin to influence Nietzsche's life.[87]

Nietzsche later attributed the anti-Semitism of his own generation and that of Wagner to the influence of Schopenhauerian philosophy.[88] Although Schopenhauer was no racist, he had the patrician's disdain for the Jewish plebe. It was not difficult for the young Schopenhauerians of Nietzsche's circle to turn the philosopher's animus toward Judaism as the optimistic religion par excellence into open hostility toward a Jewish-seeming liberal Hegelianism.

Wagner attacked the Jews before he had discovered Schopenhauer. His initial motives were largely personal. In his 1850 pamphlet "Judaism in Music" he belittled his popular Jewish rivals, Mendelssohn and Meyerbeer, with the rancor of an exile; he condemned Jewish democracy with the pathos of a repentant insurrectionary; and he imagined Jewish capital with the resentment of a spendthrift debtor. His first wife rebuked him for daring to "slander whole races which have been fundamentally helpful to you," and the composer admitted that the object of such scurrilous writings had been to purge the "poisons" within himself.[89] Nietzsche would later be the first to publicly point to the neurotic origin of Wagner's obsession with a suspicion that his stepfather, whose name he had carried in boyhood, might have been Jewish and might also have been his real father. But it was finally through Schopenhauerian metaphysics that Wagner's anti-Semitism took on ideological coherence. When he republished his anti-Semitic tract in March 1869, he did so as a Schopenhauerian anxious to have his revenge on his liberal critics. His festival ideal now incorporated the idea of an internal enemy. Nietzsche quickly fell into this attitude, hailing Wagner for working alongside "your great intellectual brother Arthur Schopenhauer" in bringing relief to the "poor Germans" plagued "by political misery, philosophical mischief, and intrusive Jewry."[90]

Yet in Triebschen Wagner was not yet the full-blown racist he was to become ten years later when he befriended Gobineau and espoused the latter's racial theories. Nor was he even the political anti-Semite of his early Bayreuth years. Religion, not race, was the pressing issue in Triebschen.

Cosima was in the process of converting to Protestantism, a step that would enable her to marry Wagner. As her conversion implied a break with the celebrated Catholicism of her father, Franz Liszt, as well as a renunciation of her French background, Cosima invested her act with symbolic meaning. She saw herself becoming a true German in embracing the Reformation. She became a partisan of Döllinger, hoping that his opposition to the doctrine of Papal Infallibility might lead to a new "German church." Only religion, Cosima advised Nietzsche, could hope to influence the "people," and to expect otherwise was only to betray insufficient understanding of Schopenhauer.[91]

Nietzsche continued to view himself as "anti-Christian" but was too critical of "increasing secularization" and too compromised by his commitment to Wagner's religion of art to offer resistance; he proceeded to invoke in himself the very cultural Protestantism he was later so much to despise. "The German spirit will return to itself," he declared, only by remaining worthy of its Lutheran heritage. Wagner, he added, was the "leader," the new *Reformator* following in the footsteps of Beethoven and Luther, destined to lead the lost back to the nation's aesthetic roots. Nietzsche and Wagner planned a magazine for their festival project entitled *Die Reformationszeitschrift.*[92]

In the nostalgic modernism Wagner was fashioning, the archaic was evoked through musical innovation, and the Jew was cast in the role of the non-believer in the new aesthetic church. As the exemplar of a militant secularism, he was to be ostracized by the "new community" that was to gather in Bayreuth. By settling in March 1870 on this small Protestant Bavarian town as the site of his *Festspiel,* Wagner also turned his back on Germany's nascent urban culture. Bayreuth was as far from Munich as was possible without leaving the confines of his protector's kingdom and was equally distant from the other major cities of Germany. To this picturesque provincial setting the faithful were expected to make their pilgrimage, shedding on their way their urban mannerisms, thereby consecrating themselves to the higher spirituality of the new aesthetic temple of Bayreuth. Nietzsche became so absorbed in this vision during the spring of 1870 that he contemplated requesting a leave of absence so he could accompany the composer to Bayreuth. There he planned to make public his conception of the imminent rebirth of agonal festivity. Cosima enthused, "Write your book in Bayreuth, and we will do the book honor."[93]

Nietzsche's Wagnerian reveries were suddenly interrupted by the outbreak of the Franco-Prussian War. Although many Europeans, Nietzsche included, had been predicting war in the preceding years, few if any, were ready when it came in the summer of 1870. Public attention was riveted on the convening of the long-awaited Vatican Council, and the Hohenzollern candidacy to the Spanish throne attracted little public notice. When war broke out, European opinion was one in condemning French belligerence as the root cause. Nietzsche suddenly felt in a "depressed mood to have to be Swiss."[94] With Cosima urging him to back Prussia's German mission to the hilt, he was uncomfortable with the thought that his old regiment was marching off to war without him.[95] He was especially moved by the act of the philology students of Kiel, volunteering *en masse*. But he still went ahead with a planned vacation, prompting Cosima to complain in her diary that Nietzsche was seeking to "escape" into the Alps.[96] Yet two weeks later, and a year and a half after renouncing his Prussian citizenship specifically to avoid such a contingency, to everyone's surprise Nietzsche requested and was granted a leave of absence in order to serve his country.

Deussen always found it inexplicable that a "cosmopolitan" like Nietzsche could throw himself into the war.[97] As the most committed of Nietzsche's fellow Schopenhauerians, it could not have escaped Deussen's notice that Nietzsche was making the opposite choice of the young Schopenhauer in 1813. By his action, Nietzsche had shown himself closer in spirit to Fichte than Schopenhauer. A startled Cosima sought to dissuade Nietzsche by urging him not to be blinded by the example of the earlier youth movement: "we don't have 1813 now."[98] But Nietzsche, who had been primed for such a moment since the war scare of 1859, who had uneasily sat out the war of 1866, now regretted the loss of his citizenship and was determined to make his patriotic stand. Since active military service was no longer possible, Nietzsche joined the medical corps instead.

The war enthusiasm of 1870 never approached the mass hysteria of 1914, but among educated Germans it did arouse the sensation of reliving the heroic legend of the war of liberation. And Nietzsche, outside Germany's borders, was especially prone to magnify the depth of this sentiment, contrasting in his mind the tepid support of the German Swiss for the German cause with what he assumed was a great wave of patriotic renewal pulsating through Germany. All the more so as Nietzsche immediately perceived the war as a contest between French and German culture. "It concerns our culture! And for this no sacrifice could be too great," Nietzsche wrote his mother at the outbreak of the war.[99] It seemed axiomatic to him that French victory would so further infect Germany with foreign influences that the needed cultural Reformation planned for Bayreuth would be set back at least another generation. Nietzsche wrote Naumburg as he left for the front, "I await all my friends in the field."[100] But a perplexed Nietzsche was forced to write Rohde inquiring, "Why did you not participate?"[101] Only Gersdorff, already an officer, fought, and he did so armed with a battlefield will that concluded: "If I die, I die a faithful, unshakable adherent of the philosophy of Schopenhauer."[102]

After a cursory ten-day training with a Protestant association of medical volunteers, Nietzsche was dispatched to join the Crown Prince's Army of the Rhine as it penetrated the Vosges mountains of Alsace and Lorraine. Nietzsche was one of the three professors dispatched in a group of 91 medical orderlies, of whom over two-thirds were students, over half of these being theologians.[103] Nietzsche left for the front with eight others on August 23rd, on the tenth and last transport sent through this organization. With him was his new friend, Adolf Mosengel, a landscape painter of the Engadine.[104] The furious battle for the Vosges dominated public attention in the first weeks with Gustav Freytag whipping up German anger at the French employment of North African "Turcos." In his war dispatches Freytag protrayed the use of these "dirty semi-apes" with their "most dangerous, sinister guillotine physiognomy" as a violation of the code of war.[105]

Nietzsche like other German medics, however, came to respect the fortitude and suffering of the wounded prisoners, especially as necessary medical supplies were often lacking and transport was long and laborious.[106] Nietzsche and Mosengel arrived at the battlefield of Gravelotte near Metz just as the decisive battle of Sedan was occurring to the north. At a time when railroad transport was overtaxed, Nietzsche was given the task of nursing eleven wounded and dying North Africans across the border in a foul cattle car. The journey took three days. By the time they arrived Nietzsche was feverish, and after a week of treatment for dysentery and diphtheria he had to be sent home to Naumburg.[107] It was several months before he completely recovered. Nietzsche's duty had been short but nasty; "the atmosphere of these experiences surrounded me like a bleak fog: for a time I heard a never ceasing cry of pain."[108]

Nietzsche would maintain a fastidious reticence about his war experiences, although he was not adverse to publicizing his participation in the *Birth of Tragedy*. He had seen, though briefly, the worst aspects of the war, the inadequate medical facilities—at one stopover he was the only French speaking orderly in the hospital full of prisoners—yet those who saw this war's most merciless aspect rarely became pacifists. Losses had been too limited for that; the war was over too soon. Moreover, there was a cloud over the performance of the medical orderlies in the first weeks of the war. Nine days before Nietzsche arrived at Pont a Mousson, 1,500 medics had swarmed over the battlefield robbing the corpses.[109] The legitimate medical participants preferred to reflect on the lack of medical preparation as a blemish that needed to be corrected. For instance, two of Nietzsche's colleagues, Basel professors of medicine, surgeons in the war, published reports on the inadequacy of field hospital medicine, convinced that their experience could be put to good use in any future war. Neither Nietzsche's experience nor his illness was untypical. Four of the eight dispatched with him became ill, almost all with dysentery. Only three were still in service by mid-October, and these returned by end of the year. Dysentery ravaged other groups of volunteers in a similar fashion.[110]

Nietzsche gathered souvenir gifts of chassepot shells on the battlefield for the homefront, but was horrified by the bloodlust he encountered when he returned. The mood of exultation simply had no relation to what he was fighting for or what he had experienced. In a Germany wild with euphoria over a victory hardly imaginable just months before, extravagant expectations filled the air. Protestants envisaged a second Reformation in the making, and even a sober outsider like Burckhardt could briefly entertain the notion that German might displace English as the world language.[111] Nietzsche's unease, vague as it was at this moment, was only shared by an isolated handful, as for instance by the painter Hans von Marées who returned from the front complaining of the "swindle."[112] With hindsight one may well agree with Michael Howard that "Germany's magnificent and well-deserved victory was, in a profound and unforeseeable sense, a disaster for herself, and for the whole world."[113] Cassandras were, however, almost impossible to find.

Nietzsche was prescient, however, in worrying that victory could destroy his plans as surely as defeat. By October the war which had begun in Nietzsche's mind as a contest between French and German culture had turned into an ugly rout which he feared threatened to affirm all that was mediocre in German cultural life. "I am beginning to lose sympathy for the present German war of conquest," he wrote his family after he returned to Basel. Hegemony, total victory, was inconsistent with the agonal idea; one contestant may win, but never totally "master" his opponent; agonism required the tension of comparability. Germany's crushing victory violated the political framework of an agonism fostered by the climate of *Realpolitik,* a concept focused on limits; 1866 was the victory of the "little German" position over the "greater German" position; 1870 compromised that sense of limits. The pomposity of victory confronted Nietzsche with a new fear, that German culture was threatened as surely in triumph as it would have been by a humbling at the hands of the French. "The future of German culture seems more endangered than ever," he concluded.[114] The French, not the Germans, promised to be the cultural beneficiaries from the war, neither softened by the spectacle of greatness nor blinded to its limits.

He might protest the materialization and the dehumanizing features of modern war, but the spiritualization of war continued to be his purpose. His rhetoric would stock up with the terminology of battle, with expressions of military tactics and strategy finding their way into his prose. Having sought to sublimate the new militarism in the aestheticism of agonism before the war, Nietzsche reacted to his experience by embracing that ideal formulation with greater intensity. "Does the contest originate in war? As artistic game and imitation?" he asked himself as he returned.[115] His aesthetic program would indicate that it did. By sublimating war into culture the Greeks, the most politicized of peoples, had saved themselves, Nietzsche would argue, suggesting that similar salvation might be found in Bayreuth for postwar Germans. The image of the Prussian soldier—and of himself, the former officer candidate—propelled him into his new role as literary polemicist.

Nietzsche gave an aesthetic meaning to the growing military institutions, and thereby helped reconcile the educated middle class to a benign view of militarism. Nietzsche was in this regard typical of a generation that affected manliness and promoted an anemic, bloodless vision of war, one that banalized and domesticated the cost of armed struggle. The generation that trotted off with the *Zarathustra* in their knapsacks in 1914 landed in trenches that had little resemblance to Nietzsche's sublime, spiritualized battlefields.

According to Elisabeth, her brother "discovered" the notion of the "Will to Power" during his war service, prompted by the sight of Prussian troops massing for battle. This legend distorts a critical juncture in Nietzsche's life, for it makes him part of that exultation he would so bitterly condemn. The "Will to Power" was a formula Nietzsche first used a decade later, and even in the highly likely event that it had first surfaced in his mind during this six-week period, it more likely was inspired by the sight of the wounded fighting for life. For Nietzsche was one of the war's victims. He experienced the great victory in its limitations, and was forced to confront his own physical limitations. Henceforth, Nietzsche was forced to produce despite illness; all his creativity was fashioned within the tension of sickness, poor eyesight, and other physical ailments. His subsequent philosophy of health, his will to health, was guided by a determination not to yield to pity, especially self-pity. This vigilance, the weeding out of resentment, and the constant inner exhortation to strength, inhibited antiwar sentiments.

The triumph of *Realpolitik* after 1866 had seemingly rendered obsolete the politicizing optimism of the liberals by insuring the primacy of the army over the rule of party. But the triumphant expectation of national greatness fueled its own form of reactionary politicism. It was the mission of the Wagnerian movement to depoliticize Germany, Nietzsche believed. In various gnomic sayings on art as the destroyer of the state, Nietzsche pitted culture against polity, thereby introducing an antipolitical element to Wagner's religion of art. However, Triebschen was in no mood to listen to Nietzsche's mournful warnings. The war had inflamed Wagner's chauvinism, he dreamed of Paris ablaze and had just finished a tasteless farce, *Die Capitulation,* when Nietzsche came to visit in November. By affecting aloofness to the events of the day—the continuing siege of Paris, the proclamation of the Reich, and the imminent annexation of Alsace and Lorraine—as well as ignoring the implications of Wagner's Imperial March, Nietzsche was able to gloss over any incipient political rift between himself and the composer. Wagner took Nietzsche's worried anxiousness as fervency for his cause and was moved to declare after Christmas that aside from the unconventional political critic Constantin Frantz, Nietzsche was the only living contemporary who "has brought me something, a positive enrichment of my outlook."[116]

Nietzsche's dilemma resembled that of the Crown Prince. As idealists both sought to validate the war through aesthetic militarism—although the liberal imperialism of the latter would be attacked as "cultural Philistinism" by the critic, and the Wagnerianism of the former was condemned as obscurantism by Friedrich III. In 1870 the commanding general and the anonymous medical orderly in his ranks dreamed great dreams for themselves and their generation. Their conception had presumed the Germans as underdogs and the French as aggressors. But in the first days, the Prussian Crown Prince realized to his horror that French lack of preparedness was going to deprive Germany of the opportunity of gaining a great defensive victory on the banks of the Rhine.[117] The war was not to be a repetition of the heroic crusade against the first Napoleon. Once Germany was forced on the offensive, Friedrich III became insistent that some new majestic symbol accompany victory. His notion was pedagogic in character, aimed at sanctifying ideals and unifying the national community. The center of European gravity might have shifted from Paris to Berlin, but it was still patent that German unification had been imposed from above as a result of victories on foreign battlefields. Only a Reich could unite north and south German, Prussian and Bavarian in a higher community. Since the North German Confederation had failed to follow up the victory of Sadowa with unifying symbolism, the opportunity afforded by Sedan must not be lost. He worked closely with Bismarck, his old nemesis, to cast the new German nation-state into an imperial mold. The Crown Prince's enthusiasm for the imperial idea overcame the liberal party's initial and instinctive resistance to it, but what his liberal conception of Empire was never became clear or certainly never actual.[118] The proclamation of the Reich did not in itself satisfy popular feeling or engender popular festivity. His father, Wilhelm I, was reluctant to assume the imperial title and did nothing to create enthusiasm for it, choosing to hold his imperial coronation, just as he had the regal coronation, far from the masses of the capital, excluding the populace from participation. This event failed to galvanize public sentiment for the newly founded German Reich. Wilhelm I insisted on viewing it as a step in the monarchy's rise to greater ascendancy rather than a national event. For instance, he crowned himself on January 18, the day commemorating the founding of the Prussian monarchy, and Prussian patriots would then preclude its future use as a national holiday by insisting that it remain a purely Prussian memorial.[119] As in 1866, lavish receptions were afforded the returning armies, but little else was done. And so like the North German Confederation before it, the new German Empire faced a festive vacuum in its hour of triumph. While Nietzsche committed himself ever more to Wagner's cause, Friedrich III would throw himself into his ceremonial role as Imperial Crown Prince, reviewing his South German troops and lavishing attention on the newly founded university of Strassburg. Both men had grandiose visions of what might come from the war, but both deferred to their "fathers," actual or spiritual, in implementing those dreams.

The war emboldened Nietzsche with the veteran's conviction of having earned the right to speak out forcefully. It also made him all the more dissatisfied with his philological career. Back at the university of Basel he leaped at the chance of changing fields and filling a soon-to-be vacant professorship in philosophy. However, aside from his lack of formal qualifications, his reputation as a Schopenhauerian effectively barred him. Frustrated in this move, Nietzsche would invest all his energy in Bayreuth. He turned from the lecture to the essay, exchanging in the process the intimacy of an immediate audience for a larger public that needed to be rallied and instructed. To his prewar lectures he now grafted a lengthy essay explicitly promoting Wagner; together they would appear at the end of 1871 as *The Birth of Tragedy*.

In his pedagogic zeal, Nietzsche sounded the clarion call of a new generational movement. The young, he felt, could be reeducated "according to new principles with the aid of the theater."[120] He wrote Rohde that "a completely new culture" would emerge if "only a few hundred people out of the next generation" gained from Wagnerian music what he had gained from it.[121] He recruited Gersdorff by telling him "that the two of us are called upon to fight in the front ranks of a cultural movement whose full significance will not be revealed to the larger masses of the public until the next generation, possibly not until a much later period."[122] The Leipzig Philological Society was informed by its former president that "we still can hope for a reawakening of Hellenic antiquity of which our fathers could not have dreamed."[123] And when Ritschl expressed disapproval, Nietzsche defiantly replied, "My first concern is to win over the younger generation of classical philologists, and I would think it shameful if I did not succeed in doing so."[124] "Together with all my friends," as members of a "new generation," we have the solemn task of making "amends" for the failure of the preceding two generations of Germans to appreciate Wagner by taking "very seriously our task to be a public," he wrote the composer.[125] Small wonder Wagner came to believe that "with and through Nietzsche I have gotten into very good company," and that he had discovered in Nietzsche "a new type of man, perhaps an entire generation."[126]

Nietzsche, the veteran, returned to his place across the border, back to his stateless condition. Although personally well received, he found "the political atmosphere frankly atrocious"; "even with calm and basically pro-German Baslers one can no longer come to any understanding. Hatred of the German is instinctive here and the joy in French victory reports is great."[127] Living at the flashpoint of German-French rivalry, he experienced first hand the dramatic swing of European opinion against Germany in the winter of 1870. There were anti-German riots in Zurich and a modest commemoration of German victory had to be canceled at the Basel university.[128] The city itself was overrun by angry Alsatian refugees, causing acute inflation and a housing shortage. Caught between his own qualms at the course of the war and lingering patriotic pride, Nietzsche sought relief in a Lugano vacation during March 1871. There, in the company of relatives of General Moltke, he celebrated—probably for the last time—a patriotic event: that of the birthday of the new Emperor, Wilhelm I.[129]

But Nietzsche returned to a Basel ever more fearful of Germany's growing power. The unification first of Italy and then of Germany had made the Swiss extremely nervous. When Italian nationalists called for the return of Italian-speaking cantons in the early sixties, the Swiss public was forcibly confronted for the first time with the thought that their state might not survive the implementation of the principle of nationality in Central Europe.[130] The federalism traditionally championed by the Swiss was crushed in 1866 by an overweening centralism all too ready to trample upon historic rights and traditions. Bismarck's humiliation of the formerly free city of Frankfurt was particularly galling to the Basel elite. With the expulsion of the Austrians from Germany, the German Swiss also began to feel shut out of a Bismarckian Germany that would in the coming decades show itself ever more hostile to the Swiss Confederacy. Nor could the Swiss take comfort in the pronouncements of German nationalists such as Treitschke who acknowledged that a neutral Switzerland played a useful role in European politics in the foreseeable future but were unwilling to make a more principled commitment to the more distant future of the Swiss state.[131] At the outbreak of the Franco-Prussian War many feared invasion as in the Napoleonic era.[132] Maintaining his optimism, the President of the Swiss Confederacy sought to interest Bismarck in the creation of a greater Switzerland, including Alsace and Lorraine, which together with the Benelux countries would form a permanent buffer zone between the belligerents. Bismarck dismissed the notion of restoring the Carolingian "middle kingdom" out of hand.[133] The Swiss public consequently emerged from the war more nervous than before, and nowhere was this anxiety stronger than in a Basel situated on the border of a Baden now absorbed into the Reich and a new Reichsland of Alsace-Lorraine.

But in the spring of 1871 even these concerns were overshadowed by reports emanating from Paris. It is said that when the false rumor of the Communards burning down the Louvre reached Basel, Burckhardt and Nietzsche spontaneously set off to console each other, and when they met both were moved to tears.[134] Nietzsche had fantasized shortly before that the war might still find its aesthetic justification if the Germans, like the Greeks pursuing Helen to Troy, "liberated the Venus from the Louvre."[135] Now the thought that this statue as well as the other treasures of the museum had been destroyed was almost more than Nietzsche could bear. He wrote Vischer, "One devotes one's whole life and one's best energies to better understand and explain a period of culture; what is this profession if one single, accursed day can turn the most priceless documents into ashes. This is the worst day of my life."[136]

He hurried to Triebschen for comfort but was hardly mollified by Wagner's nonchalant remark that an era incapable of creating anew did not deserve to possess the creative artifacts of the past. He was taken aback by the nostalgic indulgence with which the composer discussed Bakunin, then widely held responsible for the alleged blaze.[137] In Nietzsche's mind, such spokesmen of "anarchism" and "communism" had assumed a horrifying larger than life quality. Having invested the war with cultural meaning, he was quick to ascribe the most terrifying significance to the Commune.[138] Even discovering that the rumor was false did not lessen his sense of outrage. In the late seventies he would remember his reaction without irony, listing it as one of the four occasions in the past ten years that had brought him to tears.[139]

Nietzsche would continue to affect a certain radicalism, declaring, for example, that his form of terrorism would be to drive the academics from his utopia as Plato had expelled the poets.[140] But he henceforth expressed an almost Philistine fear of the "Rousseauian man" and other "Catiline existences" brought to the surface in the uprising of the Commune. He also began retreating from his previous praise of the revolutionary character of the Dionysian. If the Apollonian and the Dionysian had initially been conceived as representatives of two contrasting political orientations, Nietzsche was now at pains to depoliticize the Dionysian by identifying the political exclusively with the Apollonian. His revised version of the Dionysian in The Birth of Tragedy read: "We know now that whenever a group has been deeply touched by Dionysian emotions, the release from the bonds of individuality results in indifference, or even hostility to political instincts."[141]

The Dionysian was no longer to be an eruptive, emancipatory force capable of transforming society, but was instead to be a cult of a select and elite brotherhood. When an unwelcome radical admirer, Rosalie Nielsen, a Mazzinian and subsequent fixture of the Leipzig bohème, persisted in identifying the Dionysian with revolution, Nietzsche was greatly alarmed.[142] He had visions of the International seizing and applying his ideas. He consequently took further pains to distance himself from contemporary radicalism, from what he took to be "modern" ideas. He now saw himself fighting against his times and would entitle the essays of the coming years *Untimely Meditations*. In sociopolitical asides he nostalgically evoked the settled social order of the middle ages, and the generalization he derived from antiquity—that all higher cultures rested upon some form of slavery— was stated in ever more belligerent terms.[143]

Nietzsche placed increasing emphasis on the aristocratic character of agonal contests; it was a game in which slaves could not play, only equals. Or as Pater concluded later, apparently independently of Nietzsche, the agon was a "wholly friendly contest for prizes which in reality borrow all their value from the quality of the receiver."[144] Pater's 1876 essay, "A Study of Dionysus: The Spiritual Form of Fire and Dew," similarly sought to discount the egalitarianism of the Dionysia by remarking simply that during these festivities "even slaves have their holiday." While noting that "there were some who suspected Dionysus of a secret democratic intent," Pater insisted that the god was *"liberator* only of men's hearts."[145] For the young critics of the seventies, led by Nietzsche and Pater, Dionysus had become an antipolitical god, diffused and aestheticized.

Nietzsche thus set out to publicize Bayreuth as the future "forum of the People" while he was filled with ambivalence toward an "awakened people." But Bayreuth's ability to play successfully on this tension was the secret of its eventual success: the most aristocratic of art forms presenting itself as a force capable of harnessing the cultural energies of the people. The Founding Era of the immediate postwar years was itself rent by conflicting emotions, fearing the masses in the wake of the Commune, dividing the confessions in the *Kulturkampf*, while seeking new communal bonds that would truly unite the nation. Bayreuth presented itself as an alternative to the *Kulturkampf,* as the bearer of spiritual unification.

Although the opportunity for a formal celebration around the victory had again been missed, expectations remained high that a new cultural epoch with new forms of festivity would soon unfold.[146] Since Rousseau had first urged the Poles to hold festivals to preserve their threatened national identity, popular festivity had become such an integral part of the rise of the modern nation-state that its absence seemed inconceivable. With historians proclaiming that creativity followed power, the Founding Era began with exaggerated expectations of what was to come. Festival politics again became the order of the day. All the leading patriotic groups in the society wished to see themselves as bearers of a new national will, as "founding fathers" orienting the new state through new forms of communal festivity.

Among the first to propose a new national festival was the young Pietist leader Pastor Friedrich von Bodelschwingh. Bodelschwingh had earlier sought to stage "popular Christian festivity" in his rural parish, but now returned from the war with the vision of Sedan day festivals that could recapture the high-minded seriousness of the national day of prayer held at the outset of the war.[147] But his attempt to invest Sedan day with the somber characteristics of the Lutheran festival of the dead only deprived it of popular appeal and further alienated the Catholics, who saw themselves thereby confirmed in their second class citizenship and who consequently boycotted what they called "Satan day" festivity.[148] The nascent working class movement also took up their campaign against it—a campaign that would culminate twenty years later in the creation of their own counter-holiday, May Day.[149]

Liberals, long associated in the public mind with political festivity, lay paralyzed by the very success of their compromise with Bismarck. For instance, Sybel, the political luminary during Nietzsche's year in Bonn, declared he no longer knew what to live for now that the goals of a lifetime had been realized.[150] As junior partners in the new "liberal Empire," liberals continued to pin their hopes on the imminent succession of the Crown Prince and were thereby doomed to await that which never came. Seeking to fill the void, Sybel, like so many others, threw himself into the *Kulturkampf* against political Catholicism. But the *Kulturkampf*, unlike the liberal nationalist agitation Sybel had previously led, was by its very nature negative and unfestive. The rituals of secularization such as civil marriage helped to dismantle the old festivity without generating new forms of celebratory politics. The liberal aesthetic vision faltered as well. Freytag focused attention on "dramatic technique"; the liberal program for theater reform came to a standstill.[151] Able neither to direct nor to oppose, liberals lost mass popular support.

Nietzsche had reason to believe as he completed *The Birth of Tragedy* that for all his polemical flourishes against Socratism his book would be well received by the largely liberal reading public. He even sought through his new Basel intimate Franz Overbeck, a boyhood friend of Treitschke, to have segments published in advance in Treitschke's *Preussische Jahrbücher*. He remained undismayed by the latter's refusal. The times seemed ripe for a new intellectual impetus, and his book confronted both the bankruptcy of the liberal theater program and the growing malaise of German Hellenism. Ribbeck alerted Dilthey to its appearance, saying that its "charming madness and fermenting must" was necessary to rejuvenate "our ossified philology."[152]

Access to Vischer's patrician villa opened all the doors to Basel's aristocratic society. Nietzsche suddenly found himself courted, writing proudly to Naumburg that he had appeared at one grand ball in December 1871 as the "single German" in attendance.[153] For the first and last time in his life, he affected the manner of the dandy. After the first tentative years of acclimatizing himself, he did not share the restlessness so typical of the German academics who had preceded him. Since Nietzsche had served in 1870, he no longer suffered from the thought that he had absented himself from the great national events occurring across the border; since he had already established himself in the Basel community before 1870, he also never appeared to the Basler to be one of the new type of German academics who arrived in the seventies as arrogant and defensive *Reichsdeutsche,* alert to every slight and eager to represent at all times the great Reich to the north.[154] Much of Nietzsche's social success can be explained by the timing of his arrival and the hopes placed upon him by the Basel elite. When Vischer appointed Nietzsche in 1869 he believed he had found a man both capable of reviving the flagging fortunes of classical scholarship at the university and championing the threatened classical ideal within the city itself.

In 1867 Dilthey had summed up Basel's intellectual climate as "a lack of faith, of confidence in the world. It was a complete shock to me that a man like Burckhardt could suddenly announce: He had no hopes of any kind, Europe is becoming old, our culture is approaching its end." Dilthey attributed such sourness to a blindness to the promise of 1866 and took the first opportunity to flee what he called a remote "corner" of the German-speaking world.[155] Nietzsche, arriving a year later, proved far more susceptible to the dark mood of Basel's conservatives. He settled into his anomalous legal status as a stateless person, traveling happily on the temporary passport issued him by the Basel authorities.[156]

The city largely had owed its cultural revival to the role of the university which had been reorganized and rejuvenated by German exiles fleeing Metternich's crackdown on the German universities in the 1820s.[157] The newcomers instilled what seemed a revolutionary new classicism into the sons of the elite at the Pedagogium, and the university was feared in Germany as a source of subversion. Prussians were banned from attending the university. During the canton civil war of the 1830s, the exiles compromised their radicalism and through intermarriage rapidly became a part of the old elite. Basel had been thoroughly "Germanized" by the importation of the neo-classical ideal.

Those who were educated in the aftermath of Basel's civil war felt a special immediacy with the Hellenic world and a strong attachment to Germany. Wilhelm Vischer, Nietzsche's patron, left a scholarly travelogue of his pilgrimage to the cities of Greece and sought to make Grote's theories of Hellenic federalism popular in Germany; Arnold Böcklin distinguished himself from the over-stylized neo-classical painting of his day by bringing the landscape of antiquity to life; J. J. Bachofen wrote another memoir of his journey to Greece and published arcane studies of the mythological prehistory of the ancient world that included the novel thesis of an earlier matriarchal age; and Jacob Burckhardt left for his studies in Germany armed with the conviction that it was his task to make the German Swiss see that they were German.

The cosmopolitan mission which German Hellenism bestowed upon German nationalism enabled the Basel classicists to feel at home in Germany just as it permitted a disappointed Ritschl to declare after 1848 that Germans were destined to be the Greeks in the New French Imperium of Louis Napoleon.[158] But once Bismarck appeared on the scene, the nature of these illusions became transparent. Nationalism was stripped of its cosmopolitan trappings, and the old classical ideal began to dissolve. Intellectual interest already had begun to shift from the Greeks to the Romans, and, within Roman history itself, from the formation of the Republic to the making of Empire. Bachofen unhappily discovered when his Roman history appeared simultaneously with that of Theodor Mommsen that the new positivist history had only scorn for his interest in the myths and legends of early republican Rome. Burckhardt was also forced to see his evocation of city-state culture treated as largely irrelevant in a Germany enamored with bigness. Thus while formerly the Basel classicists had seen Germany as the beacon of their classicism, they now increasingly saw themselves as the last true guardians of German Hellenism, fighting desperately now on their own home ground. Burckhardt was their ascetic high priest. The son of the Basel Protestant church leader, he had an almost religious sense of vocation and a fierce loyalty to the "piece of ground" that was Basel and its university. In a series of public lectures, later assembled as *World Historical Reflections,* he alerted the Basel public of the crisis at hand and the need to defend the city's cultural traditions.

The university's central role within the city's constitution placed it at the heart of the political controversy. The university held two critical seats on the all-powerful seven-man Inner Council. This arrangement consolidated the peculiar symbiosis of patricians, industrialists, and academics which had dominated the city since the canton civil war.[159] The elite tended toward extended and interlocking families; double-barreled names were the norm. So numerous were the Burckhardts, for example, that a Burckhardt-Burckhardt was not uncommon; eleven of the 223 university faculty members between 1835 and 1885 were Burckhardts; Nietzsche could count eight Burckhardts among his classes at the Pedagogium; and the mayor in these years was a Burckhardt.[160]

The nemesis of Jacob Burckhardt and the conservatives was Wilhelm Klein, a one-time promising mathematics student of modest origins. Over the decades he had been the soul of the progressive movement as party activist, newspaper editor, and *Volksschullehrer*. Klein's lifelong goal was to humble the university and to strip away the neo-classical ideal that bolstered the defense of the old Basel. He led a campaign in the early seventies to democratize Basel's suffrage, to eliminate the university's political privileges, and to shift attention from the claims of higher education to mass education. His guiding principle was that "unequal distribution of knowledge was an even greater misfortune than the unequal distribution of wealth."[161] In 1851 he unsuccessfully sought to abolish the university and replace it with a national polytechnical institute. His dream was a tuition-free, eight-year *Volksschule* capable of integrating the children of Basel's social strata. He consequently sought to dismantle the Pedagogium; he saw this *"Standesschule"* functioning as the bonding mechanism of the hated "family regiment" that had ruled Basel for the last thirty-five years.[162]

Nietzsche had thus entered a highly politicized academic world. The German universities he had known had functioned as a world apart, largely indifferent to their surroundings and accountable only to periodic edicts from the Ministries of Culture. Basel's academics, however, were so identified with the old order that they had increasingly adopted a siege mentality. This was particularly true of the philologists and theologians. Vischer, who had represented the university on the Little Council since 1867, hired Nietzsche as a potential counterweight to the challenge of radical educational reform. He thought that around Nietzsche he could rejuvenate a whole department and thus guarded his "good acquisition."[163] In 1871 Nietzsche was hurriedly given a raise to discourage him from leaving to tour Greece as a guest of a wealthy aristocrat. In January 1872 the Pomeranian university of Greifswald offered Nietzsche a position, but Basel students staged a torchlight parade to dissuade him, and when he declined the new offer, he was given an academic promotion.[164] Soon thereafter Nietzsche made his highly successful public debut in the lecture series, "The Future of Our Educational Institutions."

These lectures, imaginatively constructed as a generational dialogue between an "old philosopher" and his middle-aged pupil, now a teacher, and two students, one of whom was Nietzsche himself, drew overflow crowds and positive press reviews. But even as he unraveled the central problems involved, he failed to resolve the underlying issues. On the one hand, he feared universal education as a Trojan horse of a "communism" determined to dilute and ultimately destroy the classicism of the *Bildungs-prinzip*. Yet, he was himself far too critical of the existing classicism not to make far-reaching concessions to the arguments of the opposition. Claiming ill health, Nietzsche canceled the final lecture, which had promised to spell out his own conception of the future of education. Nietzsche had documented the seriousness of the problem to his audience and to himself; the assumptions propelling the classical ideal at the beginning of the century no longer seemed to apply in a rapidly industrializing society; yet no appealing alternative presented itself. Germans thus seemed destined to continue to borrow on past greatness. The most that Nietzsche could propose was that this inheritance be rejuvenated by a new sense of artistic integrity. But even Nietzsche was unsatisfied with this solution and declined to publish the lectures on the grounds that they were too "exhortative."[165]

Nietzsche's dilemma was that he stood at the terminus of a great tradition, as the last of the poet-philologists in German culture. Like Hölderlin and the brothers Schlegel, his object was to inspire the young with a vision of antiquity at variance with the modern world. If he challenged the harmonizing conception of the Periclean age held up by earlier Hellenists, he did so in the name of a new agonal ideal rooted in the Pre-Socratic world. For all his seeming radicalism, Nietzsche never broke with the idealistic tradition of European Hellenism. Yet his own increasingly troubled philological existence was an indication of the growing difficulty of continuing to maintain the poetic and pedagogic impulse within the climate of modern "scientific" scholarship. His professional problems would begin with the publication of *The Birth of Tragedy*, which linked the cause of German Hellenism with Wagnerianism.

Nietzsche wrote Rohde, "I have formed an alliance with Wagner," an alliance which Nietzsche believed represented their mutual commitment to an avant-garde guided by the composer, inspired by his "genius," and heralded by Nietzsche as the spokesman of the younger generation.[166] When the Wagners left Triebschen in April, Nietzsche helped them pack and joined them in Bayreuth a few weeks later for the May cornerstone ceremonies, which Nietzsche called "the happiest days of my life."[167] Although he did not quit Basel for Bayreuth, Nietzsche had the solace of his pen and his efforts on behalf of the new Wagner Societies.

The music world did react appreciatively to the *Birth of Tragedy*. Liszt graciously sent his congratulations, and Hans von Bülow paid a respectful visit. The book also won a numerically tiny yet highly significant number of converts among his own generation's creative elite. The young Ferdinand Tönnies was excited when he stumbled across it, and it won the whole-hearted endorsement of the Pernersdorfer circle, a Viennese student coterie including the future leader of Austro-Marxism, Viktor Adler, the Marxist editor, Heinrich Braun, the historian Heinrich Friedjung, and the poet Siegfried Lipiner. (Sigmund Freud and Gustav Mahler were also loosely affiliated with the group in these years.)[168] But elsewhere the book was greeted with stony silence. Rohde's favorable review was rejected by one liberal journal as too partisan, others refused to touch it, and the already beleaguered Ritschl was painfully embarrassed by his protégé's "brilliant nonsense."[169] Nietzsche's challenge to an older generation of classicists in the name of a younger generation was pointedly ignored. But just as Nietzsche was beginning to despair of any critical reaction, a quite unexpected opponent suddenly emerged, his former schoolmate Ulrich von Wilamowitz-Möllendorff.

While Nietzsche and Deussen represented the one type for which Schulpforta was famous, the pastor's son who pursued scholarship with unusual eloquence and ease, Wilamowitz and the future Chancellor Theobald von Bethmann Hollweg represented the other, the aristocrat who mastered the craft and values of middle class scholarship while retaining an imperious manner. Wilamowitz had watched Nietzsche's success at Schulpforta warily, disapproving of his flamboyance. Arriving in Bonn in the aftermath of the Ritschl-Jahn dispute, he was condemned to watch a broken Jahn move rapidly toward the grave; inwardly he fumed at the "nepotism" that had brought his older rival a professorship without fulfilling the formal academic requirements.[170] This did not prevent Wilamowitz from paying Nietzsche, the young Basel professor, a friendly visit in 1869; at that time Nietzsche had no inkling that he had before him the one figure who could and would dispute his claim to represent the new generation of philologists.

Wilamowitz would be more than eager to take up the cause of the "Socratic" man. He was at the beginning of a career that would make him the dominating classicist of the next half century. His extraordinary output was sustained by his positivism and his willingness to jettison the tenets of German Hellenism. "Antiquity as a conceptual unity and ideal is gone," he would argue, "science itself had destroyed this faith."[171] When he encountered Nietzsche's flowery prose in *The Birth of Tragedy* he tore it apart, held it up for ridicule, relishing the opportunity to turn the tables on the Ritschleaner who themselves had long slighted the students of Jahn as practitioners of faulty scholarship. Nietzsche had disgraced "mother Pforte," young philologists needed to learn the "asceticism" of "scientific" scholarship, Wilamowitz asserted; he made clear that there was no longer any place for Nietzsche in the profession by mocking Nietzsche's "philology of the future" as a bygone ideal. Nietzsche should resign, Wilamowitz concluded.[172]

Nietzsche chose not to reply to Wilamowitz's polemic. Rohde's counterattacks sparkled only when he defended Schopenhauer from Wilamowitz's scorn, and when Wagner interjected himself into the controversy, he only underscored the gulf between Nietzsche and his fellow philologists. Precisely that which made Wagner so popular made the book so unacceptable to Nietzsche's philological colleagues in Germany. While one professor was telling his students in Bonn that Nietzsche had "ruined his career," Ritschl was pleading with Nietzsche to recant or, at least, return to the type of scholarship for which he had become known in Leipzig.[173] But Nietzsche felt he could no longer pursue the laborious scholarship for which he had been trained. He had come to share his Basel colleagues' fear that the historical-critical method, once the proudest creation of neo-classicism, was now turning on that ideal and destroying it. In crisis-conscious Basel to belabor was to belittle. Nietzsche's scholarly career was over almost before it actually began. He published only one philological study after he left Leipzig, "The Florentine Tractat of Homer and Hesiod, Their Generation and Their Contest," which appeared in two parts in 1870 and 1873.

As he watched his professional reputation crumble, Nietzsche harbored a grudge toward Wilamowitz as the personification of "Berlin" incarnate.[174] With the option of an academic position in Germany closed, Basel turned into a refuge and intellectual exile. His final humiliation came that winter when he failed to attract a single philologist to his lectures in Basel. Having taken the stand that Wilamowitz did not deserve a response, Nietzsche began to search for a suitable opponent for an agonal contest. He fell upon the liberals of Berlin on the occasion of the dedication of the newly Germanized university of Strassburg. Nietzsche was supposed to be Basel's delegate to the lavish June ceremony.[175] The keynote speaker was Anton Springer, his former Bonn art history teacher, a man who typified the naive character of liberal nationalism. Springer thought that the surly inhabitants of Alsace and Lorraine could be brought into the fold by simply dispensing the blessings of German culture.[176] Nietzsche was conversant enough with the mood of Alsace to see the delusions in Springer's dream of Strassburg university as a liberal showcase. But if the Liberals were smug and deluded, their optimism was only fortified by French academics rushing to emulate the German educational system after their defeat. Nietzsche remained convinced, however, that the superiority the German academe was experiencing only masked its inner decay. When *Im Neuen Reich,* the new aesthetic mouthpiece of the Crown Prince's party, attacked Wagner, Nietzsche responded by writing an angry open letter to the editor.[177] He made plans to denounce that new emblem of liberal imperialism, the university of Strassburg.

His skepticism was reinforced by his friendship with Marie Baumgartner whom he later said fought "the annexation with sonnets and books."[178]

Marie Baumgartner was a Basler married to an Alsatian industrialist and mother of his promising pupil, Adolf. Marie made it her special mission to act as a mediator between French and German culture, translating Nietzsche's books into French. She and Nietzsche worried together about Adolf, whom they feared was adopting the mannerisms of the Reich while in Prussia for his university and military training. Nietzsche started a project attacking the institution which was at the heart of the Prussian educational system, the one-year volunteer which linked educational advancement to military privileges.[179] Nothing came of this or the earlier planned "manifesto" on the university of Strassburg, but in the process Nietzsche had arrived at a new position for himself as a critic standing outside the Reich but inside German culture. Nietzsche's sense of his own academic disrepute may have spurred some desire for revenge, but *Schadenfreude* was overshadowed by his desire to demonstrate to the Germans that they were failing to live up to their own ideals.

While Nietzsche's career was being ruined by his enthusiasm, even those who had been critical of Wagner in the past and would again be so in the future were caught up in the excitement surrounding the promised Wagnerian festivity. Burckhardt, for instance, wrote at the time of the groundbreaking ceremony at Bayreuth, "something great, new, and liberating must come out of Germany, and what is more *in opposition* to power, wealth, and business."[180] And he added at the end of the year, "Things can only be changed by ascetics, by men, that is, who will be able to help the national spirit and soul express itself. For the moment Richard Wagner occupies the whole forefront of the scene." If there were some who sought to "promote" the composer to "the rank of Fool," Burckhardt wrote that "there was a time when Bismarck was called a fool."[181] Wagner launched the Bayreuth campaign with the field completely to himself. No German artist of the time could even hope to approach the composer's international stature; rival forms of festivity had failed, and the stain of scandal was expunged in the triumph of his return. Bayreuth alone would capture the imagination of the Founding Era and leave a permanent stamp upon German culture.

During a brief November meeting with Wagner in Strassburg, Nietzsche was alerted by the composer's anger to the best seller of 1872, David Friedrich Strauss's *The Old Faith and the New*. Nietzsche had found his opponent. Strauss had a genius for timing; his 1835 biography of Jesus launched the Young Hegelians; his 1859 biography of Ulrich von Hutten helped inaugurate "the era of festivals"; and his verbal duel with Ernst Renan during the Franco-Prussian War thrust him again into the limelight. He intended his final work to be the liberal manifesto of the *Kulturkampf*. Wagner had long detested this "cold-blooded critic of the gospels."[182] Thoughtful liberal critics, appalled by the tenor and presumption of the book, nevertheless kept their silence out of loyalty to the memory of the young Strauss, "the critical hero of the century." But Nietzsche interjected a deadly critique into what had been a ritualistic reunion of Strauss's lifelong enemies and friends in *David Strauss, Writer and Confessor* (1873). Since Strauss viewed himself as the representative of the "new" in battle with the "old," he was quite unprepared for Nietzsche's furious attack on him in the name of the "young," describing his treatment at Nietzsche's hands as being "first beheaded, then hung."[183]

Nietzsche had his own score to settle with the "cultural Philistines" whose "chieftain" at that moment was undeniably David Friedrich Strauss. Nor had it escaped Nietzsche's attention that Wilamowitz had used against him the very words Strauss had employed against Schopenhauer. Nietzsche effectively exposed the sterility of Strauss's "new faith" as nothing more than an eclectic mix of materialist doctrines, evolutionary theory, and the familiar pieties of the Weimar cult. Germany was indeed suffocating under a flood of these classics; no less than twenty-eight Goethe and seventeen Schiller editions were published between 1868 and 1874, but Nietzsche made clear that worship of dead genius was no substitute for the loss of the "old faith."[184] While some biographers such as Hans Grimm would show Goethe "at home" in the new Reich, Nietzsche unmasked the stale "new gospel" of the tired "Goethean man."

While Nietzsche couched his attack on "cultural Philistinism" in generational terms by singling out for ridicule the old Young Hegelian, David Friedrich Strauss, it was clear Nietzsche's main target was aesthetic pretensions of the *Kulturstaat* heralded by the Crown Prince's party. In turn, Friedrich III was offended by the cultural politics of the Wagnerian movement identified with his rival, Ludwig II, and he snubbed the Wagnerians in 1873 by visiting Bayreuth but declining to tour the composer's theater.[185] Nietzsche had wanted his "anti-Strauss" to be a "duel" between himself and the leading critic of the older generation. But he proved less a David confronting Goliath than a Hamlet distractedly striking down Polonius. Years later he admitted that the result had not been a contest as much as an "assassination."[186] But as a result Nietzsche was suddenly notorious in the university towns and intellectual centers of Germany. The liberal press which had ignored his first book overreacted to his second. *Die Grenzboten*, edited by Gustav Freytag, the Crown Prince's champion, denounced Nietzsche as "an enemy of our culture"; Emil Kuh, an Austrian critic known for his biography of Hebbel, called Nietzsche a "panderer of Wagner"; the Hegelian aesthete Friedrich Theodor Vischer dismissed the "impudent" young Basel professor; while Gottfried Keller observed that in his experience those who began their careers denouncing others as Philistines invariably ended as Philistines themselves.[187] This stage of the controversy was later likened by Albert Schweitzer to a battlefield struggle over the corpse of an already "dead book."[188] Strauss died in the following year; his last work was soon forgotten. Nietzsche had vastly overrated the staying power of contemporary "Socratism."

Nietzsche's attack did focus attention on the Swiss critique of the German nation-state. The counterattacks emanating from the Reich went beyond denigrating Nietzsche personally to open scorn for the *"Winkeluniversität"* ("cubbyhole university") of Basel which he represented. Thus while castigated in the Reich, in Basel he became a local hero.[189] He counted over nine favorable local newspaper articles; even the radical *Volksfreund* took him under its wing. If Nietzsche had initially considered publishing "the anti-Strauss" under an Italian pseudonym, he came to revel in the notoriety he was bringing the city. "Basel is becoming truly offensive," he boasted.[190] Basel was now the center of his intellectual world. Nietzsche became active in an informal Tuesday Society which brought together young academic outsiders like himself with some of the leading young intellectuals of the Basel elite. Nietzsche was also recreating his old Leipzig circle in his new setting. While unsuccessful in landing Rohde a job at the university, Romundt did establish a tenuous academic foothold; Paul Rée, Romundt's philosopher friend, arrived in 1873 to continue his studies, and two unsolicited admirers of Nietzsche, Heinrich Köselitz and Paul Widemann, also appeared. Gersdorff came for frequent visits as did Rohde who praised Basel as "an island in today's *Jetztzeit.*"[191]

For Nietzsche, however, Basel was more than a refuge of creative solace amidst general decay; it was also a prophetic vantage point, a window on the Reich. Increasingly troubled by what he saw, Nietzsche found a valuable ally in his housemate Franz Overbeck. Overbeck's *Über die Christlichkeit unserer heutigen Theologie* appeared as the "twin" of the "anti-Strauss."[192] But while the latter was essentially a polemical counter-stroke, Overbeck's work had the deeper seriousness of *The Birth of Tragedy,* challenging the assumptions of the profession in which he had been trained. Overbeck was representative of a new generation steeped in the biblical criticism pioneered by Strauss, and had been appointed in 1870 largely through the pressure of the Basel radicals who demanded a counterweight to the Pietists on the theological faculty. But in his characteristically cryptic manner he went far beyond the position of the radical party. Having lost his faith since his ordination, Overbeck had little interest in baiting the orthodox, but was rather troubled by what he took to be the nihilistic consequences of Strauss's liberal historicism. While Nietzsche challenged the assumptions of the *Kulturkampf,* Overbeck mourned its success. He allowed Nietzsche to demolish Strauss's "new faith," reflecting instead on the liberal destruction of the old faith.[193]

Christianity in Overbeck's view was less a religion than a culture. He held that "antiquity has survived to our times in the embalmed form of Christianity."[194] He consequently treated all attempts to modernize the faith as disguised repudiations of the western cultural tradition. He became in Troeltsch's phrase a "negative theologian," stoically standing guard over the grave of historical Christianity lest theological grave robbers come to tamper with the corpse.[195] Overbeck would later disappoint Nietzsche by suspending his polemical stance out of gratitude to the university for not dismissing him during the controversy aroused by his book. He did not, however, repudiate his "renunciation of my colleagues in the guild," and could reemerge out of retirement a quarter century later to unnerve a new generation of German theologians with renewed polemics. Having made himself "impossible for every theological chair in my German fatherland," Overbeck saw himself after 1873 in a "state of war" with this "country or 'Reich.' " Basel had become the "asylum of my 'theology.' "[196]

Overbeck's unusual cosmopolitan background fortified him in this stance. Raised in Russia by a German father and a French mother, he arrived in Saxony at the age of thirteen speaking imperfect German. He was a close boyhood friend of Treitschke, but remained an apolitical innocent. In Basel he studiously kept his distance from the city's political conflicts. His apoliticism caused him to despise the upsurge of nationalist ideologies, which he saw poisoning the unity of European culture. Especially abhorrent to him was a Christianity fueled by nationalism, i.e., a Christianity fused with contemporary politics. He did not hesitate to express his disapproval of Treitschke's newly found faith. He quarreled with Treitschke over Nietzsche; and Treitschke, in turn, blamed Nietzsche's "radicalism" for undermining his friendship with Overbeck. Overbeck finally broke off relations with Treitschke when the latter stooped to lead the nascent political anti-Semitism of the late seventies. Overbeck was the one confidant with whom Nietzsche freely discussed politics; in their correspondence "the Reich" always appeared in quotation marks. Overbeck, too, was "looking from afar" at "the great events of Germany" and coming to the same negative conclusions about the Empire.[197]

A German colleague pointed to the "triumvirate"—Nietzsche, Rohde, and Overbeck—and said they turned Basel into a "poisonous den."[198] While Rohde soon made his own separate peace with the Reich, and Overbeck withdrew in silence, Nietzsche continued to exploit the ancient polarity and conflict between city-state and empire in his attacks on Bismarckian Germany. This dichotomy was not without its artificiality: Basel was, after all, a small city disguising itself as a city-state with the pretensions of being a half canton, and Berlin was also playing a part, that of the Prussian capital now pretending to be the capital of a nation-state with pretensions of being an empire.[199] Nietzsche articulated a polarity that would dog the German nation-state's existence from beginning to end: the Third Reich would go to its doom by seizing the city-state of Danzig whose High Commissioner happened to be a Burckhardt from Basel.

The code word "Berlin" peppered Nietzsche's personal correspondence in the coming years. It symbolized the scholarly scientism of men like Wilamowitz, and the soullessness of an instant metropolis; Berlin embodied the pretensions of an imperial style blind to the dangers lurking in the hubris of a lopsided military victory. In 1872/73 the symbolic opposition between the two cities was dramatized by Burckhardt's refusal to accept Ranke's chair at the university of Berlin.[200] The honor was then passed to Treitschke. The cosmopolitan restraints which Ranke had placed on German historiography were consequently shattered by the one-dimensional nationalism preached by the now deaf, self-enclosed Treitschke. Burckhardt had in effect turned his back on the German nation-state before this, declining other opportunities in Germany. By ceasing to publish, he broke his connection with the German public as well. Burckhardt could not bring himself to desert the conservative cause in Basel for an uncertain future in a capital of an empire he now increasingly feared.

Burckhardt's pessimism was reflected in lectures on Greek cultural history which he was then delivering to his university classes. Nietzsche followed the lectures through the class notes prepared for him by one of his former pupils. Both Burckhardt and Nietzsche focused on agonism as the key to the understanding of ancient Greece. Burckhardt derived the "Hellenic man" from the "colonial and agonal era" when the city-states first colonized the Mediterranean and utilized the festivity of the contest system to sustain a sense of Panhellenic unity.[201] The small urban aristocracy which dominated this era Burckhardt likened to the Renaissance patriciate, and he equated the Hellenic ideal fusing wealth, birth, and the drive for excellence with the neo-classical conception of *Bildung*.[202] This was not a celebration of flowering as in Burckhardt's study of the Renaissance. He now focused on the forces dissolving the established festive tradition, unraveling the city-state world in which the "agonal man" had once thrived. At the end of this process of dissolution stood Socrates, "the gravedigger of the Attic city," whose optimistic dialectic "educated the sons of the city, but not for the republic."[203] What followed, Burckhardt concluded, was the soul-deadening imperium of the "Hellenistic man."

Under the impress of Burckhardt's ideas, Nietzsche came to perceive festivity less in terms of a specific aesthetic institution and more as an expression of the fabric of a given society. In his own lectures he began to present tragedy as "a festival of the whole urban community" and declared, "without Homer's public, no Homer."[204] Nietzsche was becoming skeptical about the real chances of Bayreuth effecting a new aesthetic beginning within the climate of the Founding Era. This does not mean, however, that Nietzsche was ready to accept Burckhardt's pessimistic conclusion that the tradition embodied in city-state festivity was destined to be swallowed up by ever larger military despotisms which would inevitably lead to the arrival of the latter-day "Scythians." Nietzsche still clung to the hope that the old festivity could be revived in the future. Consequently he was ever more eager that Wagner present himself to the nation as an "anti-Alexander" leading "a generation of anti-Alexanders" in a crusade against the falsity of the new German imperium.[205]

But once Wagner left Triebschen Nietzsche and Wagner were moving in opposite directions. One was the promised *Dichterfürst* of Bayreuth, the other the intellectual exile in Switzerland. Nietzsche now observed Wagner performing as the most effective of all the "founding fathers" save Bismarck. The composer saw himself as the bearer of an aesthetic "secret" that was the counterpart to Bismarck's "secret of the nation's political power."[206] Armed with a diagnosis of cultural stagnation, a seemingly revolutionary rhetoric calling for renewal, and a concrete goal, Wagner presented himself as the mytho-poet heralding a new national dramaturgy. Once in Bayreuth a new set of followers surrounded him. Rohde and Nietzsche dismissed the "purely musical Wagnerians" in Bayreuth for lacking an understanding of the deeper issues involved. Nietzsche became even more suspicious of the young aristocratic ideologues who were flocking to Wagner.[207] He watched Wagner's new friends turn the composer's utterances into dogma, corrupting the character of the composer's aesthetic campaign. It ceased to be purely a "movement" viewing culture as creation or a center of activity and energy and became instead ever more a "school" with a master, a method, and a sense of tradition.[208]

But Nietzsche held on to his hopes for Bayreuth in the year and a half following the cornerstone ceremony, still believing that it might engender "German unity in its highest sense."[209] He remained largely in the background, active only in organizing a Swiss Wagner Society, but he and Rohde continued to retain their importance to the cause simply because they were the most prominent "Wagner professors." Half in jest Nietzsche wrote Rohde in January 1873 that they would appear at the planned "summer Bayreuth Council" as "bishops and worthies of a new church."[210] Wagner was then campaigning for the project through the Wagner Societies and his endless concert tours. The propaganda campaign was a resounding success; throughout 1872 and 1873 Wagner captured the attention of the educated German public.[211] However, he failed to entice enough wealthy "patrons" to actually buy "shares" in the enterprise and after the terrible financial panic of 1873 seemed unlikely to do so.[212]

Few contemporaries grasped that a long wave of economic prosperity had just come to an end, and that the "Great Depression," a quarter century of slackened growth and intermittent recession, now stretched out before them.[213] But virtually all concurred in a moralistic revulsion against the style and tone of the postwar boom. The optimistic bubble of the Founding Era had burst. The much heralded Vienna World's Fair, opening four days before the Vienna stock market crash, became an expensive fiasco that threatened to pull the plans for Bayreuth down with it. Bayreuth's financial crisis was a press fixation during the summer and fall of 1873, drawing attention to the special October meeting of delegates from the Wagner Societies.

Nietzsche arrived as the most angry and determined of the thirteen delegates. At a time when Hungarians were staging an elaborate fête honoring Liszt in their capital, when Americans offered to underwrite Wagner's theater project in Chicago, the failure of the Germans to back Wagner seemed to Nietzsche particularly shameful. His manifesto, "Warning to the Germans," was rejected by the assembly as too aggressive. While Wagner was not unpleased by the draft, the delegates felt that the public could no longer be shamed or browbeaten into supporting Bayreuth. A milder appeal was drafted by the young literary historian Adolf Stern. Its lack of success gave Nietzsche little subsequent satisfaction, since he had already left Bayreuth convinced that as his own appeal had failed so had Wagner's festival plans.

Bayreuth's apparent failure had a liberating effect upon Nietzsche. "I began to examine why the enterprise was unsuccessful with the coldest detachment," he explained to Rohde in February. "I thereby learned much and now I believe I understand Wagner far better than before."[214] The failure was in part caused by the "money crisis," by the end of a "period of aesthetic agitation." The "chief thing," however, was that Wagner's art and the festivity that was to flow from it had proven "inappropriate" for "our present social and economic conditions," Nietzsche felt.[215] This analysis allowed Nietzsche to have it both ways; on the one hand, his critique of postwar German culture was confirmed—the Germans had proven unworthy of his festive ideal. On the other hand, he would now feel free to attribute Wagner's failure to all that he disliked in the cultural politics emanating from Bayreuth.

He began working on an essay that was to explain how Wagner had erred. The principal problem, Nietzsche would argue, was the composer's eagerness to be "the people's tribune and demagogue."[216] Nietzsche now looked back on Wagner's career as a string of political mistakes: failing to "see through the situation in 1849," then aligning himself too closely to Ludwig II, "thirdly insulting the Jews," initially when "he had no call to do so" and later as "revenge."[217] Nietzsche now feared that the composer was intent on fashioning a "theater-ocracy," "a tyranny with the aid of the theater masses."[218] The resulting populism was false both in the pseudoarchaic language employed by Wagner—so alien to the direct, plain idiom of Luther—and in its aesthetic purpose. Rather than reviving the Reformation, Nietzsche saw Wagner's art adhering to the spirit of the Counter-Reformation. He complained that it was precisely the composer's "most reactionary elements"—his blend of pagan myth, medieval Christianity, and Buddhist pathos, his evocation of the miraculous and a nativist national-ism—that was proving most popular in Germany.[219]

In the winter of his discontent, Nietzsche determined that "Wagner is not a *Reformator* because everything has remained as it was."[220] Nietzsche clearly preferred to see Bayreuth fail than succeed by mirroring a society gone wrong. But if Nietzsche had begun to "laugh at Wagner in secret," this laughter "bit into the heart" when the composer salvaged his threatened enterprise.[221] After failing to convince Bismarck to sponsor the Bayreuth festival as part of the fifth anniversary celebration of the battle of Sedan, the composer's old protector, Ludwig II, rescued him with the necessary finan-cial backing. Nietzsche was in a quandary.

Nietzsche sought to reestablish his independence. In *The Use and Abuse of History* (1874) he appealed directly to "the kingdom of youth" to arise and assert itself.[222] This work was more influenced by Overbeck than by either Wagner or Burckhardt. He followed Overbeck in assessing the dangers of the judgmental stance of "critical history," distancing himself from Burckhardt by attacking the practitioners of "antiquarian history" for surrounding themselves with the furniture of the past in order to shut out the future. But most striking was his critique of "monumental history" which implicitly took Wagner to task for adapting himself to the reigning style of the Founding Era. And to compound the problem, Nietzsche would condemn Wagner for having condescended to the Reich.[223] Bayreuth was predictably miffed by Nietzsche's warnings that his generation stood in danger of being crushed by a momumentalizing style imposed upon them by their elders.

Bayreuth could, however, take consolation in the fact that Nietzsche's attempt to rally the young to a "supra-historical" vision fell on deaf ears. An American observer of the German university scene returning after several years' absence was surprised at the sudden intellectual and political apathy of the postwar student body.[224] The one show of recognition, a birthday message from the Pernersdorfer circle in Vienna, was significant, but it also underscored the fact that Nietzsche's following lay among Germans living outside not inside the Reich. The one friendly critic, Karl Hillebrand, himself an exile, put it as gently as he could when he wrote that Nietzsche might appear as a latter-day Herder, but he was actually leading a *Sturm und Drang* without followers; the young had turned to more modest, practical concerns.[225] Nietzsche later acknowledged the same when he remarked that the *Untimely Meditations* "predated" the earlier *Birth of Tragedy* in the sense that they sought to recapture the pathos of his student years in Leipzig.[226] There was simply no generational movement in the making. And in any event, Nietzsche had lost touch with the postwar student world.

Schopenhauer as Educator, published in the fall of 1874, was a retrospective and, at times, sentimental evocation of his philosophical "education" in the 1860s. In this essay Nietzsche proceeded to praise that which he was in the process of abandoning. Here again he attacked the "Goethean man," distinguishing the "Schopenhauerian man" from the "Rousseauian man" as well. Wagner's program was, if anything, an attempted synthesis of Rousseau's populist General Will with Schopenhauer's ideology of will-less aesthetic contemplation; the composer, accordingly, took offense at Nietzsche's critique of Rousseau. But the overall impression of the essay was nevertheless favorable, and Nietzsche was temporarily restored to the good graces of Bayreuth.

Nietzsche would acknowledge, however, that he had little addressed the changing character of the Schopenhauerian enthusiasm. "Schopenhauer's authority became predominant in Europe in the seventies," Nietzsche later wrote, and he found that what had once seemed an avant-garde "education" was becoming an all-too-prevalent *Weltanschauung* that was increasingly assuming a morbid character.[227] Thomas Mann's depiction of Thomas Buddenbrooks's discovery of Schopenhauer is a classic portrait of the allure of the new pessimism to cultured business circles in the wake of the Great Depression. The "heroic pessimism" which Nietzsche had sought to provoke in the young gave way in the universities to a fascination with decadence. The self-destructive antics of the "Club of the Resigned" at the university of Greifswald, described by Carl Ludwig Schleich in his autobiography, was typical of a new youthful interest in Schopenhauer.[228] Notorious at the time was the case of Phillip Mainländer who committed suicide after he published his *Philosophie der Erlösung* (Philosophy of redemption) in 1876 in order, he said, to lend credence to its Schopenhauerian message. And closer to home, Nietzsche witnessed the nervous breakdown of his neo-Kantian friend Romundt, who, unable any longer to carry the burden of his uncertain academic future and Schopenhauerian pessimism, threatened to convert to Catholicism. A shaken Nietzsche and Overbeck bundled the disconsolate Romundt onto a train for the Reich where he later emerged as a popularizer of a Kantian Protestantism.[229] The bond of an atheistic brotherhood which had first attracted him to Schopenhauer was disintegrating. Most disturbing, it was being transformed by Bayreuth into a compliant faith of a pseudo-religious community dedicating itself to the new mysteries of reconciliation and redemption then being enunciated by Wagner in his new opera *Parsifal.*

For Nietzsche, 1875 was a year of quiet desperation. With the Bayreuth festival now scheduled for the following year, he found himself boxed into a corner, unable to give voice to his qualms. He found it ever more difficult to bring himself to go to Bayreuth, particularly after one unpleasant visit when he had unwisely sought to instruct the composer in the virtues of Brahms's music. He told Overbeck that epistles from Bayreuth requesting his presence touched off "half-hour cramps." His own circle was also beginning to disintegrate, with friends immersing themselves in their careers or losing themselves in romantic entanglements. His illness grew worse; teaching was ever more a burden; and Basel was beginning to lose its charm.

His pen faltered. Earlier he had planned some thirteen essays, written at a fast clip, covering sundry cultural and political topics. But he now found it impossible even to finish the fourth *Untimely Meditations,* "We Philologists," intended as his reply to his critics within the profession. Even as he sought to restate his faith in the educational mission of classical philology, he found he doubted his own remedies, and he no longer believed in the future of that mission. For Nietzsche as for Burckhardt's students, as well, the crisis of the classical ideal posed a more acute psychological and aesthetic problem. Joesph Viktor Widmann and Karl Spitteler, Burckhardt pupils of the 1860s who would dominate Swiss letters in the coming decades, continued to aestheticize neo-classicism. Spitteler's epics, composed in the vein of Tennyson's *Idylls of the King,* won him the Nobel Prize for literature in 1919. But neither Widmann nor Spitteler cared to sustain the political pathos of Burckhardt's stand; yet without it their classicism became ethereal and esoteric.

Nietzsche spurned both options which Basel seemed to hold out to him: either to follow Burckhardt in the creation of a new art history or to take the route of Spitteler into an ever detached aestheticism. Nietzsche's dilemma was echoed by Anselm Feuerbach, the neo-classical painter and son of a noted classicist, who mournfully declared that he had "imbibed classicism with my mother's milk, a classicism oriented to humane truth and greatness, but one which did not fail to turn my life into a hopeless struggle against my time."[230] Feuerbach would die prematurely in 1880 full of confused bitterness toward his German contemporaries for abandoning this same neo-classical ideal. In the mid-seventies Nietzsche seemed to be traveling on the same path.

Nietzsche's connection to Basel was also noticeably weakened after the death of Wilhelm Vischer in July 1874. Vischer's death was thought a portent of the patriciate's imminent fall from power. Nietzsche informed Gersdorff that his successor was expected to be a supporter of "the party of the *Volksfreund.*"[231] The success of Swiss liberals in amending the federal constitution the year before fueled local radical hopes of launching the final victorious campaign against the city's oligarchic constitution. The Basel·elite was reeling from the full force of economic crisis; Nietzsche wrote Rohde the "sad news" of a Burckhardt-owned firm's "great bankruptcy." "Things are bad for all of the Basel textile producers," he added.[232] But what troubled Nietzsche most was the loss of his protector who had stood by him during "the most complicated circumstances." He complained to Rohde, "We, Overbeck and I, now find ourselves in an almost sinister isolation. Here and there there are signs of a formidable opposition against us."[233]

Nietzsche exaggerated. The older classicists continued to support him with Burckhardt paying him the high compliment that Basel would never see a teacher the likes of Nietzsche again. Nietzsche had also made valuable allies among Baslers of his own generation, notably Vischer's son, an up-and-coming organizer of the local conservative party.[234] But Nietzsche was too enamored with his own "radicalism" to share the pathos of Basel conservatism making its last stand. He was especially impatient with the resurgence of local Pietist feeling which lent a religious dimension to the impending political confrontation.[235] Nor did the prospect of university reform alarm him; on the controversial issue of admitting female students he had already pointedly sided with the defeated minority favoring admission.[236] He consequently observed the election campaign of 1875 with a certain bemused detachment. He wrote Rohde in February, "There is great excitement here as the new city constitution is being debated in the Great Council. All the parties are embittered; in the spring the people will decide."[237] He was amused to have his published warnings of state power quoted in the campaign. In March he wrote home, "We have here a great constitutional conflict; the old form of government will be carried to its grave in a few months, new people will come to the top and much will change."[238] On election day he wrote Overbeck almost welcoming the triumph of the radicals.[239]

The fall of the elite was a symbolic turning point, but the radicals found themselves unable to institute sweeping changes. Conservatives regrouped under Vischer's son and others Nietzsche knew; they even managed a brief conservative restoration between 1878 and 1881. Yet there was no turning back, and Nietzsche took no part in the politics of the conservative reaction. By the mid-eighties when Carl Gustav Jung entered the Pedagogium and the nineties when Hermann Hesse arrived in the city, the "old Basel" had already receded into an almost mythological past.[240] In the eyes of a new generation Burckhardt seemed a throwback to an earlier time. The completion of the Gotthard tunnel had transformed the old textile center into a bustling depot of goods and cash. As the patrician past faded, the city became known as the home of Europe's most numerous and most anonymous millionaires. Nietzsche's youth had been involved in the defense of a latter-day city-state until he too became convinced of the pointlessness of the exercise. Unlike his advice in the *Zarathustra,* to give that which was falling a kick, he removed himself in his last Basel years, living as a recluse on the semi-rural outskirts of the city. Nietzsche's "Baselphobia" in the late seventies was not a function of his displeasure with the new Basel, but was rather a consequence of the difficulty he had in finalizing his break with the city.[241] He ignored the new regime as it regarded his earlier defense of classicism irrelevant to the city's future. Nietzsche may have had some nostalgic memories of the twilight years of the old regime, but he lost interest in memorializing the past. Burckhardt would speak of his eventual departure in 1879 as an "abdication."[242] Already by 1875 he had tired of upholding the old ideals; he felt overburdened by his teaching and contemplated his early professorship more as a curse than a blessing. His health broke down so that in early 1876 he was forced to suspend all teaching activities for the rest of the semester. He obtained a leave of absence for the coming academic year.

As his identification with Basel waned so did his desire for polemical confrontations with "Berlin." Yet instead of making peace with the Reich, he sought new contacts in the other cities of Switzerland. In the spring he traveled to Geneva to visit Hugo von Senger, the director of the local symphony, although he told Overbeck he "feared a new city almost as much as a wild beast."[243] There he became infatuated with Mathilde Trampenbach, Senger's Russian-German music pupil. On the eve of his departure he proposed marriage, apologizing in his letter for not doing so in person because he had to catch the early train back to Basel.[244] He was then highly embarrassed by the episode—as was Senger, who later married the lady after the death of his first wife. Nietzsche was clearly desperate to break out of his isolation and to chart a new course for himself.

But upon his return there was no longer any further delaying of the long-promised final essay, *Richard Wagner in Bayreuth* (1876). It proved to be the most tortured and curious of all of Nietzsche's endeavors. He proceeded to invoke the old festival ideal while implying his own hesitations and qualms. The composer was presented "not as a prophet, but as the interpreter and clarifier of the past"; his life "consists largely of comedy, not to mention burlesque," and Nietzsche spoke darkly of Wagner's "demonic magnetism."[245] Yet he still insisted that "with the name 'Bayreuth' I designate the greatest defeat suffered by the '*Gebildeten.*'"[246] Nietzsche took little pride in his tightrope walking act. Ludwig II sent his congratulations, and

Wagner responded by telegraphing, "The book is simply tremendous! Where did you learn so much about me?"[247]

Within his intimate Basel circle, Nietzsche jocularly mocked the upcoming festival. The thought of joining the Wagnerian legions amassing in Bayreuth did not please him. For all his theoretical interest in festivity, he was highly uncomfortable in such public gatherings. He found Basel's festive occasions unbearable; the constant "drumming" of the city's carnival season put him to flight.[248] He boycotted Basel's large Singers' Festival in the summer of 1875, telling Marie Baumgartner that he had so removed himself that he felt he lived "on the other side of the moon."[249] His appearance at the August Bayreuth festival was surreptitious to say the least. Fervent young Wagnerians found him a mournful presence as he strove to remain as aloof as possible.[250] His general discomfort was accidentally shared by at least one other arrival in festival week. Karl Marx, having missed a train connection, found himself stuck in Bayreuth's railway station; he relieved his frustration that night by damning the "Fools' Festival" held across town.[251]

Despite his private skepticism, Nietzsche had been unprepared for what he found. Perhaps he still hoped that Bayreuth might still be a spiritual half-way house between a now idealized Triebschen and a despised "Berlin." He clearly had not expected to find Berlin in Bayreuth in the form of a high society gathering of royalty, the aristocracy, and the upper middle class *Gebildeten*. "It was as if we were in Berlin," Anna von Helmholtz wrote home to the capital, "all our good acquaintances, all the artists, Menzel, Meyerheim, Makart, Lenbach, in short, all the nice people together."[252] Nietzsche fled before the festival ended, jotting down in his notebook: "Long live the noble traitor!"[253] His break with Wagner was to be the hinge on which life would turn.

CHAPTER FIVE

The Experimental Thinker

> I'll never
> Be such a gosling to obey instinct; but stand,
> As if a man were author of himself
> And knew no other kin.
> Shakespeare, *The Tragedy of Coriolanus*

NIETZSCHE FLED BAYREUTH on the August 27 train for Basel with a new determination to become a "free spirit" (*Freigeist*). The emancipation promised by the "free spirit" was at first a defensive posture: "free spirit out of self-defense, out of the need for power" was what he jotted down the next day or soon thereafter.[1] Nietzsche's "free spirit" was suspicious, alert to the "tyrant" in everyone, be it friend, sponsor, or teacher.[2] Nietzsche would compose successive aphorisms on "the free spirit." It would provide him with the necessary new direction and purpose he needed following his break with Wagner. His typology of the free spirit, a compendium of these aphorisms, appeared a year and a half later as *Human, All-Too-Human,* subtitled "a book for free spirits."

With self-conquest the new aim, the public display of the contest motif was accordingly devalued as hindering inner development. Agonism had externalized the anti-motif, allowing his youthful revolt to be directed toward outside forces: his clerical milieu, the older generation, the "Socratism" of the intellectual establishment. It had so personalized opposition, as in his "anti-Strauss," that even his tentative critique of his "spiritual fathers," Schopenhauer and Wagner, could only proceed through the camouflage of praise. The true conflict and intellectual challenge, he now decided, lay not without but within himself. The anti-motif turned inward, becoming a process of thinking against himself, against his earlier selves, as an attempt to free himself from the persona of his youthful rebellion.

Having previously sought "shelter in some kind of reverence or hostility," Nietzsche now sallied forth to embrace the "riddle of emancipation."[3] The new polarity was to be between the free and the fettered spirit, between the renegade breaking with his past and the slave trapped in his environment. His new ideal rejected the ecstatic festive community with its drama of integration in favor of the principles of individuation, skepticism, and sobriety. Free spirits were to be "carefree-living *(leichtlebenden)* gods," who spurned the consolations of festivity and intoxicants.[4] Nietzsche turned from Dionysus, the god of wine, and even championed the temperance movement.[5] His experience with Bayreuth's "oppressive and false 'festival' " convinced him that modern festivity had become merely a lifeless "spectacle without spectators, a banquet without guests."[6] Nietzsche now reasoned that the Greeks sought a "palliative" to misery in agonal festivity, a use preempted in the scientific modern world by focusing on "prophylactic" solutions to the cause of misery.[7]

The theme of the free spirit had appeared once before in Nietzsche's work, in September 1870, when he was disillusioned by the wave of self-satisfaction that accompanied German victory. Embittered, he had thought of rallying "the free spirit" in aesthetic opposition; he briefly considered entitling his study on music drama "Tragedy and the Free Spirits."[8] But as Nietzsche committed himself more firmly to Wagner's aesthetic idealism, the term disappeared to appear anew in the fall of 1876 when he constructed a new intellectual genealogy for himself: the Sophist was the original "complete free spirit" and Thucydides its first outstanding exemplar.[9] The Enlightenment conception of the free spirit had stalled, he continued, because it had negated too little and was too self-contained, but he believed that the present offered great possibilities for its revival. The contemporary free spirit now faced a future made seemingly limitless by the revolution in technology, and Nietzsche saw the free spirit's ultimate "mission in removing all the barriers that stand in the way of the fusion of mankind: religion; states; monarchical instincts; illusions of wealth and poverty; prejudices of health and race—etc."[10] The free spirit would necessarily be the exception, for a society of free spirits would either corrode or etherealize the fundament of culture. The free spirit could be prone to inactive skepticism that prompted "uncertainty" in the face of the active and strong in character,[11] yet he remained convinced that "the eclipse of Europe may depend on whether five or six freer spirits remain true to themselves or not."[12]

The journey of discovery displaced the contest as the ruling metaphor of his thought. He shed his stance as an "untimely" man fighting against his times, believing that in the course of the seventies he had merely become the crusader of the latest fashions. Rather than having led, he had typified his generation, he thought, conceding in 1885: "When I once wrote the word 'untimeliness' on my books, how much youth, inexperience, narrowness was expressed in this word. Today, I realize that with this type of complaint, excitement, and dissatisfaction I actually belonged to the most modern of the modern."[13] Embarrassed by the false anti-modernism of his youth, Nietzsche became determined to expose himself and his spiritual allies, however scattered they might be, to all that was timely in the present. Whereas timeliness had previously been associated with the Philistine, it was now identified with the pioneer. So he saw himself as a scout braving new intellectual territory filled with "the most curious feeling of *solitude* and *multitude*; of being a herald who hastened ahead without knowing whether the band of knights is following or not—in fact whether they are still living."[14]

Nietzsche began what he would later call his "experimental years" with élan and a new desire for camaraderie.[15] Nietzsche found his principal intellectual support in Paul Rée (1849–1901) who joined him in Bayreuth and who departed with him for Basel. Both men shared a series of common experiences: a sickly adolescence, university studies in Leipzig, a youthful enthusiasm for Schopenhauer, and a common circle of friends. Even their war experience was similar; Rée had been wounded at Gravelotte and discharged, while Nietzsche's service ended after taking the wounded from that battlefield. Nietzsche was attracted to Rée when they first met in Basel in 1873, but it was only after the appearance of Rée's *Psychologische Beobach-tungen* (Psychological observations) in 1875 that their friendship was cemented. While Rée was neither a profound nor an original thinker, he was an adventurous spirit within the academic climate of the seventies. Most appealing to Nietzsche, Rée was seeking to break out of the aesthetic and metaphysical constraints Schopenhauer had imposed upon his followers.

Nietzsche's other Schopenhauerian friends were either in crisis, such as Romundt; retreating into their studies, like Overbeck and Rohde; or presenting positions which filled Nietzsche with irritated *déja vu,* such as the stalwart Deussen in his *Die Elemente der Metaphysik* (1877). Rée, on the other hand, sought to sever Schopenhauerian pessimism from its ties to Idealist natural philosophy and root it in the new context of Darwinian and Positivist thought. He proceeded provocatively in his *Habilitationsschrift,* declaring his adherence to Schopenhauer and Darwin in the preface, discarding the traditional format of academic treatises in favor of a pointed epigrammatic style, and scouring the emerging anthropological literature for evidence to bolster his psychologically-oriented theories. Like Nietzsche's, Rée's style, tone, and intent rapidly doomed his chances for a successful academic career in Germany. But that only made him all the more a fitting ally, and Nietzsche saw to it that Rée's forthcoming work, *Der*

Ursprung der moralischen Empfindungen (1877), was published by his own new publisher, Ernst Schmeitzner. Nietzsche thanked Rée for bringing him something he had hitherto "lacked in Basel, a man with whom one can discuss man."[16]

Rée stimulated Nietzsche to rediscover Europe's contemporary intellectual life, much as Wagner had stimulated his interest in Europe's aesthetic life. Rée helped Nietzsche break out of the imprisoning Francophobia Wagner was imposing on his German followers. German access to Paris was, in any case, drastically reduced in the aftermath of the Franco-Prussian war. While France might have hitherto been regarded as the traditional enemy, these periodic convulsions of Francophobic feeling had little affected the continued flow of Germans to what was universally regarded as the capital of European culture and European renewal. The German exile community of Paris had once been so large that in 1848 they demanded the right to send a delegate to the Frankfurt Parliament. But in 1870 all this changed. Karl Hillebrand, Heine's one-time secretary, set the example for the remaining exiles by emigrating to Italy, and once the German armies withdrew behind their borders, France became *terra incognita,* particularly to younger Germans. Nietzsche had made his first plans to visit Paris in the months after the Luxemburg war scare, but he was typical in never getting closer to Paris than Nancy, Geneva, and Nice.

Rée, however, had made a Parisian journey in 1875, and returned with an infectious enthusiasm for French thought. "Positivism completely necessary," Nietzsche jotted down during the winter of 1876/77. His earlier writings, Nietzsche now came to believe, "all speak the language of fanaticism."[17] He consequently rejected all claims of party, determined to stimulate through the principle of doubt. He abandoned the programmatic statements of the "untimely" essayist addressing a compact public whose requirements he knew. Nietzsche also followed Rée in emulating La Rochefoucauld and the other aristocratic French aphorists. *Human, All-Too-Human,* his first aphoristic work, bore a motto from Descartes and was timed to appear on the centenary of Voltaire's death.[18]

In surrendering the essay, that pedagogic instrument integrating the reader into a commonly shared culture, Nietzsche finalized his break with his Wagnerian following. His previous efforts sought to galvanize his audience in common response; this new turn would atomize his readership. But while recognizing that the improvisation and discontinuity of an aphoristic style was "difficult to digest," that it would present "a stumbling block" to many, he hoped to heighten the quality and variety of the individual response, and adopted it as more consonant with his new intellectual purpose. He emulated Laurence Sterne, whom he judged "the freest writer," in whose aphoristic style he saw "the definite form continually broken, thrust aside, and transferred to the realm of the indefinite," a procedure which "arouses in the proper reader a feeling of uncertainty."[19]

Rée's fervent Darwinism also encouraged a new Anglophilia in Nietzsche. England, Nietzsche decided, was claiming what was once a German prerogative, "the intellectual leadership of Europe." He would recognize in Darwinism "Europe's last great scientific movement."[20] Mill, Spencer, Tylor, Huxley, Lecky, the Anglo-German William Rolph were all on his intellectual agenda in the coming years. He plunged into the latest natural scientific literature, seeking to recapture lost time—insofar as his failing eyesight permitted. Much of his anger with Wagner came from the belief that his association with the composer had stymied his intellectual growth for almost a decade.

As a student, Nietzsche had shared the widespread aversion to Darwin's theory, conditioned by antipathy to scientific materialism and British empiricism. While Nietzsche moderated his opposition after reading Lange's *History of Materialism,* his Wagnerian concerns took him in a hostile direction. In Basel he was also close to his neo-Lamarckian colleague, Ludwig Ruitmeyer, who was doing battle with Ernst Haeckel's popularization of evolutionary theory. Nietzsche went further and championed the controversial Leipzig astrophysicist, Friedrich Zöllner, who was attributing the decline of German science to uncritical emulation of British empiricism. "What Zöllner criticizes," Nietzsche wrote in 1872, "is the unceasing experimentation, the lack of logical-deductive energy, which is equally evident in the historical sciences as well."[21] It surprised and amused Nietzsche in 1873 when one Protestant reviewer likened his agonal theories to Darwinism translated into a musical idiom.[22]

When evolutionary theory entered Germany, it did so with little reference to the inductive tradition of Baconian "experimental philosophy," the early pragmatist Chauncey Wright observed in his 1875 essay "German Darwinism."[23] Consequently, it was highly ideological from the outset, becoming a new bone of contention in the already heated confrontation between Materialists and Idealists, which pitted a group of former radicals, primarily physicians and physiologists, against the conservative Hegelian remnant.[24] Nietzsche had, however, already reluctantly accepted the moral relativism which he believed to be inherent in the theory of evolution. Although Nietzsche would make fun of Strauss's discovery of Darwin as "the new Messiah," one critic was not off base in charging that Nietzsche's real critique was that Strauss had sought to tame the ethical implications of Darwinian theory.[25] One of the things that united Rée and Nietzsche was their common interest in the new ethical theories that were to come out of the Darwinian revolution. Nietzsche read Haeckel in 1875, objecting primarily to the mindless idealization of the strong contained in the notion of

the struggle for existence. Nietzsche argued that it was precisely the fragmented community that was most susceptible to "the infection of the new,"
that illness and inner wounds provided the impetus to creativity and that the
weak, by being less bound and hence freer, made "all progress possible."[26]

Nietzsche's new openness to evolutionary theories and the inductive
method brought him in line with younger Germans who, Dilthey observed
in 1877, were abandoning all the German philosophers save Kant in favor of
the new thought emanating from England, America, and France.[27] Encouraged by Rée, Nietzsche had begun to look outward. In the summer of 1877
he met G. Croom Robertson, the editor of the new English journal *Mind*
whose contributors, Nietzsche enthused, contained "all the philosophical
greats (Spencer, Tylor, Maine, Darwin, etc., etc.)."[28] Robertson was opening
up the pages of his journal to young German critics of the German philosophical establishment and was then publishing a lengthy piece by Wilhelm
Wundt, the proponent of a new "experimental psychology." Wundt's
account of recent German philosophy contained a critical but not hostile
reference to Nietzsche's early writings.[29] Rée had shortly before considered
obtaining his habilitation in Zurich because "Wandt [*sic*] represents there
the Darwinian orientation."[30] Nietzsche succeeded in having Robertson
favorably review Rée's book and wrote Rée that he should consider becoming a contributor to *Mind,* a magazine without equal in Germany. The whole
episode strengthened Nietzsche's belief that he was becoming a part of a
new international community of inquiry.

Wagner had intensified Nietzsche's sense of his own Germanness; now
Rée prompted cosmopolitan ideals. In October 1876, during the weeks Rée
would refer to as "the honeymoon of our friendship," Nietzsche postulated
"The Ten Commandments of the Free Spirit."[31] The first read, "You shall
neither love nor hate peoples"; the second, "You shall pursue no politics";
the fifth, "You shall take your wife from a people other than your own"; the
seventh, "You shall submit to no ceremonies of the church"; and the ninth,
"You shall, in order to speak the truth, prefer exile."[32]

Rée was Nietzsche's first Jewish friend. Short in stature with dark curly
hair, Rée bore his lonely Jewishness as a stigma and was more than incredulous when other Jews or new acquaintances such as Lou von Salomé failed
to recognize his ethnicity. Later held up as an exemplar of nineteenth
century Jewish self-hatred, Rée's case was complicated by his isolating,
pseudo-aristocratic social background. In time Nietzsche and Rée's different
religious backgrounds would divide them. It was the invariable penchant of
the clerical son to continue to declaim as from a pulpit in the expectation
that what was said would be necessarily believed, while the Jewish intellectual, Nietzsche noted, worked with the opposite premise, anticipating disbelief and therefore amassing evidence in a scientific, systematic framework.[33]

Nietzsche would eventually find Rée's dogmatism intolerable; Rée, in turn, would accuse Nietzsche of intellectual vanity, a capital sin for one who devoted the end of his life to selflessly providing medical care for the poor. Or was it a compulsory quality Rée lacked? "Man minus vanity = nullity" was one of the last epigrams Rée wrote before he fell off a mountain, a possible suicide.[34]

Nietzsche and Rée shared not only a personal diffidence that was coupled to an aggressive literary style but also a wounded love of the aristocracy that made the notion of a cosmopolitan moral aristocracy appealing to both. As a scholarship boy at Schulpforta, Nietzsche had learned to emulate the aristocratic style-setters and had cultivated his friendship with Gersdorff, the future Baron, court functionary, and member of the Prussian Upper House. He was greatly pained as a young Basel professor to have to present himself to the Grand Duchess Constantine as the son of the former family tutor. Even after his break with Bayreuth, Nietzsche would continue to court those Wagnerian aristocrats who came his way, notably the Freiherr von Seydlitz and Heinrich von Stein. The legend of Polish noble forebears became ever more attractive to him. Rée's merchant father had acquired an East Elbian estate, but unlike other entre-preneurs who benefited from the agrarian crises that were leading to a "pseudo-democratization" of Prussia's landed elite, the Rée family's Jewish-ness blocked their assimilation, particularly after the rise of the anti-Semitic agitation in the seventies.[35]

In late October the two friends traveled to Sorrento for an extended stay with Malwida von Meysenbug (Wagner's friend of twenty years) and Nietz-sche's former pupil, the gifted but ailing Albert Brenner. The Wagners, escaping another mounting financial catastrophe, were also in Sorrento. Malwida utilized all her social skills to keep friction at a minimum. The Wagners made clear their distaste for Rée, and Rée was kept at arm's length. Several years before Nietzsche had spurned the friendship of Mendels-sohn's son, an art historian, fearing that it might arouse Wagner's displea-sure. Now he bristled at the composer's innuendos that he was falling under the spell of his Jewish friend.

By mutual inclination the subject of the Bayreuth festival was studiously avoided. Wagner had been forced to abandon all thought of annual music festivals in Bayreuth for the foreseeable future. In one of the final conversa-tions, Wagner became expansive on the subject of his new opera, *Parsifal,* speaking mystically and reverently of the blood of the Savior. Nietzsche was dumbfounded, prompting the composer to ask, "Why are you so silent, my friend?"[36] While Nietzsche was aware of the new project, the manner in which Wagner was adapting himself to his religious theme was deeply disturbing—particularly at a moment when Nietzsche's Seventh Commandment enjoined the free spirit from submitting to religious ritual. Perhaps the Christian ecstasy of *Parsifal* also reminded Nietzsche as it would Eduard Hanslick "not infrequently of the versified devotional seizure of the German Pietists."[37] Eventually Nietzsche would respond to the composer's religiously conceived "stage-festival-play" by asserting that "festivity is paganism *par excellence*."[38] But during this, their last meeting, Nietzsche's stance was one of disaffection rather than confrontation, and as a final conciliatory gesture he halfheartedly agreed to contribute to the new journal the composer was planning to launch in Bayreuth.

Wagner traveled on to Rome where he met Count Gobineau, the spiritual father of modern racism. In the coming six years Gobineau would displace Nietzsche in Wagner's estimation as his single noteworthy *"Contemporain."* Before he left, Wagner unsuccessfully sought to break up the Sorrento group, urging Malwida to join him. Wagner was fiercely possessive of Malwida, and had in 1874 staged violent scenes when she extricated herself after one year's residence in Bayreuth. Several months after his departure, Wagner wrote Sorrento, recounting his dream in which Nietzsche, Rée, and Brenner had been arrested for murdering Malwida.[39]

Malwida, a sixty-year-old spinster, was an unlikely chaperone for a budding colony of free spirits, but she watched over her "three sons" with matronly care. A fervent Wagnerian who produced vapid, self-important literary exercises defending "idealism," she admired Nietzsche's earlier writings, but disapproved of Nietzsche and Rée's new concerns. Still, she was in a remarkably buoyant, receptive, and generous mood. Her recently published *Memoiren einer Idealistin,* was a critical success that was bringing her recognition as the gray eminence of an emerging, still genteel women's movement. Nietzsche was a great admirer of her autobiography, which recounted her break with her Hessian bureaucratic, aristocratic family; her forced flight to London after the revolution; her role as governess in the Herzen family; and her friendships with Mazzini, Wagner, and Michelet. Malwida, like Wagner, was shedding her radical past and would end her life as a friend of the Imperial Chancellor Bernhard von Bülow. In contrast to Cosima, however, Malwida staunchly supported the anticlericalism of the Risorgimento, attending on her way to the Bayreuth festival a major Mazzini memorial in Genoa. This mix enabled her to make the obscured world of mid-century radicalism acceptable and intriguing to Nietzsche's group.

While Rée stimulated Nietzsche's interest in French and English thought, Malwida helped complete his cosmopolitan education by serving as his guide both to Italy and to Russian radicalism. Malwida's sentimental cultivation of Mazzini's memory was particularly infectious. Nietzsche had been deeply impressed with Mazzini ever since their chance encounter shortly before the Italian's death in 1872, and although hardly sympathetic to Mazzini's national-democratic vision, in 1882 Nietzsche would hail him as the only man of the century who could be called equally good, noble, and great.[40]

Nietzsche's first contact with Russian radicalism was Malwida's translation of Alexander Herzen's memoirs. "I have learned from him to think much more sympathetically about a number of negative tendencies," Nietzsche wrote Malwida in 1872, "and perhaps I should not even call them negative because such a fiery-noble and determined soul could not simply nourish himself from negation and hatred."[41] Malwida introduced him to Herzen's children. He visited the younger Alexander, a physiologist, in Florence and composed his *Une Monodie á deux* in honor of Malwida's adopted daughter, Olga, on the occasion of her marriage to the French historian Gabriel Monod. In Sorrento Nietzsche toyed with the idea of marrying Herzen's eldest daughter, Natalie. Natalie had been the most mindful of her father's concern before his death that his children were losing their Russian identities, becoming, under Malwida's influence, cosmopolites. A few years before Natalie had thrown herself into Russian exile politics, and had been at the center of one of the most dramatic episodes of Russian radicalism, "l'affaire Nechayev."[42] She fell under the influence of Bakunin, who was especially eager to disassociate her from Malwida, "that veritable lunatic, that Wagnero-Germanizing Pommeranian [*sic*] Virgin."[43] Natalie became involved with the sinister and fanatic young nihilist Sergey Nechayev, with whom Bakunin was then composing his "Catechism of the Revolutionist." She emerged disillusioned from the experience, which ended with Nechayev's extradition and imprisonment in Russia for murder. Whether Nietzsche learned the details of the case from Malwida or from his later reading of Dostoevsky's fictional account in *The Possessed* is unclear. But in any event Russia was on the agenda in Sorrento. In addition to Herzen, the little group read Turgenev, Rée's idol, whom Rée had visited in Paris. Malwida promoted Natalie's virtues, and Nietzsche wrote Elisabeth that Natalie's manner and intellect seemed highly compatible with his own; his only fear was that she was too old, being his own age.[44] His family was pestering him to marry; the German doctor he consulted in Naples advised it, and he also desired it. He recognized that his previous intellectual orientation excluded the feminine. He noted that women had been banned from agonal festivity, and he criticized Rohde for neglecting the homosexual basis of Greek culture. Nietzsche wanted instead to make marriage and the family a central concern of his free spirit. But while Rohde was soon to marry, absolutely nothing was to come of Nietzsche and Natalie.

During the winter the little Sorrento group planned a pedagogic institute for adults of both sexes, managed by Malwida and with Nietzsche and

Rée as instructors. Such an idealized modern cloister was a vehicle for Malwida's feminism and for Nietzsche's new Enlightenment. Nietzsche was also on the verge of resigning his Basel post; Malwida encouraged the step. The institute was to provide him with an alternative outlet for his pedagogic impulse. In these months, Rée completed his manuscript, which Nietzsche ventured "probably represents a decisive turning point in the history of moral philosophy."[45] Even Brenner, mortally ill and craving peace, was able to finish his novella.

Brenner and Rée left in April; without them Malwida's humorless company was no longer tolerable. Nietzsche's health deteriorated, and he left Sorrento before Natalie arrived. But the Sorrento plans, while unrealized, did leave their mark. It seemed legitimate for Nietzsche to address his public with an aphoristic "we," a sense of camaraderie and community which, if occasionally forced, nevertheless did bring together into a coherent whole the some 2,400 aphorisms published in volumes annually over the next five years. Rée, his apostle from afar, sent encouragement in late 1877 from Berlin: "You can view yourself as the head of an invisible church whose members are far more numerous than perhaps even you believe."[46] Malwida, in turn, formed a salon in the mushrooming German colony in Rome, which drew on her former Mazzinian friends, many now in high government posts, and attracted a steady stream of young female intellectuals from abroad.

Although still vaguely committed to the idea of marrying before the year was out, Nietzsche fled into the Alps. There he relished his isolation, found that he felt more at home among the German Swiss than among Germans, and reluctantly decided to make the "experiment" of returning once more to his Basel post.[47] "In Switzerland I am more myself," Nietzsche wrote Malwida; "In the Alps I am unconquerable, namely when I am alone and have no other enemy than myself."[48] Nietzsche's identification with Switzerland, his projection of its polity as the model for European developments, could only now be said to have begun. He was thus embarrassed by the scandal caused during his absence by his young Thuringian disciple, Heinrich Köselitz (*aka* Peter Gast, 1854–1918), who had attacked Basel's music director as a "musical Philistine" in an essay modeled on the "anti-Strauss."[49] The dense Köselitz had not yet grasped Nietzsche's alienation from Wagner and the Reich. From their first meeting in 1875, Nietzsche had sought to impress on Köselitz the superiority of Switzerland's freer intellectual climate over the stultifying atmosphere in the Reich and had praised the German Swiss for retaining those traditional German virtues which Germans across the border were so busily abandoning. But Köselitz's cosmopolitan, anti-nationalist pose was without substance. In this essay Köselitz had attributed the "unmusicality" of the Swiss to their republican institutions. In 1877 he could not resist scorning the pettiness of Swiss conditions, and in 1914 he would be among the first to herald the German advance.

To Western Europeans Switzerland might appear to be merely a tourist mecca of the new Alpinism, a land of "theologians and waiters" as Wilde would put it. But Nietzsche would identify with Switzerland's more sinister reputation, and the drama of his politics would feed on the growing hostility toward the Swiss manifested by the conservative states and proponents of national and racial purity. Gobineau, Wagner's new mentor, considered it "a place of rendezvous of all who are dangerous." Switzerland was in his mind a loathsome "kind of promised land or mother-country which revolt and treachery need but touch to regain strength."[50] Gobineau understood his pessimistic racial prophecies to be "a natural consequence of my horror and disgust at equality and democracy."[51] While Nietzsche was not without a similar revulsion, he suspected the drive to racial purity fed democratic populism, with racial purity but a symptom of decadence and degenerate inbreeding. It was not racial degeneracy and doom but rather racial experimentation, specifically the emergence of a European race through ethnic intermingling, that now excited his imagination.

Nietzsche identified himself with a Switzerland which Erich Gruner has recently called "the experimental field" of nineteenth century European politics.[52] After 1830 the Swiss polity became the laboratory of liberal institutions, evolving the first ideological mass parties on the Continent and introducing both the plebiscite and recall referendum. The Swiss also remained in a curious insider/outsider role vis-à-vis their neighbors, for, unlike the Dutch who had similarly broken away from the Holy Roman Empire, they had developed no distinctive national culture. Nietzsche would proceed on the assumption that the German Swiss were destined to play the same role within German affairs as the French Swiss had done in the preceding century of French ascendancy. Nietzsche assumed a stance toward the Reich and European politics comparable to that taken by Rousseau, Madam de Staël, and Benjamin Constant toward France.

Nietzsche's similarity to Rousseau—as a kind of Rousseau in reverse—was most marked in the manner in which Nietzsche exploited his association with Switzerland, the haven of radical and subversive thought. While Rousseau fought absolutism by idealizing nationality, republican virtue, and the small state, Nietzsche envisaged the cosmopolitanism of the Swiss model eventually enveloping the European nation-states. The loss of nationality was a sacrifice only of backwardness, of "barbarism." He echoed Burckhardt's view of 1870 that "the men of today have gradually and unconsciously given up nationality and really hate every form of diversity," but without embracing the latter's fatalistic conclusion "that the final end might be an Imperium Romanum (only when we are dead, to be sure) and after numerous Assyrians, Medes, and Persians."[53] He did not, at least not in the aphoristic period, accept Burckhardt's projection of this *'beata tranquillitas,"* enforced by the soldiery and a centralized administration. Instead Nietzsche's concept circled back to Rousseau's vision of small states: the contemporary nation-states would swallow up the petty states, and in turn would be consumed by a coming European "monster state," which, however, in the absence of external enemies, would eventually "split up into atomistic state structures."[54]

During the 1870s and 1880s, the locus of conservative fear of Switzerland shifted eastward. Dostoevsky sought to underscore the western origin of European nihilism by having his arch-nihilist character, Stavrogin, sign his suicide note "a citizen [of the canton] of Uri." Nietzsche, in contrast, was delighted when *Human, All-Too-Human* was banned in Russia, a fact immediately advertised on the dust jacket.[55] With German politics veering sharply to the right, Nietzsche became increasingly convinced that Switzerland was the only possible abode for the German free spirit. He relished that which was banned or banished from the Reich. He found "very instructive" Harry von Arnim's 1875 brochure, "Pro Nihilo," presenting his case against Bismarck, for it confirmed Nietzsche's increasingly negative view of the Chancellor's character and influence.[56] After the passage of the anti-Socialist legislation, Nietzsche wrote Overbeck requesting the address of a Zurich book dealer from whom he could obtain a catalogue of banned socialist literature.[57]

In turning from Wagner, Nietzsche was drawn into liberalism's deepening crisis; his free spirit addressed the disheartened liberal intellectual. Nietzsche now recognized that even if his youthful polemics against liberal rationalism, historicism, and the "cultural Philistine" had been justified, they did more harm than good. With German liberalism abandoning the cultural politics of the *Kulturkampf,* in retreat on all fronts, Nietzsche took up some of its lost causes, especially anticlericalism. While Nietzsche prided himself in attacking that which seemed victorious, he was less comfortable championing that which seemed defeated. More often than not he would turn on the vanquished in the hope of provoking some resistance, some sign of life. Thomas Mann, in associating Nietzsche with liberalism, would correct Nietzsche's self-characterization as "anti-liberal to the point of malice" to read anti-liberal "out of malice, out of perversity"[58]—one might add, out of frustration.

Nietzsche was ill equipped to penetrate the forces bringing on Bismarck's anti-liberal "Change of Course." Nietzsche's own "Change of Course" was to abandon aesthetics in favor of ethics. The predominance of economic issues during the Great Depression was foreign and distasteful to his nature. He saw only selfish interest at play in the raging dispute between free traders and protectionists that was fatally dividing the liberal movement in Germany. He fitfully consulted economic writers, such as the American protectionist H. C. Carey, but with little effect.[59] But he had grasped, as in one key aphorism of the chapter "A View of the State," the polarization of European politics into two camps, the nationalist and the socialist, and was determined to arm the free spirit with a set of political aphorisms to meet the contemporary crisis. In the aphorism he still referred to national-liberalism in the printed manuscript, but then deleted liberalism from his dichotomy in the recognition, no doubt, that it had ceased to be a viable mediating force. Liberalism, he suggested, had been consumed in its embrace of nationalism; the alliance of commercial and dynastic interests may have freed social life from certain "oppressive castes" flourishing under particularism, but the growth of state power and the separation of the nation-states from each other had served to betray liberalism's cosmopolitan goals. Nationalism and war, he concluded, functioned now merely as weapons against the alleged threat of revolution.[60]

Nietzsche's condemnation of nationalism flowed naturally from the failure of his own attempted reconciliation of nationalist and cosmopolitan ideals. His position toward the other camp, the socialist, was produced by no former infatuation and was consequently less developed. For almost a decade his instinctive disdain for socialism had been fortified by his Schopenhauerian rejection of optimism, his caste-conscious Hellenism, and his emulation of the lingering paternalism of the Basel industrialists. His recognition of the social question had extended only to curiosity about flamboyant radical leaders, such as Lassalle, Bakunin, and Herzen, or about Wagner's submerged socialist past. The Commune was, moreover, a profound shock that seemingly confirmed all his fears of the cultural barbarism of the lower classes. But the specter of proletarian uprisings gradually dimmed, with Bakunin conceding in 1875, "the revolution for the moment has returned to its bed; we have fallen back into a period of evolution, that is to say one of subterranean revolutions, insensible and even often imperceptible."[61]

The changed situation demanded a new response from Nietzsche. He was anxious to disassociate himself from the reactionaries who were manipulating the fear of socialism to undermine Bismarck's collaboration with liberalism. Nietzsche was thus disconcerted when criticized by a Mr. Cook, a disciple of Proudhon, in an 1875 encounter.[62] The present economic crisis of capitalism, engendering calls for state intervention, moreover, lent new credibility to socialist ideas among intellectual circles. Nietzsche proceeded to place socialism on his intellectual agenda in order to question, or at least, examine the motives of his own youthful anti-socialism.

He did so during the confused ideological hiatus that existed between

Lassalle's death and the doctrinal triumph of Marxism in the 1880s. Aside from his cursory perusal of Bebel's *Woman under Socialism* (1883), Nietzsche read no work by a committed Marxist.[63] John Stuart Mill's article "Socialism" (1879), marked, chronologically and ideologically, the terminus of Nietzsche's examination of socialism.[64] He no doubt came across Marx's name. He would own Albert Schäffle's *Quintessence of Socialism* (1874), a conservative but straightforward popularization of socialist theories which social democrats would themselves distribute in the late seventies. References to Marx, primarily dismissive, also occur with some regularity in the seven volumes of Eugen Dühring which Nietzsche would eventually possess.[65] Like so many of his contemporaries, Nietzsche was dazzled by Dühring's meteoric rise to prominence, accepting at face value Dühring's claim to represent socialism. Neither Dühring nor Mill shared Marx's economic determinism; Mill considered all who worked to transform society to the benefit of the lower classes to be socialists; Dühring worked with a similar inclusive, morally based conception of socialism. Nietzsche was able to meet such moral arguments more or less on his own ground. To portray Nietzsche as an intellectual opponent of Marx is thus quite misleading; he would become, at most, an "anti-Dühring."

Dühring had a negative influence on Nietzsche, offering too easy a target and precluding a more sophisticated understanding of the socialist movement. Neither Mill's socialist liberalism nor Dühring's racist national socialism facilitated Nietzsche's comprehension of the new political polarity he had himself foreseen. Both were—like his own variant, aristocratic radicalism—attempts to deny, synthesize, or overcome the dichotomy of nationalism and socialism. Setting aside Nietzsche's obvious neglect of socialist economic theory, Nietzsche was never moved to contrast the new proletarian internationalism with his own cosmopolitanism which optimistically projected the coming ascendancy of the intelligentsia. The socialist critique of imperialism, that is to say, the new nationalism of the nation-states, quite eluded him. Lukács's harsh critique is justified on this point. Nietzsche was in this respect a man of his epoch whose concentration on socialism was easily deflected onto the then-thriving parallel movements of anarchism, "nihilism," and radical populism. As Mill became the foil of a hypocritical commercialism, so Dühring became the classic exemplar of the resentment motivating anti-Semitism, subversive movements and "slave morality" in general. Dühring was "the anarchist," the "Berlin apostle of revenge" whose derivation of justice from revenge Nietzsche happily reapplied back upon Dühring, the self-proclaimed "Rousseau of the nineteenth century."

Nietzsche had first become aware of Dühring during his Leipzig years. Nietzsche then believed the popular, blind *Privat-Docent* at the university of Berlin to be a Schopenhauerian, but Dühring had merely adopted the philosopher's sarcastic, denunciatory style. As Nietzsche later discovered, Dühring was, in fact, an "amalgamist" who borrowed freely from positivism, from Carey's optimistic economic individualism, and from socialist theorists including Marx. Politically he was an amalgamist as well, blending the anti-Semitism of the right with positions he told his followers stood to the left of Marx.[66] After failing to win Bismarck's backing for his social program in 1868, he became conspicuous in the early seventies through his outspoken defense of the Commune. He enjoyed great popularity among German social democrats as much for his frenetic attacks on the educational establishment as for his eclectic, abstruse writings. Eduard Bernstein was drawn to "his emphasis on the liberal element in socialism"; Bebel hailed him as "the new communist"; and crypto-anarchists such as Johann Most embraced his theory of force as the oppressive engine of history.[67]

Nietzsche turned to Dühring in the summer of 1875, subjecting an early work, *Das Werth des Lebens* (1865), to an extensive analysis. As Nietzsche was then seeking an avenue out of his own Schopenhauerian idealism, he focused primarily on the book's positivist critique of pessimism. Dühring's socialist evolution envisaged a "perfect type of human being." But Nietzsche balked, for even to raise the question of "the value of life" seemed symptomatic of a declining feeling for life, and in any case, defied the type of collectivist answer that Dühring was seeking. Nietzsche was also repelled by Dühring's pugnacious, self-important pose and would exploit this repugnance to construct a portrait of the socialist as a twisted, narrow personality who, if successful, could only reduce happiness on earth.

Yet in characterizing socialism's determination to destroy tradition, custom, and restraint in which well-being naturally resided, Nietzsche could also acknowledge socialism as a partial ally in his own campaign against the "fettered spirit." He was thus able to praise socialism as an intellectual stimulus, bringing the lower classes into "a kind of practical-philosophical dialogue" with the rest of society.[68] The "inspiring power" of socialism, he recognized, lay in the doctrine of equality or rather the determination to overlook the inequalities between men, a procedure Nietzsche now conceded was justified insofar as Europeans were becoming basically similar.[69] He even speculated that as the cultures of the employers and employees approximated each other, backward peoples would have to be imported to undertake society's more menial and unpleasant tasks.

Nietzsche's attitude toward socialism mirrored his ambivalent view of capitalism. While he embraced the technological revolution ushering in a new age of experimentation, he, like the other *Gebildeten* of the period, did not have a principled commitment to liberal capitalism. To the extent that he considered it, state economic intervention as such did not alarm him. Yet he did despair of the new industrial centers and scorned the coming of a new popular mass culture. It was a self-consciously "aristocratic" position, spoken in the name of an emerging intellectual stratum in "the vanishing voice of olden times." He proposed that the intelligentsia be guaranteed the necessary leisure to originate a "higher culture," an alternative schema, of "the caste of compulsory labor and the caste of free labor." He dealt with the capitalist/socialist dichotomy by contrasting the employer/employee with that of the noble/slave relationship, asserting that the slave of antiquity worked less and with more security than the modern worker or that the modern businessman lacked the leadership qualities and cultural instincts of the nobleman.[70]

Nietzsche was among the first to project such high hopes upon the intelligentsia; an 1878 fragment speaks of "the beginning of the rule of the writer."[71] Unlike Karl Mannheim a half-century later, conceiving of the intelligentsia as a free-floating stratum mediating between the conflicting classes, Nietzsche at this early point fantasized the subordination of society to the interests of the culturally creative. The 1878 aphorism "My Utopia" visualized "the most sensitive"—thereby the most suffering and creative— at the tip of the social pyramid as the receptacle of society's hopes.[72] Nietzsche could be tolerant of socialism when he reflected on its actual effect as, for instance, when he called it "merely an agitational means of individualism," an unconscious method of organizing numerous individual wills for one common purpose.[73] But when his attention turned to social- ism's moral and utopian aspirations, Nietzsche immediately sensed a rival and threat.

Nietzsche countered with anti-utopianism, a principled rejection of collective human goals and visions of social stasis. His brief foray into socialist thought had only more sharply delineated his own intransigent individualism, his belief that future values rested in exemplars rather than collectivities. Burckhardt once recommended Thomas More's *Utopia* to Nietzsche as a counterweight to Machiavelli's *The Prince,* saying that the former's concern with the future compensated for the latter's emphasis only on the past and the present.[74] Nietzsche did not pursue the suggestion and would remain strictly a Machiavellian in his approach to politics. Moral claims were smoke screens, the socialist principle of justice could only follow not precede the agreements reached in the coming power struggle, Nietzsche argued. He took a militant stand against the statism he detected in the socialist bid for power. In 1875 he noted "the ideal state of which the socialists dream destroys the fundament of the great intellects, the great energy"; two years later he repeated his doubts about whether humanity would thrive under "the ordered situation which socialists" demand; these positions would be amplified in a string of aphorisms beginning with "The Contradiction of Genius and the Ideal State."[75] Socialism was the heir and "younger brother of an almost expired despotism." It "desires (and under certain circumstances furthers) the Caesarian despotism of this century" so as to better install its own brand of state terrorism. As a movement it is "in the deepest sense reactionary," one which "aims at the complete annihilation of the individual."[76]

But even as Nietzsche was using Dühring to differentiate his "radicalism" from socialism, he found himself gradually drawn into the web of Dühring's varied influence. In 1876, Rée befriended one of Dühring's most promising converts, the young aristocratic aesthete Heinrich Freiherr von Stein (1857–1887). While Engels was attacking Dühring in the socialist press of 1877/78 as "the Richard Wagner of philosophy—but without Wagner's talents," Wagnerians were flocking to embrace Dühring. "The conversion of the German student to social democracy" was due to Dühring, Engels would admit. In his *Die Ideale des Materialismus* (1878), an aphoristic work admired by Rée and Nietzsche, Stein characterized his development: "At fifteen I was a believer in Jesus, at eighteen an atheist, at twenty a materialist. At first a lie, then a conversion, and then a religion."[77] The "Prussian socialism" Engels despised in Dühring with its violent anticlericalism and vicious anti-Semitism attracted the young Franconian nobleman whose political radicalism had definite limits. In the summer of 1877 when Dühring was stripped of his post and right to teach for accusing Germany's most eminent scientist, Hermann von Helmholtz, of plagiarism, Stein joined the thousands of protesting students and socialists, filled with the mission of taking "philosophy to the people."[78]

Malwida, from afar, shared the sense of outrage at Dühring's dismissal, writing Nietzsche of her admiration of the man who had dared take on the "old professorial clique" of Berlin. She found Dühring to be highly compatible with her own agnostic idealism; he was "good for the young," and she was convinced that "Schopenhauer would have acknowledged him as Dühring acknowledges Schopenhauer."[79] Through Rée she soon met Stein whom, in turn, she introduced to the Wagners. Immediately installed as the Wagner family tutor and literary warhorse of the new *Bayreuther Blätter,* Stein would function as a substitute Nietzsche, the new philosophical exponent of Wagner's aesthetic religiosity. On the way to his new residence in Bayreuth, Stein visited Dühring who approved of the step, calling Wagner "a kind of national Reformator" and "my ally" in battle against the Jews.[80] Nietzsche did not meet Stein until 1884, and although the men enjoyed each other's company during the three-day stay, the meeting had a predictable outcome: Stein had come with the intention of coaxing Nietzsche back into the Wagnerian fold, while Nietzsche was determined to lead the young "Junker" aesthete out of the "swamp" in which Dühring and Wagner had plunged him.[81]

Nietzsche also saw his young Thuringian protégé Paul Widemann fall under Dühring's spell. Widemann had accompanied Köselitz to Basel in 1875 in order to study under Nietzsche. Widemann, more philosopher than musician, was at first favored by Nietzsche over Köselitz. But Widemann left Basel after six months for his military service and then continued his philosophical studies in Germany. Since Widemann and Köselitz were close friends and advisors of Nietzsche's publisher, Widemann and Nietzsche kept in close touch. In 1879 Dühring became affiliated with Schmeitzner's publishing house, and Schmeitzner and Widemann thereafter sought to link Nietzsche with Dühring. Widemann had written Köselitz of his great desire "that Nietzsche would also become acquainted with Dühring. (And finally he will have to if he continues on his path.)" Widemann added that it was high time "Nietzsche emancipated himself from the historical standpoint and the influence of developmental natural science" since Dühring had already "solved the old duality between philosophy and natural science" and had indeed "overcome Kant and all metaphysics."[82] To Nietzsche's great disgust, Schmeitzner and Widemann then contrived to promote Dühring and Nietzsche as the dual pillars of the short-lived *Internationale Monatsschrift* of 1881/82.

By the mid-eighties, Dühring was a renegade without a following; this sinister, embittered figure would continue his flight into the fringe racism of the right, dying in 1921 surrounded by a handful of obscure disciples who later became prominent in the SS.[83] The brief Dühring enthusiasm on the left and the right was symptomatic of the confusion of fronts that accompanied Bismarck's "Change of Course" that effectively realigned German politics for the next forty years. The new integral alliance between agrarians and industrialists reduced left liberalism to a rump and established political Catholicism as a political broker, while isolating social democracy. Within this new constellation, anti-Semitism represented a volatile force manipulated by fringe elements anxious to break out of the constricting political reality. Dühring's anticlerical, anti-Semitic socialism was one such attempt, the anti-Semitic Christian Socialism of the Pietist Pastor Adolf Stöcker, then Court Preacher, was another. As Nietzsche discovered when he was completing *Human, All-Too-Human*, Bayreuth was becoming a platform for these racist dissidents.

Nietzsche may have broken intellectually with Wagner but many personal ties still bound him to Bayreuth. There was his halfhearted promise to contribute to the composer's planned magazine; Schmeitzner was to be its publisher. Nietzsche's old friends were almost all Wagnerians, and Elisabeth had insinuated herself into the Bayreuth fold. During 1877 Nietzsche used his illness to avoid meeting Wagner and he seldom wrote to Bayreuth, but through Schmeitzner and others he kept abreast of the growing crisis in

Bayreuth. The composer lamented that although his works were being performed everywhere, "no one wants to come back to Bayreuth."[84] It was known that the festival audience of 1876 had responded to music drama no differently than audiences in the court theaters; therefore, artists were unwilling to make the sacrifice of low wages, and the huge remaining deficit precluded annual productions. Unwilling to see Bayreuth become a private theater with occasional performances, Wagner, albeit fatalistically, gave the signal for another publicistic campaign to secure state intervention. Bayreuth, he insisted, should become "the property of the nation."[85]

The choice of Hans von Wolzogen, a sycophant whose fondest dream was to ally Bayreuth with Stöcker's Christian Socialism, as editor of the *Bayreuther Blätter* duly alarmed Nietzsche. Wagner gave his blessing to its reactionary tack in his first piece, "Modern," where he attacked democracy as a "triumph of the modern Jewish world."[86] Since subscribers were the members of the Wagner Societies, it was evident that the journal intended to instill ideological purity among the most committed Wagnerians. After Wolzogen rejected Köselitz's contributions on the grounds that they were written in a "purely atheistic" spirit, Nietzsche added a passage to his manuscript denouncing "romantic retreat and desertion" as "a soiling of one's intellectual conscience."[87] Yet he was still reluctant to flaunt opposition, and he considered publishing under a pseudonym until Schmeitzner's objections finally dissuaded him. On January 4, 1878, one week before he completed the manuscript, Nietzsche received the text of *Parsifal* from Wagner who mockingly added the title "Ecclesiastical Councilor" to his inscription. In response, after months of silence, *Human, All-Too-Human* arrived in Bayreuth. Nietzsche later likened the exchange to the crossing of two swords.

Wagner could at first not bring himself to read what he termed *Human and Inhuman,* then felt compelled to do so; in August he published his response, attacking Nietzsche, although not by name. The composer vented his anger toward a skepticism which emulated the experimental process of physical science and which dared to "cast overboard the entire idea of *genius* as a radical error." He upheld the intuitions of the "people" over the "progress" of the academics; the folk "does not reason, still it knows; it knows its great men and loves the Genius those others hate; and finally to them an abomination, it honors the divine."[88] Nietzsche accepted his "excommunication" with a certain relief, assigning Wagner's polemic to the "all-too-human."[89]

"It is difficult," Nietzsche wrote that summer, "to attack Wagner on specifics and not score points; his art form, life, character, his opinions, his preferences and aversions all have their glaring vulnerabilities. But as a totality the phenomenon is equal to every attack."[90] Wagner was then complicating his persona by both politicizing his following and depoliticizing his art. He fashioned a political legacy that would place his Bayreuth followers at the forefront of the *völkisch* movement in Germany and Austria until 1945; yet in his final work, *Parsifal,* "the political world is completely absent." Recent critics have thus approached the late Wagner from opposing directions. Carl Schorske treats the later career as a disillusioned retreat from revolutionary "social politics," and "Wagner-Parsifal becomes the psycho-therapeutic artist-redeemer,"[91] while Robert Gutman's biography focuses on the composer's manipulation of his fame to further his own bizarre "musical *Realpolitik*" of blood and race.[92]

One of the consequences of Wagner's attempt to force his following into the straightjacket of nationalism was that German Wagnerianism was stultified, made orthodox, and isolated from the rest of European Wagnerianism. In contrast to the parochialism of the *Bayreuther Blätter, Revue Wagneriènne* became the literary vanguard of the French Symbolists and even *The Meister* of London had a more creditable literary impact. If Germans were thereby spared some avant-garde snobbishness, they were left with the choice of purely musical appreciation or a politicized cult of the composer. A serious literary Wagnerianism was virtually nonexistent in Germany after Nietzsche's defection. The one exception, Thomas Mann, lived within the Wagner-Nietzsche tension until he too denounced Bayreuth in 1933 as the "court theater of Nazism."[93] The fury of Nietzsche's later attacks was largely occasioned and conditioned by what Wagner had done to his German following; with some notable exceptions only the German Wagnerians felt the need to respond in kind. Indeed, non-Germans, Auden for example, often came to appreciate Wagner's importance only through Nietzsche's polemics. Nietzsche was a renegade turning on a former renegade. He thereby became the champion of some of Wagner's earlier principles, if not his socialism then certainly his cosmopolitanism.

The surprise, consternation and anger which *Human, All-Too-Human* was bound to arouse among Wagnerians and Nietzsche's previous admirers—as well as the satisfaction it could be expected to bring the critics of Bayreuth—should have ensured the book's *succès de scandale,* Schmeitzner certainly expected this. But the book appeared at the worst possible moment, simultaneously with the pathetic attempt on the life of Wilhelm I by a confused plumber on May 11. "An uproar is made over completely empty events such as the attempted assassination," Nietzsche complained, "the press is a permanent false alarm."[94] Nevertheless, not since the news of the Commune was Germany gripped with such paranoia and hand-wringing. When Dr. Karl Nobiling then seriously wounded the Emperor on June 2, a new paroxysm of indignation ensued. It was hardly the conducive climate to rally "free spirits" to the new skepticism.

Socialists would bear the brunt of the reaction, but there was also a generalized revulsion against the tenor and relativism of contemporary intellectual life. Bismarck had already begun attacking "nihilists"; the appearance of an assassin with a doctorate seemed to confirm the worst, while liberal intellectuals began to blame themselves for the spread of subversive doctrines.[95] Dilthey worried in the *Westermanns Monatsheften* that "the innermost life of the nation was beginning to be poisoned"; "everywhere one looks, above in the salons of the aristocracy and bourgeoisie or below in the workshops and bars of the workers" one came to the conclusion that "gradually all spheres of society are showing themselves infected with skepticism, nihilism, and materialism."[96] Four days after Nobiling's act, Otto Ribbeck wrote: "the worst is that this whole way of thinking is destroying so many of the better natures like a deadly poison," citing as his example the destructive, "disgusting new book by Nietzsche."[97]

There was no scandal. The book received scant public attention, but it did mark a parting of the ways; first, from his estranged friends: Cosima wrote Gersdorff that she would remain "loyal to the dead Nietzsche" by ignoring the new Nietzsche; Rohde was "painfully amazed" to find "instead of Nietzsche now suddenly Rée"; Seydlitz found "everything is very much Réeal" and asked Nietzsche when he would again write a "Nietzschean book";[98] Romundt announced his opposition; Adolf Baumgartner expressed disappointment in his former teacher, and the former Viennese admirer Siegfried Lipiner sent a thirty-two page letter attacking Rée. "All my friends are unanimous that my book was written by you," Nietzsche wrote Rée, adding defiantly: "Long live Réealism and my good friend!"[99]

The book also precipitated a break with Elisabeth, who continued to court Bayreuth, and in fact met her future husband in that circle. Although she avoided falling under Bayreuth's ban, her residual sibling loyalty was more than offset by her displeasure at her brother's new turn. As relations with Naumburg worsened, Nietzsche's Basel world was also shriveling up. It was no longer the rendezvous of old friends, and new ones were scarcely forthcoming. With Brenner's death, the dissolution of the nine-month household with Elisabeth, the departure of Köselitz for Venice, and his inability successfully to carry out even his reduced teaching load, it became apparent that it would now only be a matter of months before he resigned his post and left the city.

Still his intellectual isolation and the critical failure of what he then called his "main work" should not be exaggerated.[100] Burckhardt's praise was a source of great encouragement; Overbeck stood by him; and the alliance with Rée was stronger than ever. *Human, All-Too-Human* was also more widely read than the lack of reviews would indicate. The book was admittedly difficult to grasp. If Nietzsche had hitherto utilized dueling pistols to strike at one target, he now employed a shotgun approach, scattering aphorisms in his path. As the crisis mood of 1878 slowly faded, Nietzsche's skepticism again had its attractions. Dilthey's brief but laudatory review in 1880 "greeted with joy" Nietzsche's new psychological and historical perspective; Nietzsche was a thinker "everyone who reflects independently upon the present must respect."[101]

Schmeitzner, however, was greatly disappointed. He took little comfort in Karl Hillebrand's belief that Nietzsche's present obscurity would be but temporary, and that within a decade he would be more than compensated with fame.[102] The impatient Schmeitzner dreamed of founding his fledgling publishing house on Nietzsche's imminent fame and even supposed that the coming Nietzscheanism would completely displace Bayreuth. But the plan of rallying support for a Nietzsche yearbook soon had to be dropped with Schmeitzner complaining of the tendency of Nietzsche's admirers to praise Nietzsche in private while remaining silent in public.[103] Even the friendly Hillebrand declined to review the new work, saying he had already sufficiently praised Nietzsche in print. Schmeitzner's attempt to arouse the interest of Wagner's critics in Nietzsche also failed. Bayreuth now seemed an anticlimactic issue; anti-Wagnerians were losing their zeal, the old *Kulturkampf* belligerence had waned and intellectuals were no longer so ready to scorn aesthetic religiosity.

Nietzsche's intellectual aboutface may have seemed shocking to old admirers, but to new critics the new Nietzsche only seemed more in conformity with contemporary trends and thereby less strikingly original. At the Easter book fair of 1879, instead of the hoped-for thousand copies, only 150 were sold.[104] Schmeitzner then developed the plan of founding a journal around Nietzsche. While Schmeitzner was neither an intellectual nor, as it turned out, a man of clear political principles, he did approach various dissident liberals during 1879 and 1880, among them the young Ferdinand Tönnies who immediately concluded "an alliance" with the publisher.[105] Schmeitzner indicated that in addition to Nietzsche, Rée, and Overbeck, he had also garnered the idiosyncratic old Young Hegelian Bruno Bauer and perhaps the equally eccentric cultural critic Paul Lagarde. Tönnies was to gather his friends, notably Friedrich Paulsen, an admirer of *Human, All-Too-Human*. Tönnies was convinced that the new philosophical journal was to be "unique" and would "mark the beginning of the formation of a community of thinkers in Germany; and it would have an impact: among students, high school teachers, etc." He added that its special mission would be to "guide and edify" those young people who were turning to the Zurich *Social Democrat* out of frustration and bitterness.[106]

Nietzsche had at this point ceased to concern himself with Schmeitzner's various strategies. The connection with the Tönnies group soon fell through. Nietzsche was already resigned to addressing an audience of hypothetical rather than actual "free spirits" just as in his own life he had decided that the "free spirit" was fated to "fly alone" and not marry.[107] He continued writing aphorisms: *Mixed Maxims and Opinions* appeared in 1879, *The Wanderer and His Shadow* in 1880; together they were later reissued as the second volume of *Human, All-Too-Human*. Political aphorisms were now more infrequent, less prominently displayed, and only occasionally did he comment directly on contemporary issues, such as on the anti-socialist laws which he observed were aimed at striking down "the democrats and anti-dynasts" rather than the socialists themselves.[108]

He was no longer connecting himself to the external world. What goaded Nietzsche on was his own deteriorating health, which was now constantly alerting him to the provisional, "experimental" nature of existence. Despite years of diagnoses and treatments by various specialists, his malady only worsened, bringing him to the verge of death in 1879. In the spring he finally resigned, was generously awarded a modest pension from three university endowments, and returned to Naumburg like a wearied Candide intent on cultivating a fruit and vegetable patch. That winter the rumor that he had died spread from Germany to Switzerland and the German colony in Italy. His life was now one of constant interruption; headaches that came without warning, shortsightedness sometimes approaching partial blindness, constant stomachaches bringing forth in Nietzsche the sensation of brevity—brevity in life, thought, and expression. The aphoristic mode became the only means of utilizing those pain-free hours that a day brought him. He wrote his latest physician as he completed *The Wanderer and His Shadow*. "My existence is a *terrible burden*; I would have thrown it over long ago, if I were not making in this condition of suffering and almost total deprivation the most instructive probes and experiments in spiritual-intellectual areas—this joyous thirst for knowledge brings me to the heights where I conquer all pain and hopelessness."[109]

In his acute struggle for life, Nietzsche embraced the experimental idea as a new therapeutic philosophy of health. This was an abrupt change. A decade of inveighing against "experiment" as hostile to the stylistic norms and unifying style which his festival ideal had sought to engender was not easily surmounted. Even the 1878 aphorism, "The Revolution in Poetry," only halfheartedly conceded that once the thread of development was broken "even the most gifted only succeeded by continuously experimenting." The revolutionary implications in the modern poet's "plunge into a sort of Rousseau-like state of nature and experiments" remained troubling.[110] But the physical crisis of 1879 overcame his politically inspired distrust of the principles of the inductive method. Nietzsche now saw the principle of change and the search for change as vital to his own recovery.

Experimentation was his antidote to a debilitating Schopenhauerian pessimism which preached a doctrine of compassion that only trapped the pitied in a static existence. At the end of his aphoristic period, Nietzsche declared that "the thought that life may be an experiment for the thinker . . . was the day on which the great liberator broke my fetters."[111] The experimental laboratory—the hated site of the vivisection of animals in the Wagnerian imagination—became in his mind the arena of self-renewal. Armed with the anti-motif, Nietzsche began to vivisect himself: "we others who thirst after reason are determined to scrutinize our experiences as severely as a scientific experiment—hour after hour, day after day. We ourselves wish to be our own experiments and guinea pigs."[112]

His new motto became: "Skepticism! yes, but the skepticism of experiments! not of indolence and despair."[113] From the observation that "every action (act of will) is an experiment whether our judgment (in willing) was correct," Nietzsche derived the admonition: "Your life [is] an experiment and monument of your experiment."[114] In this self-inquisition, the journey of discovery replaced the contest as the ruling metaphor of his thought. The seeker discovering autonomy through constant disillusionment was the theme of "A Fable," an aphorism dealing with "the Don Juan of Knowledge," while the poem "The New Columbus," would chart the voyage to that intellectual New World from which Nietzsche would proclaim "the experimental philosophy" to be "the philosophy of the future."[115] *Versuch* and *Experiment* were key to his new vocabulary. *Versuch* with its meanings of tempt, attempt, and experiment was used with rhetorical flourish as when Dionysus reappears as the *Versucher-Gott*, while *Experiment* was reserved for a more programmatic enunciation of the *Experimental-Philosophie*.

Nietzsche brushed aside the restraints the Idealist tradition had placed before experimentalism. Kant had viewed experiment as merely a secondary device for resolving dispute, while Hegel flatly termed the whole notion of an experimental philosophy "erroneous and fruitless" since "the true philosophy rejects the principle of experiment" because "every experiment is unknowing as to the aim of the true philosophy."[116] Experimentalism would remain for this tradition but a form of preliminary speculation to be engaged in, if at all, before the real effort of systematizing philosophical thought began. Many of Nietzsche's interpreters have been similarly unwilling to follow him in his repudiation of the "bewitching deceptive power" of "those glittering mirages called 'philosophical systems'" or to hold with him that "the will to a system is a lack of integrity."[117] Walter Kaufmann, for instance, criticized Nietzsche for having "overlooked the possibility that systematization might be one of the most useful tools of the experimentalism he envisaged" since "experiment is stopped prematurely if systematization is not eventually attempted."[118]

Nietzsche, however, was determined to place his thought within the experimental process itself. Experimental inquiry begins with the rejection of authority; experiment aims at new knowledge, Nietzsche argued, by throwing doubt on accepted formulations, by making the "known" world "unknown"; and consequently experiment loses its experimental status once results are deemed successful. Codification, systematization, and verbal disputation seemed to him signs of intellectual weariness, a reluctance to follow any longer the tentative, the provisional, and the unprecedented. The departure from accepted certainties rather than the arrival at new truths became now Nietzsche's overriding concern. Living out what he took to be an experimental life, wherein his choices and remedies could have mortal consequences, Nietzsche was unwilling to trivialize and domesticate experiment as a diagnostic technique. The distinction between the laboratory setting and the 'real' world had been dissolved. Experimentalism as seen through the perspective of his anti-motif had become a philosophy of risk which he believed could restore a "heroic mood" to science and instill new "pride" in modern man.[119]

Dawn (1881) and *The Gay Science* (1882), products of a seeming recovery and convalescence, marked the triumph of the experimental ideal in his thought. His aphoristic works became a passage through darkness in which the shadow was dispelled by the light of dawn and the wanderer armed once only with "mixed maxims and opinions" found the new method of the gay science. Nietzsche's "Réealism" took a correspondingly optimistic turn, concerned no longer with simply eliminating metaphysics. His new Enlightenment assimilated evolutionary thought in order to proclaim not with Spencer a mechanistic theory of progress but rather a process of continuous experimentation. Evolution was a series of "experimental stations"; Darwinism indicated that man, too, was now subject to experimentation. The "free spirits" were not seen "experimenting with different types of life"; they situated themselves on the "experimental-stations of humanity."[120] In the same mood Nietzsche was willing to recognize in socialism a force heralding "innumerable state-experiments," or in Wagner one of the first to begin "experimenting" with the unification of the arts.[121] He would later look back on his Wagnerian phase as his "most dangerous experiment," "my strongest test of character."[122] What has been called Nietzsche's "perspectivism," his doctrine that there are no facts only interpretations, was guided by an experimental futurism, a determination to meet the demands of "the age of experiments" in which contemporary man found himself.

Nietzsche was never so timely as when he inscribed the word experiment upon his philosophical banner. Experiment was the magical, leading idea of the age, rediscovered and imbued with new meaning by each of the new intellectual movements then vying for influence. Positivists were following Claude Bernard in the exploration of man's "inner environment" which *An Introduction to the Study of Experimental Medicine* (1865) indicated could only proceed by disturbing nature through the "*observation provoquée.*"[123] But it was Darwin who, as Dewey said, "emancipated, once for all, genetic and experimental ideas as an organon of asking questions and looking for explanations."[124] In the quarter century following the publication of *Origin of Species* in 1859, a new generation experienced their philosophical education with Dewey as a path from "absolutism to experimentalism."[125] During Nietzsche's six "experimental years," Wilhelm Wundt formally launched his "experimental psychology," Hans Vaihinger formulated his "philosophy of the as-if," Emile Zola espoused the writing of the "experimental novel," and C. S. Peirce worked out a pragmatism that sought to embody "the experimentalist's view of assertion."[126] In the late seventies and early eighties, German, French, and Anglo-American thought seemingly converged in a new generation's effort to effect "the transfer of experimental method from the technical field of physical experience to the wider field of human life."[127] "We are," Zola wrote in his 1880 manifesto, "experimental moralists showing by experiments in what fashion a passion behaves in a social milieu"; as "experimental moralists," Zola added, "we work with the whole age at that great task which is the conquest of nature, the unleashing of man's power."[128]

Nietzsche's rivals contained their notions of experimentalism to certain restricted spheres. Wundt's experimental psychology flowed naturally into behaviorism by limiting investigation to the normal and testable and by excluding the pathological and the personal. Zola urged upon his fellow Naturalists a new intellectual content but stopped short of proposing experiments in form and style. Vaihinger held back his theory of constructive fictions for over thirty years, publishing it only after completing his perceptive study of Nietzsche. Peirce, an original mind matching Nietzsche's effusiveness with a logician's parsimony, focused on a philosophy of inquiry, venturing rarely into the realms of psychology or aesthetics.

Nietzsche's experimental approach labored under no comparable inhibitions; his "adventures in speculation" sought to encompass psychology, philosophy, aesthetics, even politics under the rubric of the experimental process. He asserted an experimental ideal that bridged the instrumentalism of the laboratory and the iconoclasm of the avant-garde. Nietzsche could well have spoken Henry James's words of 1878: "being 'very artistic,' I have a constant impulse to try experiments in form."[129] Nietzsche's aphoristic mode, once forced on him by circumstance, found its justification as the memories which cropped up at decisive moments in the 1880s. In July 1881 he reacted to the news of Pastor Theobald Oehler's death by commending outcomes, and trap the reader into ambiguous, provisional responses. This technique provided him with the means of carrying on experimental activity that proceeded without the promise of successful resolutions since Nietzsche's experimental speculations engendered no objective criteria for assessing success or failure.

But having arrived at his central theme, Nietzsche still had to come to terms with his public or lack of it. He had earlier attacked experimentation precisely because it severed ties to the public and tradition. He had warned of rootlessness. Having now embraced the self-ostracizing stance of the experimenter, he predictably found that he had exchanged imprisoning affiliations for a troubling isolation. He felt apart from his age, ahead of it, but somehow not of it. He came to engage, stylistically as well as intellectually, in that violent "polemic against the public" which was so characteristic of late nineteenth century thought.[130] Unwilling to compromise with contemporary fashion or taste, he still did not reconcile himself to a lack of contemporary influence, warning himself in the aphorism "Posthumous Fame" "not to speak so readily in favor of haughty solitude" since "not to be recognized is always interpreted by posterity as lack of power."[131] He resorted ever more to aphorisms that evoked the first person plural: "We beginners," "We Gods in exile," "We artists," "We incomprehensible ones," "We who are homeless."[132] The less the immediate response, the more he projected a sense of future camaraderie.

The dilemma of defining the social role of the experimental thinker was faced by other experimenters as well. Zola sought to compensate for the alienation of the experimenter by preaching a similar vanguardism; he appealed to a "new literary generation," and promised that a "new literary age is about to begin."[133] But as Lukács argued, unfairly perhaps, Zola's experimental method "hampered not only Zola himself but his whole generation" by reinforcing the writer's sense of isolation as "mere spectator and chronicler" of society.[134] Yet Zola's sense of group mission subsequently allowed him to break with his own theoretical detachment, and he became the very model of the politically engaged artist during the Dreyfus affair. While Zola, following Bernard, made the experimental synonymous with the scientific, Strindberg added a restless, psychological, and "artistic" element by "experimentally" adopting all possible intellectual positions until finally in the 1890s he was left alone with the final "experiment" of a religious reconversion, a return to the initial community he had abandoned.[135]

Wundt, in contrast, institutionalized the experimenter's role. Experimentalism became a procedure, technique, and byproduct of the new research science of physiological psychology. By isolating experimentation in the laboratory as a form of harmless trial runs in which errors of judgment could easily and painlessly be corrected, Wundt domesticated experimentalism.[136] It now became a means of filling gaps in specialized knowledge. Wundt's program also completed his own retreat from his youthful political involvement in the Workers' Educational Movement of the 1860s by offering him the substitute of an apolitical, highly respectable academic movement in which he could play a leading role.[137]

But it was Peirce's notion of the "community of inquiry" which most consciously sought to overcome the experimenter's isolation. By addressing the future thoughts of other men, the experimenter found membership in an infinite community, Peirce argued. Experimentalism became thereby a moral undertaking, dependent upon the concept of the community. As in Nietzsche, there developed an "eerie dialogue" in the isolated, philosophical stance." "Shut out of one concrete community after another," Peirce responded by formulating "the most thoroughgoing and radical ideal of community in American or European letters."[138] Nietzsche and Peirce shared a common starting point in the transcendental individualism of Emerson. Peirce grew up in the Emersonian milieu, while Nietzsche discovered Emerson in Schulpforta and would consider the Concord sage to be a "brother soul" well into the 1880s. As neither Peirce nor Nietzsche was willing to accept the new Darwinian benediction, they sought to salvage their Emersonian heritage by grounding the new experimentalism in a new ethical ideal.

They proceeded in quite different ways. Peirce abandoned Emerson's individualism as a prey of the new capitalist and Darwinian philosophies of "greed."[139] In Peirce's terminology, Darwin's "struggle for existence" fell into the category of Secondness. In his attempt to rethink the Hegelian categories (thesis, antithesis, synthesis), Peirce attributed certain characteristics to each, e.g., originality and naiveté to Firstness, effort and negation to Secondness, prediction and mediation to Thirdness.[140] Secondness was the category of conflict which Peirce's sought to overcome. With the aid of Lamarckian ideas, he espoused a doctrine of "evolutionary love"; neo-Christian ideals were thus intended to motivate the experimentalism of the "community of inquiry." Peirce, steeped in Kant, mathematics, and chemistry, aspired to a logical religion of science. By contrast Nietzsche, with his Schopenhauerian education of music and art, was convinced that "our sciences of physiology and medicine, society and solitude" can provide "the foundation-stones of new ideals (but not the ideals themselves)."[141]

Nietzsche may have shared Peirce's notion of values located "in a universe of chance," but he did not see his purpose in fixing belief in a higher form of community. His experimentalism as method, artistic strategy, and form of skepticism inclined toward fostering aloof pride and intellectual adventurism. Individuation not integration remained his goal.

In the present "moral interregnum" his injunction to his fellow "free spirits" was: "We are experiments! Let us will it so!"[142] Nietzsche found in Emerson's concept of the "over-soul"—translated in German as the *"Überseele"*—a recipe for his own heightened individualism.[143] The *Übermensch* was to provide a collective goal or aspiration fot the new individualism; "we experiment on behalf of the *Übermensch*," Nietzsche proclaimed at the end of his aphoristic period.[144] Yet lest his "superman" be confused with the future society of higher beings envisaged by Dühring, Nietzsche was quick to lock his isolated superman in conflict with his ultimate antagonist, the subman of mass society, *der letzte Mensch*.

Nietzsche and Peirce reacted to the intense present-mindedness of experimentation and the future-directedness of experimentalism with opposing, weighty, fantastic speculations. The metaphysics of Peirce's "evolutionary love," Nietzsche's "eternal return" have accordingly been met with more embarrassment than acceptance. "How can such ideas be *thought about?*" an exasperated Valéry complained of Nietzsche's eternal return; anyone doing so would destroy it.[145] Nietzsche himself did little more than hint at the enigmatic doctrine that he supposed marked "a turning point of history." Critics have been quick to discount both ideas.[146]

Although dubious as scientific propositions, both notions were consistent attempts to deal with the crisis of ethics brought on by the collapse of transcendental individualism, the Darwinian revolution and the onset of the new experimentalism. As Peirce sought to ground his pragmatic experimentalism in the community of love, so Nietzsche saw in the eternal return the ethical underpinnings of his own experimental philosophy. He embraced it at the height of his aphoristic period, in August 1881, proclaiming it to be "the highest formulation of affirmation that can ever be attained." The theory of time in which "there is no end," the freezing and recapitulation of momentary existence was to inspire the experimenter with the ethics of heroic fatalism, of the *amor fati*.[147] By forever returning the individual to the same problems and conflicts, the eternal return became the apotheosis of Nietzsche's anti-motif. As time had no conclusion, so society would find no ordained harmony; the principle of struggle was thus harnessed to the wheels of history. Peirce, in contrast, postulated a coming harmony that could dispel the "unlovely hardness" of late nineteenth century civilization.[148] Peirce's distrust of individualism was thus matched by Nietzsche's fear of utopianism.

In this setting, Nietzsche's experimentalism was gradually displaced. Gone was the turbulence of the late seventies, the rupture with Wagner, the painful break with the Academe, the near-fatal illness. By 1880 he was already weary of being a "mere aphorism man" and aware of his publisher's disillusionment with such works.[149] Having exalted the futurism of the experimental moment, having sought to place himself within it, Nietzsche now began a drift toward prophetic certainty and a new oracular style. It was to be his greatest "test," or so he thought. "In the beginning of August 1881, 6,000 feet above the sea and far higher above all human things," Nietzsche had his peak experience, his sudden receptivity and avowal of the doctrine of Eternal Return of the Same.[150] It was, he decided, "the greatest teaching." He followed his earlier advice not to become an "observer" of his experience but rather gave himself up to it.[151] "Several times" in the following two weeks he was too embarrassed to leave his room because his "eyes were inflamed" from having "wept too much on my previous day's walk, not sentimental tears but tears of joy; I sang and talked nonsense, filled with a glimpse of things which put me in advance of all other men." Ideas had arisen on his horizon which he had not seen before. "I will not speak of them, but will keep my unshakable peace," he continued in a letter to Köselitz. Evident was his exhiliration: "I really shall have to live a few more years!" And also a troubling concern: "sometimes the idea runs through my head that I am living an extremely dangerous life, for I am one of those machines which can explode."[152]

Hesitant to communicate his vision but anxious to memorialize it, Nietzsche reacted to his prophetic insight with mixed feelings. He had been seized by a thought which had flashed up "with necessity, without hesitation regarding its form—I never had any choice"; an involuntary "gale of a feeling of freedom, of unrestrictedness, of power, of divinity" had engulfed him, he recalled in 1888. Yet for all its rapture, its sense of privilege, "the experience of inspiration" left him with the thought of being merely an instrument, "merely incarnation, merely mouthpiece, merely a medium of overpowering forces."[153] He pressed on, convinced that he stood before his greatest experiment. "The individual as experiment" had been among the themes listed in the original plan of the Eternal Return, and later that month he wrote of the contemporary world as "the age of experiments" in which "Darwin's hypotheses are put to the test—through experiments," and in which one could envisage "experiments of thousands of years."[154]

Nevertheless, the new doctrine was to be "the heaviest burden" not simply because of its dark, troubling implications but also because it aroused apprehensions or premonitions of future madness.[155] The nightmare of hereditary and syphilitic madness haunted the eighties. It was a coincidence, but nonetheless fitting, that Ibsen completed *Ghosts* that summer.[156] In Nietzsche's diagnosis of his mysterious malady, he seems completely oblivious to its probable syphilitic origins. His father dying deranged, the madness of his regal namesake were, however, disturbing memories which cropped up at decisive moemnts in the 1880s. In July 1881 he reacted to the news of Pastor Theobald Oehler's death by commending his uncle for preferring suicide to life in an insane asylum. The remark proved offensive to Naumburg, and he hastily recanted, accepting the official version of a heart attack in the bath tub.[157] Nietzsche was not insensitive to the suspicions of his contemporaries concerning his mental equilibrium, although it is unlikely that Overbeck ever told him of Treitschke's angry outburst in September 1881 accusing Nietzsche of "megalomania, the most contemporary of vices."[158] Treitschke spoke jealously, angry that he had lost Overbeck's friendship to Nietzsche.

A new line of attack has been suggested by F. D. Luke, who posits a Nietzschean "Icarus complex" on the basis of the sudden predominance of the imagery of height and flight that accompanies his turn to prophecy.[159] No longer is the etiology of Nietzsche's disease at the forefront but rather the manic-depressive moods that accompanied his creative bursts. Nietzsche was himself no longer a youth exercising his wings for the first time; he was in his mid-thirties when, as he once put it, "hot and cold currents tend to rush together, so that spray and delicate clouds and under favorable conditions and glimpse of sunshine, magical rainbow-pictures emerge.[160]

A year before his prophetic experience, Nietzsche had himself depicted "The Moral Insanity of Genius": the "painful and in part terrible spectacle" of the lack of harmony between "most productive states, flights aloft and into the far distance" and the defective apparatus of genius, all too prone to inflate a "narrow and narrowing disposition." When genius takes hold of us, Nietzsche continued, "we are full of audacity, yea almost mad and heedless of health, life, and honor." But "let genius once leave us . . . we feel as if we were in the midst of shelterless rocks with the tempest raging round us."[161]

The imagery of the storm which Nietzsche associated with inspiration aptly suggested the inner turbulence of Nietzsche at the moment of his prophetic experience while also recapturing the peculiar mood that seemed to jell in the freak summer weather of 1881. Exceptional, changeable weather, Nietzsche had shortly before observed, turned men "suspicious even of others" while making them ripe for "innovation" by depriving them of their accustomed routines. It was the weather of "despots," Nietzsche concluded,[162] and also of the despotism of metaphysical speculation. Following a cold winter, sharply rising temperatures turned northern Italy into a cauldron by late spring. As Nietzsche fled into the Swiss Alps, Burckhardt descended into the sweltering region where in August he, too, would be reflecting on the Pythagorean teaching that "in earlier life . . . I must have been here before."[163]

Nietzsche discovered that "the exceptional weather" had followed him to Sils. "Continuous change of atmospheric conditions," he wrote Overbeck in late July.[164] Such weather, he added, would drive him from Europe. Throughout much of August biting winds swept down the long, high and narrow valley of the river inns, skies remained cloudy, thunderstorms were frequent, and "finally even a whole day of winter snow."[165] In these weeks the new notion of himself as a "weather prophet" began to emerge. He imagined himself an "exhibit" at the Paris Electrical Exhibition being "perhaps more receptive in this point than anyone else, to my misfortune!"[166] He wrote asking his mother how the "Nietzsches" had reacted to unusual weather conditions.[167] A month later at the end of his stay, he wrote Overbeck in Latin on a postcard: "What months, what a summer I have had! My physical agonies were as many and various as the changes I have seen in the sky. In every cloud there is some form of electrical charge which grips me suddenly and reduces me to complete misery."[168] In October he requested a work on meteorology so that he could better understand "the terrible effect of atmospheric electricity upon me."[169] The association of receptivity, electricity, misfortune, and prophecy was then enunciated in the aphorism "Prophetic human beings," written that winter. He now likened the prophetic faculty to animals reacting to "the electricity in the air and the clouds"; when a strong positive charge turned suddenly into negative electricity "these animals behave as if an enemy were drawing near . . . an enemy whose hand they already *feel.*"[170]

The hand which Nietzsche felt in Sils was that of his new prophetic persona, Zarathustra, who, as he later put it, "invaded" him there.[171] On or about August 26, he conceived the plan of infusing a philosophical poem with Zarathustra's prophetic voice.[172] It was in part a defensive measure. Zarathustra was to be the buffer warding off prophetic immediacy and also the mask and mouthpiece of the inner struggles of Nietzsche, the prophet emergent. The figure of the sage was then very much alive in his mind as he had just discovered a "most abnormal and lonely thinker," Spinoza, whom he hailed as a "precursor." "Of course," he wrote Overbeck in late July, "the differences are enormous, but they are differences more of period, culture, field of knowledge. *In summa:* my solitariness which, as on very high mountains, has often, often made me gasp and lose blood, is now a solitude of two." A month later Zarathustra displaced Spinoza in this "solitude of two."[173]

Zarathustra long remained within him; a year and a half interval separated the conception from the actual writing of the *Zarathustra. The Gay Science* of 1881/1882 concluded with a hint of what was to follow. In the penultimate aphorism a "demon" introduces the idea of Eternal Return in a "what if" construction. Had he stopped here, Nietzsche would have joined the swelling ranks of those who offered speculative asides regarding Return. His first public espousal was distinguished by the element of dread and the religious imagination at play. But without the flowing speech of a philosophical epic, without Zarathustra descending from the heights—the theme of the final aphorism, "Incipit tragoedia"—Nietzsche's avowal would hardly have capped and climaxed the late nineteenth century's fascination with the question of Eternal Return.[174]

Nietzsche was aware that aside from the ancients other "earlier thinkers" had wrestled with the notion of Return. Did Nietzsche think here of Bruno in the Renaissance, Schopenhauer and Heine in the first half of the century, or perhaps some of his own contemporaries? We know now that he would, at least, hear of the most significant of recent affirmations, jotting down in his notebook of the fall of 1883:

A. Blanqui
    l'eternité par les astres
        Paris 1872.[175]

But whether Nietzsche actually read Blanqui's account of his prison vision of Return, given his reading habits at the time, is uncertain, perhaps unlikely. Nor would it have greatly mattered. The chief merit of Blanqui's speculations on Return lay in conveying the mood of spiritual crisis that followed the fall of Commune. Blanqui died January 1, 1881, famed for the political martyrdom of his final years. The veteran revolutionary's attempt to legitimize the ancient notion of Return by associating it with the latest findings in astronomy was, moreover, widespread in the decades preceding Einstein's advent. Father Secchi, the Vatican astronomer, discussed the theory in *Le Soleil* (1870), a work which prompted Friedrich Engels to embrace Eternal Return at the end of the decade in *Dialektik der Natur*.[176] In addition Julius Bahnsen, a minor Schopenhauerian, championed it in 1872; Le Bon mentioned it in 1881; and the Zurich natural scientist Nageli stated the "proof" later used by Nietzsche already in 1878. Many felt compelled to pass judgment on the matter; Fouillée and Dühring in opposition; Peirce and Poincaré in favor.[177] The discussion was prone to matter-of-fact, quasi-scientific reasoning. Thus although Nietzsche's own contributions were sparse and intermittent, his interjection of the religious, poetic, and prophetic element overshadowed their speculations.

Nietzsche wrote as a convert, having rejected the original Pythagorean notion of Return in his early lectures of the Pre-Platonic philosophers. He even formulated his argument against monumental history as a form of history that "lives by false analogy" by alleging that it was ultimately rooted in the theory that "the earth always began its drama again after the fifth act," a notion, he observed, requiring astronomers to become "astrologers again."[178] Nietzsche's sudden reversal seven years later would correspondingly weaken his inhibitions about the monumentalizing tendencies within himself. If Nietzsche had once unmasked monumentalism as a masquerade of "hatred of present power and greatness," he would in the course of the 1880s make of himself a monument, a sphinx-like "posthumous man" whose ultimate authority over the future lay precisely in not being understood.[179]

CHAPTER SIX

The Posthumous Man

... to Mount *Marvel*, where they looked, and beheld a man at a distance, *that tumbled the hills about with Words.*

Bunyan

IN THE EIGHTIES Nietzsche reached his zenith and terminus. The personal catastrophe toward which he was headed made him alive and receptive to the imaginings of disaster which bedeviled the surface calm of that decade. Constantly recurring crises dissolving into episodes, intermittent war scares, the moodiness of deflationary economic distress, all found their resonance in Nietzsche's staggering productivity—at least one work a year, and a trunkload of notebooks left behind. Nietzsche began the decade by assuming a prophetic persona and then enunciated a vision of *"grosse Politik"* as his "bird's-eye view" of European politics.[1] Throughout the eighties he assumed the manner of the sage, living apart; yet as *the* philosopher of the railway age he was also forever on the move, darting in and out and between an empire, a dual monarchy, a kingdom, and two republics. He seemed to his old associates to be everywhere and nowhere.

Ironically, just as Nietzsche was determined to assert his separateness, just as he was mobilizing his anti-self against the world of his contemporaries, he found himself entangled as never before in the web of contemporary politics. The new political anti-Semitism seemed to strike at him personally, following him unaware, attaching itself to him surreptitiously, infecting and poisoning his personal relations and private sanctuaries. The political complications facing the prophet emergent cannot be simply or solely blamed on Elisabeth Nietzsche, as extensive and as stupid as were her later forgeries and insinuations. Nietzsche's publisher, Ernst Schmeitzner, had already sought to ride the rising wave of political anti-Semitism. Overbeck first sounded the alarm in the spring of 1880, troubled by his own association with the publisher.[2] Overbeck was more sensitive and fearful of the new demagoguery, for his origins lay in that tiny, foreign community within Russia whose vulnerability and cosmopolitanism bore some resemblance to the exposed Jewish communities of Europe. Overbeck had long affected the role of the rootless, apolitical cosmopolite. He was disturbed when Treitschke, soon after a friendly visit in September 1879, unexpectedly and dramatically promoted a new heresy for liberals, anti-Semitism. Nietzsche sent word through Köselitz that he fully endorsed Overbeck's renunciation of his old friend but that he personally did not want to be distracted into publicly entering the debate over the Jews; he had more important things on his mind.[3]

The politics of the new ethnicity would, however, dog Nietzsche's tracks. He arrived in Marienbad in late July 1880, two and a half weeks after Franz Josef concluded a controversial tour of Bohemia. Intended as a new conciliatory gesture toward the Slav minorities, the imperial presence also brought German-Czech tensions to the boiling point. The Viennese newspapers Nietzsche read that vacation fanned the controversy surrounding the creation of a separate Czech university, and the press highlighted the opposition of Ernst Mach, then Rector of the German university of Prague.[4] Small wonder that on the Emperor's birthday, the sight of all the black and yellow Habsburg flags made him think of something "terrible": "the birthday of the plague."[5] He complained to his mother that three-quarters of the guests in Marienbad were Jewish. Some Polish tourists at Marienbad hailed him as a fellow Pole and acted surprised and disbelieving when he declared himself to be Swiss—an incident he would embellish and embroider in the coming years.[6] The long-dormant Polish legend of his childhood was thereby reawakened and would come to complement his Swiss identity as a camouflage and foil to his Prussian-German origins.

He traveled north to Naumburg where he found his sister circulating the controversial, nation-wide anti-Semitic petition. Elisabeth had been recruited by her old beau, Bernhard Förster, one of Wagner's aging angry young men, whom she had met at the Bayreuth festival of 1876.[7] In league with Professor Zöllner, the Leipzig maverick Nietzsche had once admired, Förster sought to pressure the government to curb Jewish immigration and Jewish presence in the bureaucracy and the academe. The monster petition failed to garner big names, the Meister cagily refused, only the impulsive Hans von Bülow signed, and it did not achieve its immediate objective. Yet the petition publicized a new style of politics and allowed the government to display in liberal eyes a fatal ambiguous tolerance of the new force.[8]

Burckhardt had noted with *Schadenfreude* at the beginning of the year that the identification of liberalism with the "Semites" had delivered into the hands of the Catholics and Conservatives "the most popular trump that exists." And at the end of the year he predicted that liberalism would eventually be forced to discard Jewish emancipation from its intellectual baggage "even if it breaks its heart, for I believe it will break no one else's."[9] Germany, he continued, had reached a spiritual standstill; it was no longer possible to live off the mood and memories of 1870; disunity was again rife; the only promising portent lay in Wagner's *Parsifal* which seemed destined to rally "the divided souls" in renewed communal feeling.[10]

What was most disturbing to Nietzsche was that the new wave of anti-Jewish feeling in Germany seemed a perverse rendering of his own Pietist origins. The Reich's leading anti-Semite, Court Preacher Pastor Adolf Stöcker, had begun his career closely affiliated with the Pietism of the Basel Mission; Treitschke, beset by domestic tragedies, turned on the Jews in the heat of a religious conversion; Bernhard and his brother Paul, another anti-Semitic politician prominent in the eighties, were sons of a pastor whose widow was a close friend of Nietzsche's mother. Franziska sensed something unnatural in Bernhard's "inflamed hatred of the Jews" and was appalled when hotheaded Bernhard assaulted a Jew on a Berlin street car, an act which led the Berlin City Council to remove him from his teaching post.[11] Mother and son, agreeing on little else, concurred in dismay over Elisabeth's choice of Bernhard as beau, fiancé, and husband. Nietzsche avoided Bernhard as long as possible, meeting him only once in 1884, all too aware that Förster, public promoter both of Nietzsche's works and *Parsifal,* importunely dreamed of reconciling both.[12] The crisis of evangelical Christianity was at hand, Nietzsche sensed, when the absence of a genuine religious revival led to fanaticism without faith, when the descendants of the broken Christian state ideal racialized their inheritance and when there was universal blindness to the "anti-Protestant" message lurking in Wagner's *Parsifal.*

Cowardice and resentment, Nietzsche discerned, were the motivating factors of the new anti-Semitism in Germany. Cowardice because for all the temporary ascendancy of Jews in business and journalism—Nietzsche went far in accepting contemporary stereotypes of "Jewish influence"—the fact remained that the new chosen "enemy" was the archtypal non-warrior, allowing for cheap victories for heroic, "Aryan" virtues and a fatal underestimation of the real dangers facing Germany. The cry for Jewish exclusion was insofar justified, Nietzsche would later write, in that the "weak," uncertain German character could ill digest foreign or different elements. He had "never met a German who was well disposed toward the Jews."[13] Nietzsche disdained most philo-Semitism as sentimental; and Nazis would certainly find their quota of disparagement of contemporary and historical Jewry in his oeuvre. When his Caesarism and anti-Christian atheism were inflamed, harsh invective would flow toward the Jews. Yet anti-Semitism remained for him the most acute symptom of the "nationality madness" sweeping Europe, and correspondingly, he increasingly conceived of European Jewry as a key component of his Europeanism and as a trump against the Reich.

As 1881 began Europe seemed to be breathlessly awaiting some great event. Burckhardt, as usual, was predicting general war in the spring; German Socialists touring America spoke of the "dagger" that would soon unleash upheaval in Russia; Nietzsche, his eye also on Russia, sensed anarchy loose in the world.[14] Fittingly Kropotkin's anarchist tabloid in Geneva was the first to hit the streets in the west with the news of the assassination of Czar Alexander II.[15] The same day a Viennese literary evening honoring the German editor of the *Deutsche Rundschau* became an emotional remembrance of 1848, and after police dissolved the meeting the gathering surreptitiously regrouped elsewhere to talk excitedly through the night.[16] Engels foresaw European revolution and predicted the Swiss would soon begin mass expulsions of foreign radicals.[17] In Zurich the newly arrived Lou von Salomé observed demonstrations by her fellow Russian students demanding clemency for the perpetrators of "the propaganda of the deed."[18] The British eventually jailed the exiled German anarchist Johann Most for his editorial, "Finally!" Conservatives were duly alarmed by the prospect of revolution, European war, or both at the same time. Henry James's *The Princess Casamassima* (1886) sought to recapture the strange panic of those months when "subterraneous politics" displaced the specter of barricades and street fighting which the Commune had foisted on the preceding decade.[19] Revolutionary politics had become something far more sinister and unseen; the crisis of "nihilism" seemed at hand.

To comprehend the mysteries of the new terrorism, Nietzsche returned to Dühring's works, a not wholly inappropriate choice since Dühring was among the authors favored by members of the Executive Committee of the People's Will.[20] The vapid bombast and verbal violence found in Dühring only betrayed, however, what was most puzzling to contemporaries about the new political "nihilism": its lack of ideological substance or coherence. Just as the master conspirator of James's novel never appears but only lurks in the background, so nihilism, once merely a police label, became in the western imagination an inchoate force terrifyingly capable of suddenly overturning society.

The notoriety of the Russian case, where the term became a defiant catchword of a quasi-socialist, populist revolutionary movement, largely defined popular perception of nihilism as a sinister, mysterious, and dangerous force. The debate among the major Russian writers—Turgenev, Herzen, Dostoevsky, and Tolstoy—over nihilism as a generational legacy, personalized crisis, and subversive modernism inspired Nietzsche's conception of himself during the 1880s as "Europe's first complete nihilist."[21]

The Russian association of philosophical nihilism with political terrorism dramatized the challenge facing Nietzsche's generation. In more muted forms, the appearance of nihilism as a spiritual crisis of the post-Darwinian generation was experienced throughout the western world.

Peirce's Metaphysical Club at Harvard, for example, was sharply divided during the 1870s over the implications of Chauncey Wright's "nihilistic" doctrine of the absolute neutrality of science. "Nihilism," Wright argued, "is rather a discipline than a positive doctrine; an exorcism of the vague; a criticism of questions which by habit have passed beyond the real practical grounds of causes of questions."[22] Wright's refusal to enter into any "anticipations of nature" was unacceptable both to Peirce's experimental futurism and to William James who countered Wright's "anti-religious" skepticism with his doctrine of "the will-to-believe" in his paper "Against Nihilism."[23]

Nietzsche affirmed an experimental ideal that could counter the specter of "nihilism" that was haunting his generation. The concept of nihilism had previously made its appearance in post-revolutionary periods of exhaustion, disillusionment, and revulsion. At the beginning of the century, the Catholic philosopher Franz von Baader had denounced Fichte's transcendental egoism as "nihilism," while Karl Gutzkow painted a despairing portrait of the defeated revolutionaries in his novel *Die Nihilisten* (1850).[24] But between 1860 and 1890 nihilism came to be widely perceived as the peculiar destiny and fate of the mid-century generation. Turgenev launched a European-wide debate by contrasting the idealistic "men of the forties" with the new nihilistic "men of the sixties" in *Fathers and Sons* (1862). Herzen reluctantly endorsed this assessment in his memoirs: "What has our generation bequeathed the coming one? Nihilism."[25]

In Germany the debate over nihilism began primarily as a critical reaction to the popularity of Schopenhauerian pessimism. In his lengthy review of *Schopenhauer as Educator,* Franz Hoffmann, a disciple of Baader, prophesied that Nietzsche would soon be driven beyond Schopenhauerian pessimism to a full exploration of "nihilism."[26] Only in 1888 did Nietzsche acknowledge how "thought-provoking" the review had been, accepting Hoffmann's prophecy of "a great destiny for me—bringing about a kind of crisis and ultimate decision in the problem of atheism whose most instinctive and relentless type he divined in me."[27]

Like Tolstoy, his spiritual opposite and elder contemporary, Nietzsche began his dialogue with European nihilism only after he had broken with Schopenhauerian pessimism. In repudiating his own Schopenhauerian phase and his earlier agnosticism, Tolstoy declared himself to have been "for thirty-five years a nihilist in the real meaning of that word, not a Socialist or revolutionary, but a nihilist in the sense of the absence of any belief."[28] At precisely the same moment when Nietzsche discovered his experimental ideal, Tolstoy registered his disillusionment with "the experimental sciences" which could only provide "counterfeit answers" to life's central questions.[29] Whereas Tolstoy returned to Christianity, Nietzsche pressed on with his goal of imbuing his experimentalism with a new ethical religion. Nietzsche had begun his aphoristic period by appealing to "the free spirits"; over the years the free spirits had become experimenters, at once naively optimistic and joyful. "We fearless ones" must rally together to engage in the more somber and darkening problems lurking ahead, he was saying at the close of his aphoristic years.

With the future of Russian autocracy cloudy, the whole structure of Germany's defensive alliance system seemed vulnerable and in doubt. To mobilize against terrorism and dampen speculation of a possible Russo-German war, Bismarck hastily constituted the League of the Three Emperors in the summer of 1881. At this moment the Reich, just ten years old, became the symbol of the "principle of the almighty State" to the terrorists. "If the German Empire fails to come out victorious from a war," Kropotkin would argue, "this will not only be the defeat of European reaction; it will also be the defeat of the principle of the State."[30]

The new anarchism of the eighties, heralded by Prince Kropotkin, a scholarly, pacific type, became inarticulate in its love affair with dynamite. With German social democracy playing a waiting game, retrenched but determined to outlast Bismarck, anarchism, although never strong in Germany, had its moment in the eighties. Reinsdorf's unsuccessful attempt to blow up Emperor and Chancellor at the unveiling of the Niederwald Monument in 1884, the murder of Police Inspector Rumpf, and the scattered bombings were acts of a minuscule band of adventurers determined—as one of their number put it at his trial—to wait no longer.[31] The Reich was to be blasted away.

Bismarck put increasing pressure on Switzerland. In August 1881 Swiss authorities expelled Kropotkin after his return from a much-publicized international anarchist congress in London. Six months before, the newly elected President of the Swiss Confederacy had committed suicide, stung, it was said, by charges of his former radical friends that he was bargaining away the historic rights of Swiss asylum.[32] Henceforth foreign pressure to curb and expel exiles became the key emotional issue of Swiss politics in the eighties. It was an issue which agitated Nietzsche, particularly in his final months of sanity when German pressure was especially acute.

However, the actual effect of Czar Alexander's assassination was a long hiatus in the Russian revolutionary movement. In Western Europe, the trauma and prophetic speculations of the early 1870s were similarly put aside. The French exchanged Rimbaud's vision of a deranged world for Maupassant's elegant but cynical mirroring of the uneasy equilibrium. The future might still seem bleak but a respectable intellectual nihilism promised at least to make it palatable, if not enjoyable. British political prophets of the eighties, such as Seeley, might raise alarm about England's future but the decline that beckoned was hardly catastrophic, save to inflated pride. Americans were becoming determinedly innocent, oblivious to future terrors and even to the horrors of their recent Civil War, as was exemplified in Bellamy's utopian novel of 1887, *Looking Backward,* which portrayed the men of 2000 in the manner now reserved for the depiction of benign, superior beings from other planets.

It was Central Europe and specifically the German Empire, then seemingly the strongest, most successful, most "satisfied" of European powers, that was beset with prophetic uncertainty in the eighties. It did not come from the Viennese who did not yet dare to contemplate possible German collapse, and chose instead to embrace their former rival. In Germany, the thought if not the fear of political decline was taboo. Nevertheless, the post-Bismarckian era was awaited anxiously. With stiff bravado seeking to repress troubling speculations and expectations, the storm clouds of prophecy gathered overhead.

"Germany's temporary political ascendancy" was not to be sustained, Nietzsche believed as he entered the eighties. Her superiority rested too exclusively on the talents and will power of one moody, passionate individual who had so exploited his perception of "the weak character of all Germans that he feared neither parties nor princes." Bismarck might be ranked with Richelieu, the founder of the modern French state, but the inheritance he was about to leave harbored a "great danger" of having overinflated national expectations and aspirations. For all her justifiable pride in the excellence of her organization and discipline, Nietzsche added, "seldom were born in this land the commanding spirits and even more seldom those who could command with insight."[33]

Bismarck, facing a Reichstag election with an unpopular program of higher taxes, took no high-minded stand against political anti-Semitism; Jews and their left-liberal allies seemed decidedly on their own; anti-Semitism became the one emotional issue of the fall campaign. Moreover, Russian reaction to the assassination provoked a wave of pogroms which had a spillover effect in Germany. Anti-Jewish violence in Pomerania during the summer of 1881 recalled similar rioting in 1848 and before. Wagner, inspired by Gobineau, his summer house guest, publicized an optimistic, "redemptive" version of the latter's racism in "Heroism and Christianity"; Treitschke gloated that his anti-Jewish stand had won him the enthusiastic backing of the Protestant peasantry in his electoral district; and Stöcker won national attention by taking the issue directly into the left-liberal bastion of Berlin. In September Nietzsche learned that Schmeitzner was seeking to do the same in the socialist stronghold of Chemnitz (Karl-Marx-Stadt) but with the difference that the publisher was proclaiming a new irreligious, 'radical' 'free-thinking' anti-Semitism.[34]

The election, however, proved a setback to Bismarck's rightward course, presenting the Chancellor with the most perplexing internal stalemate in almost twenty years. The Crown Prince was too shaken by the mobilization of anti-Jewish hysteria—"the greatest disgrace of the nineteenth century"— to take much consolation in the results; he rightly sensed the vulnerability of the left liberal notable parties to the new style of politics now set in motion. Engels accepted the socialist vote loss in his relief that the party had finally expanded beyond its traditional base, the volatile, quasi-urban voters of Saxony and Thuringia whose susceptibility to anticapitalist demagoguery he greatly feared.[35] The anti-Semites had been denied their breakthrough; their vote totals and representation would grow in the coming decade, thanks to the economic distress of rural and semirural areas, but their attempt to penetrate the urban centers had been turned back. Bismarck would not again be tempted to play the anti-Semitic card.

In his Genoese hideaway Nietzsche determined to distance himself from Schmeitzner and was particularly annoyed that the publisher had been using his name to solicit contributors to his new journal, *Die Internationale Monatsschrift*.[36] Yet Nietzsche also became intrigued with the figure in whose hands Schmeitzner had placed the direction of the magazine: the idiosyncratic, aging Young Hegelian Bruno Bauer. Nietzsche and Bauer shared the same Thuringian, Prussian, and Pietist antecedents, and their intellectual paths had already crossed in parallel joint attacks on David Friedrich Strauss a decade before. The older man, Bauer, "the hermit of Rixsdorf" (a town just outside Berlin) thought of Nietzsche, the "wanderer" in the south, as his young intellectual ally.[37]

Bauer began his career in the 1830s as a violent orthodox critic of Strauss, only to turn around and attack him even more violently as a radical atheist in the early 1840s. Having critically "demolished" Christianity, Bauer turned with even greater fury on Judaism, prompting Marx to write his essay on the Jews in response. Consistently hostile to socialism, Bauer became after 1848 a publicist of the reaction. In that capacity, Bauer wrote anti-Jewish polemics; one notable outburst appeared at the height of Lassalle's agitation. Thereafter he became fascinated with "Disraeli's romantic imperialism" as the alternative and counterpoint to "Bismarck's socialist imperialism." Bauer differed from the new racial fanatics, however, in that he had other issues on his mind. In his final months during the winter 1881/82, he ignored the Jews, focusing solely on his prophecy of Europe's future.[38]

Bauer was a minor prophet and soon forgotten; he remained too much a polemicist and journalist to present a moving and powerful vision of the future, even though he anticipated the views later popularized by Spengler. He was, of course, not alone in drawing the analogy between the late nineteenth century and the final days of antiquity or in foreseeing a Caesaristic imperialism. What was distinctive about Bauer was the degree his political vision remained shaped by the Crimean War; in the process of describing that war for a German-American audience he had approached a Tocquevillian conception of Russia and America as the coming superpowers. Such views were no longer topical in Bismarckian Germany, and Bauer was relegated to publicistic obscurity, writing occasionally on behalf of the conservative and even at times the liberal opposition. A quarter century after the Crimean War, his hour seemed again to have struck; Russia was again on the public agenda. Having no confidence in the staying power of the Reich, he took the opportunity to chastise German nationalism, lecturing Treitschke and mockingly holding up to him the example of Nietzsche's enlightened cosmopolitanism.[39]

Nietzsche was well pleased by the Europeanist program enunciated by Bauer in the first volume of the *Internationale Monatsschrift,* and he was flattered by the admiring, straightforward review of his latest works in that issue.[40] He impulsively dispatched a set of poems (later appended to the second edition of *The Gay Science*) which appeared in the following issue as "Idylls from Messina."[41] The brief hopes Nietzsche entertained for the still obscure journal were quite illusory, however. The new cosmopolitanism was effective only as a critique of nationalism. Europe was not about to be panicked or cajoled into unity, and the satisfaction derived by Bauer in the emergence of international associations and European cooperation in such matters as the mails was as naive and hopelessly idealistic as Nietzsche's vaunted "good European." The bubble broke soon enough; Bauer died in May 1882 and was replaced by Dühring, Nietzsche's intellectual nemesis— the "frothing fool" of the *Zarathustra*.[42] To Nietzsche's understandable disgust, the journal found a new content for its Europeanism: an international crusade against Jewry. After a few more issues the magazine passed away unmourned.

Although Nietzsche's exposition of the component of resentment in anti-Semitism was insightful, his comprehension of the general crisis of European liberalism in which anti-Semitism was both a symptom and a cause was fraught with limitations.[43] Liberals were less critical of Nietzsche during his aphoristic years, no doubt, because the seventies had shattered their faith in the old certainties once trumpeted by David Friedrich Strauss. Nietzsche's old champion Karl Hillebrand, the dean of liberal critics, encouraged him in the name of an older generation; the young Hermann Pachnicke, who would begin his political career as a left-liberal Reichstag deputy in 1890, hailed him as his personal educator and guide, dedicating his dissertation to Nietzsche; and Nietzsche coyly wrote his contemporary Theodor Curti, leading Swiss democrat and editor of the *Züricher Post,* of his surprise "that my political-social ruminations could arouse the serious interest of a political-social thinker [such as yourself]. "[44] As episodic as these contacts were, they show that Nietzsche was no longer the young literary lion of conservative Basel stalking an over-inflated liberalism. More pointedly, he had estranged Burckhardt, a rival if private prophet, one determined to stand in final defense of a doomed "Old Europe." Burckhardt responded to *Dawn* by likening Nietzsche to one scrambling up the steep granite face of a high mountain, gradually compelling the gathering of admirers in the valley below. His one-time mentor made it clear to Nietzsche that it was a "community" he did not intend to join.[45] Nietzsche's stopovers in Basel became ever more strained and infrequent. A few old-timers recalled him nostalgically as the most "elegant" of recent German transplants; newer arrivals regarded his aphorisms as unworthy effusions of excess leisure and uncertain health. Among the most pressing anxieties weighing upon Nietzsche as the decade progressed was the fear that his writings and reputation might jeopardize the generous pension granted him by the Basel authorities.

Nietzsche began to look to liberal Zurich as a compensating source of intellectual associations. He undertook a determined courtship of Burckhardt's political opposite, Gottfried Keller, his critic of a decade before. The wary, earthy, and self-enclosed Keller responded with some reserve to Nietzsche's flattering letters—the only such Nietzsche was writing in the early eighties. Their eventual meeting in the fall of 1884 brought no closeness, yet the whole operation was not without its rewards. Nietzsche thereby became a presence in the German Swiss literary world, a compensation of sorts for German neglect, and he fashioned what Overbeck termed his "Zurich circle," his one notable social success of the decade.[46] Zurich was then by far the most radical city in the German-speaking world: the headquarters of outlawed German Social Democracy and the new center of the Russian exile community. Yet even this citadel of European liberalism was not immune to the pressures of the conservative ascendancy. Keller's acceptance of Nietzsche was as much a function of the poet's political despair as Nietzsche's gesture of conciliation was an expression of his growing political homelessness.

Keller's powerful political poem of 1878, "Die öffentlichen Verleumder" ["The Public Slanderers"], was no less prescient in being prompted not by public defamation of the Jews but rather by conservative libels of the director of the local insane asylum. Its bleak conclusion—the good have disappeared, the bad stand amassed—evoked the emptiness of shabby times, of popular folly and betrayed ideals:

... einen Streit
Um nichts, ein irres Wissen,
Ein Banner, das zerrissen,
Ein Volk in Blödigkeit.
[... a struggle
Over nothing, a confused wisdom,
A banner torn,
A people in stupidity.]

This poem would sustain the White Rose in its resistance during the dark days of 1942/43.[47] Keller's final rambling novel of the eighties, *Martin Salander,* written more in sorrow than in anger, utilizes the generational theme to show how the "sons" have corroded political liberalism from within, leaving only its empty husk intact. Nietzsche could not accuse Keller as he did Burckhardt of "holding back out of desperation"; they might meet and Keller reluctantly bestow his blessing; but between the weary disappointments of the one and the burgeoning prophecies of the other there could be little true communication.

The dream of a cosmopolitan "third way" between nationalism and socialism proved elusive. He turned away from the Reich, spending less than one year of the eighties in Germany (discounting the eleven months of 1889 spent in a Jena asylum). The eight summer seasons (1881–1888) in the Swiss Alps, his primary and nominal contact with the German-speaking world, alternated with winter seasons in Italy (1880/81–1883/84, 1888/89) and France (1884/85–1887/88). Yet one cannot say that Nietzsche's gift for being in the right place at the right time deserted him in his final decade. Having lived his boyhood in the archetypal home town of the reactionary fifties, having been caught in the cross-currents of Bismarckian unification during his student years of the sixties, having been stationed on the border of Franco-German conflict and tension in the seventies, Nietzsche, the traveler, now accompanied the locus of European power politics as it shifted southward to the Mediterranean basin.

As he completed *The Gay Science* in early 1882, Nietzsche stood hesitating on the threshold, undecided whether to go ahead and enunciate the prophetic experience of the preceding summer or to plunge anonymously into a period of renewed studies. But what was uppermost in his mind was a craving for some great new adventure—a journey to Mexico or North Africa or "better still a war."[48] Köselitz, now living in Venice, suggested he enlist as a medical orderly in the Habsburg forces then suppressing resistance to their occupation of Bosnia-Herzegovina.[49] While hardly what Nietzsche had in mind, the suggestion was symptomatic of the new focus of political passions. Convinced that the great political eruption would soon take place across the Adriatic in the form of a great war with Russia, Köselitz was a partisan of Germanic penetration of the Balkans and on one occasion became so annoyed with a British naval demonstration in the area that he fantasized about shooting Gladstone.[50]

In February Paul Rée descended from the north, full of stories of his recent trip to America, anxious to put behind him recent family tragedies, and eager to indulge his gambling mania in Monte Carlo. The visit buoyed Nietzsche; he decided to travel alone by ship from Genoa to Messina. A year before he had been in the midst of preparations for a journey with Gersdorff to Tunis when the French suddenly occupied the city, making travel there impossible. Italy had herself long coveted the region, and Burckhardt, visiting Genoa a few months later, was struck by the virulence of anti-French feeling.[51] Nietzsche had experienced its outbreak first hand, and he now insistently sought to persuade Köselitz to take advantage of Italy's dramatic new embrace of Germany by seeking out the Italian queen as the patroness of his unfinished opera.[52] He arrived in Messina in an exalted state, writing friends that some messenger must have preceded him, smoothing his way, so friendly was the reception he encountered.[53] Some interpreters have detected mental imbalance in this reaction, yet Sicilians were in fact in a joyous, exuberant mood at this moment, having just celebrated the 600th anniversary of the Sicilian Vespers which was capped by a ferociously anti-French speech by Garibaldi.

No sooner had he arrived than Nietzsche received urgent messages to hurry to Rome and meet Rée's great new discovery: an extraordinary, enchanting Russian.[54] Nietzsche was ready to leave, suffering from the sirocco and perhaps also from Wagner's troubling proximity in Palermo. Rée stage-managed the first meeting with Lou von Salomé in St. Peter's. Lou, just twenty-one, dressed in the black costume of the Russian student, was a most striking and unusual figure. The blood she was coughing up in these months highlighted her dramatic appearance. She was also brilliant. As Köselitz put it later, one felt oneself in the presence of a female intellect that only recurred five or six times in any century.[55] At that moment she was the star attraction of Malwida's Roman salon.

Wherever she went in these years, Lou aroused the greatest expectations. The feminists of Zurich claimed her, passing her on to Malwida in Rome. Malwida in turn immediately saw Lou as her long-awaited heir apparent—a ludicrous misunderstanding, perhaps, for between the staid "idealism" of old-maidish Malwida and the defiant radicalism of the provocatively virginal Lou lay an unbridgeable clash of generational styles. Still, despite the almost immediate and inevitable break, there was a certain continuity. Lou, for all her superior gifts, was also to be significant primarily as a presence and catalyst, and not without reason did she emulate the success of Malwida's salon in the coming years.[56]

Since the Sorrento winter of 1876/77 Malwida had established herself as a critical personage in a new Rome that was rapidly becoming the capital of European café society. Malwida's Wagnerianism brought her into close proximity to Liszt who was after Pio Nono's death the real spiritual patriarch of the new Italian capital; her fluent Italian and intimate friendship with Donna Laura Minghetti, the wife of the intellectual leader of the Italian Right, brought her access to ruling circles; her cultivation of the influential Scandinavian colony around Ibsen, her annual trips to Paris, the constant visits of feminists from the north, all made her the person to know in the extensive German colony of Italy. Legions of young Germans from the hapless Gersdorff to the future Imperial Chancellor Bernhard von Bülow made use of her matchmaking services; an indefatigable correspondent, she kept in touch with those who came and went or were merely absent. In the spring of 1882, she was playing her new role to the hilt.[57]

Malwida's motherly feminism was threatening to no one. It was backward-looking, concerned with establishing a respectable tradition; her radical past was now no more than a storehouse of anecdotes and impressions. Lou, in contrast, was intent on living out the life of the new independent, intellectual woman, bringing to her role the sexual egalitarianism then theoretically promoted by the Russian radical movement. She seemed intent on flaunting herself as an exotic type not yet common in the West, at least not outside Paris. She was politically minded only in the sense of sharing the essentially religious sensibility of revolutionary populism. The daughter of a Russian general decorated for suppressing the Poles in 1830, she had kept hidden in her desk a picture of Vera Zasulich, the terrorist heroine of 1878.[58] The terrorist's devotion to a cause, the self-sacrifice and martyrdom, appealed to her imagination, but she herself skirted direct involvement. A refugee of sorts, she left Russia after her father's death with no intention of returning, intent on adopting German culture. Over the next half-century in print and in friendship with Nietzsche, Rilke, and Freud—to name merely the most famous—she remained active as unofficial spiritual guide to the Slavic east and the new femininity. She was determined to be free and equal, but never hesitated to use every feminine wile to press her advantage or illustrate her ascendancy. The jealousy of others was her constant companion. Not surprisingly such prudish German women as Malwida or Elisabeth Nietzsche were first impressed, then overwhelmed, and finally horrified by Lou.

Nietzsche confided to Lou his still secret prophecy of Eternal Return the day after he met her. A new horizon of exciting, expanding possibilities seemed to open up for a Nietzsche frantically bored with his own loneliness—studies with Lou and Rée in Munich or Vienna, a joint trip to Paris, even marriage to Lou. But the threesome's northern journey that Parsifal summer of 1882 only precipitated a series of devastating confrontations and crises that left Nietzsche more constricted and isolated than before.

They traveled into a cultural landscape then totally dominated by Wagner. The six-year hiatus following the first disappointing Bayreuth festival lent a retrospective nobility to the enterprise which effectively silenced once-vocal critics. The composer was clearly at the end of his career; *Parsifal* was to be the final statement; his legions amassed once more, swollen now by an even younger generation again seeking to trump the cultural establishment by identifying itself with soon-to-be-disappearing greatness. During their stopover at the lake of Lucerne, Nietzsche relived in melancholy tones his Wagnerian experience for Lou's benefit. Nietzsche had been telling friends and would-be intermediaries from Bayreuth that he would only attend the upcoming event if some gesture of reconciliation—a personal invitation—was forthcoming; none was extended. Nietzsche then arranged that at least Lou and Elisabeth would be present, while he secluded himself in the Thuringian village of Tautenburg. To be conspicuously absent was painful, but far worse was in store for Nietzsche. In the aftermath of the festival he heard (from Elisabeth?) of Wagner's "murderous insult": an unsolicited diagnosis offered to Nietzsche's physician some years before attributing Nietzsche's malady to his supposed sexual proclivities. Nietzsche presumed this to mean homosexuality, although Wagner apparently had in mind onanism.[59] Such an accusation coming just as Nietzsche was self-consciously courting Lou was not easily shrugged off; the sense that he was the object of general contempt began to gnaw away at him.

More trouble lay ahead; Elisabeth, upstaged by Lou, affected indignant outrage at the younger woman's provocative manner, melodramatically declaring that were she a Catholic she would enter a nunnery to atone for her brother's philosophy of sin. She alarmed Franziska, who in a nightmarish scene accused her son of being a curse on his father's grave. With "the virtues of Naumburg" aroused against him, Nietzsche fled the next morning to Leipzig, only to be told that official disapproval of blasphemous passages in his most recent works precluded his obtaining even a temporary teaching position at Leipzig or any German university, all this by his former Schulpforta tutor and Basel colleague the neo-Kantian philosopher Max Heinze.[60] Nietzsche in turn found his publisher deeply immersed in the first international Anti-Semitic Congress held in Dresden.[61] The Prussian elections of October 1882, which strengthened the right and checked the liberal gains of the preceding year, only further underscored the inhospitable climate for any new publications by Nietzsche.

Yet Nietzsche clung to his high enthusiasms in this, his "festival year."[62] The passionate religious conversations of the preceding five months allowed him to relive his own break with evangelical Christianity; Lou's religious search fueled his own value-creating mission. Lou, it seemed, was to be the midwife at the birth of "his son Zarathustra" whom Lou enthused was destined to be "the prophet of a new religion."[63] But as quickly as a spiritual communion had been established between them, Lou would as suddenly seek refuge in Rée's morose positivism. Rée, wracked with jealousy and habitual self-doubt, had grown ever more rigid and dogmatic since the Sorrento winter, his "priestly" self-righteousness curiously feeding on his philosophical paeans to selfishness. The threesome was shattered in November when Lou and Rée left for Berlin. The unraveling of intimacy, always tawdry, haunted Nietzsche for the next year and a half, flaring up in streams of letters conveying hurt, anger, or regret, and finally climaxing in an absurd challenge to a duel. In a comic repetition of Nietzsche's trip to Messina when he failed to contact Wagner in Palermo, Rée and Lou encamped near Sils in the summer of 1883, dispatching Ferdinand Tönnies as mediator. To Lou's great disgust, however, Tönnies became speechless upon encountering Nietzsche and passed him by. For all his melodramatics it was Nietzsche, Rudolph Binion observes, who emerged from the affair the least scathed and most able to put the experience to good use.[64]

What had once seemed a new opening had brought dramatic closure. The prophet emergent had reaped the reactions to his anti-motif: no last-minute reconciliation with Bayreuth was to be forthcoming; contact with home would be possible now only on the most superficial and infrequent terms; and "the Bismarckian atmosphere" of the Reich effectively quelled any illusions of a professional comeback in Germany. Each was to be expected and was, in fact, to some degree already anticipated by Nietzsche, but their dramatic confluence in the context of an unhappy romance vividly marked the end of the wandering quest for the "free spirit." The exile of the "posthumous man" had begun with the subtitle of the *Zarathustra*, "a book for all and none," effectively defining his new stance vis-à-vis his audience.

Nietzsche would don the mantle of prophecy just as the great prophets of the age were making their exits. Darwin, Marx, and Wagner died a year apart from each other in 1882/83. A series of national prophets also passed away in the early eighties: Carlyle and Dostoevsky in 1881; Emerson and Gobineau in 1882; Turgenev in 1883. The climax of the funereal mood came with the burial of Victor Hugo in 1885. While Nietzsche mourned Emerson as the century's wisest sage, it was, of course, Wagner's death that had the greatest impact on Nietzsche and his immediate world. Köselitz was among the first to mill around before Wagner's Venetian villa that day; in Basel a British friend observed to Overbeck that the composer's absence left "a big hole in human existence." Nietzsche heard the news as he completed the first book of the *Zarathustra*.[65] Among other emotions, he felt the burden of six years of opposition lifted from him and even briefly fancied himself the heir to Wagner's immense following. Not since Schiller had any German cultural figure so dominated the imagination of the young; at that moment "every young person was a Wagnerian. He was one even before he heard a single bar of his music," Hermann Bahr would recall.[66] Little popularity would accrue to Nietzsche from the younger generation's attempt to turn mourning into a rebuke of contemporary cultural life. Instead there was a heightened sense of the spiritual vacuum left by the departed, an emptiness that weighed heavily on the psyche of the eighties.

In the coming years Nietzsche undertook the graveyard work of delineating and at times caricaturing "the generation of 1830." In contrast, his own type of which he was the greatest exemplar, the generation of 1866, seemed ever more paralyzed and anonymous. Nietzsche was himself entering almost complete obscurity and was forced to publish the last books of the *Zarathustra* at his own expense. Schmeitzner's attempt to lead the Alliance Antijuive Universelle in league with Hungarian anti-Semites dissipated his fortune and bankrupted his firm. Nietzsche's meeting with Josef Paneth, Freud's colleague and friend, in early 1884 opened his eyes to the damage his association with the anti-Semitic publisher was doing to his reputation. He wrote Overbeck in April, "The accursed anti-Semitism is ruining all my chances for financial independence, pupils, new friends, influence; it alienated R[ichard] W[agner] and me; it is the cause of the radical break between myself and my sister etc., etc., etc."[67] He would now enter a long, acrimonious legal struggle to wrest his works from Schmeitzner's clutches.

Yet his life was also assuming a calming regularity which mitigated against the consequences of viewing himself a "mystical separatist."[68] Reserved, sickly, and more secluded than ever, Nietzsche had chosen the Riviera as his winter quarters—the hub of the new European social whirl. Burckhardt's macabre vision of the Riviera "becoming in a few years nothing more than a forty-hour-long hotel in which all of rich and sick Europe" would gather in the winter conveys the changes brought by the new boom in tourism.[69] Cheap railway transport made the seaside and the mountains accessible and affordable even to those of moderate income. By exchanging Genoa for Nice, Nietzsche settled into the cosmopolitan capital of the Riviera. Nice, predominantly Italian, ceded to France only a quarter of a century before, enabled Nietzsche's tentative foray into the French cultural realm. If his spoken French was not much better than his clumsy Italian, his reading knowledge was superior, and at such sites as Visconti's bookstore he could keep abreast of the latest Parisian trends while unknowingly rubbing shoulders with vacationing notables such as Fouillée and Guyau who frequented the place.[70] His Francophilia, hitherto theoretical with contact restricted to fleeting visits to Geneva, gained actuality.

In the summers he recruited a series of Lou substitutes—a tamer variety to be sure—among the feminists of Zurich of which the Swiss aristocrat Meta von Salis and the Austrian Resa von Schirnhofer were the most notable.[71] Among the habitués of Sils he established another set of primarily female companions which included the Anglo-German writer Helen Zimmern.[72] And if the world was not beating a path to his door, he could at least observe it every summer trooping by into the high country. Alpinism was reaching its crest in the eighties. The Zarathustra landscape, already familiar in Tennyson's "The Voice and the Peak" and as the setting of C. F. Meyer's novellas, was the expression of a triumphant new aesthetic. Poets and writers seemed to have burrowed into every nook and cranny of the Alps eager to soak up inspiration. Scientists emulating Tyndall and Helmholtz, clambered over the glaciers and the high rock formations; Giovanni Segantani arrived to make the Upper Engadine the "El Dorado of landscape painting," and Brahms complained in 1887 that he could no longer go hiking in the mountains without some companion exclaiming at some new view: "that is just as in your third symphony."[73]

For émigrés fleeing nationality and fatherland, such as Strindberg, Switzerland was simply the "ideal land" even though they soon came to think twice of life in "Hotel-Schweiz."[74] Here, the principal nationalities, the English and Germans, engaged in subtle warfare for control of the lobbies and drawing rooms; an unofficial "Hotel Boss" acted as master of ceremonies, and to some observers, such as Brandes in 1885, the social interactions among this new milieu were at least as intriguing as the scenery outside, perhaps more so.[75] Nietzsche's initial reaction to his first Alpine season in St. Moritz resembled Robert Louis Stevenson's sense of being

> Into an Alpine valley shut;
> Shut in a kind of damned Hotel,
> Discountenanced by God and man.[76]

At times the major resorts resembled "the last Day, or universal judgment. Such heaps of unexpected persons keep turning up," Edward Lear complained in 1882, "I constantly expect to see the Sultan, Mrs. Gladstone, Sir Joshua Reynolds, and the twelve apostles walk into the Hotel."[77] In quieter Sils, known as a rendezvous of German professors and boasting one local celebrity, the mountain guide Christian Klucker, Nietzsche would invariably bump into old acquaintances or run into some prominent figure such as

Paul Bourget.[78] As J. V. Widmann, the preeminent social chronicler of the Alpine world, said of Nietzsche, "Who knows but that his bitterest and most anti-human expression, that of the 'Many too many,' may not have been provoked by the sight of the tourists who overrun the Engadine in swarms every summer?"[79]

As Nietzsche was himself one of those "many" who were putting into place that world of cosmopolitan exchange so brilliantly portrayed a generation later in Thomas Mann's *The Magic Mountain,* his telling-it-on-the-mountain has a certain saving, self-conscious air. Topicality and clownishness intrude into the *Zarathustra* as in the parody of Bayreuth as the Festival of Asses, or Zarathustra the purveyor of dulcet didacticism. The actual prophecy of Eternal Return slips unobtrusively into the work, never overwhelming it. Nietzsche said he wrote "comme poèt-prophète"; and as Henry David Aiken notes, "whatever its imperfections either as philosophy or as imaginative literature, the form in which *Thus Spake Zarathustra* was cast made possible a fuller and freer projection of, as well as release from, the tensions between Nietzsche and his 'anti-self' than he could usually achieve in his more imaginative 'prose' writings."[80]

The first three books of the philosophical poem were composed at breakneck speed in ten-day bursts during 1883, with months of reflection and self-doubt following each literary effort, much as the hangover follows revelry. The last book was written at the beginning of 1885. Paneth, who met Nietzsche during one such lull, was surprised that "there is not a trace of false pathos or any pose of the prophet about him, despite what I had feared from his latest works; his manner is, on the contrary, innocuous and natural." Nietzsche told him "without the slightest affectation and quite unself-consciously, that he always felt he had a mission that now, as far as his eyes would allow it, he wanted to work out what was in him."[81] The *Zarathustra* is an exposition of that sense of mission; it displays man and mind at play and not, as Aiken put it, "the aphoristic distillate."

Dissatisfaction followed each bout with prophecy; the "posthumous man" was gripped with a yearning to say something pertinent to the present. Did he suspect himself of lack of seriousness, of too easy an exit from the world of his contemporaries? In 1884 he dreamed of some polemical comeback that could rivet the attention of his countrymen as he had once done in his attack on Strauss. He wrote a horrified Overbeck in January of his planned "great frontal attack on all types of present German obscurantism (under the title, 'New Obscurantists')."[82] His cautious friend warned that it would be folly to attempt to stir up that "swamp."[83] The visit that summer of his Wagnerian admirer, Heinrich von Stein, then also a prominent member of Lou's Berlin salon, only convinced Nietzsche of the degree the new obscurantism was infecting even the "higher," talented natures. He was again planning his polemical response, this time to be entitled simply "The Germans" or "German."[84]

All-encompassing and overwhelming as was Nietzsche's critique and rejection of Germany in the eighties, he lacked the focus of a defined target. Although again mocking German pretensions, these pretensions, even though advertised more loudly than ever, were no longer products of blinding success but rather props used to disguise troubling inner stalemate and a deteriorating position abroad. He might protest the conformity and overconformity of the late Bismarckian era, but he could do little against the sluggishness that fostered and protected it. His absence from the Reich and his disdain for keeping abreast of current events in the press was only part of the problem and nothing new. He seemed to have lacked the journalistic tenacity to go after specific public issues, as when a decade before he had abandoned a planned exposé on the intertwining of higher education and the one-year volunteer, which he had correctly blamed for militarizing the educated young.

The real problem was that he thought he could find no worthy intellectual opponent with whom to do battle. No new David Friedrich Strauss, blatantly seeking to encapsulate the public mood, offered himself up to Nietzsche—save the posthumous Wagner. Dühring was beneath contempt and a source of irritation only because Nietzsche had allowed his publisher and others to associate his name with the "Berlin apostle of revenge." He contented himself with scornful asides mocking Treitschke as a court historian; perhaps it was the mutual friendship with Overbeck which kept Nietzsche from doing open battle with his generation's pugnacious version of David Friedrich Strauss. The rest of his German coevals seemed in bondage to decaying philosophical and aesthetic schools or simply lying low and hedging their bets. The generational expectations which fueled Nietzsche's initial polemics seemed now as misplaced as the self-congratulatory pathos of the Founding Era. The prideful unanimity which the nation experienced at that moment would not reappear until the outbreak of the Great War. Nietzsche's turn from the essay to the aphorism during the seventies was itself a function of the failure of the Reich and his generation to form a compact, articulate public capable of responding to the essay as a form of intellectual discourse. The stirrings of the new generation, the self-proclaimed "Youngest Germany," were too stridently naturalistic and inarticulate to provoke Nietzsche's serious attention, at least in the mid-eighties.[85] With the process of social fragmentation only intensifying, the revival of the essay format seemed even more illusory. In *Beyond Good and Evil* (1886), Nietzsche did achieve some success by lengthening his aphorisms and arranging them more cohesively in the manner of an essay.

His focus was less scattered, his points more consistently pursued, yet it was only in his final months when he confronted Wagner's ghost directly that Nietzsche once again came into his own as a polemicist.

Nietzsche's failure to affect the mid-eighties as he had done the early seventies was ultimately due, however, to the fact that he largely if perversely shared the ethos of the new conservatism. While conservatives soon came to see him and his following in the nineties as the principal and most dangerous opponent of their orthodoxy, Nietzsche's effectiveness against them derived from his dispassionate analysis of their decline. Even his atheism was couched in the language of regret: God is dead; we have killed him; nihilism, alas, is our fate; let us be strong and go forward, etc.. Nietzsche might be "anti-liberal to the point of malice" but toward conservatives he assumed the pose of the far-sighted decadent who recognized that the game was up, that lapses into resentful demagoguery were dishonorable and ultimately self-defeating. He transposed and etherealized the conservative enthusiasms of the moment. His cult of aristocracy focused on spirit, not genealogy; he justified the coming ruling class in the name of European unity, not national greatness; he attributed social unrest not to race-mixing, but the mixing of classes. He was antidemocratic, not so much in the sense of wanting to thwart democracy's rise, but rather in assuming the stance of a postdemocratic critic anxious to undermine its hegemony. His anti-feminism similarly assumed the triumph of the new woman; like Strindberg, half in love, half in fear, completely obsessed with the new type, he called for resistance. To be a "modern spirit" and simultaneously avoid the pitfall of Darwin's "liberal theology" necessarily meant one had to be conservative, Strindberg wrote in 1886.[86]

Unlike the avant-garde of the turn of the century which was elitist as to the present but democratic in its expectations for the future, Nietzsche resisted placing any such hopes in the prospects for mass culture. Yet here as elsewhere he was inconsistent, for he, too, dreamed of the millions who would one day read the *Zarathustra*. His style, temptingly accessible to all, was like a tonic for the daily routine, an escape from the strictures of scientific analysis. His elitism was ultimately too affected by his atheistic religiosity to bar access to his new church. Yet at the same time he kept alive the distinctive pathos of the eighties which pitted the one against the many. Bruno Bauer had begun the decade depicting the "isolated," a tiny, knowing group who had fathomed the onset of the new age of imperialist structures and conflicts.[87] In 1884 Nietzsche would write Overbeck, "I am now, very probably, *the most independent man in Europe*. My aims and tasks are more embracing than anyone else's; and what I call *grosse Politik* gives at least a good standpoint and bird's-eye view for things of the present."[88]

The various and inconsistent renderings of Nietzsche's concept of *grosse*

Politik as "high," "grand," or "great" politics have, at least for readers in English, dissipated its meaning and hidden the course of Nietzsche's usage. In German the term has a familiar, majestic ring, one rooted in the then fashionable conviction of the primacy of foreign policy, of a higher form of politics specifically addressing European and world power conflicts in contradistinction to a presumably lesser form of politics dealing with internal matters. German historians in the 1920s would entitle their compilation of prewar diplomatic documents *Die Grosse Politik der Europäischen Kabinette, 1871–1914.* It was during the celebration of the success of the "great statesman" in the 1870s that the term became a popular article of faith. In his 1878 aphorism *"Grosse Politik* and Its Drawbacks" Nietzsche first responded to its vogue by asserting that "the political growth of a nation almost necessarily entails an intellectual impoverishment and lassitude, a diminished capacity for the performance of works that require great concentration and specialization."[89] Here, as in countless reformulations over the next decade, Nietzsche interjects a seesaw theory, an either-or choice, between politicization and cultural flowering that challenged the cherished conviction that cultural splendor necessarily and eagerly follows in the train of military success.

The aphorism *"Grosse Politik"* in *Dawn* continues to examine the psychology of the politicizing urge, of the "need for the feeling of power," and why in particular "The time comes again and again when the masses are ready to stake their lives and fortunes, their consciences, and their virtue, in order that they may secure that highest of all enjoyments and rule as a victorious, tyrannical, and arbitrary nation over other nations (or at all events think that they do)." Conscious of the mass appeal of such a "state of exaltation," of "feelings of prodigality, sacrifice, hope, confidence, extraordinary audacity, and enthusiasm" all couched and camouflaged by the leader's "pathetic language of virtue," Nietzsche began to associate his own call for depoliticization with the promise of a coming "age of festivity" in which such emotions could find peaceful expression.[90]

Nietzsche had so far stood outside the concept. He mocked the *grosse Politik* of the Reich in view of impending European unity as a new form of "petty politics," much as nationalists such as Treitschke were then scorning the superseded age of "petty" particularism.[91] But during the writing of the *Zarathustra,* Nietzsche began to internalize the concept of *grosse Politik* as a component of his own prophetic mission. *Grosse Politik* appears as a cryptic heading in a notebook of the winter of 1884/85 and then again in the late spring.[92] There, while reflecting on "the higher Europeans, the precursors of *grosse Politik,*" and then again after stating that the "new philosopher" can only emerge in conjunction with a "ruling caste, as its highest spiritualization," he jots down: "the *grosse Politik*, government of the earth imminent; complete lack of principles on its behalf."[93]

Nietzsche embraced the concept of *grosse Politik* precisely at the moment when Germany was suddenly creating her colonial empire. It is not merely a historian's superstitious belief in simultaneity to suggest that this was no coincidence, no accident. Bismarck's dramatic about-face, his acquisition of the Cameroons in July 1884, German South West Africa in August, New Guinea in December, and finally German East Africa in May 1885 put into place a colonial empire where a year before none had existed at all. Nietzsche had hitherto made desultory remarks about European colonization, urging here and there mass migration of Europe's poor as a solution to the social problem and toying himself with the idea of joining a Swiss colony in Oaxaca, Mexico. In the mid-eighties, Nietzsche, like his European contemporaries, turned outward onto what he saw as the coming struggle for "the mastery of the earth."[94]

It was not that Nietzsche took German prospects in this conflict seriously or that he ever troubled himself with the motives of Bismarck's puzzling, overnight adoption of imperialism. The prevailing explanations for the emergence of German imperialism have entailed a misreading of the mood and circumstance of the eighties, Wehler has recently argued. To view the colonial acquisitions as another super-subtle foreign policy stratagem designed to conciliate France and alienate England is to project Bismarck's diplomatic mastery of the 1870s into the unsettled 1880s; to see it as a concession to overflowing German economic strength is to read the expansiveness of the Wilhelmian era back into the troubled economic climate of the eighties.[95] The slogans of the still nascent German colonial movement, colonies as the answer to over-production and over-population, betray the underlying anxieties of economic stagnation and massive German emigration. To be sure, Bismarck sought to extract foreign policy advantages from his colonial policy; more importantly, however, he had found an issue on which to campaign against the left liberal opposition, one which proved far more effective than the half-hearted flirtation with anti-Semitism in the preceding national election. Nationalist fears of being outdistanced in the world arena came into play for the first time in the fall election of 1884. Although anti-Semitism continued to infect social attitudes, it declined as a political force, and Bernhard Förster, ever alert to new trends, placed himself in the forefront of the colonial agitation. Nietzsche even affected a certain lukewarm interest in Bernhard's projected German colony in Paraguay, impressed in part with Bernhard's backers, which included the Mecklenburg aristocrat and Africa traveler Hermann von Maltzan, a leader of the German Colonial Association.[96] But he would view Bernhard and Elisabeth's departure from Europe with misgivings, and tried to distance himself from the project, turning a deaf ear to subsequent pleas for financial help for the shaky enterprise.[97]

Nietzsche's own reflections on the coming world conflict presumed German eclipse, indeed general European decline. The Reich owed its European pre-eminence to its ascendancy over "tired, old peoples"; French decline was symptomatic of European decadence; Russia and the Anglo-Saxon powers were the only true protagonists on the world stage, he argued in 1884/85.[98] He shared enough of the new anti-English feeling in Germany to favor Russia in the coming struggle. His greatest fear was that the Russians would themselves become infected with the mediocrity which he attributed to British parliamentarianism.[99] He briefly consoled himself with the thought that Americans, so involved in haste, would use themselves up before America could become a world power.[100] Elsewhere he raised the cry: "No American future!"[101] His hope lay in Germany as a way station to a Pan-Slavic Europe, in Europe as the new Greece to a Russian Rome.[102] It was imperative that Russia gain control of India and China, etc.[103] Such was the drift of Nietzsche's speculations during the scramble for colonies in the mid-eighties, but with the onset of the Bulgarian crisis in the fall of 1885 and the traumatic specter of general European war, Nietzsche's thoughts again became centered on Europe. The great conflicts and wars which Nietzsche had so happily prophesied for the twentieth century suddenly seemed to be approaching with alarming speed.

The mood of the great war scare of the late eighties found its ultimate expression in Nietzsche's final apocalyptic writings. The anti-motif, having turned prophetic, would seek final repose in presiding over the imminent disaster. By 1888 Nietzsche had become the self-styled "man of calamity."[104] His perception of his writings as a portent and potential cause of spiritual upheaval became imperceptibly merged with apprehensions of the political and military convulsions about to seize Europe. External events seemed to constantly reinforce the drama of Nietzsche's prophetic purpose: the initial prophecy came to him amid the wild summer storms of 1881; Wagner died just as he completed the first part of the *Zarathustra;* the island of Ischia, his mental model of the "blissful isle," suffered a calamitous earthquake with 1,700 dead just after he completed the second part of the *Zarathustra;* and he had experienced the great Riviera earthquake of 1886.[105] He entered into "a fight with the lies of a millennium"; consequently, "we shall have up-heavals, a convulsion of earthquakes, a moving of mountains and valleys, the like of which has never been dreamed of." Nietzsche's antipolitics, his insistent protest of politicization, of the politicized secularization of the highest values, would conclude by drawing politics back irresistibly into his prophetic vision. "The concept of politics will have merged entirely with a war of spirits," he asserted, "all power structures of the old society will have been exploded—all of them based on lies: there will be wars the like of which have never yet been seen on earth. It is only beginning with me that the earth knows *grosse Politik.*"[106]

Such assertions seemed bizarre and exotic in the following quarter century; the guardians of Nietzsche's fame withheld the *Ecce Homo* in which this passage appears until after Nietzsche's death in 1900. Averted catastrophes arouse interest and regret only amid even greater calamities, and it was only in and after World War I that the prophecies of *grosse Politik* had a resonance. Other gloomy prognoses of the late eighties and early nineties were then also recalled to memory: Engels's belief that "world war" was about to rend Europe asunder; Moltke's warning that the coming conflict, far from adhering to the pattern of the wars he had recently conducted, might last seven, even thirty years; the pessimism of the elderly who, as Fontane put it, were wondering whether "the whole glorious edifice created between 1864 and 1870" might not soon come tumbling down.[107]

The chimerical character of the great war scare of the late eighties brought such fears to the surface only to dissipate them once the immediate crisis passed. By 1889 it was becoming clear that Bismarck had manipulated the panic to achieve his smashing electoral triumph of 1887, that Wilhelm II, for all his hawkish bluster, was loath to begin his reign with a dangerous military adventure, and that none of the European antagonists had faith in their capacity to wage war successfully. The militarism of the eighties was too colored by deflated expectations and too conscious of economic weakness to conclude in anything but a resigned stalemate. None of the international crises which followed, such as over Morocco in 1905 and 1911, threatened to spark the tinderbox of Eastern Europe. The protagonists of the political drama of these years were quickly eclipsed. Alexander of Battenberg's semi-comic tenure as the King of the Bulgars was soon forgotten; the backstage intrigues of Moltke's warlike heir-apparent, General Waldersee, unraveled; and the comet-like flamboyance of that apostle of *revanche,* General Boulanger, suddenly disappeared from sight. Yet this crisis, even though it may have ended on a note of absurdity, was still the closest Europe would come to a general war before 1914, and it was within its anxious atmosphere that Nietzsche fashioned his final political vision.

The wars of Nietzsche's youth retained a heroic and idealistic gloss even as they seemingly affirmed the Machiavellianism of modern politics. Military vitality and cultural creativity had then seemed alternating rungs in the ladder of European greatness. How different was the mood when Henry Adams, returning after an absence of two decades, declared, "Europe seemed to have been stationary for twenty years."[108] Nothing seemed to have happened save within the expectations and self-perception of the European psyche. The inspiring hopes and illusions of 1870 now seemed overlaid by a blanket of lies; stagnant lies which Nietzsche with prophetic majesty, or Max Nordau with journalistic verve, sought to unmask.[109] Uncovered truths were dark and gloomy. Europeans had betrayed their essential character by the manner in which they had sought to colonize the world, Nietzsche argued in 1884, for they had shown that they were at heart "beasts of prey."[110] Consequently war, especially war within Europe, assumed a new sinister aspect. As truthfulness became equated with ruthlessness, ascendant Social Darwinism no longer promised progress but harked back to a Hobbesian struggle of existence. But whereas Hobbes had sought to imprison the underlying barbarism of social life in cold rationality, the Darwinians of the late nineteenth century were driven to harness the dynamism of unleashed irrationality. In her worried Continental preeminence, Germany, more than any other power, internalized the new mood. Subsequent German historians, such as Dehio, have argued that the German bid for hegemony was negatively distinguished from those which preceded it by its lack of mission.[111] But the new truthfulness contained its own sense of mission; the German young of the eighties, at the helm in 1914, saw themselves as fearlessly illusionless, bowing to no false idealism.

While Nietzsche was the most eloquent iconoclast, he was also the most troubled by the spiritual vacuum which the illusionless man was entering. Nietzsche might continue to exalt the Iron Chancellor as the exemplar of "Machiavellianism pure and simple," but lines of communication between the practicing Machiavellian, Bismarck, and the theoretical Machiavellian, Nietzsche, were bound to collapse.[112] The image of the fearless, superior leader which had so gripped Nietzsche and his generation in their youth became problematic when it turned into an inheritance seeking legitimation in a world deprived of idealism. Greatness had become a burden to Nietzsche's generation, an enforced tribute and a confession of having to follow as epigones. For Nietzsche's age group, then in their forties and fifties, Bismarck was already a living icon; he, much like Goethe in the 1820s, dominated the decade simply by his presence, negatively more for past deeds than present actions. Obeisance to "the great Chancellor," "the great statesman" had become such a ritualized feature of all political oratory, except that of the socialists, that it was considered daring, even provocative, when only one such reference was made at the funeral oration of Bismarck's leading liberal opponent in 1884.[113] Rumors floated of the Chancellor's imminent departure no longer evoked consternation; rather they were heard with a resigned fatalism. Yet no viable alternative seemed to be presenting itself. For all of Bismarck's talk after 1880 of a "Gladstone Ministry" waiting in the wings, the liberal Crown Prince had long before abandoned any plan of removing the Iron Chancellor from office. Bismarck's dismissal finally in 1890 by Wilhelm II, a mere youth, seemed a sacrilege and an impiety, much like a schoolboy throwing snowballs at a monument.

Nietzsche's fantasy of Bismarck hurling the complimentary copy of *Human, All-Too-Human* against the nearest wall had been indirectly confirmed by reviewers of that work, who had detected in Nietzsche the very "nihilist professor" whose presence Bismarck was then warning the nation augured a crisis of values.[114] The Machiavellian obsession with ideals—their evasion, decline, sustenance, and creation—necessarily made Nietzsche and Bismarck spiritual opposites in the eighties.

The decade of the 1880s has hidden in Nietzsche's fame and has primarily influenced the spiritual life of the twentieth century through Nietzsche, the herald of its deepest and darkest thoughts. Nietzsche was well positioned to become the ultimate prophet of the decade. The typical prophet, Nietzsche once remarked, was but "the satirist of the hour."[115] Was there not in Nietzsche's prophetic message of Eternal Return an ironic comment on the eventlessness of the eighties, were not Nietzsche's "will to power" and final megalomania perhaps an unconscious parody of the sense of powerlessness which haunted the eighties?

Nietzsche memorialized the stalemate of his time. The birth of the new in decay, prophecy in stagnation, the assertion of a dangerously volatile radicalism in what was clearly the most ideologically conservative decade of the nineteenth century were all features of Nietzsche's final program. Unlike the previous conservative ascendancies, the eighties lacked the pathos of restoration which moved the 1820s or the prosperity to make reaction palatable as in the 1850s. To hurdle back over Napoleon and 1789 was, at least theoretically, possible in the agrarian setting of the twenties, but to reverse the industrial revolution half a century later was not. Bismarck's League of Three Emperors was necessarily a pale copy of Metternich's Holy Alliance and soon broke up. Gone, too, was the experience of religious revival which had given Nietzsche's father's life its direction. The conservatism of Nietzsche's generation would be deadened by their failure to create successful conservative institutions. Protestantism in particular was on the defensive; at a loss in the cities, embarrassed by the outcome of the *Kulturkampf,* the orthodox struggled in the Luther festivities of 1884 to preserve their image of the Reformation from telling critiques by Catholics and renegades like Nietzsche.[116] Nor could the conservatives of the eighties don the higher cynicism of the 1850s when post-revolutionary discontent could be safely channeled into economic activity.

The deflation of ideals as of currency was to become a peculiar hallmark of the eighties. Nietzsche's remark that what is falling deserves a shove conveys the frustration, indeed the resentment, of a spiritual life caught in seeming suspended animation. In the course of the decade, Nietzsche was to declare himself a "decadent" and "Europe's first complete nihilist."[117] Nihilism means, Nietzsche wrote in 1887, that "the highest values" "devalue" themselves.[118] "Decadence" was to be accepted and lived through, Nietzsche would argue, so that one could arrive at a promised "revaluation of all values." The metaphors of biology and capitalism met in Nietzsche's conception; life like the market was either ascending or descending. Sentiment, pity, indignation were of no avail. The moment for enunciating higher values in the fullness of triumph had passed, Germany was pulled down with the West into a spiritual trough, Nietzsche believed. Forced with his contemporaries on this seemingly downward path, Nietzsche did not so much rebel as envisage new heights, thereby positioning himself to become in the eyes of succeeding generations the mystagogue of modernity.

After the turbulent boom-bust cycle of the seventies, the economy of the eighties stayed virtually in place. Three years of partial recovery from 1879 to 1882 were followed by a four-year recession; renewed recovery after 1886 was reversed by another painful recession in 1890. While liberal finance capitalism was effectively discredited by the crash of 1873, the new protectionist alliance between heavy industry and agrarian capitalists brought little economic advance and only a modicum of social harmony. The industrial sector which had borne the brunt of the economic crisis of the late seventies entered the new decade with a relative advantage; it consolidated, forming between 1879 and 1890 200 of the 275 cartels in place in 1900; the new chemical and electrical industries began their rapid ascent; overseas trade continued to grow; and most significantly, workers benefited from falling prices.[119] Real weekly wages which had risen sharply in the seventies, reaching 84 in 1875 (1913: 100), plunged to 70 in 1881, only to start a steady, gradual rise over the next decade and a half.[120] The peculiarity of the economic crisis since 1873, one economist observed in 1888, was that it was "a crisis more of the rich than the poor despite all the unemployment and the frequent though not universal wage reductions."[121]

The hardest hit were the large agrarian producers of East Elbia, the very group determined to leave the decade with a conservative imprint. The agrarian depression began in earnest in the early eighties. Falling prices, interest rates, and real estate values combined with new overseas and Russian competition to darken the rural landscape with peasant flight and noble intransigence lending an anxious tone to the new conservatism.[122] The now Baron Carl von Gersdorff, unhappily managing his Silesian estate, complained to Köselitz and Nietzsche of the constricted, oppressive character of his aristocratic milieu.[123] As Kehr noted, the attempted "refeudalization" of German political life occurred precisely when the aristocratic monopoly of the officer corps and the higher bureaucracy was no longer tenable. Ideology was thus impressed into service to compensate for real strength, for the falling away of the primacy of the aristocracy's social and economic base. The "Puttkamer system" (1881–1888) operated by purging liberals from the bureaucracy and then fashioning a new type of official, loyal in word and deed to the government in power and the status quo. The reserve officer, bound to an anachronistic code of honor, was mobilized to serve as a pseudo-aristocratic, military missionary among the civilian population.[124] Most importantly, conservatives abandoned previous constraints and went to the people; the success of the Catholic Center Party of the seventies goaded them on; during the eighties conservative parties, organizations, and alignments were the coming force; the Reichstag election of 1887 would mark the greatest electoral success of the German Right until the election of 1932.[125]

As Bismarck turned to conservatism as his ideological buttress, Nietzsche felt himself ever more hounded by the censor. In 1885 he was forced to deal with skittish printers afraid of being charged with blasphemy; friends warned caution at every turn; and finally in the vivid works of Nietzsche's mental twilight he sought to lash back by defiantly courting the charge of lèse majesté.

The mature Nietzsche found himself cast into the wilderness as the prophet of an unwanted Europeanism. Convinced that "the world economy" would inevitably bring the "world literature" and European unity envisaged by Goethe and Napoleon, Nietzsche enunciated his *"grosse Politik"* in defiance of his would-be audience. Unwilling to play either the role of the "charlatan" to the wider public or the "virtuoso" to a small circle of admirers, Nietzsche consoled himself with the thought that he had the backing of the handful who mattered. These were men primarily of the older generation, Nietzsche wrote Taine in July 1887, aside from Wagner, mentioning Burckhardt, Bauer, and Keller.[126] This was, of course, largely bluff; the rightist Bauer was long deceased, and the conservative Burckhardt and the liberal Keller, far from approving or even interesting themselves in Nietzsche's later works, simply preferred to avoid an open break with their admirer. Taine was soon included in their company, and when Rohde chose to mock the value of Taine's advocacy Nietzsche broke off contact with his long estranged friend.[127] Yet despite the obviously painful isolation and loneliness of his post-aphoristic years, Nietzsche had in his independence achieved a certain personal stability and sense of direction.

George Brandes's sudden appearance as Nietzsche's champion, ready to herald his name on the European stage in late 1887, altered everything, bringing into play a new Nietzsche eager to mobilize his imminent fame in final battle with the new Rome. Brandes found himself in sympathy with

Nietzsche's political outlook. He was, if ever there was one, a "good European"; a Danish Jew, he epitomized the cause of Jewish assimilation and as literary grandee would later dispute the merits of Zionism with Herzl.[128] For a decade, various publishers and friends of Nietzsche had sought to interest Brandes in Nietzsche's works. Brandes had long moved in Nietzschean influenced circles and had known Rée, Lou, and Tönnies. He now turned to Nietzsche when he was at the height of his international influence. As a young man he had brought attention to a forgotten Kierkegaard. His positivistic literary histories had a European format; and he had just returned with a report on the literature of the east in his *Impressions of Russia*. Brandes was hurt when Nietzsche called him a "cultural missionary," but the decline of his critical reputation has confirmed Nietzsche's not-all-that-unkindly-meant designation.[129] Brandes would remain a superficial critic of Nietzsche's endeavors, but bringing him into correspondence with Strindberg lent new credibility to Nietzsche's Europeanism.

Since the death of Karl Hillebrand in 1883, Nietzsche had accustomed himself to his role as a radical outsider. The one subsequent significant critique of his work, the 1886 review of *Beyond Good and Evil* by the former Burckhardt pupil J. V. Widmann in his Swiss journal, *Bund*, under the title, "Nietzsche's Dangerous Book," had only confirmed Nietzsche's idiosyncratic standing.[130] It made him uncomfortable that in Sils many read that his thought was "dynamite." And he began to speak ironically of his seductive, mysterious, and subterranean influence on "all the radical parties (Socialists, nihilists, anti-Semites, Christ. orthodox, Wagnerians)."[131] But with Brandes lecturing on Nietzsche in Copenhagen, the floodgates barring his fame seem to have been lifted. He could now step forward on his own. Scattered admirers seemingly began to cohere as a new force. Widmann's struggling friend Carl Spitteler sought out his help and offered his literary services; Nietzsche established contact with the young editor of the *Kunstwart,* Ferdinand Avenarius; Karl Knortz, a German American professor of literature, announced his presence from overseas; Nietzsche cultivated the editor of the *Journal des Débats,* and interest among the younger literary generation was finally heralded by the appearance of the young naturalist critic Leo Berg.[132] In the spring of 1888 a new activating concept entered Nietzsche's vocabulary: "counter-movements" which he ultimately saw himself leading into battle against the prevailing "movements" of his time.[133]

By proclaiming art as the great "counter-movement," one embodying the "victorious will" and thus capable of countering the "nihilist movement" of the present in its two wings, the Buddhist and the Christian, Nietzsche was in effect announcing the advent of the European avant-garde.[134] In time he would become the first great culture hero of the international avant-garde. He also spoke of religion as a "counter-movement," specifically his latter day Dionysianism which promised to restore "pride" to modern man.[135] In addition he posed himself as the "anti-Darwin" bringing relief to a decade suffocating under a new environmental determinism.[136] Yet these themes were but variants of long standing arguments, only more insistently professed. What was distinctive was the degree to which the new activistic Nietzsche allowed himself to be drawn into the political drama of the *Drei-Kaiser-Jahr*.

The unfolding dynastic tragedy of the House of Hohenzollern absorbed European attention from the autumn of 1887 through 1888. Not since the assassination of the Czar had the problems and pathos of imperial power been so starkly posed or so uppermost in the European mind. The Boulangist agitation then reaching its crest, the sinister worsening of Russo-German relations, the triumph of the German Right in the war scare elections of February 1887, all receded before the import of the great succession crisis of Imperial Germany. The Bismarckian system faced its first real test. The passing of the hoary Wilhelm I had been expected for years but the news of the Crown Prince's cancer of the throat came as a jolt. The birth years of the four Hohenzollerns in direct succession—1797, 1831, 1859, 1882—corresponded so neatly to the recurring waves of generational feeling that Germans naturally accustomed themselves to identifying with the Hohenzollern closest in age.

Nietzsche was no exception. He had initially shared the liberalism of the Crown Prince when it seemed he might accede at an early age to the throne during the Prussian Constitutional Crisis; he had served in the Crown Prince's army group in the Franco-Prussian War; and in 1886 he noted with pleasure the Crown Prince's remark that he felt nowhere better in the world than on the Italian Riviera.[137] Their maladies, their physical proximity in the winters, their mutual disgust at anti-Semitism, their waiting-in-the-wings made the figure of the Crown Prince understandably sympathetic to Nietzsche. The shocking drowning of Ludwig II and his physician, presumably a case of murder-suicide, in the summer of 1886 was a foreshadowing of what was to follow. Nietzsche had been deeply upset by the death of the other great Wagnerian of his generation.[138] He felt privy to the king's personal history; he had met the Bavarian sovereign, and Ludwig had admired Nietzsche's literary Wagnerianism. The impending tragedy of the Imperial Crown Prince, then the only significant political figure symbolic of his generation, would be equally troubling to Nietzsche.

At first, however, as was his wont, Nietzsche was annoyed by the intrusive news of the Crown Prince's fatal malady. Having placed his imagination amid "the mechanics of *grosse Politik*," he resented hearing the blaring "Christian fanfare" which had so often accompanied "victory bulletins or imperial addresses to the people." "'The Adam's apple of the Crown Prince' is no affair of God,"[139] he wrote irritably. Yet that winter Nietzsche was not insensitive to the Crown Imperial suffering in nearby San Remo which was made all the more poignant by the liberal press's desperate hopefulness. Nietzsche was even more alarmed by the dramatically changed political situation within the Reich's ruling elite. Instead of the traditional struggle between the ascendant Bismarckian party and an oppositional Crown Imperial camp, a third grouping around the twenty-eight-year-old Prince Wilhelm seemed suddenly on the verge of gaining power. These were men of Nietzsche's age—the dreamy favorite, Philip Eulenburg, the brilliant diplomatic schemer Baron von Holstein, and the clique around General Alfred von Waldersee, the first political general in the Prussian army's high command since Bismarck's predecessor as Chancellor, General Edwin von Manteuffel. Waldersee was the leading proponent of preventive war; he had little trust in the military strength of Austro-Hungary and wanted to strike before Czarist Russia and republican France overcame their qualms and entered into a formal alliance. Just as he successfully used the institution of the military attaché as a political weapon in pursuing his foreign policy objectives, he sought internally to prepare his ascendancy through the propaganda efforts of the conservative publisher of the *Kreuzzeitung,* Baron von Hammerstein, and his close ally the Court Preacher Adolf Stöcker. At the "Waldersee assembly" in late November 1887 Prince Wilhelm seemingly gave his public blessing to their efforts.[140]

The Court Preacher stood out as the symbolic representative of the coming new force in a public mind not privy to backstage intrigues and perplexed by vague talk of a German-Slav war. "Berlin is in a warlike mood now and yet I do not know exactly why, for there does not seem to be any real reason for a general war," a military advisor wrote the ailing Crown Prince.[141] Amid this confused uneasiness, Nietzsche became preoccupied with Stöcker's rhetorical revival of the "Christian state" ideal which had been so formative in his own childhood development. Since Stöcker had refrained from interjecting himself and his anti-Semitic cause into the recent election out of "patriotic" considerations (and deference to his superiors), his prominence six months later suddenly revived what had seemed a fading cause of anti-Semitism.[142] Nietzsche had wanted to believe that anti-Semitic energies could be deflected as in the case of his brother-in-law's colonial endeavors; the court's promotion of the religious right now seemingly brought the Court Preacher backdoor access to power. Aware that Schmeitzner had sought several years before to reconcile Stöcker to Nietzsche's works, Nietzsche now expressed his disgust at the proximity of "the court preacher-canaille" to the highest circles.[143]

"With immodest Protestantism, the Court Preacher, and the anti-Semitic speculators" reasserting themselves in the succession crisis, the pathos of the "Christian state" crept back into politics for the first time since its expulsion in Nietzsche's youth.[144] An alarmed Nietzsche imagined himself responding with "A tractatus politicus" which would explicate "the politics of virtue" from the standpoint of Machiavellianism as "perfection in politics."[145] Memories of his own youthful repudiation of religious politics were made more vivid by renewed contacts with his Schulpforta friends, Deussen and Gersdorff. Deussen, the leading Indologist and scholarly cosmopolite, visited him in September with a "somewhat Jewish" wife, while the weary, liberal-conservative Gersdorff thanked Nietzsche for having helped "cure" him of the anti-Semitism of his Wagnerian youth.[146] In January 1888 with Stöcker publicly exulting that "the old Progressives were dying out," and that the young had entered the ranks of the Christian-Social "movement," Gersdorff served in the ceremonial retinue of the Empress Augusta, complaining to Nietzsche afterward of the foul politicization of all public life in which one was rendered "suspect" if one detached oneself from politics without making, at least, some profession of faith in "practical Christianity."[147] Nietzsche, for his part, was convinced that the dynasty was flirting with disaster, for "what has hurt the court more than the Court Preacher?"[148]

Nietzsche welcomed the attack on his works in the *antisemitische Correspondenz,* although he conceded in December 1887 that it may have "come ten years too late."[149] He now recognized that "nothing stands more in the way of my influence than for the name Nietzsche to be associated with such anti-Semites as E. Dühring."[150] The growing number of negative reviews of his last two works was a sign to him that he was becoming again an "influence" in Germany. While such characterizations as "pathological," "psychiatric," and especially "eccentric" rankled, he felt confident that the new support heralded by Brandes would help him make clear to those "gentlemen" exactly where he and his thought was "centered."[151]

Nietzsche felt unusually buoyant during his last winter season in France. He accepted an "empty," rainy Nice with a habitué's nonchalance and took a native's pride in a city sprucing up after a devastating earthquake.[152] He had nothing but praise for his twenty-five fellow guests and patients with whom he shared meals; he dreamed of winning big in the local lottery.[153] The festive was again in the forefront of his mind. After failing to entice Köselitz on a common journey to Corsica, Nietzsche held out the prospect of upcoming music festivals in Bologna and Stuttgart; he himself indulged his passion for Italian and French music by going to a Monte Carlo concert which was also attended by the Emperor of Brazil.[154] He lauded the festivities surrounding a congress of astronomers underwritten by a Jewish philanthropist as a commendable expression of "Jewish luxury in the great style."[155] He laughed when his mother wrote that he seemed to be living the life of a count.[156] His outsider's world was filling with new relevance. His table companion, a Baroness Plāncker, relative of a key figure in the Crown Prince's entourage in San Remo, gave him an insider's view of the unfolding tragedy when the ugly quarrel between the Prince's English and German doctors over the appropriate cure became public in the weeks preceding the March 9 death of Wilhelm I.[157]

A Franco-Italian customs war, felt most immediately and acutely in the border town of Nice, fittingly climaxed that winter's fascination with the interplay of Italian and French cultures. In April he crossed over to the old Piedmontese capital of Turin and was delighted to find himself at home in its austere, aristocratic, seventeenth-century setting. He established his presence by making contacts through the large trilingual bookstore, taking daily strolls in the palace gardens, and settling in the city center near imposing governmental structures. The city, while no longer the capital, had retained the military high command, and the mix of officers and university students encountered everywhere on the streets and the cafés appealed to Nietzsche's new polemical mood. Turin was also an unusually apt location to vicariously experience the 99-day reign of the speechless Emperor, Friedrich III, ruling uneasily in Potsdam.

Historians have grown impatient with the "what if" associated with Friedrich's name.[158] Yet this "what if" was also his one significant political achievement; not that the discouraged sovereign believed himself capable of changing Germany's course. Already in 1882 he had felt that "the young are reactionary through and through and against Bismarck nothing can be done"; that even if he could rule on his own his own son would soon enough reverse everything; and that it might thus be better to abdicate upon his father's death so as to ensure continuity.[159] While he lacked the sterner, if unlovely, stuff of his English wife, he, too, finally chose to play out his symbolic role on his faltering throne by addressing his people in a liberal vein, by decorating a Jewish Minister, and by dismissing Minister Puttkamer, the architect of the internal reaction. He thereby bequeathed German liberalism a final, mournful legend.

The dynastic gerontocracy of the eighties, the sense of stagnation and the vogue of celebratory politics, had made a fetish of power. Power had seemingly become alienated from its object; paralyzed, it had to be activated, "willed," striven after. Apparently absent in the present, it entered the imagination as a desideratum but one coupled to a guiltily desired catastrophe. The death of the father—be it as "the death of God" or as the theory of the Oedipus Complex (then germinating in the mind of the young Freud)—was viewed as the great turning point in universal or personal history. The drama of the doomed Crown Prince thus played directly to the heart of that decade. It transcended national lines; it seemingly beckoned in

England where a bored, philandering Edward waited with an unbalanced Duke of Clarence behind him; in the spring of 1888 it got top billing in the theater of European politics; it was acted out again with melodramatic flourish by Rudolf in Mayerling six months later.

The tragedy of Friedrich III was excruciatingly drawn out. Daily press bulletins, the visit of Queen Victoria, added to the drama, while the obvious impatience of the heir apparent and the Anglophobic calumnies directed at the Empress Victoria aroused apprehensions for the future. Bismarck, the old opponent, was moved to say, "The poor Emperor is worthy of tears not only from the human point of view but from that of politics as well. His death will be a misfortune. It is always bad when a link is missing in the dynastic chain."[160] Bismarck spoke with the belated concern of an elder generation which had just buried its own symbolic exemplar. Meanwhile Wilhelm II acted with the impetuosity of youth clamoring for a new dawn. The middle generation, symbolically skipped in its prime, mourned the most by mourning themselves as the now missing generation of German history. George Meredith composed an ode to the dead Emperor. Nietzsche, by then in Sils, wrote Köselitz, "The death of Emperor Friedrich moved me; in the end he was a little shimmering light of free thought, the last hope for Germany. Now begins the regiment of Stöcker; I am drawing the consequences and know already that my "Will to Power" will now be confiscated in Germany."[161]

Nietzsche's relation to his fatherland had hitherto resembled that of the obedient son turned defiant. His political "eccentricities" still mirrored the pathos of an age group which had long seemed out of place, and which now had no center. Bismarck, his onetime hero, had become for Nietzsche as for Friedrich another obstacle in his path. Nietzsche's adult life was one long flight from the patriarchal politics of the Reich. Only in the ninety-nine days did his shrillness moderate. Aware of his own ascendancy, he ceased to court the old and remained cool to the overtures from the young. Since the early spring he wrote with new expressionistic freedom and authority; the time had come to make the definitive polemic against Wagnerianism and to enunciate the twilight of the old. No wonder that in June 1888, on the verge of writing what he believed would be his masterpiece, "The Will to Power," Nietzsche suspected that the new regime of Wilhelm II was out to cheat him of his fame and influence.

Nietzsche's reaction was to outflank the Reich by actively recruiting potential English, French, and Italian translators for his future works. He mobilized his new Swiss ally, Spitteler, and correctly divined that *The Case of Wagner* would be a *succès de scandale*. His anathemas came from on high but with a new biting urgency and timeliness. He was no longer the exile looking in critically from afar, no longer the heir awaiting his moment;

nor was he content to be "everywhere ... discovered; but not in the shallows of Europe, Germany."[162] Aristocratic pride and autocratic sense of self dictated the tone of his final, frantic six months.

With the publication of his "declaration of war" on Wagner, Nietzsche sought to impose the force of his personality directly upon contemporary German culture. His countrymen were to hear his low opinion of the spirituality of Imperial Germany. He put off work on his planned master-piece whose working title was now "The Revaluation of all Values." The brief vita he had written for Brandes in the spring was expanded into an extraordinarily provocative autobiography, *Ecce Homo.* He hastily wrote *Nietzsche contra Wagner* to correct the impression that he had just broken with Bayreuth. *Twilight of the Idols* flowed from his pen as effortlessly as *The Antichrist* which he saw testing the limits of the Reich's censorship laws. The rhetoric of war, of military virtue quickened the pace of his polemical onslaught.

His "counter-movement" was launched at a moment of great political uncertainty. The Bismarckian era had in effect come to an end; the true succession crisis, the struggle to replace Bismarck, was already at hand; and Nietzsche, sensing the mood, henceforth treated the Chancellor as a mere fixture in the new obscurantist order. During the summer Nietzsche viewed the new Emperor with patronizing disdain and was delighted to hear of the public uproar caused by Brandes when the Danish critic expressed his reservations about the volubly anti-Jewish Wilhelm II, then sailing about the Baltic.[163] Nietzsche could not resist trumping the Christian anti-Semites by asserting the Jewishness of Christianity, the ingrained subversive and anti-imperial character of Christianity, and the inferiority of both "slave reli-gions" to the aristocratic Aryanism of the Brahmins—attitudes which played into the hands of irreligious racism.[164] *The Book of Manu,* which he had discovered in Turin that spring, had become his codex of the higher morality by the time he returned in the fall.

Nietzsche saw himself attacking the Wagnerian "movement at its peak," as "recently the young German Emperor described the whole affair as a national matter of the first importance, and placed himself at the head of it—reasons enough for permitting oneself to move into battle."[165] But when Wilhelm II permitted traditional conservative spokesmen to express his distance to the "Waldersee Assembly" of the year before, Nietzsche's atti-tude softened. He now found the young sovereign more appealing: "virtu-ally every week he takes steps to show that he does not want to be confused with either the *Kreuzzeitung* or the *Antisemiterei.*"[166] Gersdorff wrote hope-fully that the "young, fiery Caesar" was showing signs of becoming cured of his Wagnerian "sickness."[167]

Nietzsche briefly assumed the pose of tutor by including thinly veiled passages addressed to the twenty-nine-year-old leader.[168] It was an attitude to which the German professoriat was particularly prone and never, perhaps, more than at this moment. Nietzsche's father and Max Heinze, Nietzsche's former teacher and colleague, as well as Hans Delbrück, Nietzsche's Berlin admirer, had all once played similar roles. It was a conceit which reflected Nietzsche's sense that a new literary generation was about to become his captive audience. Wilhelm's anger at the publication of his father's wartime diary and the prosecution of the elderly Professor Geffcken which followed soon shattered that illusion. It was an ugly episode, displaying Wilhelm's immaturity and rancor toward his mother and dead father. "The repulsive conflict over the grave of the poor martyr Friedrich III" revolted Malwida and many others.[169] Seeing the new regime in its most squalid light rekindled Nietzsche's fear that his works would be suppressed in the Reich. The Geffcken case was on his mind to the end, demonstrating, or so he thought, that the Reich was built on a tissue of lies.[170]

Fancy was now merging ever more with fantasy, criticism with the sense of direct involvement and control. He acted as a man taking charge of destiny, flinging in the face of those who slighted his importance the fact that he was "the foremost mind of the century" (as in his note to Hans von Bülow on October 9).[171] It was a gesture he now allowed himself, he explained to Köselitz.[172] In November he wrote Brandes that once his polemics were completed he would turn to his main task and "that in two years we shall have the whole earth in convulsions. I am a man of destiny."[173] Politics was no longer a province closed and foreign to him; his antipolitics had become receptive and suggestive, reacting to every passing political event. Returning to a Turin absorbed in regal pomp, Nietzsche became obsessed with the festive happenings of the House of Savoy. He arrived just after the Duke d'Aosta, formerly King of Spain, married Princess Laetita Buonaparte, "our new lady of Turin."[174] In November he mourned the death of Count Robilant—foreign minister the year before and "actually also a son of King Carlo Alberto"—as the loss of "a premier for whom people had been waiting with impatience—and whom nobody can replace." The death of Eugene, Prince of Savoy-Carignano, had him awaiting another "great funeral" in December.

As his anti-German campaign reached its crescendo, Nietzsche reveled in his incognito, writing Overbeck that "nobody yet has taken me for a German."[175] His "Polishness," once a sentimental conceit, took on, like everything he now touched, a politicized meaning. Since Bismarck's decision in 1885 to pursue a policy of forced evacuation and resettlement of Poles in Prussia's eastern provinces, German-Polish relations had sunk to a new low point; hence all the more reason to flaunt his ethnic solidarity with the new enemies of the Reich.[176] Ever more sensitive to the shifting focus of public concern, Nietzsche also shared the sudden anxiety and fascination with the criminal. That autumn Jack the Ripper had terrorized London, and the Parisian paper Nietzsche avidly read was filled with similar lurid crimes. If the buffoon had accompanied the prophet within him, so now the criminal followed in the footsteps of the figure of the potentate forming in his mind. The great literary prize to which he now aspired was the charge of lèse majesté; only then could he be sure that his blows had struck home. The vision of *grosse Politik,* once intended to provide prophetic detachment, now became one with the imminent catastrophe about to engulf him.

His war of words became synonymous with a war of deeds. With all Europe nervously awaiting Boulanger's *coup d'état,* Nietzsche made his own move against the Reich. At Christmas he concluded the preface of *Nietzsche contra Wagner* by admonishing Crispi to no longer pursue the Italian alliance with Germany as it could only result as a "mésalliance."[177] On December 28 Overbeck received a letter declaring:

> I myself am working on a memorandum for the courts of Europe, with an anti-German league in view. I mean to sew up the Reich in an iron shirt and to provoke it to a war of desperation. I shall not have my hands free until I have the young Emperor, and all his appurtenances, in my hands.[178]

His final notebook of December-January begins with the section *"Die Grosse Politik."* Here he repeated that he was bringing war not between peoples but between the ascendant and the descendant, between the will to power and the spirit of revenge and resentment. *Grosse Politik* was to make physiology the mistress of human thought and values. He called for a "party of life, strong enough for *grosse Politik*," able to make an end of all the parasitic and ill-formed.[179] "Reichs" and "Triple Alliances" were now to him mere "houses of cards" to be brushed aside; he envisaged the founding of "organizations everywhere in order to give me at the right moment millions of followers."[180] It was essential to win over "officers and Jewish bankers" as "both represent together the will to power."[181] (On December 9 he had written Köselitz that he needed "all of Jewish high finance for my international movement.")[182] The notebook then ends with a furious section entitled "War to the Death to the House of Hohenzollern" in which he pours out his scorn for the dynasty with the single exception of "the unforgettable Friedrich the Third, the most hated, most libeled of the whole race."[183] Bismarck appears as a mere "instrument," "the Idiot par excellence among all statesmen."[184] He stigmatized the "criminal insanity" of dynastic and priestly institutions. With the old God abolished and Europe arming herself for destruction, he declared himself ready "to rule the world."[185] The line, "insofar as I annihilate the Hohenzollern, I annihilate the lie," concluded the notebook.[186]

By now he was addressing epistles to the King of Italy, the secretary of the Vatican, the House of Baden. He drew up a manifesto calling upon the Poles to rise as their liberator, Nietzky, was here. Strindberg received a note declaring, "I have ordered a convocation of princes in Rome—I mean to have the young emperor shot." It was signed "Nietzsche Caesar."[187] Overbeck was informed, "I am having all the anti-Semites shot."[188] His self-identifications multiplied; he was Dionysus and the Crucified; he was Herzen; he identified himself with recently convicted Parisian criminals and with de Lesseps in his final rambling letter to Burckhardt. But his wild mind always revolved back to his central political passion—his long submerged, lifelong connection with the House of Hohenzollern. He again recalls his imperial coeval in his final letter: "I too was crucified at great length last year by the German doctors. Wilhelm Bismarck and all the anti-Semites done away with."[189] Nietzsche would come full circle in madness, announcing to an attendant after he was institutionalized that he, Nietzsche, was Friedrich Wilhelm IV.[190]

CHAPTER SEVEN

The Defeatist

NIETZSCHE ENDED AS an enemy of the Reich, as the first defeatist of the German nation-state. Such defeatism was the flip-side of the new militarism that had come of age in Nietzsche's youth. This militarism promoted a domesticated vision of war, a humanized carnage, for the wars of the 1860s had bolstered national currencies and epitomized liberal expansiveness. In contrast, pacifism—its ostensible opponent—seemed anemic, carping, and mean-spirited. Defeatism cut closer to the bone by accepting the either/or of militarism—either giving battle or shameful capitulation—and opting for the latter. Like militarism, defeatism assumed the primacy of foreign policy. Nietzsche concurred with the militarist spirit of his age. He thought in terms of struggle and contradiction, promoted the ideal of martial valor in times of peace, and equated pacifism with powerlessness and harmony. Nietzsche was, Vagts pointed out, "a representative of the still rather new phenomenon—the militaristic civilian—who preached the 'Will to Power,' a politicization if not militarization of Schopenhauer's 'Will to Live.' "[1]

After the failure of revolution in 1848, politicization came to Germany as militarization in the war of 1866. Militarism substituted for political discourse. Pacifism fell outside the political spectrum, unable or unwilling to marshall a mass following. Nor was it ever really at home in the nineteenth century. Pacifism thought in Enlightenment terms of social and cosmopolitan bonds, of juridicial contracts and harmonizing reason. During the first great European war scare, when revolution was upstaged by war or the threat of war, even the pacifists failed to project a threatening image of war. The most terrifying aspect of Bertha von Suttner's classic pacifist novel of 1888, *Lay Down Your Arms!* is not the depiction of war itself which remains relatively benign, but rather the bloodthirsty mob welcoming its arrival. Nietzsche's fearful portrait of the stampeding "herd" trampling the solitary man reflects the uneasiness with which the "people" were viewed in the deadlocked immobility of the eighties.

The urban demonstrations of the late eighties had a wild, unpredictable quality quite unlike the disciplined proletarian parades of the nineties or even the organized insurrections of the seventies. Le Bon's bleak mass psychology of the "crowd" captures the fear which developed during the Boulangist agitation. The border town of Nice where Nietzsche spent his winters, peripheral as it was, nevertheless had been drawn into the political passions convulsing France. With the economic monoculture ruined by phylloxera, Mediterranean France was undergoing a novel and profound politicization, with radicalism everywhere ascendant after 1885.[2] The new political phenomenon of the 1880s, the interplay of the urban crowd and would-be leader, revived a Bonapartism which liberals had once hoped lay buried at Sedan. Stimulated by Stendhal, Nietzsche plunged into the latest Napoleonic literature which the Bonapartist revival was offering the public. Nietzsche's walks on the quays of Nice revived the Napoleonic legend his grandmother had recounted in his childhood. Nietzsche's cult of the superior man was in keeping with the spirit of a decade that could no longer believe in the liberal dream of the gradual creation of an enlightened public opinion guided by the educated element in society and which had not yet seen the emergence of a self-conscious European avant-garde. He made endless, unfullfilled plans to cross over to Corsica, imagining himself resuming Goethe's fight on behalf of the Corsican. "How easily you become for a moment a little part of your own tremendous notion of Napoleon," Kafka once remarked after reading Bonaparte.[3]

Nietzsche's Caesaristic critique of democracy prompted his furious polemic against "the four great democrats"—Socrates, Christ, Luther, and Rousseau.[4] It was due to their influence that the "highest human beings," their freedom of will, and the strongest instincts of life were falsified and belittled. Against them he ranged Heraclitus, Machiavelli, Voltaire, or the great activists, Alexander, Caesar, Muhammed, and Napoleon. World history was made to hinge on their implicit or explicit quarrels; the Reformation was pitted against the Renaissance, and the clash between Voltaire and Rousseau was seen determining the character of the nineteenth century. Against the deflating leveling of a "democratic epoch," he upheld those types envisaging the "elevation of man"—the hero, the prophet, the Caesar, savior, and shepherd.

Nietzsche's distrust of the popular will extended to the popular leader, thereby complicating, compromising, and ultimately undermining his own Caesaristic affirmations. He commended Taine for offering a "kind of explanation and solution to that immense problem of the inhuman and the superhuman" embodied in Napoleon. Taine responded that those two

German words *"Unmensch* and *Übermensch"* perfectly captured the meaning of his essay on Napoleon.[5] Nietzsche had recognized "the antecedent form of *every* Caesar" was to be found in the demagogic, revolutionary conspirator Catiline; that the sense of freedom is most intense when the anti-motif is most active in overcoming resistance; and that the habitat of the Caesar is "five steps from tyranny, near the threshold of the danger of servitude."[6] He consequently lauded Caesar's "maximum of authority and discipline toward himself" as this was the necessary self-protection "against the extreme vulnerability of that subtle machine working at the highest pressure which is called genius."[7] Nietzsche's youthful cult of genius, long subject to intense self-criticism, finally reemerged in a troubled psychological Caesarism that bound into one the tyrant and the rebel. "Almost every genius knows, as one of the phases of his development, the "'Catilinarian existence,' a feeling of hatred, revengefulness, and revolt against everything which already *is*, which is no longer *becoming.* . . ."[8]

George Brandes had characterized Nietzsche's position as "aristocratic radicalism," with Nietzsche responding by calling the designation "the shrewdest remark that I have read about myself till now."[9] Brandes also considered himself to be an aristocratic radical, writing that "Caesarism, hatred of pedantry, and admiration of Beyle [Stendhal]" were the three issues most closely linking him with Nietzsche.[10] Thus Brandes's dismay when he read Nietzsche praising Shakespeare for having become Brutus' accomplice, for having prostrated himself "before the whole figure and virtue of Brutus."[11] Brandes demurred, *Julius Caesar* was a *"Majestätsverbrechen,"* a crime against the sovereign, glorifying "a miserable fellow who could do nothing else but stick a knife into a great man."[12] Nietzsche had, however, been long fascinated with the conspiracy which had brought "a Stoic and an Epicurean" in league against the all-powerful leader;[13] Nietzsche's anti-motif was too active for him to remain content with a Carlylean hero worship; and his own repudiation of his one-time father figure and mentor, Richard Wagner, necessarily fostered a Brutus complex within him.

In Nietzsche's mental world of slaves and tyrants, the Brutus-like figure offered the antidote to the personified dominance of a Wagner in the arts or a Bismarck in politics. The noble rebel, vainly evoking lost aristocratic arcadias, played to Nietzsche's pathos of being the "last" to resist the pretensions of imperial politics. The would-be intellectual dictator was also the frantic literary conspirator seeking to puncture Wagner's inflated fame. He struggled to reject the disciplehood which militarism had imposed on himself and his generation: Wagner's triumph had meant Nietzsche's subservience; 'Nietzsche contra Wagner' was his response. In rallying a countermovement, he praised his anti-Wagnerian precursors: "Among us Germans" such resistance to the composer "cannot be esteemed too highly or honored too much. He was resisted like a sickness—not with reasons—one does not refute a sickness—but with inhibition, mistrust, vexation and disgust, with a gloomy seriousness, as if he respresented some creeping danger."[14]

Nietzsche can be said to have played out his Brutus-like role vis-à-vis the Meister, to have fallen on his pen like Brutus on his sword, by rendering the composer a "case study" of the preceding generation's illusions, contributing to the Wagner legend—albeit negatively. Yet Nietzsche's antipolitics reflects neither Brutus's nobility nor Caesar's authority. Brutus looked backward, Caesar forward; Nietzsche's antipolitics was an imprisoning perception of the politics of his time. What he offered was neither restoration nor affirmation but a prophetic verdict on the existing power constellation. Exasperation was his final impetus.

The new public spectacle of imperial greatness demanded by pseudo-democratization contravened and denied the "tragic" and elitist element so important to Nietzsche's initial cultural program. The triumphalism of the Founding Era, its worship of victory, challenged Nietzsche's neo-Hellenic cultural revival. Rather than enlivening the arts, a great victory posed a great danger, Nietzsche was warning by 1873. As informer of the hollowness of victory, pronouncing a prophetic verdict on the destruction of a mighty political system, Nietzsche placed himself beyond the frontier of his generation. Nietzsche's defeatism began as the disbelief in the promise of victory and would end during the late 1880s as an anticipation of the great crisis of World War I.

Rather than being disassociated from time and place, Nietzsche was emblematic of the second self-conscious generation in German history: a proud but failed generation whose youthful expectations of the sixties had met frustration in the eighties and oblivion with the death of Friedrich III. The new doctrine of the Oedipus Complex cast these sons of mid-century and fathers of the century's end into the role of the archetypal father, one who was alarmingly ineffective yet disturbingly proud and wooden. Nietzsche was quickly lost to his generation. Historically unmoored, the post-humous contemporary became a key arsenal against his age group in the revived generational ideologies of the 1890s. Already in Hermann Conradi's 1889 brochure, "Wilhelm II and the Young Generation," Nietzsche's stylistic influence was integral to the would-be avant-garde message.[15] Turning his back on the bedside of dying emperors, Conradi asserted a new political and aesthetic role for those born between 1855 and 1865. Nietzsche was the one member of the older generation made prominent in the essay, with bits and pieces of his writing strewn here and there. Nietzsche's impact was too sudden, too contradictory, and too international to be swallowed whole; his thought was employed unsystematically, leading to a myriad of dilutions.

Precisely because Nietzsche was so difficult to grasp, so multitudinous, his interpreters have also inevitably sought to capture *their* Nietzsche by highlighting some personified analogy, be it a Caesar, a Faust, or a Hamlet. Shaw's *Man and Superman* captured the spirit of the turn of the century. His anarchistic Nietzschean is the figure of the erotic revolution, the witty, self-styled "Don Juan of Knowledge" of the aphoristic years now dutifully enrolled in the war between the sexes. The Nietzsche reception deflected the negativity of Nietzsche's antipolitics. By 1900 the problem of "Nietzsche contra Wagner" seemed less vital than the desire to absorb both as "founding fathers" of a new cultural revival.

During World War I, the apocalyptic, over-lucid mood of Nietzsche's final year became relevant, all-too-relevant. No longer the playful cavalier, within Germany the new Nietzsche was the tablet-breaking prophet striking at the rickety architecture of the Reich. Nietzsche's following grew and became politicized with Nietzscheanism dividing into Left and Right factions. The *Aktivists* of the antiwar Left used the posthumous Nietzsche as a spur and a catalyst; wartime censorship and more importantly their own frenetic pace rendered fragmentary their explication of Nietzsche's antipolitics. Defeat in war and revolution prompted a postwar, interwar Nietzsche of the Right, the mythic Caesar of the George Circle, the brutal fascistic Nietzsche of the *Decisionists* and the Nazis. Nietzsche's rejection of the Second Reich was now understood in Hegelian terms as anticipation of a Third Reich. Similarly, the uprooting of Nietzsche as a precursor of fascist aestheticism became for Lukács and his generation on the left an embittering verdict on the Nietzscheanism of their youth.

With the fall of the German nation-state, Nietzsche hovered between banishment and ahistorical restoration. Heidegger and others sought to salvage a Nietzsche-as-Zarathustra, guilty perhaps of "biologism," but nevertheless a solitary Existentialist sage, aloof from time and place. Since the Zarathustra figure focused on the camouflaged politics of an "unpolitical" philosophy, it could not address the polemical Nietzsche seeking, not hiding, from the flow of historical time. Thomas Mann's *Doctor Faustus* addressed the issue more acutely when he placed his Nietzsche-like protagonist, Adrian Leverkuhn (born 1885, mad 1933, dead 1940), squarely in the center of the German problem and in the ranks of Mann's own generation. But as antidote and afterthought, Mann restored Nietzsche to his actual age group in "Nietzsche in the Light of Recent History," arguing that Nietzsche was profoundly unpolitical, and suggesting that he be cast in a "Hamlet role."

Hamlet's burning consciousness of the politics of the moment makes him more of a personified metaphor of Nietzsche's antipolitics than, for instance, the cavalier individualism of a Don Juan, or the secret, self-destructive pact of a Faust. The latter are in flight from native realms; the antipolitical is, however, a willful, interjective mode of discourse. The overt crisis of 1888 provoked Nietzsche to call himself antipolitical, articulating the motivating supposition on which his inner world was constructed. Not evasion but the dangerous imperatives of his counter-statement trapped him into succumbing to the spell of his apocalyptic thesis and dark intuitions, until the oracle in prose became the megalomaniac in sickness.

There is among Shakespeare's characters one who speaks more directly than Hamlet to the interplay between Nietzsche's anti-motif and Bismarckian politics: Coriolanus, the man of pride in revolt against his origins who fell in his last futile campaign against the Reich. He, too, was no callow youth but the apostate, full of renounced ambitions, defeated hopes. Hamlet takes center stage as *deus ex machina* of his political world, while Nietzsche, like Coriolanus, is a figure offstage, whirling in clandestine persistence against the imperial order that has banished him. As renegades once sharing native errors, once preaching inflammatory stupidities, they strove to adjure real or imaginary fatherlands. Through scorn, ridicule, mockery, and denunciation they moved from protest to betrayal of the new national Gods, seeking to annihilate in themselves the last reflex of the citizen by overt acts of treason.

Coriolanus was the Shakespearean protagonist who spoke most directly to Bismarck. The Iron Chancellor was fascinated by the patrician rebel who abhorred the banner of homogeneity and scorned the dotage of the many—attitudes thinly veiled, or veiled not at all, in the architect of the Reich, who had come into power and remained there through the manipulation of the chastened crowd. But Coriolanus also represented the final option of playing the counter-revolutionary undoing the system from outside. Nietzsche never mentioned Coriolanus; nor would the drama of narcissistic detachment and self-destructive betrayal have recommended itself to Nietzsche's worried psyche. But Coriolanus' futile treason has a resonance in the pathway to Nietzsche's final separation in madness. And more importantly, Coriolanus' aristocratic revolt seems to speak to Nietzsche's crushing verdict against his nation-state.

The first to feel remorse for the once vital hopes that had spurred his intellectual generation, he was the first to unmask false victory. The philosopher of the great deflation that followed the victory of 1870/71, he was the skeptic who admonished and would strip bare what soon became a depressed peace. By divorcing himself from imperial society, by seeking to exist without political roots, Nietzsche was driven to exploit his own rages and frustrations. His antipolitics were an exegesis of failure: the Reich failed

German culture by weakening and perverting its existence. Nietzsche denied creativity its home within the Reich, and the imperial academe ostracized him as "impossible." Nietzsche traded the delusions of victory for the unsociable truth that the failure of the Reich was at hand. "There is much in Nietzsche," Kenneth Burke observed, "to indicate that his maladjustments arose from his searching perception of issues which were wholly unnoted by his more 'fit' contemporaries. Is it a sign of 'weakness' to see with such intensity that one can disclose 'conflicts' and encounter 'defeats' where hackmen find nothing?"[16]

In Nietzsche's final proud frenzy, full of cocky assurance and bitter exhaustion, he came to resemble a noontime Diogenes with a lantern—searching futilely for enlightenment during the false zenith of the German nation-state. Like Diogenes the Cynic, Nietzsche was stateless, everywhere alien, without home and without hope for the reigning political system.[17] Cynicism presumed the end, the failure of the polis; defeatism projected the collapse of latter-day empire. By Christmas 1914 Nietzsche's defeatism was no longer a recapitulation of the succession crisis of Bismarckian Germany as insinuated by its most over-lucid mind. It had become the creed of the avant-garde, one step ahead of the public. With triumphalism in retreat, defeatism became a treasonous liberation. In France *defeatisme* became a crime; revolutionary defeatism became the new tactic of the Bolsheviki; in Germany anti-war defeatism pointed to a structural flaw inherent in the Reich's formation.

Encapsulated by victory bulletins, censorship, and spy-haunted paranoia, Central European defeatism before defeat was antipolitical in Nietzsche's sense: isolated courage led to a species of withdrawal, a withdrawal not from history but within it. The prophetic awareness of the catastrophe hanging over the Reich spurred the antiwar *Aktivismus* of the Left Nietzscheans. Paramount were exposure, rejection of disciplehood, and defiance of social controls opposed to innovation. Defeatism was the fruit of experimentalism under acute pressure and was twisted with resentment. The cultural fruits of defeat—Weimar culture—were not to be enjoyed but sacrificed to the misery of suicidal hardness. The interwar defeatism of the *Decisionists*—the Right Nietzscheans—stripped experimentalism bare, leaving nihilism and a lynch mob mood.

Nietzscheanism was stood on its head: cultural flowering, political decline were traded for blood-soaked visions of victory. All of Nietzsche's Social Darwinian pomposities, racist asides, and other stupidities were plundered for meaning. Nietzsche's political defeatism was translated into cultural defeatism that paraded the virtue of neo-barbarism.

Two centuries before, the jurist Pufendorf had despaired of the many

Germanies of the Holy Roman Empire, calling the system a "monstrum";[18] Nietzsche had suspected the same of the Second Reich of the German nation-state. But just as Nietzsche found it impossible to think of Socrates without associating him with the fall of Athens, today "Silberblick," the former Nietzsche archive in Weimar, looks out across the valley to Buchenwald, and Nietzsche's megalomania seems the fitting epitaph for the monstrous system on its knees in 1944, the year of the Nietzsche Centennial.

NOTES

ABBREVIATIONS

BAB = Friedrich Nietzsche, *Briefe: Historisch-Kritische-Gesamtausgabe.* 4 volumes, Munich, 1938–1942.

BAW = Friedrich Nietzsche, *Werke. Historisch-Kritische-Gesamtausgabe,* 5 volumes, Munich, 1933–1940.

GB = Friedrich Nietzsche, *Gesammelte Briefe,* 5 volumes, Leipzig, 1907–1909.

KGB = Friedrich Nietzsche, *Briefwechsel. Kritische Gesamtausgabe,* edited by G. Colli and M. Montinari, 18 volumes, Berlin, 1975ff.

KGW = Friedrich Nietzsche, *Werke. Kritische Gesamtausgabe,* edited by G. Colli and M. Montinari, Berlin, 1967ff, approximately 30 volumes.

Mus.A = Friedrich Nietzsche, *Gesammelte Werke,* "Musarionausgabe," 23 volumes, Munich, 1920–1929.

SL = Friedrich Nietzsche, *Selected Letters of Friedrich Nietzsche,* edited by Christopher Middleton, Chicago, 1969.

1. THE ANTI-MOTIF

1. *Ecce Homo,* "Why I Am So Wise," #3.

2. The recent claim, "perhaps no opinion has been so generally accepted about Nietzsche as that he was 'anti-political,'" can easily be misconstrued, since a false consensus camouflages contradictory activist and quietist definitions. Tracy Strong, "Nietzsche and politics: parables of the shepherd and his herd," in Robert Solomon, ed., *Nietzsche* (Garden City, 1973), 258. Failure to come to grips with the concept of antipolitics has promoted an abstract and ahistorical discussion in Tracy Strong, *Friedrich Nietzsche and the Transfiguration of Politics* (Berkeley, 1975).

3. Walter Kaufmann, *Nietzsche. Philosopher, Psychologist, Antichrist* (New York, 1968), 418, 412. The ascendancy of this view prompted Henry David Aiken to characterize it as an interpretation which "has insisted with what looks to be admiration, that Nietzsche's philosophy is essentially apolitical. That in sum, is just the trouble with it." "An Introduction to Zarathustra," in Solomon, *Nietzsche,* 130.

4. *Europe in the Twentieth Century* (New York, 1972), 152.

5. *The Concept of Ideology* (New York, 1967), 235.

6. *Twilight of the Idols,* "The Problem of Socrates."

7. *The Rights of Man* (New York, 1961), 57.

8. Julius Froebel, *Die Gesichtspunkt und Aufgabe der Politik* (Leipzig, 1878; repr. Aalen, 1971), 340. Julius Froebel (1805–1893) was a son of a Thuringian pastor who as a professor of natural science in Zurich in the 1830s and 1840s emerged as a leading spokesman of resurgent radicalism. In 1848 he was elected delegate to the Frankfurt Parliament and was condemned to death with his fellow deputy Robert Blum for his participation in the Vienna Revolution in the fall of 1848. Unlike Blum he was pardoned, and he emigrated to the United States. Between 1859 and 1863 Froebel returned to German political life as the principal champion of a greater German position with the financial backing of the Austrian government. His aim was the creation of a supra-national federal state in Central Europe. After 1871 he made his peace with the Bismarckian system and was awarded a consulship in Algiers. He is primarily remembered for his cosmopolitan political vision and his sharp rejec-

tion of the "national swindle." On Froebel see his autobiography, *Ein Lebenslauf,* 2v. (Stuttgart, 1890–91); Hans Rosenberg, "Honoratiorenpolitiker und 'Grossdeutsche' Sammlungsbestrebungen im Reichgründungsjahrzehnt," *Jahrbuch für die Geschichte Mittel- und Ostdeutschland,* v.19 (1970), 155–233; Heinz Gollwitzer, *Europabild und Europagedanke* (Munich, 1964), 305–315; Wilhelm Mommsen, "Julius Froebel. Wirrnis und Weltsicht," *Historische Zeitschrift,* v.181 (1956), 497–532.

9. It is highly unlikely that Nietzsche ever came across Froebel's concept of antipolitics. Froebel had collaborated with Wagner in publishing a journal in Munich during the mid-1860s, and he was not one to underestimate the composer's possible impact on the body politic. He accused Wagner of seeking to reverse the secularization of art, of introducing "a political religion [that] was laced with a dogmatic chauvinism, more concerned with satisfying its cultish requirements than becoming more closely connected to the dramatic-pragmatic spirit of politics." *Die Gesichtspunkt und Aufgabe der Politik,* 341. As Froebel believed that Europe could only compete with Russia and America by creating a United States of Europe, he saw in Bayreuth's aesthetic chauvinism and nationalism a dangerous stumbling block to this goal.

10. *Culture and Anarchy* (Cambridge, 1957), 204.

11. *Twilight of the Idols,* "What the Germans Lack," #4 (Hollingdale trans.). Words with special, specific meanings, such as *Kulturstaat* and *Grosse Politik,* have been retained in the original.

12. *The Gay Science,* #31; *Beyond Good and Evil,* #251; *Human All-Too-Human,* v.1, #481.

13. *Human All-Too-Human,* v.1, #481.

14. Jacob Burckhardt, *Weltgeschichtliche Betrachtungen* (Pfullingen, 1949), 55–100. Nietzsche heard the lecture "Of the Three Potencies" in 1870/71.

15. The most notable case and the source of many errors is Thomas Mann, *Betrachtungen eines Unpolitischen* (Frankfurt/M., 1968 [1st ed., 1918]), 106, 181. Ironically Mann makes much use of the concept of antipolitics which he identified with a conservative and nationalist standpoint; "One feels oneself antipolitical insofar as one feels conservative-national(ist)," 196. His work concludes with the lame confession, "I do not know if the antipolitician is also a politician," 406. Fritz Stern also misquotes Nietzsche: "there was pride as well as truthfulness in his oft-repeated assertion that he was the last 'unpolitical German.'" *The Politics of Cultural Despair* (Berkeley, 1961), 285–286.

16. Irving L. Horowitz, ed., in his introduction to *The Anarchists* (New York, 1964), 15.

17. P. A. Kropotkin, *Selected Writings on Anarchism and Revolution* (Cambridge, Mass., 1970), 505. After quoting the Nietzsche passage on the conflict of culture and state, the anarchist Rudolf Rocker wrote that Nietzsche's "inner disharmony and his constant oscillation between outlived authoritarian concepts and truly libertarian ideas all his life prevented him from drawing the natural deductions from it." *Nationalism and Culture* (New York, 1937), 83.

18. This point has been insufficiently stressed. Kaufmann, for example, argues that both Nietzsche and Hegel "found a single word that epitomized their entire dialectic; and the two words, though not identical, have literally the same meaning. . . . Nietzsche's sublimation actually involves, no less than does Hegel's *aufheben,* a simultaneous preserving, canceling, and lifting up." *Nietzsche,* 236. But Nietzsche's use of the term sublimation hardly warrants the place which Kaufmann assigns to it. It neither approached Freud's usage nor rivaled the place which *aufheben* assumed in Hegel's work. Ernst Nolte's conception of "resistance to the transcendence" as the fundamental category of Nietzsche's thought seems more justified. *Three Faces of Fascism* (New York, 1966), 441, 446. One need not concur with Nolte's conclusion that such a viewpoint represents "the political ontology of fascism" to recognize that "resistance" rather than "sublimation" served as the

propelling agent of Nietzsche's dialectic. See the excellent study by Alfred Schmidt, *Zur Frage der Dialektik in Nietzsches Erkenntnistheorie* (Frankfurt/M., 1963).

19. *Ecce Homo,* "The Birth of Tragedy," #1.

20. Jackson Matthews, ed., *The Collected Works of Paul Valèry,* v.9 (Princeton, 1968), 339.

21. *Twilight of the Idols,* "Morality as Anti-Nature," #3 (Hollingdale trans.).

22. SL, 336 (12 XII 88).

23. *Beyond Good and Evil,* Part 3, #48 (Hollingdale trans.).

24. *Beyond Good and Evil,* Part 4, #76 (Kaufmann trans.).

25. Michael Hamburger, *Contraries. Studies in German Literature* (New York, 1970), 215. Hamburger adopts the Yeatsian expression "anti-self" which was itself a product of Yeats's period of Nietzschean enthusiasm.

26. Max Weber, *The Sociology of Religion* (Boston, 1964), 226.

27. Weber, *The Sociology of Religion,* 122, 126.

28. *Politics and Vision* (Boston, 1960), 414–419. For Wolin "the anti-political impulse was an old one, with roots deep in the very beginnings of political speculation," 414. He traces antipoliticism back from managerialism through Durkheim, Marx, Proudhon, St. Simon, Hobbes, and Luther to Plato's reaction to the Sophist postulation of the "political" as a definable field of study, 30–31, 109–111, 144, 280–281, 305, 361, 414–419. As Nietzsche's antipolitics has been seen leading to fascist irrationalism, so Plato's antipoliticism, his attempt to expel politics from his ideal polity, has been interpreted as the first idealization of the totalitarian state. Nietzsche and Plato's antipoliticism have been understood in diametrically opposite ways; Plato has been accused of seeking to purge conflict, Nietzsche of introducing new conflicts into the political realm. If as Wolin suggests, "the central weakness in Plato's philosophy lay in the failure to establish a satisfactory relationship between the idea of the *political* and the idea of *"politics,"* one can say the opposite of Nietzsche, that he failed to establish a nexus between the reality of politics and the idea of the political. See also the exchange between Wayne A. R. Leys, "Was Plato Non-Political?" and F. E. Sparsshott, "Plato as Anti-Political Thinker," in Gregory Vlastos, ed., *Plato. A Collection of Critical Essays,* v.2 (Garden City, 1971), 166–184.

29. *Politics and Vision,* 416.

30. *Politics and Vision,* 423. For two contrasting interpretations of the contemporary antipolitical impulse see John H. Bunzel, *Anti-politics in America* (New York, 1967), a critical account of the political radicalism of the 1960s and Jacques Ellul, *The Political Illusion* (New York, 1967).

31. *Richard Wagner in Bayreuth,* #10; SL, 330 (7 XII 80).

32. KGW, v.8:2, 185 (Kaufmann trans.).

33. *Human All-Too-Human,* v. 1, #481.

34. *Dawn,* #189.

35. KGB, v.3:1, 497 (21 IV 84).

36. Ecce Homo, "Why I Am a Destiny," #1.

37. Ecce Homo, "Why I Am a Destiny," #1.

38. Ecce Homo, "Why I Am So Wise," #3 (Kaufmann trans.).

39. KGW, v.8:3, 457–461.

40. *Die Boheme* (Stuttgart, 1968), 280.

41. Without entering the thorny problem of defining "Nietzscheanism," it is clear that the familiar distinction between "tough" and "tender" Nietzscheans which Crane Brinton introduced in *Nietzsche* (New York, 1965 [1st ed., 1941]), depoliticized the problem. The tough/tender continuum identified Nietzsche solely with the Right and trivialized the problem of the Left Nietzscheans. It deals only with the differences between the Fascist and Existentialist interpretations of Nietzsche and does not take into account the earlier political history of Nietzscheanism. But it was in the crisis of the Expressionist movement during World War I that the left-right

dichotomy first emerged. The contrasting politicization of Nietzsche is reflected in the quarrel between Heinrich and Thomas Mann with the former treating Nietzsche as *a politique et moraliste* and the latter seeking to restore the cultural trinity of Schopenhauer, Wagner and Nietzsche. In Kurt Hiller's *Aktivist* program Nietzsche's final apocalyptic mood was channeled in a revolutionary direction. While Thomas Mann had sought to salvage a conservative Nietzsche, one who opposed "politicization"; the *Decisionists,* in the aftermath of defeat and failed revolution, assimilated the politicized Nietzsche of the *Aktivists* into a counter-ideology of prophetic Caesarism. The political history of Nietzscheanism in Germany has yet to be written. Gisela Deesz, "Die Entwicklung des Nietzsche-Bildes in Deutschland" (diss., Würzburg, 1933), presents an uncritical survey, while George Lukács, *Die Zerstörung der Vernunft* (Berlin, 1955), writes a brilliant polemic which ignores (or discounts) the Left Nietzscheans.

42. *Human All-Too-Human,* v.2, "The Wanderer and His Shadow," #100.

2. THE CLERICAL SON

1. Quoted in Karl Barth, *Protestant Theology in the Nineteenth Century* (Valley Forge, 1973), 516. On the educational milieu in which Ludwig Nietzsche was trained see Hans Rosenberg, "Geistige und politische Strömungen an der Universität Halle in der ersten Hälfte des 19. Jahrhunderts," *Politische Denkströmungen im deutschen Vormärz* (Göttingen, 1972), 52–68.

2. Quoted in Richard Blunck, *Friedrich Nietzsche. Kindheit und Jugend* (Basel, 1953), 29.

3. See Robert M. Bigler, *The Politics of Protestantism. The Rise of the Protestant Church Elite in Prussia, 1815–1848* (Berkeley, 1972).

4. Adalbert Oehler, *Nietzsches Mutter* (Munich, 1941); Erich F. Podach, *Gestalten um Nietzsche* (Weimar, 1932), 7–32; *Der kranke Nietzsche. Briefe seiner Mutter an Franz Overbeck,* ed. Erich F. Podach (Vienna, 1937).

5. Erwin Rohde in his August 4, 1889 letter to Franz Overbeck in Ernst Staehlin, ed., *Overbeckiana, I. Teil, Die Korrespondenz Franz Overbecks* (Basel, 1962), 162.

6. August Langen, *Der Wortschatz des deutschen Pietismus* (Tübingen, 1968).

7. Carl Hinrichs, *Preussentum und Pietismus* (Göttingen, 1971); Hans Patze and Walter Schlesinger, eds., *Geschichte Thüringens,* v.4, *Kirche und Staat in der Neuzeit* (Cologne, 1971); Hartmut Lehmann, *Pietismus und weltliche Ordnung in Württemburg* (Stuttgart, 1969).

8. Quoted in Bigler, *The Politics of German Protestantism,* 50.

9. The publicist Jarcke, quoted in Hans Rosenberg, "Theologischer Rationalismus und vormärzlicher Vulgärliberalismus," *Politischer Denkströmungen,* 43.

10. R. Bohley, "Nietzsches Taufe. 'Was, meinst du, will aus diesem Kindlein werden?'" *Nietzsche-Studien,* v.9 (1980), 399.

11. Ludwig Feuerbach, *Kleine Schriften* (Frankfurt/M., 1966), 225.

12. BAW, v.1, 4; he also recalled the bivouacking of Hussar troops, BAW, v.1, 279.

13. *Ecce Homo,* "Why I Am So Wise," #3.

14. Elisabeth Förster-Nietzsche, *Der junge Nietzsche* (Leipzig, 1912), 18.

15. KGW, v.8:1, 293.

16. *Ecce Homo,* "Why I Am So Wise," #3 & #1.

17. BAW, v.1, 6.

18. BAW, v.1, 33.

19. BAW, v.1, 1.

20. BAW, v.1, 33; Ernst Borkowsky, *Naumburg a.d. S. Eine Geschichte deutschen Bürgertums, 1028 bis 1928* (Jena, 1928), 100.

21. KGW, v.4:1, 270, where Nietzsche in 1875 recalled: "Then on Neugasse [the new home], where I always heard father's warning voice."

22. Blunck, *FN*, 21–22; Elisabeth Förster-Nietzsche, *Der junge Nietzsche*, 4–7.

23. BAW, v.1, 7.

24. Hans Herzfeld, "Ernst Ludwig von Gerlach," *Mitteldeutscher Lebensbilder*, v.5 (Magdeburg, 1926), 275–298.

25. Hermann Niebour, "Die Abgeordneten des Provinz Sachsen in der Frankfurter Nationalversammlung," *Thüringisch-Sächsische Zeitschrift für Geschichte und Kunst*, v.4 (1914), 45–60; Kurt Wassermann and Fritz Hege, *Naumburg. Stadt und Dom* (Dresden, 1952), 28; Borkowsky, *Naumburg*, 45–60.

26. This was a general phenomenon; Mack Walker observes that "the political environment that had nourished the home town was destroyed between 1855 and 1870," and that "hometownsmen were most notable in the politics of the Second Reich for their absence." *German Home Towns; Community, State, and General Estate 1648–1871* (Ithaca, 1971), 405, 425.

27. Borkowsky, *Naumburg*, 100.

28. SL, 293 (10 IV 88).

29. After losing 48% of its population in the Thirty Years War, Naumburg did not equal its population of 1600 until the nineteenth century. Armgard Ritter, "Der Einfluss des Dreissigjahrigen Krieges auf die Stadt Naumburg," *Thüringisch-Sächsische Zeitschrift für Geschichte und Kunst*, v.15 (1926), 3–96.

30. *Human All-Too-Human*, v.2, "Mixed Maxims and Opinions," #324.

31. Hans Engel, *Musik in Thüringen* (Cologne, 1966).

32. He wrote, however, in the spirit of Enlightenment rationalism, receiving his doctorate in 1817 from the University of Königsberg when Erdmuthe's brother was Professor of theology there; Blunk, *FN*, 21–22.

33. *Ecce Homo*, "Why I Am So Wise," #3.

34. Particularly as the province of Saxony was still a source of irritation in Saxon-Prussian relations; the Prussian Ambassador in Munich, Freiherrn von Werthern, wrote in March 1877, "I believe that we will manage to get along tolerably with Bavaria, but not with Saxony. Saxony is the intellectual author of all resistance to the Reich, and since the annexed province—to which I have the honor of belonging—is always before its eyes . . . the hatred toward Prussia will become stronger rather than weaker." Hans Philippi, "Preussisch-sächsische Verstimmungen im Jahrzehnt nach der Reichsgründung," *Jahrbuch für die Geschichte Mittel- und Ostdeutschlands*, v.15 (1966), 225.

35. KGB, v.1:1, 308 (1852).

36. KGW, v.4:4, 350.

37. BAW, v.1, 8.

38. Oehler, *Nietzsches Mutter*, 66.

39. *Beyond Good and Evil*, #247.

40. Of the 765 poets listed in the *Allgemeine Deutsche Biographie* between 1525 and 1900 whose father's occupation was given, 195 were clerical sons and eight clerical daughters. Albrecht Schoene, *Säkularisation als sprachbildende Kraft. Studien zur Dichtung deutscher Pfarrersöhne* (Göttingen, 1958), 7–28.

41. KGW, v.5:1, 712 (1880).

42. BAW, v.1, 312–327, 333–337.

43. The genealogical tables are assembled in Max Oehler, *Nietzsches Ahnentafel* (Weimar, 1938).

44. KGB, v.1:1, 305 (1851) and 310 (1852).

45. BAW, v.1, 26 (1858).

46. KGB, v.1:1, 12 (1 XI 57).

47. See Eugene N. Anderson, *The Social and Political Conflict in Prussia, 1858–1864* (Lincoln, 1954).

48. On Peter see Ernst Weymar, *Das Selbstverständnis der Deutschen. Ein Bericht über den Geist des Geschichtsunterrichts des höheren Schulen im 19. Jahr-*

bundert (Stuttgart, 1961), 194–196; Hermann Peter, "Peter: Karl Ludwig," *Allgemeine Deutsche Biographie,* v.53 (1907), 21–23; Wilhelm Roessler, *Die Entstehung des modernen Erziehungswesens in Deutschland* (Stuttgart, 1961), discusses the peculiar ethos of the princely schools exemplified by Schulpforta, 109–115. See also Lenore O'Boyle, "Klassische Bildung und soziale Struktur in Deutschland zwischen 1800 und 1848," *Historische Zeitschrift,* v.207 (1968), 584–608.

49. The term "classical liberal" has distinguished liberal spokesmen of the 1850s and early 1860s from the "social liberals" of the 1840s who attacked the government for failing to solve the problems of pauperism and economic depression. With the economic expansion of the post-revolutionary period, classical liberals no longer needed or wanted to present a revolutionary challenge. The term is also used to differentiate the classical liberals from the "national liberals" who accommodated themselves to Bismarckian policies after 1866. Often, as in the case of the Saxon political leader, Karl Biedermann, in whose house Nietzsche would board in 1868, the progression from "social" to "classical" to "national" liberalism represented three phases in the same career. See Hans Rosenberg, *Rudolf Haym und die Anfänge des klassischen Liberalismus* (Munich & Berlin, 1933); Heinrich Heffter, *Die deutsche Selbstverwaltung im 19. Jahrhundert* (Stuttgart, 1950), 349– 372; D. G. Rohr, *The Origins of Social Liberalism in Germany* (Chicago, 1963); Karl Biedermann, *Mein Leben und ein Stück Zeitgeschichte,* 2v. (Breslau, 1886).

50. Matthew Arnold, *Higher Schools and Universities in Germany* (London, 1874), 130.

51. Arnold, *Higher Schools,* 131.

52. KGB, v.1:1, 50 (II 59).

53. KGB, v.1:1, 50 (II 59).

54. Paul Deussen's phrase, *Mein Leben* (Leipzig, 1922), 60–79; see also Ulrich von Wilamowitz-Möllendorff, *My Recollections, 1848–1914* (London, 1930), 66–94.

55. BAW, v.5, 252.

56. Quoted in Blunck, *FN,* 49; see also Reiner Bohley, "Über die Landesschule zu Pforta," *Nietzsche-Studien,* v.5, 298–320 (1976).

57. KGB, v.1:1, 53 (23 III 59).

58. KGB, v.1:1, 64 (V 59).

59. BAB, v.1, 355.

60. BAW, v.1, 116.

61. BAW, v.1, 115.

62. BAW, v.1, 116.

63. "Die Schiller-Feier der alten und neuen Welt" (Leipzig, 1860), 2. Cited in Alex Gehring, *Genie und Verehrergemeinde* (Bonn, 1968), 75. See also pp. 72–87, 96–114 for an analysis of the Schiller rhetoric of these years.

64. See Franz Schnabel, "Die Denkmalkunst und der Geist des 19. Jahrhunderts," *Abhandlungen und Vorträge, 1914–1965* (Basel, 1970), 134–150; Thomas Nipperdey, "Nationalidee und Nationaldenkmal im Deutschland im 19. Jahrhundert," *Historische Zeitschrift,* v.206 (1968), 529–585; on the role of symbolic politics see George L. Mosse, *The Nationalization of the Masses, Political Symbolism and Mass Movements in Germany from the Napoleonic Wars through the Third Reich* (New York, 1975); also Alice Freifeld, "The Chastened Crowd in Liberal Hungary" (forthcoming diss., University of California, Berkeley).

65. BAW, v.1, 152; the Pietist tradition had long been a source and stimulus to both the concept of Bildung and cultural nationalism. See Gerhard Kaiser, *Pietismus und Patriotismus in literarischen Deutschland* (Wiesbaden, 1961); Koppel Shub Pinson, *Pietism as a Factor in the Rise of German Nationalism* (New York, 1934); Hans Weil, *Die Enstehung des deutschen Bildungsprinzip* (Bonn, 1930); Rudolf Vierhaus, "Bildung" in O. Brunner, W. Conze, R. Kosselleck, eds., *Geschichtliche Grundbegriffe,* v.1 (Stuttgart, 1972).

66. BAW, v.1, 186 and 188.

67. Friedrich Heinrich Ranke, *Jugenderinnerungen mit Blicken auf das spätere Leben* (Stuttgart, 1886), 42–43.

68. KGB, v.1:1, 342.

69. KGB, v.1:1, (20 X 60).

70. Quoted in Fritz Fischer, *Moritz August von Bethmann-Hollweg und der Protestantismus* (Berlin, 1937), 227; see also Friedrich Wilhelm Kantzenbach, "Zur geistig-religiösen Situation der christlichen Konfessionen zwischen 1850 und 1860," *Zeitschrift für Religions- und Geistesgeschichte,* v.18 (1966), 193–219.

71. Goethe-Schiller Archiv, Nietzsche papers, #361.8.

72. Blunck, *FN,* 62.

73. KGB, v.1:1, 97.

74. KGB, v.1:1, 97.

75. KGB, v.1:1, 137 (14 I 61) and 349.

76. Carl Spitteler, *Autobiographische Schriften* (Zurich, 1947), 175.

77. Heinrich Wilh. Rob. Buddensieg, "Gedächtnisspredigt für Se. Maj. Friedrich Wilhelm IV am Sonntage Invocavit 1861," *Erinnerungen an Heinrich Wilh. Rob. Buddensieg* (Eckartsberga, 1861), 38.

78. KGB, v.1:1, 141–148 (I–III 61).

79. KGB, v.1:1, 350 and 352.

80. BAW, v.1, 280.

81. Deussen, *Mein Leben,* 70.

82. BAW, v.1, 135–243 (24 III 61).

83. Goethe-Schiller Archiv, Nietzsche papers, #361.8. The complaints were also repeated in reports of 1863 and 1864 (#361.8).

84. KGB, v.1:1, 188.

85. KGB, v.1:1, 278 (20 IV 64).

86. Deussen, *Mein Leben,* 68.

87. Paul Deussen, *Meine Erinnerungen an Friedrich Nietzsche* (Leipzig, 1901), 20.

88. KGB, v.1:3, 44–45; Blunck, *FN,* 114–117.

89. KGB, v.3:1, 326 (10 II 83).

90. KGB, v.3:1, 256 (9 IX 82).

91. Hans Rosenberg, ed., *Ausgewählte Briefwechsel Rudolf Hayms* (Berlin, 1930), 23.

92. Karl Kupisch, *Vom Pietismus zum Kommunismus. Zur Jugendentwicklung von Friedrich Engels* (Berlin, 1953).

93. Quoted in Walter Nigg, *Franz Overbeck. Versuch einer Würdigung* (Munich, 1931), 67.

94. A decade earlier another Norwegian friend called him a "disguised Pietist." Quoted in the preface by Mary Sandbach in her edition of August Strindberg, *Getting Married* (New York, 1972), 13.

95. Michael Hamburger, *Contraries* (New York, 1970) 203–235.

96. Friedrich Paulsen, *An Autobiography* (New York, 1938), 39; nowhere was this trend more marked than in the birthplace of the Reformation, Patze and Schlesinger, *Geschichte Thüringens,* v.4, 44.

3. THE GENERATION OF 1866

1. For example, Theodor Schieder, "Nietzsche und Bismarck," *Historische Zeitschrift,* v.196 (1963), 320–342, fails to probe the real tensions between the two men.

2. Adolf Silberstein, *Im Strome der Zeit,* v.3 (Budapest, 1895), 128–129.

3. Goethe-Schiller Archiv, Nietzsche papers, #361.8.

4. KGB, v.1:1, 183 (21 X 61).

5. BAW, v.2, 434. The précis was dated "January 13, 1862, the day of the opening of the legislature."

6. Mus A, v.1, 65.

7. KGB, v.1:1, 194 (11 I 62).

8. KGB, v.1:1, 194 (11 I 62).

9. BAW, v.2, 4.

10. BAW, v.2, 430.

11. BAW, v.2, 23.

12. "Studien zur römischen Geschichte mit besonderer Beziehung auf Th. Mommsen," *Einladungsprogram zu der 23 Mai 1861 stattfinden Stiftungsfeier der Königlichen Landesschule Pforta* (Naumburg a/S, 1861), 1–68.

13. Wilhelm Dilthey, *Gesammelte Werke,* v.11, 221.

14. H.-U. Wehler, ed., *Grundsätze der Realpolitik* (Frankfurt/M., 1972); see H. Gollwitzer, "Der Cäsarismus Napoleons III im Widerhall der öffentlichen Meinung Deutschlands," *Historische Zeitschrift,* v. 173 (1952), 23–75.

15. BAW, v.2, 28, 23.

16. BAW, v.2, 28, 23.

17. BAW, v.2, 28, 23.

18. BAW, v.2, 90.

19. KGB, v.1:1, 386–387; Paul Deussen, *Mein Leben* (Leipzig, 1922), 69–73.

20. KGB, v.1:1, 388, 390–391.

21. KGB, v.1:1, 388, 390–391. Of the 16 expulsions between 1862 and 1864 most were for drinking and visiting the forbidden taverns. Goethe-Schiller Archive, Nietzsche papers, #361.8.

22. KGB, v.1:1, 237 (16 IV 63).

23. See Walter Reichle, *Zwischen Staat und Kirche. Das Leben und Wirken des preussischen Kulturministers Heinrich v. Mühler* (Berlin, 1938).

24. Goethe-Schiller Archiv, Nietzsche papers, #361.8. Report of September 3, 1863.

25. This was the high water mark of the school's oppositional stance. A conservative reaction soon set in within the school itself, with one teacher supposedly declaring that "for years Pforta had delivered the state only atheists, democrats, or drunkards." KGB, v.1:3, 199 (26 III 67). In Gersdorff's same letter he consoled Nietzsche with the thought that they had, at least, experienced the "setting sun" of the school's greatness.

26. BAW, v.2, 193–200.

27. BAW, v.2, 170.

28. KGB, v.1:1, 268–269 (6 XII 63).

29. Paul Deussen, *Mein Leben,* 79.

30. KGB, v.1:1, 277 (20 IV 64).

31. G. Bocke, *Vom Niederrhein ins Baltenland. Erlebnisse und Beobachtungen eines deutschen Schulmeisters* (Hannover, 1925), 18.

32. KGB, v.1:2, 143 (12 VII 66).

33. BAW, v.3, 74.

34. BAW, v.3, 64–66.

35. KGB, v.1:2, 65 (VI 65).

36. KGB, v.1:2, 26 (XII 64).

37. KGB, v.1:2, 54 (25 V 65).

38. KGB, v.1:2, 15 (24/25 X 64); Dilthey, *Gesammelte Werke,* v. 11, 222; Friedrich Meinecke, "Treitschke und die deutsche Burschenschaft" (1914), *Zur Geschichte der Geschichtsbeschreibung* (Munich, 1968), 187–205.

39. *Die Aufgabe und Stellung der heutigen Burschenschaft. Eine Festgabe zum funfzigjährigen Burschenschaftsjubilaum* (Jena, 1865), 9.

40. Friedrich Paulsen, *An Autobiography* (New York, 1938), 172.

41. Rudolf Eucken, *His Life Work and Travels. By Himself* (London, 1921), 40.

42. See Hermann Haupt and Paul Wentzcke, eds., *Hundert Jahre Deutscher Burschenschaft* (Heidelberg, 1921), 218–256.

43. *Die Aufgabe und Stellung der heutigen Burschenschaft* (Jena, 1865), 10.

44. O. F. Scheuer, *Friedrich Nietzsche als Student* (Bonn, 1923), 16–47.

45. BAW, v.3, 78.

46. BAW, v.3, 81.

47. BAW, v.3, 90.

48. Scheuer, 36–37.

49. KGB, v.1:2, 66 (VI 65).

50. KGB, v.1:2, 18 (10–17 XI 64).

51. See Hellmut Seier, "Sybels Vorlesung über Politik und die Kontinuität des 'staatsbildenden' Liberalismus," *Historische Zeitschrift,* v.187, (1959), 90–112.

52. KGB, v.1:2, 18 (10–17 XI 64).

53. Otto Ribbeck, *Friedrich Wilhelm Ritschl,* v. 2 (Leipzig, 1881), 332–381.

54. Norbert Andernach, *Der Einfluss der Parteien auf das Hochschulwesen in Preussen, 1848–1919* (Göttingen, 1972), 37–40.

55. Paul Egon Hübinger, "Heinrich v. Sybel und der Bonner Philologenkrieg," *Historisches Jahrbuch,* v.83 (1964), 162–216.

56. BAW, v.3, 291.

57. KGB, v.1:2, 61–64, 66–67 (VI 65). Heinrich von Sybel, "Am Denkmal Arndt's in Bonn," *Vorträge und Aufsätze* (Berlin, 1874), 267–276; for the mood of the time, see J. Droz, *L'opinion publique dans la Province Rhénane a cours du conflict austro-prussien 1864–1866, Rheinisches Archiv,* v.22 (Bonn, 1932). Nietzsche registered his praise for Sybel's speech in a letter to Gersdorff on 4 VIII 65, KGB, v. 1:2, 76.

58. KGB, v.1:2, 74 (10 VII 65).

59. BAW, v.3, 294; KGB v.1:2, 79–80 (30 VIII 65).

60. KGB, v.1:2, 88.

61. BAW, v.3, 292; Goethe-Schiller Archiv, Nietzsche papers, #341.8.

62. BAW, v.3, 294.

63. Roscher, a founder of the "historical" school of political economy, had a negative influence on Nietzsche's interest in economics, although Roscher's son was a central member of Nietzsche's student philological circle. KGB, v.1:2, 257 (16 II 68).

64. KGB, v.1:2, 326 (18 X 68).

65. BAW, v.3, 298.

66. KGB, v.1:2, 121 (7 IV 66).

67. BAW, v.3, 295.

68. I.e., Wilhelm I. KGB, v.1:2, 109 (31 I 66).

69. Robert Weber, *Geschichte des klassisch-philogischen Vereines zu Leipzig von 1865–1890* (Leipzig, n.d.), 4.

70. Goethe-Schiller Archiv, Nietzsche papers, #2807.

71. By the mid-seventies the organization had lost its creative edge, becoming a more typical reading circle. By the late eighties it had become a social club, almost indistinguishable from other fraternities. Weber, *Geschichte des klassisch-philogischen Vereines* (Leipzig, n.d.), 11–13.

72. On Rohde see Otto Crusius, *Erwin Rohde. Ein biographischer Versuch* (Tübingen, 1902); Ernst Seillière, *Nietzsches Waffenbruder, Erwin Rohde* (Berlin, 1911).

73. "Hueffer was a rather bulky but not a tall man, of very Teutonic physiognomy . . . a believer in Schopenhauer; and, though not a melancholy person in his ordinary demeanor, had a certain tinge of hypochondria in his outlook on life." *Some Reminiscences of William Michael Rossetti,* v.2 (London, 1906), 332–333. Hueffer

was the father of the novelist Ford Maddox Ford; see also Max Moser, *Richard Wagner in der englischen Literatur des XIX. Jahrhunderts* (Diss., Bern, 1938), 10, 15, 18, 29–30, 54.

74. KGB, v.1:2, 128 (27 V 66).

75. *Human All-Too-Human,* v.2, #271.

76. *Bilder aus dem Geistigen Leben unserer Zeit,* v.1 (Leipzig, 1870), 1–41; Wilhelm Scherer responded a few weeks later affirming this analysis in his own article, "Die neue Generation," reprinted in *Geist und Gesellschaft der Bismarckzeit, 1870–1890,* ed. Karl Heinrich Höfele (Göttingen, 1967), 335–339; K. Rosenkranz, *Hegel als deutscher Nationalphilosoph* (Leipzig, 1870), regretfully concluded that Schopenhauer's popularity was a sign that contemporaries had grown tired of philosophizing, pp. 270–281; on the depoliticization of philosophy in the Bismarckian era, see Hermann Lübbe, *Politische Philosophie in Deutschland* (Basel, 1963).

77. Quoted in J. P. Stern, *Re-interpretations* (London, 1964), 191.

78. KGB, v.1:2, 134–135 (VII 66).

79. KGB, v.2, 58 (VII 66).

80. KGB, v.1:2, 136 (VII 66); KGB, v.1:2, 126 (IV 66).

81. KGB, v.1:2, 140 (11 VII 66).

82. KGB, v.1:2, 138 (5 VII 66).

83. KGB, v.1:2, 140–141 (12 VII 66).

84. KGB, v.1:2, 144 (12 VII 66).

85. KGB, v.1:2, 150 (15 VIII 66). See Richard Dietrich, "Der Kampf um das Schicksal Sachsens in der öffentlichen Meinung 1866/67," *Neues Archiv für Sächsische Geschichte und Altertumskunde,* v.58 (1937), 202–222; Hellmut Kretzschmar, "Das Sächsische Königtum im 19. Jahrhundert," *Historische Zeitschrift,* v.170 (1950), 470–493; Hans Blum's *Lebenserinnerungen,* v.1 (Berlin, 1907), 256–272, recounts how the son of the principal martyr of 1848 became one of Leipzig's leading partisans of Treitschke and Bismarck in 1866/67.

86. KGB, v.1:2, 138 (VI 66).

87. KGB, v.1:2, 143 (12 VII 66).

88. KGB, v.1:2, 143 (13 VII 66).

89. KGB, v.1:2, 178 (31 X 66); KGB, v.1:2, 198–200 (20 II 67); KGB, v.1:2, 181 (XI 66). The election proved a disaster for greater German populism as well, Joachim Müller, "Der Historiker Johann Heinrich Wuttke als Politiker," *Karl-Marx-Universität Leipzig, 1409–1959,* v.1 (Leipzig, 1959), 341. Dietrich, "Der Kampf um das Schicksal Sachsens. . . ," 215–222; Hans Philippi, "Preussisch-sächsische Verstimmungen im Jahrzehnt nach der Reichsgründung," *Jahrbuch für die Geschichte Mittel- und Ostdeutschlands,* v.15 (1966), 225–268, discusses the tenacity of anti-Prussian sentiment which lasted well into the 1870s; further details in Fritz Dickmann, "Bismarck und Sachsen zur Zeit des Norddeutschen Bundes," *Neues Archiv für Sächsische Geschichte,* v.49 (1928), 255–288.

90. Heinrich von Treitschke, *Heinrich von Treitschkes Briefe,* ed. Max Cornicelius, v.3 (Leipzig, 1920), 48 (17 VII 66).

91. The liberal journalist Julius v. Eckardt decades later recalled the excited mood of the pro-Prussian young in Leipzig in these months: "Never in my life have I breathed fresher, more envigorating air than that which blew through the north in the late fall of 1866. National feeling generated a more powerful and prouder current in 1870, when an electric charge went through the world carrying with it all resistance. Yet the more moderate, all absorbing warmth of the political temperature of the fall, 1866 had a quiet magic which cannot be compared to any other. One stood at the threshold of a new period, an epoch which still promised miracles." *Lebenserinnerungen,* v.1 (Leipzig, 1910), 56–57; Karl-Georg Faber, "Realpolitik als Ideologie. Die Bedeutung des Jahres 1866 für das politische Denken in Deutschland," *Historische Zeitschrift,* v.203 (1966), 1–45.

92. Gustav Freytag, *Reminiscences of My Life,* v.2 (London, 1890), 151.

93. Quoted in Walter Bussmann, *Treitschke, Sein Welt- und Geschichtsbild,* (Göttingen, 1952) 387; Walter Bussmann, "Gustav Freytag, Massstäbe seiner Kulturkritik," *Archiv für Kulturgeschichte,* v.34 (1952), 261–287.

94. BAW, v.4, 213.

95. The list included Haupt, Lahers, Bergk, Mommsen. KGB, v.1:2, 284 (2 VI 68).

96. KGB, v.1:2, 316 (IX 68).

97. KGB, v.2:2, 67 (23 X 69); KGB, v.2:2, 112 (1 I 70); Paul Deussen, "Wie ich zu Schopenhauer kam," *Erstes Jahrbuch der Schopenhauer Gesellschaft* (Kiel, 1912).

98. *Philosophische Monatsheft,* v.14 (1878), 32; Arthur Schopenhauer, *The World as Will and Idea,* v.1 (London, 1957), 461; see also A. Leslie Wilson, *A Mythical Image: The Ideal of India in German Romanticism* (Durham, 1964).

99. KGB, v.1:2, 158 (16 II 68); 211 (6 IV 67).

100. KGB, v.1:2, 211 (6 IV 67).

101. "Philosophy in Germany," *Mind,* v.2 (1877), 503.

102. Alexander Dru, *The Letters of Jacob Burckhardt* (New York, 1955), 122 (16 III 56).

103. See Gustav Mayer, *Johann Baptist von Schweitzer und die Sozialdemokratie* (Jena, 1909), 32–45.

104. Karl Marx, *Das Kapital,* v.1 (Berlin, G.D.R., 1962), 27 (Nachwort zur zweiten Auflage, 1873).

105. Frederick Engels, *Ludwig Feuerbach and the Outcome of Classical German Philosophy* (New York, 1970), 9.

106. *Beyond Good and Evil,* #204 (Kaufmann trans.).

107. See William J. Brazill, *The Young Hegelians* (New Haven, 1970); Albert Levy, "Stirner et Nietzsche" (Diss., Paris, 1904), demonstrated that Nietzsche had read Stirner in Basel and that he was anxious not to be confused with him; cf. R.W.K. Paterson, *The Nihilistic Egoist Max Stirner* (Hull, 1971).

108. KGB, v.1:2, 83 (IX 65).

109. BAB, v.2, 258–259 (27 X 68).

110. Karl Birker, *Die Deutschen Arbeiterbildungsvereine, 1840–1870* (Berlin, 1973), 126, 171–172; Gerhard Albrecht, "Der junge Schmoller und die Arbeiterfrage," *Schmollers Jahrbuch,* v.79 (1959), 1–20.

111. As elsewhere, the Leipzig student body was recruited primarily from the *Bildungsbürgertum,* 46% of Leipzig students in the six years prior to Nietzsche's arrival were the sons of higher officials, jurists, professors, teachers, clergymen and doctors. Franz Eulenberg, *Die Entwicklung der Universität Leipzig in den letzten hundert Jahren* (Leipzig, 1909), 205.

112. BAW, v.3, 301.

113. BAW, v.3, 301.

114. BAB, v.3, 388 (journal of W. Wisser 12 & 19 XII 66).

115. KGB, v.1:2, 199 (20 II 67).

116. KGB, v.1:2, 257 (16 II 68).

117. KGB, v.1:2, 257 (16 II 68).

118. Quoted in Gustav Mayer, "Die Trennung der proletarischen von der bürgerlichen Demokratie in Deutschland, 1863–1870," *Radikalismus, Sozialismus und bürgerliche Demokratie,* H.-U. Wehler, ed. (Frankfurt/M, 1968), 175.

119. Dawn, #176 (J. M. Kennedy trans.).

120. See Manfred Riedel, *Wandel des Generationsproblems in der modernen Gesellschaft* (Düsseldorf, 1969); Juan Marias, *Generations,* (University, 1972); Herbert Butterfield, "The Discontinuities between the Generations in History," *The Rede Lecture 1971* (Cambridge, 1972); Lewis Feuer, *The Conflict of Generations* (New York, 1969); Karl Mannheim, "The Problem of Generations," *Essays on the Sociology of Knowledge* (London, 1952), 276–320.

121. *The Eighteenth Brumaire of Louis Bonaparte,* 2nd paragraph.

122. See Eugenii Lampert, *Sons against Fathers; Studies in Russian Radicalism and Revolution* (Oxford, 1965). The literary theme of generational conflict was posed most starkly in Russia but also in England, less so in Germany. George Meredith's *The Ordeal of Richard Feverel. The Story of Father and Son* (1859) and Matthew Arnold's poem "Sohrab and Rustum," dealing with slaying of son by father, were followed by the retrospective accounts of Samuel Butler's *The Way of All Flesh* (1882–1904) and Edmund Gosse's autobiography, *Father and Son* (1907). In German the theme was most evident in historical reflections such as Wilhelm Kiesselbach's "Drei Generationen," *Socialpolitische Studien* (Stuttgart, 1862), 193–249, or in the disillusioned tradition of the *Bildungsroman* as exemplified in Gottfried Keller's *The Green Henry* and *Martin Salander* (1886). On the young Freud's early fascination with the problem see Heinz Politzer, *Hatte Oedipus einen Oedipus-Komplex?* (Munich, 1974).

123. Gustav Rümelin, "Über den Begriff und die Dauer einer Generation," *Reden und Aufsätze,* v.1 (Freiburg, 1875); Friedrich Meinecke, "Ranke in der Auffassung von Ottokar von Lorenz und die Generationslehre," (1891), *Zur Geschichte der Geschichtsschreibung* (Munich, 1968), 41–49; Wilhelm Dilthey, "Die Generation von 1830," *Gesammelte Schriften,* v.11 (Stuttgart, 1960), 219–220; Wilhelm Dilthey, "Über das Studium der Geschichte der Wissenschaften von Menschen, der Gesellschaft und dem Staat" (1875), *Gesammelte Schriften,* v.5 (Stuttgart, 1957); Dilthey first developed the generational concept in his 1865 essay on Novalis, see Detlev W. Schuhmann, "Cultural Age-Groups in German Thought," PMLA, v.51 (1936) 1180–1207.

124. *Human All-Too-Human,* v.2, "The Wanderer and His Shadow," #216.

125. Karl Löwith, *From Hegel to Nietzsche* (New York, 1964).

126. Alfred North Whitehead, *Science and the Modern World* (New York, 1960), 96.

127. KGW, v.8:1, 205–206, 293; KGW, v.8:2, 261, 361; KGW, v.8:3, 208.

128. *Hartmann, Dühring, und Lange* (Iserlohn, 1876), 2, 206; Adalbert von Hanstein, *Das jüngste Deutschland* (Leipzig, 1905).

129. See Friedrich Meinecke, "Drei Generationen deutscher Gelehrtenpolitik," *Historische Zeitschrift,* v.125 (1922), 248–283; Richard Hamann, "Die Heroisierung des Schlichten und die jüngere Generation der 70er Jahre," *Die deutsche Malerei im 19. Jahrhundert* (Leipzig, 1914), 231–244; Carlton J. H. Hayes, *A Generation of Materialism, 1871–1900,* (New York, 1941).

4. THE SPECTACLE OF GREATNESS

1. Quoted in Otto Pflanze, *Bismarck and the Development of Germany, 1815–1871* (Princeton, 1963), 417; Elisabeth Fehrenbach, *Wandlungen des deutschen Kaisergedankens 1871–1918* (Munich, 1969), 14–88.

2. KGB, v.1:2, 218 (27 V–3 VI 67); KGB, v.1:3, 202–203 (23 V 67).

3. KGB, v.1:2, 210 (6 IV 67).

4. BAW, v.3, 230–244.

5. *Philosophy in the Tragic Age of the Greeks,* #5 (M. Cowan trans.).

6. "Homer's Contest," last sentence; BAW, v.3, 230–244.

7. *The Crown of Wild Olive* (London, 1906), 116, 210.

8. *Greek Studies* (London, 1901), 281, 270, 279, 295.

9. See Karl Griewank, "Wissenschaft und Kunst in der Politik Kaiser Wilhelms I. und Bismarcks," *Archiv für Kulturgeschichte,* v.34 (1952), 302–307.

10. *Psyche. Seelenkult und Unsterblichkeitsglaube,* (Leipzig, n.d.), 16–17, 80–81, 250–251.

11. *Re-interpretations* (London, 1964), 173.

12. KGW, v.7:2, 59.

13. Quoted in George Rapall Noyes, *Tolstoy* (New York, 1968 [1st ed., 1918]), 139.

14. KGB, v.1:2, 311 (21 VIII 68).

15. KGB, v.1:2, 239 (24 XI–1 XII 67).

16. Throughout his philological career, Ernst Windisch (1844–1918) promoted the now discredited theory that Greek tragedy influenced Indian drama; see Johannes Hertel, "Nekrolog auf Ernst Windisch," *Berichte über die Verhandlungen der Sächsischen Akademie der Wissenschaften. Philogisch-historische Klasse*, v.73 (1921), 9–24.

17. KGB, v.1:2, 225–226 (4 X 67).

18. KGB, v.1:2, 247 (1–3 II 68).

19. KGB, v.1:2, 258 (16 II 68).

20. Otto Ribbeck, *Ein Bild seines Leben aus seinem Briefen 1846–1898* (Stuttgart, 1901), 234 (2 II 65).

21. KGB, v.1:2, 4 (27 IX 64).

22. KGB, v.1:2, 133–134 (VI 66).

23. See Friedrich Schulze, *Hundert Jahre Leipziger Stadttheater,* (Leipzig, 1917), 161–201; Georg Hermann Müller, *Das Stadt-Theater zu Leipzig von 1. Januar 1862 bis 1. September 1887* (Leipzig, 1887).

24. See Frederick R. Love, *Young Nietzsche and the Wagnerian Experience* (Chapel Hill, 1963), 31–36.

25. BAW, v.3, 303–304.

26. *Young Nietzsche and the Wagnerian Experience,* 80.

27. Richard Wagner, *Mein Leben,* v.1 (Munich, 1969), 48.

28. See Jack M. Stein, *Richard Wagner and the Synthesis of the Arts* (Detroit, 1960); Carl Dahlhaus, *Wagners Konzeption des musikalischen Dramas* (Regensburg, 1971).

29. See Lore Lucas, *Die Festspiel-Idee Richard Wagners,* (Regensburg, 1973).

30. Wagner, *Mein Leben,* v.1, 381–382, 388.

31. See Wilhelm Widmann, *Theater und Revolution* (Berlin, 1920), 59–124.

32. *Correspondence of Wagner and Liszt,* ed. W. Ashton Ellis, v.1 (New York, 1973), 25 (5 VI 49). The letters were translated by Nietzsche's Leipzig friend, Francis Hueffer.

33. Lucas, *Die Festspiel-Idee,* 39 (letter of 12 XI 51).

34. *Correspondence of Wagner and Liszt,* v.1, 32 (19 VI 49).

35. Theo Gantner, *Der Festumzug. Ein volkskundlicher Beitrag zum Festwesen des 19. Jahrhunderts in der Schweiz* (Basel, 1970) 25.

36. Wilfrid Blunt, *The Dream King. Ludwig II of Bavaria* (New York, 1970); Hans-Josef Irmen, "Richard Wagner und die öffentliche Meinung in München bis zur Uraufführung des Tristan," in Carl Dahlhaus, ed., *Richard Wagner. Werk und Wirkung* (Regensburg, 1971), 127–146.

37. Robert W. Gutman, *Richard Wagner, The Man, His Mind, and His Music* (New York, 1968), 241.

38. "What Is German?" *Richard Wagner's Prose Works,* ed. William Ashton Ellis, v.4 (London, 1895), 166–167.

39. "A Music School for Munich," *Wagner's Prose Works,* v.4, 222.

40. Blunt, *The Dream King,* 6.

41. See Lucas, *Die Festspiel-Idee,* 47.

42. Hermann Baumgarten, *Der deutsche Liberalismus. Eine Selbstkritik* (1866), ed. Adolf M. Birke (Frankfurt/M., 1974), 116.

43. KGB, v.1:2, 240 (24 XI-1 XII 67).

44. KGB, v.1:2, 322 (8 X 68).

45. KGB, v.1:2, 322 (27 X 68).

46. KGB, v.1:2, 322 (8 X 68).

47. KGB, v.1:2, 331 (27 X 68).

48. KGB, v.1:2, 336 (9 XI 68).

49. KGB, v.1:2, 373 (II 69).

50. KGB, v.1:2, 341 (9 XI 68).

51. KGB, v.1:2, 352–353 (9 XII 68).

52. KGB, v.1:2, 346 (25 XI 68).

53. See Eduard Vischer, *Wilhelm Vischer. Gelehrter und Ratsherr, 1808–1874* (Basel, 1958), 118–128; Johannes Stoux, *Nietzsches Professur in Basel* (Jena, 1928), 15–55.

54. KGB, v.1:2, 323 (8 X 68).

55. Goethe-Schiller Archive, Nietzsche papers, #2807.

56. KGB, v.1:2, 381 (7 III 69).

57. BAW, v.5, "Homer und die klassische Philologie," 283–305; Walter Bussmann, "Gustav Freytag. Massstäbe seiner Zeitkritik," *Archiv für Kulturgeschichte,* v.34 (1952), 270–272.

58. BAW, v.2, 319 (10 V 69).

59. Jacob Burckhardt, *Briefe,* v.5 (Basel, 1963), 105 (20 VII 70) was the first such usage in his letters.

60. Emil Durr, *Jacob Burckhardt als Politischer Publizist. Mit seinem Zeitungsberichten aus dem Jahre 1844/5* (Zurich, 1937) 43–56.

61. "Gedächtnisrede auf Schiller," in *Kulturgeschichtliche Vorträge* (Stuttgart, 1959), 35–41.

62. *The Civilization of the Renaissance in Italy,* v.2 (New York, 1958), 401, 353.

63. *The Civilization of the Renaissance in Italy,* v.2, 401.

64. M. Gregor-Dellin and D. Mack, eds., *Cosima Wagner's Diaries* v.1, *1869–1877* (New York, 1976), 96.

65. *Cosima Wagner's Diaries,* v.1, 103–104, 148, 162, 177; for these dates see Curt Paul Janz, *Die Briefe Friedrich Nietzsche* (Zurich, 1972), 162–171.

66. Ludwig August von Rochau, *Grundsätze der Realpolitik,* part 2 (1869), H.-U. Wehler, ed. (Frankfurt/M., 1972), 230–231.

67. Courbet, who attended, remarked: "In Germany good painting is all but unknown. There they are completely caught up in the negativity of art; one of the most important things in their eyes is perspective. The whole day is spent talking about it . . . Painting is approaching the anecdotal." Quoted in Alfred Langer, *Wilhelm Leibl* (Leipzig, 1961), 24; on the general problem see Gert Schiff, "Teutons in Togas," in *Academic Art,* Thomas B. Hess and John Ashbery, eds. (New York, 1971), 51–84.

68. Julian Schmidt, "Richard Wagner, 25 März 1869," *Bilder aus dem geistigen Leben unserer Zeit,* v.2 (Leipzig, 1871), 417.

69. August Bebel, *Ausgewählte Reden und Schriften,* v.1 (Berlin, G.D.R., 1970), 40, 666; Erich Gruner, "Die Schweiz als Schauplatz internationaler Macht- und Prinzipienkämpfe in der ersten Internationale," *Historische Zeitschrift,* v.204, 305–322.

70. Johann Jakob Bachofen, *Gesammelte Werke,* v.10, *Briefe* (Basel, 1967), 433.

71. Karl Marx–Friedrich Engels, *Werke,* v.16 (Berlin, G.D.R., 1973), 370, 371, 372.

72. See Martin Schaffner, *Die Basler Arbeiterbevölkerung im 19. Jahrhundert* (Basel, 1972).

73. BAB, v.2, 368 (28 IX 69).

74. See Martin Vogel, *Apollinisch und Dionysisch. Geschichte eines genialen Irrtums* (Regensburg, 1966), 69–148.

75. KGW, v.3:2 ("Die dionysische Weltanschauung"), 48, 47, 80, 55.

76. KGW, v.3:2, 48.

77. See Max L. Baeumer, "Nietzsche and the Tradition of the Dionysian," in *Studies in Nietzsche and the Classical Tradition,* ed. James C. O'Flaherty (Chapel Hill, 1976), 165–189.

78. KGW, v.3:2, 9–13.

79. KGW, v.3:2, 6.

80. KGW, v.3:2, 22.

81. KGW, v.3:3, 296; KGW, v.3:2, 25–41.

82. *Twilight of the Idols,* "The Problem of Socrates," #8.

83. KGW, v.8:3, 69.

84. *Die Briefe Cosima Wagners an Friedrich Nietzsche,* ed. Erhart Thierbach, v.1 (Nietzsche Archiv, 1938), 27 (5 II 1870).

85. BAW, v.1, 254–255.

86. Sung to the satisfaction of Pastor Friedrich von Bodelschwingh, who discerned "a special judgment of God on Frankfurt" and "its Jewish money-aristocracy." *Ausgewählte Schriften* (Bielefeld, 1955), 267.

87. BAW, v. 4, 304.

88. *The Gay Science,* #99.

89. Cited in Gutman, *Richard Wagner,* 135.

90. KGB, v. 2, 320 (22 V 69).

91. *Die Briefe Cosima Wagners an Friedrich Nietzsche,* v.1, 28 (5 II 70).

92. See Martin Vogel, "Nietzsche und die Bayreuther Blätter," *Beiträge zur Geschichte der Muskikkritik,* ed. Heinz Becker (Regensburg, 1965), 55–68.

93. *Die Briefe Cosima Wagners an Friedrich Nietzsche,* v.1, 52 (24 VI 70).

94. BAB, v.3, 62 (19 VII 70).

95. *Cosima Wagner's Diaries,* v.1, 245.

96. *Cosima Wagner's Diaries,* v.1, 246.

97. Paul Deussen, *Erinnerungen an Friedrich Nietzsche* (Leipzig, 1901), 78.

98. KGB, v.2:2, 237 (9 VIII 70).

99. BAB, v.3, 62 (19 VII 70).

100. BAB, v.3, 67 (20 VIII 70).

101. BAB, v.3, 88 (23 XI 70).

102. KGB, v.2:2, 249 (10 X 70).

103. August Ebrard, *Bericht des Erlanger Vereins für Felddiakonie über seine Tätigkeit im Kriege 1870/71* (Erlangen, 1871).

104. On Mosengel (1837–1885) see Friedrich von Boetticher, *Malerwerke des Neunzehnten Jahrhunderts,* v.2 (Leipzig, 1901), 79–82; Richard Voss, the novelist, recounts his experiences as a medical volunteer. *Aus einem phantastischen Leben* (Stuttgart, 1920), 41–60; for Nietzsche's brief wartime journal see KGW, v.3:3, 89–93.

105. Gustav Freytag, *Auf der Höhe der Vogesen . . . Kriegsberichte von 1870/71* (Leipzig, 1914), 19. Violation of this code of war would become a much more incensing issue with the guerrilla tactics of the Franc tireurs.

106. On sanitary conditions see G. A. Zimmermann, *Kriegs-Erinnerungen* (Milwaukee, 1895), 493–567.

107. BAB, v.3, 70–72 (11 IX 70).

108. BAB, v.3, 78–79 (20 X 70).

109. August Ebrard, *Bericht des Erlanger Vereins* (Erlangen, 1871), 4, 52, and 57.

110. August Ebrard, *Bericht des Erlanger Vereins* (Erlangen, 1871), 40–41.

111. J. R. de Salis, *Switzerland and Europe* (London, 1971), 150; on the Protestant response, see Karl Hammer, *Deutsche Kriegstheologie, 1870–1918* (Munich, 1971).

112. Cited in Julius Meier-Graefe, *Hans von Marées,* v.1 (Munich, 1910), 43 (29 I 73).

113. *The Franco-Prussian War* (New York, 1961), 456.

114. BAB, v.3, 93 (12 XII 70).

115. KGW, v.3:3, 430.

116. *Cosima Wagner's Diaries,* v.1, 319.

117. Margarethe von Poschinger, *Diaries of the Emperor Frederick* (London, 1902), 195–205.

118. Elisabeth Fehrenbach, *Wandlungen des deutschen Kaisergedankens 1871–1918* (Munich, 1969).

119. See Theodor Schieder, *Das Deutsche Kaiserreich von 1871 als National-staat* (Cologne, 1961), 72–87, 125–153.

120. KGW, v.3:3, 98.

121. BAB, v.3, 178 (21 XI 71).

122. BAB, v.3, 206 (4 II 72).

123. BAB, v.3, 135 (14 VII 71).

124. BAB, v.3, 202 (30 I 72).

125. BAB, v.4, 7 (20 V 73).

126. *The Nietzsche-Wagner Correspondence,* ed. E. Förster-Nietzsche (New York, 1949), 140 (Wagner letter to Rohde).

127. BAB, v.3, 81 (29 X 70).

128. See above. Peter Stadler, "Die Schweiz und die deutsche Reichsgründung," *Geschichte in Wissenschaft und Unterricht,* v.25 (1974), 209–227.

129. BAB, v.3, 114–115 (22 III 71).

130. See Guido Hunziker, *Die Schweiz und das Nationalitätsprinzip im 19. Jahrhundert* (Basel, 1970).

131. *Politics,* ed. Hans Kohn (New York, 1963), Ch. "The Democratic Republic," 227.

132. Bachofen wrote two days before, "A century's experience demonstrates that when things become desperately serious, everything is turned upside down, and Basel, an indefensible open city, is devoured by the stronger enemy. . . . The eventual fate of a neutral is determined naturally by the victor. If this is Prussia, it will be bad for us." Johann Jakob Bachofen, *Gesammelte Werke,* v.10, *Briefe* (Basel, 1967), 446.

133. See Peter Stadler, "Die Schweiz und die deutsche Reichsgründung," 213–219.

134. GB, v. 3, 167. The story may be apocryphal or highly embellished as it stems from Elisabeth; Burckhardt did write in a letter of July 2, 1871 of the "terrible days . . . a month behind us. . . . Yes, petroleum in the cellars of the Louvre and the flames in other palaces are an expression of what the Philosopher calls 'the will to live'; it is the last will and testament of mad fiends desiring to make a great impression on the world. . . . The great harm was begun in the last century, mainly through Rousseau, with his doctrine of the goodness of human nature." Dru, *Letters of J. Burckhardt,* 147; Edgar Salin, *Vom deutschen Verhängnis. Gespräch an der Zeitenwende: Burck-hardt-Nietzsche* (Hamburg, 1959), 57–58; Günter Grützner, *Die Pariser Kommune, Macht und Karriere einer politischen Legende. Die Auswirkungen auf das politische Denken in Deutschland* (Cologne, 1963.)

135. KGW, v.3:3, 166.

136. BAB, v.3, 121 (27 V 71). Three years before he had made plans to study at the Louvre.

137. *Cosima Wagner's Diaries,* v.1, 369.

138. Cf. KGW, v.3:4, 182, where Nietzsche writes that "Bakunin wants to destroy history and the past in his hatred against the present. Now it would be necessary to destroy all the past in order to exterminate mankind; but he only wants to destroy culture as it has existed up to now, that is to say, the whole continuation of life."

139. KGW, v.4:3, 441.

140. KGW, v.3:3, 172.

141. *The Birth of Tragedy,* #XXI.

142. Curt Paul Janz, *Friedrich Nietzsche. Biographie,* v.1 (Munich, 1978), 540–541, 547–551; BAB, v.4, 18 (18 X 73).

143. "Fünf Vorreden zu Fünf Ungeschriebenen Büchern," Ch. "Der Griechische Staat"; *Human All-Too-Human,* v.1, #452.

144. *Greek Studies. A Series of Essays* (London, 1901), 279.

145. *Greek Studies,* 22.

146. See Karl Heinrich Höfele, "Sendungsglaube und Epochenbewusstsein in Deutschland," *Zeitschrift für Religions- und Geistesgeschichte,* v.15 (1963), 265–276; Wolfgang Frhr. von Löhneysen, "Der Einfluss der Reichsgründung von 1871 auf Kunst und Kunstgeschmack in Deutschland," *Zeitschrift für Religions- und Geistesgeschichte,* v.12 (1960), 17–44.

147. Hartmut Lehmann, "Friedrich von Bodelschwingh und das Sedanfest. Ein Beitrag zum nationalen Denken der politisch aktiven Richtung im deutschen Pietismus des 19 Jahrhunderts," *Historische Zeitschrift,* v.202 (1966), 542–569.

148. Schieder, *Das Deutsche Kaiserreich als Nationalstaat,* 129.

149. Harald Müller, "Die deutsche Arbeiterklasse und die Sedanfeiern. Zum antimilitarischen Kampf der Sozialdemokratischen Arbeiterpartei in den ersten Jahren nach der Reichsgründung," *Zeitschrift für Geschichtswissenschaft,* v.17 (1969), 1554–1564.

150. See Fritz Martini, *Deutsche Literatur im bürgerlichen Realismus, 1848–1898* (Stuttgart, 1962), 8.

151. See Helmut Schanze, *Drama in bürgerlichen Realismus,* (Frankfurt/M., 1973), 19–36, 74–77.

152. Otto Ribbeck, *Ein Bild seines Leben aus seinem Briefen, 1846–1898* (Stuttgart, 1901), 298.

153. BAB, v.3, 174 (3 XII 71).

154. See, for instance, Karl Bücher, *Lebenserinnerungen,* v.1 (Tübingen, 1919).

155. Clara Misch, ed., *Der junge Dilthey. Ein Lebensbild in Briefen und Tagebüchern* (Stuttgart, 1960), 237.

156. He had the prospect of becoming eligible for citizenship in Basel after eight years of accumulated teaching. His tie was to the city and not the Swiss state, a function of Basel's quasi-autonomous status. He remained untroubled by his ambiguous legal status, periodically renewing his Basel passport, but rarely speaking of it, so that even his Basel intimate, Franz Overbeck, was unaware of the complications of arranging public institutional care for the insane Nietzsche in 1889. See Eduard His, "Friedrich Nietzsches Heimatlosigkeit," *Basler Zeitschrift für Geschichte und Altertumskunde,* v.400 (1941), 159–186.

157. Andreas Staehelin, *Geschichte der Universität Basel, 1818–1835* (Basel, 1959), 113–148.

158. Otto Ribbeck, *Friedrich Wilhelm Ritschl,* v.2 (Leipzig, 1881), 168.

159. See Paul Burckhardt, *Geschichte der Stadt Basel* (Basel, 1957), 254–309; Eduard His, *Basler Gelehrte des 19. Jahrhunderts,* (Basel, 1941); Eduard His, *Basler Handelsherren des 19. Jahrhunderts,* (Basel, 1929).

160. Albert Teichmann, *Die Universität Basel in den fünfzig Jahren seit ihrer Reorganisation im Jahre 1835* (Basel, 1885); Hans Gutwiller, "Friedrich Nietzsches Lehrtätigkeit am Basler Pädagogium, 1869–1876," *Basler Zeitschrift für Geschichte und Altertumskunde,* v.50 (1951), 147–224. Of the 128 pupils he taught in these years, 42 planned to study theology, 25 law, 20 medicine, 6 each philosophy and philology, 5 philology-history, 4 natural science, 2 business; 17 died, withdrew, or did not list future occupational endeavors.

161. Heinz Isenschmid, *Wilhelm Klein, 1825–1887. Ein freisinniger Politiker* (Basel, 1972), 146.

162. Ischenschmid, *Wilhelm Klein,* 5, 140–172.

163. Eduard Vischer, *Wilhelm Vischer. Gelehrter und Ratsherr, 1808–1874, im Spiegel seiner Korrespondenz mit Rudolf Rauchenstein* (Basel, 1958), 128 (12 V 69) and 120 (16 II 69).

164. BAB, v.3, 198 (24 I 72).

165. BAB, v.3, 357 (II 73).

166. BAB, v.3, 199 (28 I 72).

167. BAB, v.3, 368 (5 IV 73).

168. Ferdinand Tönnies, *Der Nietzsche-Kultus* (Leipzig, 1897), v; William J. McGrath, *Dionysian Art and Populist Politics in Austria* (New Haven, 1974), 53–83.

169. BAB, v.3, 461 (Ritschl diary, 2 II 72).

170. Ulrich von Wilamowitz-Möllendorff, *My Recollections, 1848–1914* (London, 1930), 96, 150–152.

171. Quoted in Heinz Haffter, "Geschichte der klassischen Philologie," in Fritz Wehrli, ed., *Das Erbe der Antike* (Zurich, 1963), 28; see also Ernst Howald, *Friedrich Nietzsche und die klassische Philologie* (Gotha, 1920).

172. Karlfried Gründer, ed., *Der Streit um Nietzsches 'Geburt der Tragödie.' Die Schriften von E. Rohde, Wagner, U. v. Wilamowitz-Möllendorff* (Hildesheim, 1969), 36, 55.

173. BAB, v.3, 302 (25 X 72); 341–342 (4 I 73).

174. BAB, v.3: Wilamowitz "must still be very immature—clearly he has been used, stimulated, incited—everything breathes Berlin." 247 (8 VI 72); "this disgusting Berliner from [the city district] Gesundbrunn [mineral spring]," 251 (18 VI 72); to Ritschl Nietzsche wrote, "In any event I have elicited a cry of anger from the Berliners—that is also something," 255 (26 VI 72); Wilamowitz is a "presumptuous, Jewish infected fellow!" 267 (24 VII 72).

175. In the end he did not attend. KGW, v.3:3, 266–267; KGW, v.3:4, 88, 93, 99.

176. Anton Springer, *Aus meinem Leben* (Berlin, 1892), 290–305, 328–346. See Dan P. Silverman, *Reluctant Union. Alsace-Lorraine and Imperial Germany, 1871–1918* (University Park, 1972).

177. KGB, v.3:2, 287–291.

178. KGB, v.2:5, 19 (7 II 75).

179. BAB, v.4, 41–42 (18 I 74).

180. Dru, *The Letters of Jacob Burckhardt,* 151 (21 IV 72).

181. Dru, *The Letters of Jacob Burckhardt,* 157 (31 XII 72).

182. Wagner, *Prose Works,* v.4, 336.

183. David Friedrich Strauss, *Ausgewählte Briefe* (Bonn, 1895), 570 (19 XII 73). "I only find puzzling the patron's psychological problem; how does he arrive at such anger against someone who has never encroached on his preserve—in short, I do not comprehend the actual motive of his passionate hatred."

184. Wolfgang Leppmann, *The German Image of Goethe* (Oxford, 1961), 82.

185. *Cosima Wagner's Diaries,* v.1, 677, 718.

186. *Ecce Homo,* "The Untimely Ones," #2.

187. Carl Albrecht Bernoulli, *Nietzsche und die Schweiz* (Leipzig, 1922), 31.

188. *Geschichte der Leben-Jesu-Forschung,* v.1 (Munich, 1966), 115.

189. BAB, v.4, 23–24 (27 X 73); 28 (14 X 173); 31 (21 XI 73).

190. BAB, v.3, 375 (18 IV 73).

191. Otto Crusius, *Erwin Rohde. Ein biographischer Versuch* (Tübingen, 1902), 76.

192. Franz Overbeck, *Über die Christlichkeit unserer heutigen Theologie* (2nd ed., Leipzig, 1903; repr. Darmstadt, 1963), 18.

193. *Über die Christlichkeit,* 72–109.

194. *Über die Christlichkeit,* 22.

195. Cited in Jacob Taube, "Entzauberung der Theologie: Zu einem Porträt Overbecks," introduction to Franz Overbeck, *Selbstbekenntnisse,* (Frankfurt/M., 1966), 7–8; see also Franz Overbeck, *Christentum und Kultur* (Basel, 1919; repr. Darmstadt, 1973).

196. *Über die Christlichkeit,* 168.

197. *Über die Christlichkeit,* 15.

198. *Overbeckiana*, v.1, 112 (I 75).

199. See Wolfgang Sauer, "Das Problem des deutschen Nationalstaates," *Moderne deutsche Sozialgeschichte*, ed. H.-U. Wehler (Cologne, 1966), 407–436.

200. See Friedrich Meinecke, "Ranke und Burckhardt," (1948), *Zur Geschichte der Geschichtschreibung* (Munich, 1968), 93–121.

201. *Griechische Kulturgeschichte*, v.3 (Stuttgart, 1952), 46–108, 240–241, 418–421.

202. *Griechische Kulturgeschichte*, v.3, 65–66.

203. H. Spiegelberg, ed., *The Socratic Enigma* (Indianapolis, 1964), 242.

204. "Geschichte der griechischen Literatur," Mu. Aus., v.5, 110, 224.

205. *Richard Wagner in Bayreuth*, #4.

206. Wagner, *Prose Works*.

207. Winfried Schüler, *Der Bayreuther Kreis von seiner Entstehung bis zum Ausgang der Wilhelminischen Aera* (Münster, 1971).

208. On the distinction between "movement" and "school" see Renato Poggioli, *The Theory of the Avant-Garde* (New York, 1971), 16–40.

209. *Use and Abuse of History*, #4.

210. BAB, v.3 (31 I 73).

211. In Dresden and Leipzig, for instance, the Bayreuth plans touched off intense debate among artistic circles, see Julius Meier-Graefe, *Hans von Marées*, v.1, 226.

212. See Michael Karbaum, *Studien zur Geschichte der Bayreuther Festspiele (1876–1976)*, 19–20.

213. See Hans Rosenberg, *Grosse Depression und Bismarckzeit* (Berlin, 1967).

214. BAB, v.4, 52 (II 74).

215. KGW, v.3:4, 377.

216. KGW, v.7:3, 409 (1885).

217. KGW, v.3:4, 380.

218. KGW, v.3:4, 389.

219. KGW, v.4:1, 266.

220. KGW, v.3:4, 377.

221. KGW, v.7:3, 405 (1885).

222. #X.

223. "What did I never forgive Wagner? That he condescended to the Germans—that he became reichsdeutsch." *Ecce Homo*, "Why I Am So Clever," #5 (Kaufmann trans.).

224. James Morgan Hart, *German Universities. A Narrative of Personal Experiences* (New York, 1874), 166–167.

225. *Zeiten, Völker und Menschen*, v.2 (Berlin, 1875), 315; Friedrich Kapp was then observing that "the future of Germany no longer [rests] with its students, the young wandering around the universities, but with the young technicians, manufacturers and advanced artisans," quoted in H.-U. Wehler, "Vom radikalen Frühsozialismus des Vormärz zur liberalen Parteipolitik der Bismarckzeit: Friedrich Kapp, 1842–1884," *Krisenherde des Kaiserreichs* (Göttingen, 1970), 246.

226. *Human All-Too-Human*, v.2, Preface, #1.

227. *The Genealogy of Morals*, "What Is the Meaning of Ascetic Ideals?" #5.

228. *Besonnte Vergangenheit. Lebenserinnerungen, 1859–1919* (Leipzig, 1977), 131–132.

229. KGB, v.2:5, 27–28 (28 II 75); 40–41 (17 IV 75).

230. *Ein Vermächtnis* (Berlin, 1912), 1.

231. BAB, v.4, 86 (9 VII 74).

232. BAB, v.4, 123 (13 XII 74).

233. BAB, v.4, 84 (4 VII 74).

234. Wilhelm Vischer the younger (1833–1886) and Andreas Heusler the

younger together founded in 1875 the conservative "Eidgenössischen Verein" to combat ascendant radicalism, Eduard His, *Basler Gelehrte des 19. Jahrhunderts,* 256–257 and 268.

235. KGB, v.2:5, 38 (26 III 75); after an American "swindler" stirred up the local Pietists, Nietzsche wrote, "Ever since it has tolerated this streetcorner Christianity, Basel society disgusts me." 44 (19 IV 75).

236. Werner Kaegi, *Jakob Burckhardt, Eine Biographie,* v.4 (Basel, 1967), 77–78.

237. KGB, v.2:5, 26 (28 II 75).

238. KGB, v.2:5, 32 (12 III 75).

239. KGB, v.2:5, 59 (30 V 75); Burckhardt, *Geschichte der Stadt Basel,* 310–327; Walter Luthi, "Die Struktur des Baseler Grossen Rat von 1875 bis 1914 nach politischer Parteizugehörigkeit und sozialer Schichtung." *Basler Zeitschrift für Geschichte und Altertumskunde,* v.62 (1962), 125–165 and v.63 (1963), 125–177.

240. In announcing the death of the younger Vischer in 1886, Overbeck wrote, "The old Basel is dying out at the university in a disturbing way." R. Oehler and C.A. Bernouilli, eds., *Friedrich Nietzsches Briefwechsel mit Franz Overbeck* (Leipzig, 1916), 334.

241. KGB, v.2:5, 402 (3 IV 79).

242. Jacob Burckhardt, *Briefe,* v.7 (Basel, 1969), 33 (16 VI 79).

243. KGB, v.2:5, 146 (5 IV 76).

244. KGB, v.2:5, 147 (11 IV 76).

245. *Richard Wagner in Bayreuth,* #11, #3 & #7.

246. KGW, v.4:1, 290; *Richard Wagner in Bayreuth,* #4.

247. KGB, v.2:6/1, 362 (13 VII 76).

248. BAB, v.3, 359 (24 II 73); KGB, v.2:5, 31 (12 III 75).

249. KGB, v.2:5, 76 (14 VII 75).

250. Hans von Wolzogen, *Lebensbilder* (Regensburg, 1923), 93–94.

251. Yvonne Kapp, *Eleanor Marx,* v.1 (London, 1972), 174.

252. Ellen von Siemens-Helmholtz, *Anna von Helmholtz,* v.1 (Berlin, 1929), 204.

253. KGW, v.4:2, 404.

5. THE EXPERIMENTAL THINKER

1. KGW, v.4:2, 387.

2. KGW, v.4:2, 401 and 413.

3. *Human All-Too-Human,* v.1, Preface, #7.

4. KGW, v.4:2, 406 and 477.

5. KGW, v.4:2, 477.

6. KGW, v.4:3, 438 and 447.

7. KGW, v.4:2, 553.

8. KGW, v.3:3, 101 & 107.

9. KGW, v.4:2, 443.

10. KGW, v.4:2, 402.

11. KGW, 4:2, 407.

12. KGW, 4:2, 434.

13. KGW, v. 8:1, 163.

14. KGW, v.2:5, 299 (draft to R. & C. Wagner I 78).

15. Preface to *Human All-Too-Human,* v.1, #3.

16. KGB, v. 2:5, 138 (3 III 76); this letter, hitherto misaddressed, is missing from the otherwise useful compendium, Ernst Pfeiffer, ed., *Friedrich Nietzsche, Paul Rée, Lou von Salomé. Die Dokumente ihrer Begegnung* (Frankfurt/M, 1970).

17. KGW, v.5:1, 377.

18. KGW, v.4:2, 462.

19. *Human All-Too-Human,* v.2, "Mixed Maxims and Opinions," #113; on Nietzsche's new rhetorical style, see Bernard Greiner, *Friedrich Nietzsche: Versuch und Versuchung in seinen Aphorismen* (Munich, 1972); Helmut Schoeck, *Nietzsches Philosophie des 'Menschlich-Allzumenschlichen': Kritische Darstellung der Aphorismen-Welt der mittleren Schaffenszeit als Versuch einer Neuorientierung des Gesamtbildes* (Tübingen, 1948); Joachim Groh, *Nietzsche und die Rhetorik* (Tübingen, 1970).

20. KGW, v. 4:2, 562.

21. KGW, v.3:4, 243.

22. BAB, v.3, 369 (5 IV 73).

23. *Nation,* v.31, 168; see Philip P. Wiener, *Evolution and the Founders of Pragmatism* (Philadelphia, 1972), ch. 3.

24. See Fritz Bolle, "Darwinismus und Zeitgeist," *Zeitschrift für Religions- und Gesitesgeschichte,* v.14 (1962), 143–178; Hedwig Conrad-Martius, *Utopien der Menschenzüchtung. Der Sozialdarwinismus und seine Folgen* (Munich, 1955); Hans-Günter Zmarzlik, "Der Sozialdarwinismus in Deutschland," *Vierteljahrshefte für Zeitgeschichte,* v.11 (1963), 246–273.

25. *David Strauss, #9*; Franz Hoffmann, *Philosophische Schriften,* v.5 (Erlangen, 1878), 431–435.

26. KGW, v. 4:1, 334.

27. Wilhelm Dilthey, *Gesammelte Werke,* v.17 (Göttingen, 1974), 363.

28. KGB, v.2:5, 268 (4 VIII 77).

29. "A prominent representative of this pessimistic strain in our literature is Prof. Friedrich Nietzsche of Basel, the successive parts of whose *Unzeitgemässe Betrachtungen* have drawn much notice. In the writings of Nietzsche and others of the same stamp, the pessimistic mood is combined in a very peculiar way with an enthusiastic devotion to certain ideas closely related to religious mysticism. Richard Wagner and his music are ardently worshiped by this sect of pessimists." *Mind,* v.2 (1877), 509.

30. Pfeiffer, *FN, PR, LS,* 23.

31. KGB, v.2:6/2, 717 (10 X 77).

32. KGW, v.4:2, 462.

33. *The Gay Science,* #348.

34. Paul Rée, *Philosophie* (Berlin, 1903), 192.

35. Hans Rosenberg, "Die Pseudodemokratisierung der Rittergutsbesitzerklasse," *Probleme der deutschen Sozialgeschichte* (Frankfurt/M., 1969), 7–49.

36. Robert W. Gutman, *Richard Wagner* (New York, 1968), 359–360.

37. "*Parsifal*' (Letters from Bayreuth, July 1882)," *Music Criticisms, 1846–99,* ed. Henry Pleasants (London, 1963), 195; see also Adolf Nowak, "Wagners *Parsifal* und die Idee der Kunstreligion," *Richard Wagner. Werk und Wirkung,* ed. Carl Dahlhaus, (Regensburg, 1971), 161–174.

38. KGW, v.7:2, 219.

39. Malwida von Meysenbug, *Im Anfang war die Liebe. Briefe an ihre Pflegetochter* (Munich, 1926), 76–77, 316. On Wagner's relation to Gobineau see, E. J. Young, *Gobineau und der Rassismus* (Meisenheim am Glau, 1968), 224.

40. KGW, v.5:2, 578.

41. BAB, v.3, 284 (27 VIII 72).

42. See Michael Confino, ed., *Daughter of a Revolutionary. Natalie Herzen and the Bakunin/Nechayev Circle* (Lasalle, 1973).

43. Confino, *Daughter,* 166.

44. KGB, v.2:5 (31 III 77).

45. KGB, v.2:5, 208 (to Schmeitzner, 18 XII 76).

46. KGB, v.2:6/2, 769.

47. KGB, v.2:5, 264 (VIII 77).

48. KGB, v.2:5, 284 (3 IX 77).
49. Frederick R. Love, "Prelude to a Desperate Friendship: Nietzsche and Peter Gast in Basel," *Nietzsche Studien,* v.1 (1972), 261–285.
50. Michael D. Biddiss, *Father of Racist Ideology. The Social and Political Thought of Count Gobineau* (New York, 1970), 85.
51. Biddiss, *Father,* 177.
52. "Die Schweiz als Schauplatz internationaler Macht- und Prinzipienkämpfe in der Ersten Internationale," *Historische Zeitschrift,* v.204 (1967), 322; see also Erich Gruner, *Die Parteien in der Schweiz* (Bern, 1969).
53. Alexander Dru, ed., *The Letters of Jacob Burckhardt* (New York, 1955), 142 (20 VII 70).
54. KGW, v.4:2, 440.
55. "In a few shop windows," Rée wrote Elisabeth, "I saw advertised on a large wrapper in inch-high letters: 'Banned in Russia.'" Pfeiffer, *FN, PR, LS,* 64 (VIII 79).
56. KGB, v.2:5, 127 (8 XII 75).
57. KGB, v.3:1, 17 (18 IV 80).
58. "Nietzsche's Philosophy in the Light of Recent History," *Last Essays* (London, 1959), 174.
59. KGW, v.4:3, 445; KGW, v.4:4, 484.
60. *Human All-Too-Human,* v.1, #480; KGW, v.4:4, 229.
61. Quoted in James Joll, *The Anarchists* (Boston, 1964), 113.
62. KGB, v.2:5, 42 (17 IV 75).
63. GB, v.4, 226 (21 VIII 85); 228 (22 IX 85).
64. Karl Brose, "Nietzsches Verhältnis zu John Stuart Mill," *Nietzsche-Studien,* v.3 (1973), 152–174.
65. E. Förster-Nietzsche, "Friedrich Nietzsches Bibliothek," ed. Arthur Berthold (Berlin, 1900), 429–444.
66. Christoph Cobet, *Der Wortschatz des Antisemitismus in der Bismarckzeit* (Munich, 1973), 14–151.
67. Quoted in Peter Gay, *The Dilemma of Democratic Socialism. Eduard Bernstein's Challenge to Marx* (New York, 1962), 103fn; cf. 24–26, 94–103; Gustav Mayer, *Friedrich Engels. Eine Biographie,* v.2 (Cologne, n.d.), 282–295, discusses the Dühring vogue in the socialist camp; Vernon L. Lidtke, *The Outlawed Party. Social Democracy in Germany, 1878–1890* (Princeton, 1966) treats it as a "passing influence," 61–62.
68. KGW, v.4:2, 579.
69. KGW, v.4:2, 578.
70. *Human All-Too-Human,* v.1, #439.
71. KGW, v.4:3, 426.
72. *Human All-Too-Human,* v.1, #462.
73. KGW, v.8:2, 169.
74. KGB, v.2:5, 469 (11 XII 79).
75. KGW, 4:1, 169; *Human All-Too-Human,* v.1, #235.
76. *Human All-Too-Human,* v.1, #473.
77. Heinrich von Stein, *Idee und Welt,* ed. Guenter Ralfs (Stuttgart, 1940), 40.
78. Stein, *Idee,* 49.
79. *Briefe von und an Malwida von Meysenbug,* ed. Berta Schleicher (Berlin, 1920), 68 (2 II 80).
80. Stein, *Idee,* 55.
81. R. Stackelberg, "The Role of H. v. Stein in Nietzsche's Emergence as a Critic of Wagnerian Idealism and Cultural Nationalism," *Nietzsche-Studien,* v.5 (1976), 178–193.
82. KGW, v.4:4, 89.
83. Gerd-Klaus Kaltenbrunner, "Vom Konkurrenten des Karl Marx zum Vor-

läufer Hitlers: Eugen Dühring," in *Propheten des Nationalismus,* ed. Karl Schwedhelm (Munich, 1969), 36–54.

84. Quoted in Michael Karbaum, *Studien zur Geschichte der Bayreuther Festspiele (1876–1976),* v.1 (Regensburg, 1976), 29.

85. See Susanna Grossmann-Vendrey, ed., *Bayreuth in der deutschen Presse,* v.2 (Regensburg, 1977).

86. *Wagner's Prose Works,* v.6 (London, 1897), 41–49.

87. KGW, v.4:4, 187; *Human All-Too-Human,* v.1, #109.

88. *Wagner's Prose Works,* v.6, 73–74, 77.

89. KGB, v.2:5 (3 IX 78).

90. KGW, v.4:3, 394.

91. Carl E. Schorske, "The Quest for the Grail: Wagner and Morris," K. Wolff and B. Moore, eds., *The Critical Spirit. Essays in Honor of Herbert Marcuse* (Boston, 1967), 230–231.

92. *Richard Wagner. The Man, His Mind, and His Music,* 301–361.

93. Quoted in Karbaum, *Studien zur Geschichte,* 2.

94. KGW, v.4:3, 345.

95. Günter Grützner, *Die Pariser Kommune. Macht und Karriere einer politischen Legende* (Cologne, 1963), 129–131.

96. Wilhelm Dilthey, *Gesammelte Werke,* v.17 (Göttingen, 1974), 367, 366.

97. Otto Ribbeck, *Ein Bild seines Lebens aus seinen Briefen,* (Stuttgart, 1901), 309.

98. *Die Briefe des Freiherrn Carl von Gersdorff an Friedrich Nietzsche,* v.3, ed. Karl Schlechta (Weimar, 1936), 124 (12 I 79); KGB, v.2:6/2, 896 (16 VI 78) and 901 (19 VI 78).

99. KGB, v.2:5, 346 (10 VIII 78).

100. KGB, v.2:5, 292 (3 XII 77).

101. Dilthey, *Gesammelte Werke,* v.17, 390.

102. KGW, v.4:4, 77–78.

103. KGW, v.4:4, 572.

104. KGB, v.2:5, 419 (15 VI 79).

105. O. Klose, E. G. Jacoby, I. Fischer, eds., *Ferdinand Tönnies-Friedrich Paulsen Briefwechsel, 1876–1908* (Kiel, 1961), 75.

106. Klose, et al., *Tönnies-Paulsen,* 75.

107. *Human All-Too-Human,* v.1, #426.

108. *Human All-Too-Human,* v.2, "Mixed Maxims and Opinions," #316.

109. KGB, v.3:1, 3 (I 80).

110. *Human All-Too-Human,* v.1, #221.

111. *Joyful Wisdom,* #324 (Reinhardt trans.).

112. *The Gay Science* (Kaufmann trans.), #319.

113. KGW, v.5:1, 617.

114. KGW, v.5:1, 365; KGW, v.7:1, 185.

115. *Dawn,* #327; KGW, v.5:1, 8, 30, 108; KGW, v.8:3, 288.

116. Quoted in R. Kuhlen and U. Schneider, "Experimentalphilosophie," *Historische Wörterbuch der Philosophie,* v.2 (Basel, 1972), 873.

117. *Twilight of the Idols,* "Maxims and Arrows," #26.

118. Walter Kaufmann, *Nietzsche. Philosopher, Psychologist, Antichrist* (New York, 1968), 93–94.

119. KGW, v.5:1, 481 and 679–680.

120. KGW, v.5:1, 344.

121. KGW, v.5:2, 425; KGW, v.5:1, 764.

122. SL, 280–281 (N-Fuchs, 14 XII 87).

123. See Reino Virtanen, *Claude Bernard and His Place in the History of Ideas* (Lincoln, 1960).

124. John Dewey, *The Influence of Darwin on Philosophy* (Bloomington, 1965), 9.

125. John Dewey, "From Absolutism to Experimentalism," *On Experience, Nature, and Freedom,* ed. J. Bernstein (New York, 1960), 3–18.

126. Wilhelm Wundt, "Die Aufgaben der experimentellen Psychologie," (1882), *Essays* (2nd ed., Leipzig, 1906), 187–213; Hans Vaihinger, *Die Philosophie des Als Ob* (Leipzig, 1922).

127. See Richard Hofstadter, *Social Darwinism in America* (Boston, 1944).

128. Emile Zola, "The Experimental Novel" in George J. Becker, ed., *Documents of Modern Literary Realism* (Princeton, 1963), 177, 181.

129. Quoted in Sergio Perosa, *Henry James and the Experimental Novel* (Charlottesville, 1978), 5; see also Stephen Donaldo, *Nietzsche, Henry James, and the Artistic Will* (New York, 1978).

130. Erich Auerbach, *Mimesis* (Garden City, 1957), 437; in Germany Nietzsche "was the first to experience the conflict between author and public which is to be observed very much earlier in France," 458.

131. *Human All-Too-Human,* #375.

132. *Dawn,* #533, #425; *The Gay Science,* #59, #351, #377.

133. Becker, *Documents of Literary Realism,* 187 and 210.

134. Georg Lukács, "The Zola Centenary" in *Studies in European Realism* (New York, 1964), 41.

135. Quoted in Ludwig Marcuse, *Amerikanisches Philosophieren, Pragmatisten, Polytheisten, Tragiker* (Hamburg, 1959), 41; see, for example, the change that takes place between Strindberg's *Entwicklung einer Seele* ([1st ed., 1885], Leipzig, 1916) and his writings of the nineties, such as *Inferno, Alone and Other Writings,* ed. Evert Spinchorn (New York, 1968).

136. On Wundt see the classic study of Edwin G. Boring, *A History of Experimental Psychology* (New York, 2nd ed., 1950), 317–346.

137. Like Wilamowitz in philology, Wundt swamped his opposition through an inexhaustible barrage which emanated from his Leipzig laboratory, his journal and his own wide-ranging philosophical writings. He fostered a new school and redefined experimentalism largely in his own image, prompting William James to complain in 1887: "He aims at being a Napoleon of the intellectual world. Unfortunately he will never have a Waterloo, for he is a Napoleon without genius and with no central idea which, if defeated, brings down the whole fabric in ruin." Quoted in Boring, *A History,* 346. On Wundt's turn from politics see his autobiography, *Erlebtes und Erkanntes* (Stuttgart, 1920), 13–30.

138. R. Jackson Wilson, *In Quest of Community. Social Philosophy in the United States, 1860–1920* (London, 1968), 52 and 48.

139. Wiener, *Evolution,* 65.

140. Eugene Freeman, *The Categories of Charles Peirce* (Chicago, 1934), presents a schematic overview.

141. *Dawn,* #453.

142. *Dawn,* #453.

143. See Stanley Hubbard, *Nietzsche and Emerson* (Basel, 1958); Ernst Benz, "Das Bild des Übermenschen in der Europäischen Geistesgeschichte," in Ernst Benz, ed., *Der Übermensch. Eine Discussion* (Zurich, 1961), 23–146.

144. KGW, v. 7:1, 176.

145. Jackson Matthews, ed., *The Collected Works of Paul Valéry* (Princeton, 1968), v.9, 339.

146. Lovejoy, for instance, pointed to the inconsistency between Peirce's claim that the cosmos was moving toward ever greater order and his notion of evolution as a theorem of probabilities. Arthur O. Lovejoy, "A Note on Peirce's Evolutionism," appendix E of Wiener, *Evolution,* 227–230. Nietzsche's doctrine of the "eternal

212 • *Notes 136–143*

return of the same" similarly defies the principle of entropy which dictates that the universe is heading for a final state of general disorder.

147. See *Ecce Homo,* "Thus Spoke Zarathustra," #1; *The Gay Science,* #276; Joan Stambaugh, *Nietzsche's Thought of Eternal Return* (Baltimore, 1972); Karl Löwith, *Nietzsches Philosophie der ewigen Wiederkehr des Gleichen* (Stuttgart, 1956).

148. Wilson, *In Quest of Community,* 56.

149. KGB, v.3:1, 122 (VIII 81).

150. KGW, v.5:2, 392.

151. *Human All-Too-Human,* v.2, "The Wanderer," #297.

152. SL, 178 (14 VIII 81).

153. *Ecce Homo,* "Zarathustra," #3.

154. KGW, v.5:2, 395 and 406.

155. *The Joyful Wisdom,* #341 (Reinhardt trans.).

156. See Michael Meyer, *Ibsen: A Biography* (Garden City, N.Y., 1971), 473–492.

157. KGB, v.3:1, 102 (9 VII 81) and 104 (13 VII 81).

158. Heinrich v. Treitschke, *Heinrich von Treitschkes Briefe,* ed. Max Cornicelius, v.3 (Leipzig, 1920), 535 (11 IX 81).

159. "Nietzsche and the Imagery of Height" in Malcolm Pasley, ed., *Nietzsche: Imagery and Thought* (Berkeley, 1978), 104–122.

160. *Human All-Too-Human,* v.2, "Miscellaneous Maxims," #271.

161. *Dawn,* #538.

162. *Dawn,* #320.

163. Jacob Burckhardt, *Briefe,* v.6 (Stuttgart, 1969), 267 (10 VIII 81).

164. SL, 177 (30 VII 81).

165. KGB, v.3:1, 125 (end of VIII 81).

166. KGB, v.3:1, 119 (21 VIII 81).

167. KGB, v.3:1, 121 (24 VII 81).

168. SL, 179 (18 IX 81).

169. KGB, v.3:1, 137.

170. *The Gay Science,* #316 (Kaufmann trans.).

171. *Ecce Homo,* "Thus Spoke Zarathustra," #1.

172. KGW, v.5:2, 417–418.

173. SL, 177 (30 VII 81).

174. *The Gay Science,* #341 and 342.

175. KGW, v.7:1, 588; this as a corrective to the discussion by Henri Lichtenberger, *Die Philosophie Friedrich Nietzsche* (Dresden, 1899), 204–209.

176. Nietzsche mentions Secchi in the spring of 1884, KGW, v.7:2, 144; see also Gustav Mayer, *Friedrich Engels: Eine Biographie* (Cologne, n.d.), 324–328.

177. *Nietzsche Studien,* v.9 (1980), 434.

178. *Use and Abuse of History,* #2.

179. *Use and Abuse of History,* #2; KGW, v.8:2, 39.

6. THE POSTHUMOUS MAN

1. KGB, v. 3:1, 497 (30 IV 84).

2. KGB, v.3:2, 71 (28 V 80).

3. Ernst Staehelin, ed., *Overbeckiana,* v.1, *Die Korrespondenz Franz Overbecks* (Basel, 1960), 130 (12 V 80).

4. John T. Blackmore, *Ernst Mach: His Work, Life and Influence,* (Berkeley, 1972), 73–76.

5. KGB, v.3:1 (18 VIII 80) 35.

6. KGB, v.3:1, 32 (27 VII 80) and 37 (20 VIII 80).

7. H. F. Peters, *Zarathustra's Sister: The Case of Elisabeth and Friedrich Nietzsche* (New York, 1977), 51.

8. See Peter G. J. Pulzer, *The Rise of Political Anti-Semitism in Germany and Austria* (New York, 1964), 94–101; Paul W. Massing, *Rehearsal for Destruction. A Study of Political Anti-Semitism in Imperial Germany* (New York, 1949); Christoph Cobet, *Der Wortschatz des Antisemitismus in der Bismarckzeit* (Munich, 1973); Hans Liebeschütz, *Das Judentum in deutschen Geschichtsbild von Hegel bis Max Weber* (Tübingen, 1967).

9. Jacob Burckhardt, *Briefe,* v.7 (Basel, 1969), 131 (2 I 80).

10. Burckhardt, *Briefe,* v.7, 204 (2 XII 80).

11. KGB, v.3:2, 72 (31 V 80).

12. Bernhard Förster, *Parsifal-Nachklange* (Leipzig, 1883); on Förster see Peters, *Zarathustra's Sister*; Erich Podach, *Gestalten um Nietzsche* (Weimar, 1938).

13. *Beyond Good and Evil,* #251.

14. Burckhardt, *Briefe,* v.7, 165 (14 VII 80) and 182 (1 IX 80); Karl Marx-Friedrich Engels, *Werke,* v.35 (Berlin, G.D.R., 1967), 174; KGW, v.5:1, 690.

15. George Woodcock, *The Anarchist Prince: Peter Kropotkin* (New York, 1971), 177.

16. Julius Rodenberg, *Aus seinem Tagebüchern* (Berlin, 1919), 115–116.

17. Marx-Engels, *Werke,* v.35, 175 (30 III 81).

18. Lou Andreas-Salomé, *Lebensrückblick,* ed. Ernst Pfeiffer (Frankfurt/M., 1974), 62–63.

19. In his preface James says, "My scheme called for the suggested nearness (to all our apparently ordered life) of some sinister anarchic underworld, heaving in its pain, its power and its hate, a presentation not of sharp particulars, but of loose appearances, vague motions and sounds and symptoms, just perceptible presences and general looming possibilities," (Middlesex, 1977), 21–22. See also the study of the English novelist W. H. Mallock, John Lucas, "Conservatism and Revolution in the 1880s," in John Lucas, ed., *Literature and Politics in the Nineteenth Century* (London, 1971), 173–219. See also Lionel Trilling, "The Princess Casamassima," *The Liberal Imagination: Essays on Literature and Society* (New York, 1950), 58–92.

20. Franco Venturi, *Roots of Revolution* (New York, 1960), 680 and 829.

21. KGW, v.8:2, 432.

22. Quoted in Wiener, *Evolution,* 39.

23. Wiener, *Evolution,* 39.

24. Dieter Arendt, "Der Nihilismus-Ursprung und Geschichte im Spiegel der Forschungs-Literatur seit 1945," *Deutsche Vierteljahrsschrift für Literaturwissenschaft und Geistesgeschichte,* v.43 (1969), 346–369, 544–566; Walter Hof, *Pessimistisch-nihilistische Strömungen in der deutschen Literatur vom Sturm und Drang bis zum Jungen Deutschland* (Tübingen, 1970).

25. Dwight Macdonald, ed., *My Past and Thoughts. The Memoirs of Alexander Herzen* (New York, 1973), 639.

26. Franz Hoffmann, *Philosophische Schriften,* v.5 (Erlangen, 1878), 430; cf. 410–447.

27. *Ecce Homo,* "The Untimely One," #2 (Kaufmann trans.).

28. Leo Tolstoy, *A Confession. The Gospel in Brief and What I Believe* (London, 1971), 307.

29. Tolstoy, *A Confession,* 25.

30. Quoted in Woodcock, *The Anarchist Prince,* 186.

31. See Andrew R. Carlson, *Anarchism in Germany,* v.1 (Metuchen, N.J., 1972).

32. See Burckhardt, *Briefe,* v.7, 215 (29 XII 80) and 469–470.

33. KGW, v.5:1, 713.

34. KGB, v.3:2 (Köselitz 8 IX 81).

35. Marx-Engels, *Werke,* v.35, 237–238 (30 XI 81).

36. KGB, v.3:1, 148 (12 XII 81).

37. See Ernst Barnikol, *Bruno Bauer: Studien und Materialien* (Assen, 1972).

38. Bruno Bauer, *Zur Orientierung über die Bismarck'sche Aera* (Chemnitz, 1880; reprint Aalen 1969); Bruno Bauer, "Die socialpolitische Bilanz d.J. 1881," *Internationale Monatsschrift,* v.1 (1882), 6–37; Barnikol, *Bruno Bauer,* 375–414.

39. Bauer, *Zur Orientierung,* 287–288.

40. KGB, v.3:1, 167 (5 II 82); R. Lehmann, "Friedrich Nietzsche, Eine Studie," *Internationale Monatsschrift,* v.1 (1882) 253–261 and 306–322.

41. *Internationale Monatsschrift,* v.1 (1882), 269–275.

42. Theodor Lessing, *Untergagng der Erde am Geist* (Hannover, 1924), 429.

43. For a discussion of Nietzsche's concept of resentment, see Max Scheler, *Ressentiment* (Glencoe, 1961); Svend Ranulf, *Moral Indignation and Middle Class Psychology* (New York, 1964); Helmut Schoeck, *Envy. A Theory of Social Behavior* (New York, 1970).

44. KGB, v.3:1, 241 (VII/VIII 82).

45. KGB, v.3:2, 178 (20 VII 81).

46. *Friedrich Nietzsches Briefwechsel mit Franz Overbeck,* R. Oehler and C. A. Bernoulli, eds. (Leipzig, 1916), 290 (28 III 85).

47. *Gesammelte Gedichte* (Stuttgart, 1914), v.1, 283; see Karl Fehr, "Die öffentlichen Verleumder. Zu einem Altersgedicht Gottfried Kellers," *Gottfried Keller: Aufschlüsse und Deutungen* (Bern, 1972), 162–173.

48. KGB, v.3:1 (4 III 82) 174.

49. KGB, v.3:2, 230.

50. KGB, v.3:2, 227–228 (12 II 82); 117 (21 X 80).

51. Burckhardt, *Briefe,* v.7, 261 (5/6 VIII 81).

52. KGB, v.3:1, 182 (20 III 82).

53. KGB, v.3:1, 190 (8 IV 82).

54. KGB, v.3:2, 251 (20 IV 82).

55. In 1896 in a letter to the critic Josef Hofmiller, quoted in Rudolph Binion, *Frau Lou, Nietzsche's Wayward Disciple* (Princeton, 1968), 163fn.

56. Binion, *Frau Lou,* 35–171.

57. Malwida von Meysenbug, *Der Lebensabend einer Idealisten* (Berlin, 1898).

58. Andreas-Salomé, *Lebensrückblick,* 62; cf. H. F. Peters, *My Sister, My Spouse: A Biography of Lou Andreas-Salomé* (New York, 1974), 42–43.

59. KGB, v.3:1, 337 (to Overbeck 22 II 82); Curt Paul Janz, *Friedrich Nietzsche. Biographie,* v.2 (Munich, 1978), 173–176.

60. KGB, v.3:2, 389 (19 VIII 83).

61. H. Schulthess, ed., *Europäischer Geschichtskalender,* v.23 ([1882] Nördlingen, 1883), 160–162. This congress in which Bernhard Förster played a conspicuous role elected Schmeitzner "plenipotentiary" of a standing committee directed to create an international organization, an Alliance Antijuive Universelle. Pulzer, *Rise of Political Anti-Semitism,* 103–104.

62. KGB, v.3:1, 268 (1 X 82).

63. Ernst Pfeiffer, ed., *Friedrich Nietzsche, Paul Rée, Lou von Salomé, Die Dokumente ihrer Begegnung* (Frankfurt/M., 1970), 184 (diary entry 18 VIII 82).

64. Binion, *Frau Lou,* 116–117 and 111.

65. KGB, v.3:2, 337 (16 II 83); Ernst Staehelin, ed., v.1, *Overbeckiana* (Basel, 1962), 141.

66. Hermann Bahr, *Selbstbildnis* (Berlin, 1923), 139.

67. KGB, v.3:1, 493 (2 IV 84).

68. KGB, v.3:1, 507 (21 V 84).

69. Burckhardt, *Briefe,* v.7, 288 (10 IX 81).

70. Fouillée's preface to J. M. Guyau, *Sittlichkeit ohne 'Pflicht'* (Leipzig, 1909), 8–9.

71. See Meta v. Salis-Marschlins, *Philosoph und Edelmensch. Ein Beitrag zur Charakteristik Friedrich Nietzsches* (Leipzig, 1897); Resa v. Schirnhofer, "Vom

Menschen Nietzsche," *Zeitschrift für Philosophische Forschung,* v.22 (1968), 250–260 and 441–458.

72. See David S. Thatcher, *Nietzsche in England, 1890–1914* (Toronto, 1970), 21–22.

73. Franz Friedrich Leitschuh, *Die Schweizer Landschaft in der deutschen Malerei* (Leipzig, 1924), 69; G. R. de Beer, ed., *Travellers in Switzerland* (London, 1949), 391–392.

74. August Strindberg, *Die Entwicklung einer Seele* (Munich, 1916), 219 and 297.

75. de Beer, *Travellers,* 396; Georg Brandes, "Gletscher (1885)," *Gesammelte Schriften* v.9 (Munich, 1906), 395–401.

76. de Beer, *Travellers,* 371.

77. de Beer, *Travellers,* 378.

78. GB, v.3:2, 640 (to Malwida 4 X 88).

79. de Beer, *Travellers,* 432.

80. GB, v.4, 212 (21 III 85); Henry David Aiken, "Introduction to Zarathustra," *Nietzsche. A Collection of Critical Essays,* ed., Robert Solomon, (Garden City, 1973), 116.

81. SL, 220fn.

82. KGB, v.3:1, 467 (25 I 84).

83. KGB, v.3:1, 474 (6 II 84).

84. R. Stackelberg, "The Role of H. v. Stein in Nietzsche's Emergence as a Critic of Wagnerian Idealism and Cultural Nationalism," *Nietzsche-Studien,* 178–193; KGW, v.7:3, 175–179, 268, 297.

85. See Adalbert von Hanstein, *Das jüngste Deutschland* (Leipzig, 1905).

86. Strindberg, *Die Entwicklung einer Seele,* 257.

87. Bauer, *Zur Orientierung über die Bismarckische Aera,* 181–190.

88. KGB, v.3:1, 497 (30 IV 84).

89. *Human All-Too-Human,* v.1, #481.

90. *Dawn,* #189.

91. "The time for petty politics is over: the next century will bring the fight for the dominion of the earth—the *compulsion* to *grossen Politik." Beyond Good and Evil,* #208 (Kaufmann trans.); *Ecce Homo,* "The Case of Wagner," #2.

92. KGB, v.7:3, 132 and 204.

93. KGW, v.7:3, 254–256.

94. KGW, v.7:2, 37.

95. H.-U. Wehler, *Bismarck und der Imperialismus* (Cologne, 1969), 412–423; the contrasting interpretation in A.J.P. Taylor, *Germany's First Bid for Colonies, 1884–1885. A Move in Bismarck's European Policy* (London, 1938).

96. Wehler, *Bismarck und der Imperialismus,* 162–163.

97. In an unpublished letter to his mother on November 13, 1886, Nietzsche wrote that Overbeck advised that it would be most foolish to contribute financially to Förster's Paraguay colony. "The whole idea of making me a landowner in Paraguay also has the drawback, that then I would no longer be granted a pension in Basel; I could not even claim it. One or the other. 'Nietzsche has half a mile of land with cattle'—that would be enough of an argument in frugal and rational Basel for them in clearest conscience to *withdraw* the pension." Curt Paul Janz, *Die Briefe Nietzsches* (Zurich, 1972), 57.

98. KGW, v.7:2, 37–38.

99. KGW, v.7:2, 237.

100. KGW, v.7:2, 213.

101. KGW, v.7:2, 237.

102. KGW, v.7:2, 118.

103. KGW, v.7:2, 38.

104. *Ecce Homo,* "Why I Am a Destiny," #1.

105. "I just heard that once again I have escaped death: for a time it was highly likely that I would spend the summer at Ischia, in Casamicciola." KGB, v.3:1, 419 (to Gast 3 VIII 83); "The fate of Ischia shocks me more and more. . . . Hardly was I finished with my poem then the island collapsed.—You know that in the hour that I completed the first Zarathustra in the printed-manuscript—Wagner died." 429 (to Gast, 16 VIII 83); the major earthquake of February 23, 1887 struck Nice six hours after carnival concluded. "What pleasure when the old houses rattle over one like a coffee grinder! when the streets become filled with terrified half-dressed figures and frazzled nervous systems!" GB, v.1, 483 (to v. Seydlitz 24 II 87).

106. *Ecce Homo,* "Why I Am a Destiny," #1.

107. Fontane continued in his letter of 1893 "while the ever new six-figure armies and millions are sanctioned, nobody has the least faith that our position is secure," quoted in J. P. Stern, *Re-Interpretations* (London, 1964), 233; Nietzsche wrote Malwida 13 XII 86 from Nice, "The season is here in high gear and full brilliance, the last, one hears and senses everywhere—the last season before 'the war.'" GB, v.3:2, 622.

108. *The Education of Henry Adams* (New York, 1931), 318.

109. Max Nordau's *Die Conventionellen Lügen der Kulturmenscheit* ran through four editions in the fall of 1883; to Overbeck's apparent query (in a lost letter) Nietzsche replied, "the name 'Nordau' is unknown to me." KGB, v.3:1 (6 II 84); the Wagnerian Richard Pohl wrote in "Der Fall Nietzsche," *Musikalisches Wochenblatt,* v. 19 (1888): "Nietzsche is the counterpart to Max Nordau; he translates *Die Conventionellen Lügen der Culturmenscheit* into Wagnerisms." Pohl's critical review of *The Case of Wagner* is reprinted in Janz, *Nietzsche,* v.3, 272.

110. KGW, v.7:2, 52.

111. Ludwig Dehio, *The Precarious Balance. Four Centuries of European Power Struggle* (New York, 1962), 224–268.

112. "Bismarck's Machiavellianism with a good conscience, his so-called 'Realpolitik,'" *The Gay Science,* #357.

113. See the account of Eduard Lasker's funeral in Julius Rodenberg, *Aus seinem Tagebüchern* (Berlin, 1920), 131 (29 I 84).

114. KGW, v.4:4, 53; KGB, v.2:5, 345 (6 VIII 78).

115. *The Antichrist,* #25.

116. Max L. Baeumer, "Lutherfeiern und ihre politische Manipulation," in Reinhold Grimm and Jost Hermand, eds., *Deutsche Feiern* (Wiesbaden, 1977), 46–61.

117. KGW, v.8:2, #432.

118. KGW, v.8:2, 14.

119. W. O. Henderson, *The Rise of German Industrial Power 1834–1914* (Berkeley, 1975), 179; Hans Rosenberg, *Grosse Depression und Bismarckzeit* (Berlin, 1967), 22–57.

120. Rosenberg, *Grosse Depression,* 46–47.

121. See Julius Wolf, quoted in Rosenberg, *Grosse Depression,* 47–48.

122. See Hans Rosenberg, "Zur sozialen Funktion der Agrarpolitik im Zweiten Reich," *Probleme der deutschen Sozialgeschichte* (Frankfurt/M., 1969), 51–80.

123. KGB, v.3:2, 385 (2 VIII 83); *Die Briefe des Freiherrn Carl von Gersdorff an Friedrich Nietzsche,* v.4, E. Thierbach, ed. (Weimar, 1937), 36 (22 VII 81), 38–39 (21 VIII 81).

124. Eckart Kehr's classic essays, "Zur Genesis des Königlich Preusischen Reserveoffiziers" and "Das soziale System der Reaktion in Preussen unter dem Ministerium Puttkamer," reprinted in *Der Primat der Innenpolitik,* ed. H.-U. Wehler (Berlin, 1965), 53–86.

125. Rosenberg, *Grosse Depression,* 143–153.

126. SL, 268 (4 VII 87).

127. GB, v.2, 580–581 (21 V 87); 582–583 (23 V 87); 583–584 (11 XI 87).

128. See Franz Kobler, ed., *Juden und Judentum in Deutschen Briefen aus Drei Jahrhunderten* (Vienna, 1935), 377–378 (XII 96); in 1903 Brandes wrote a friend, "As for me, I am a European, perhaps I should use Nietzsche's designation of me, 'a good European,'" 381.

129. GB, v.3:1, 274 (2 XII 87); 277 (from Brandes, 15 XII 87); 279–280 (8 I 88); René Wellek, *A History of Modern Criticism: 1750–1950*, v.4., *The Later Nineteenth Century* (New Haven, 1965), 357–369.

130. Reprinted in Curt Paul Janz, *Friedrich Nietzsche. Biographie*, v.3 (Munich, 1979), 282–291.

131. GB, v.4, 267 (31 X 86); *Friedrich Nietzsches Briefwechsel mit Franz Overbeck*, 371 (24 III 87).

132. Carl Spitteler, *Autobiographischer Schriften* (Zurich, 1947), 493–518.

133. KGW, v.8:3, 27, 33, 57, 85, 88, 95, 99–100, 104, 147–148, 212.

134. KGW, v.8:3, 59–60.

135. KGW, v.8:3, 99–101.

136. KGW, v.8:3, 95–97, 107–109.

137. GB, v.4, 267 (31 X 86).

138. *Friedrich Nietzsches Briefwechsel mit Franz Overbeck*, 337 (20 VI 86).

139. KGW, v.8:2, 70.

140. See Heinrich Heffter, "Die Kreuzzeitungspartei und die Kartellpolitik Bismarcks," (Diss., Leipzig, 1927).

141. General Blumenthal, quoted in Egon Caesar Conte Corti, *The English Empress. A Study in the Relations between Queen Victoria and her Eldest Daughter, Empress Frederick of Germany* (London, 1957), 258.

142. Walter Frank, *Hofprediger Adolf Stöcker und die christsoziale Bewegung* (Hamburg, 1935), 160–169.

143. KGW, v.8:2, 334.

144. KGW, v.8:2, 150.

145. KGW, v.8:2, 267.

146. Unpublished postcard of 4 IX 87 to his mother, Janz, *Die Briefe Friedrich Nietzsches*, 89; *Die Briefe des Freiherrn Carl von Gersdorff an Friedrich Nietzsche*, v.3, Karl Schlechta, ed. (Weimar, 1936), 74–75 (23 IX 88); v.4, 36–37 (to Gast 22 VII 81).

147. *Die Briefe des Freiherrn Carl von Gersdorff*, v.3, 73 (4 III 88).

148. KGW, v.8:2, 168.

149. Suppressed part of letter of 19 XII 87, Janz, *Die Briefe Friedrich Nietzsches*, 59; Kummel, *Nietzsche und der deutsche Geist*, 65–66; Anton Groos, "Nietzsche und die Antisemitische Correspondenz," *Deutsche Rundschau*, v.86 (1960), 333–337.

150. Suppressed part of letter of 29 XII 87, Janz, *Die Briefe Friedrich Nietzsches*, 58.

151. GB, v.1, 493 (to Deussen, 3 I 88).

152. GB, v.4, 339 (24 XI 87); 331 (27 X 87).

153. GB, v.4, 339 (24 XI 87); 351 (1 II 88).

154. GB, v.4, 356 (13 II 88); 347 (6 I 88).

155. GB, v.1, 483 (24 II 87); GB, v.4, 331–332 (27 X 87).

156. GB, v.5:2, 772 (31 III 88).

157. GB, v.5:2, 767 (20 III 88); *Nietzsches Briefwechsel mit Overbeck*, 414–415 (22 II 88).

158. See Andreas Dorpalen, "Emperor Frederick III and the German Liberal Movement," *American Historical Review*, v.54 (1948), 1–31, and Michael Freund, *Das Drama der 99 Tage. Krankheit und Tod Friedrichs III* (Cologne, 1966). A complete biography of Friedrich III, one weighing equally internal and external political factors, has yet to be written. M. v. Poschinger's *Kaiser Friedrich*, 3 vols.

(Berlin, 1898–1900), is a useful compendium, shedding light on the Crown Prince's ceremonial role. The literature has focused either on the proposed Anglo-German alliance favored by the Crown Prince and his wife or on Friedrich III's final year. Recent treatment has continued to place the Crown Prince in the shadow of his English wife, as in Ladislas Farago and Andrew Sinclair, *Royal Web. The Story of Princess Victoria and Frederick of Prussia,* (New York, 1982), and John Van der Kiste, *Frederick III* (Gloucester, 1981).

159. Paul Wentzcke, ed., *Im Neuen Reich 1871–1890. Politische Briefe aus dem Nachlass liberaler Parteiführer* (2nd ed., Osnabrück, 1970), 391.

160. *Memoirs of Prince von Bülow,* v.4 (Boston, 1932), 618–619.

161. GB, v.4, 389 (20 VI 88).

162. *Ecce Homo,* "Why I Write Such Good Books," #2.

163. GB, v.1, 518 (26 VII 88).

164. SL, 297–298 (letter to Köselitz, 31 V 88). Middleton notes here Nietzsche's confusion of "the two castes of 'sage' and 'warrior'" so that he came in *The Antichrist* to classify the sage "as the 'strongest man,' not as the 'magnanimous man' of original [Brahman] doctrine." 298fn.

165. SL, 311 fn. (letter to Burckhardt, fall 88).

166. GB, v.4, 403–404 (16 IX 88).

167. *Die Briefe der Freiherrn Carl von Gersdorff,* v.3, 75 (23 IX 88).

168. GB, v.4, 403 (16 IX 88).

169. Berta Schleicher, ed., *Briefe von und an Malwida von Meysenbug* (Berlin, 1920), 275.

170. KGW, v.8:3, 460.

171. SL, 312.

172. GB, v.4, 409 (14 X 88).

173. SL, 326 (20 XII 88).

174. SL, 323 (letter to Overbeck, 13 XI 88).

175. *Friedrich Nietzsches Briefwechsel mit Franz Overbeck,* 451 (XII 88).

176. See Martin Broszat, *Zweihundert Jahre deutsche Polenpolitik* (Frankfurt/M., 2nd ed., 1972), 142–152; Helmut Neubach, *Die Ausweisungen von Polen und Juden aus Preussen, 1885/86* (Wiesbaden, 1967).

177. *Nietzsche contra Wagner,* Preface.

178. SL, 341 (28 XII 88).

179. KGW, v.8:3, 452.

180. KGW, v.8:3, 455–456.

181. KGW, v.8:3, 456.

182. Suppressed sentence quoted in Curt Paul Janz, *Die Briefe Friedrich Nietzsche* (Zurich, 1972), 20.

183. KGW, 8:3, 457.

184. KGW, v.8:3, 457.

185. KGW, v.8:3, 459–460.

186. KGW, v.8:3, 461.

187. SL, 344.

188. SL, 346 (7 I 89).

189. SL, 348 (6 I 89).

190. "Finally I was Friedrich Wilhelm IV," Möbius, *Nietzsche,* 185; Paul Ignotus, *The Paradox of Maupassant* (London, 1968), 85 and 242.

7. THE DEFEATIST

1. Alfred Vagts, *A History of Militarism* (rev. ed. New York, 1959), 220.

2. See Leo A. Loubère, *Radicalism in Mediterranean France. Its Rise and Decline, 1848–1914* (Albany, 1974).

3. *Diaries, 1910–1913* (New York, 1949), 101.

4. KGW, v.8:2, 12.

5. SL, 267 (4 VII 87); GB v.3:1, 202 (12 VII 87).

6. *Twilight of the Idols,* #45 (Hollingdale trans.).

7. *Twilight of the Idols,* #31 (Hollingdale trans.).

8. *Twilight of the Idols,* #45 (Hollingdale trans.).

9. GB, v.3:1, 275 (2 XII 87); the phrase was "well said and felt," he wrote Gast, GB, v.4, 344 (20 XII 87); *Friedrich Nietzsches Briefwechsel mit Franz Overbeck,* R. Oehler and C.A. Bernoulli, eds. (Leipzig, 1916), 443 (3 II 88).

10. GB, v.3:1, 278 (15 XII 87); 284 (11 I 88).

11. *The Gay Science,* #98.

12. GB, v.3:1, 296 (3 IV 88).

13. *Use and Abuse of History,* #2; *Schopenhauer as Educator,* #8.

14. *The Case of Wagner,* "Postscript."

15. Hermann Conradi, *Wilhelm II und die junge Generation eine zeitpsychologische Betrachtung* (Leipzig, [1889]).

16. *Counter-statement* (New York, 1931), 92.

17. See Klaus Heinrich, *Parmenides and Jona. Vier Studien über das Verhältnis von Philosophie and Mythologie* (Frankfurt/M., 1966).

18. Wolfgang Sauer, "Das Problem des deutschen Nationalstaates." *Moderne deutsche Sozialgeschichte,* ed. H.-U. Wehler (Cologne, 1966).

BIBLIOGRAPHY

I. NIETZSCHE

Nietzsche's published books

1872 *Die Geburt der Tragödie (The Birth of Tragedy)*
1873–1875 *Unzeitgemässe Betrachtungen (Untimely Meditations)*
1873 *David Strauss, der Bekenner und Schriftsteller, (David Strauss, the Confessor and Writer)*
1874 *Vom Nutzen und Nachteil der Historie für das Leben (The Use and Abuse of History)*
1874 *Schopenhauer als Erzieher (Schopenhauer as Educator)*
1876 *Richard Wagner in Bayreuth*
1878–1880 *Menschliches, Allzumenschliches (Human, All-Too-Human)*
1878 *v.1*
1879 *v.2:1 Vermischte Meinungen und Sprüche (Mixed Opinions and Maxims)*
1880 *v.2:2 Der Wanderer und sein Schatten (The Wanderer and His Shadow)*
1881 *Die Morgenröte (Dawn)*
1882 *Die Fröhliche Wissenschaft (The Gay Science/The Joyful Wisdom)*
1883–1885 *Also Sprach Zarathustra (Thus Spoke Zarathustra)*
1886 *Jenseits von Gut und Böse (Beyond Good and Evil)*
1887 *Zur Genealogie der Moral (On the Genealogy of Morals)*
1888 *Der Fall Wagner (The Case of Wagner)*
   Die Götzen-Dämmerung (The Twilight of the Idols)
   Der Antichrist (The Antichrist)
   Ecce Homo
   Nietzsche contra Wagner

Unpublished sources

Goethe-Schiller Archiv. Nietzsche papers. Weimar.

Published sources

Allison, David B., *The New Nietzsche: Contemporary Styles of Interpretation.* New York, 1977.
Benz, Ernst. "Das Bild des Übermenschen in der Europäischen Geistesgeschichte." In *Der Übermensch: Eine Discussion,* ed. Ernst Benz. Zürich, 1961.
Bernoulli, Carl Albrecht. *Franz Overbeck und Friedrich Nietzsche: Eine Freundschaft.* 2 vols. Jena, 1908.
———. *Nietzsche und die Schweiz.* Leipzig, 1922.
Bertram, Ernst. *Nietzsche: Versuch einer Mythologie.* Berlin, 1918.
Blunck, Richard. *Friedrich Nietzsche: Kindheit und Jugend.* Basel, 1953.
Bohley, Reiner. "Nietzsches Taufe. 'Was, meinst du, will aus diesem Kindlein werden?'," *Nietzsche-Studien* 9 (1980).
———. "Über die Landesschule zu Pforta," *Nietzsche-Studien* 5 (1976).
Brinton, Crane. *Nietzsche.* New York, 1965. 1st ed., 1941.
Brose, Karl. "Nietzsches Verhältnis zu John Stuart Mill," *Nietzsche-Studien* 3 (1973).
Danto, Arthur C. *Nietzsche as Philosopher.* New York, 1965.

Deesz, Gisela. "Die Entwicklung des Nietzsches-Bildes in Deutschland." Dissertation. Würzburg, 1933.

Donaldo, Stephen. *Nietzsche, Henry James, and the Artistic Will.* New York, 1978.

Förster-Nietzsche, Elisabeth. "Friedrich Nietzsches Bibliothek," ed. Arthur Berthold. Berlin, 1900.

———. *Der junge Nietzsche.* Leipzig, 1912.

Gilman, Sander L., ed. *Begegnungen mit Nietzsche.* Bonn, 1981.

Greiner, Bernard. *Friedrich Nietzsche: Versuch und Versuchung in seinen Aphorismen.* Munich, 1972.

Groh, Joachim. *Nietzsche und die Rhetorik.* Tübingen, 1970.

Gründer, Karlfried, ed. *Der Streit um Nietzsches 'Geburt der Tragödie': Die Schriften von E. Rohde. Wagner, U. v. Wilamowitz-Möllendorff.* Hildesheim, 1969.

Gutwiller, Hans. "Friedrich Nietzsches Lehrtätigkeit am Basler Pädagogium, 1869–1876." *Basler Zeitschrift für Geschichte und Altertumskunde.* 50 (1951).

Hamburger, Michael. *Contraries. Studies in German Literature.* New York, 1970.

Heidegger, Martin. *Nietzsche.* 2 vols. Pfullingen, 1961.

Hillebrand, Karl. *Zeiten, Völker und Menschen.* Vol. 2. Berlin, 1875.

His, Eduard. "Friedrich Nietzsches Heimatlosigkeit." *Basler Zeitschrift für Geschichte und Altertumskunde* 40 (1941).

Hoffmann, Franz. *Philosophische Schriften.* Vol. 5. Erlangen, 1878.

Howald, Ernst. *Friedrich Nietzsche und die klassische Philologie.* Gotha, 1920.

Hubbard, Stanley. *Nietzsche und Emerson.* Basel, 1958.

Janz, Curt Paul. *Die Briefe Friedrich Nietzsche.* Zurich, 1972.

———. *Friedrich Nietzsche: Biographie.* 3 vols. Munich, 1978–1979.

Jaspers, Karl. *Nietzsche: Einführung in das Verständnis seines Philosophierens.* Berlin, 1936.

Kaufmann, Walter. *Nietzsche: Philosopher, Psychologist, Antichrist.* 3rd ed. New York, 1968.

Kessler, Harry. "Erlebnis mit Nietzsche." *Die Neue Rundschau.* 46 (1935).

Krummel, Richard Frank. *Nietzsche und der deutsche Geist: Ein Schrifttumsverzeichnis der Jahre 1867–1900.* Berlin, 1974.

Lehmann, R. "Friedrich Nietzsche: Eine Studie." *Internationale Monatsschrift* 1 (1882).

Levy, Albert. "Stirner et Nietzsche." Dissertation. Paris, 1904.

Lichtenberger, Henri. *Die Philosophie Friedrich Nietzsche.* Dresden, 1899.

Love, Frederick R. "Prelude to a Desperate Friendship: Nietzsche and Peter Gast in Basel." *Nietzsche Studien.* 1 (1972).

———. *Young Nietzsche and the Wagnerian Experience.* Chapel Hill, 1963.

Löwith, Karl. *From Hegel to Nietzsche.* New York, 1964.

Lukács, Georg. *Die Zerstörung der Vernunft.* Berlin, 1955.

Mann, Thomas. "Nietzsche's Philosophy in the Light of Recent History." *Last Essays.* London, 1959.

Möbius, P. J. *Nietzsche.* Leipzig, 1904.

Nietzsche, Friedrich. *Briefe: Historisch-Kritische-Gesamtausgabe.* 4 vols. Munich, 1938–1942.

———. *Briefwechsel: Kritische Gesamtausgabe,* ed. G. Colli and M. Montinari. 18 vols. Berlin, 1975ff.

———. *Friedrich Nietzsches Briefwechsel mit Franz Overbeck,* ed. R. Oehler and C. A. Bernoulli. Leipzig, 1916.

———. *Gesammelte Briefe.* 5 vols. Leipzig, 1907–1909.

———. *Gesammelte Werke,* "Musarionausgabe." 23 vols. Munich, 1920–1929.

———. *Selected Letters of Friedrich Nietzsche,* trans. and ed. Christopher Middleton. Chicago, 1969.

————. *The Nietzsche-Wagner Correspondence*, ed. E. Förster-Nietzsche. New York, 1949.

————. *Werke: Historisch-Kritische-Gesamtausgabe.* 5 vols. Munich, 1933–1940.

————. *Werke: Kritische Gesamtausgabe*, ed. G. Colli and M. Montinari. Approximately 30 volumes. Berlin, 1967ff.

Oehler, Max. *Nietzsches Ahnentafel.* Weimar, 1938.

Pasley, Malcolm, ed. *Nietzsche: Imagery and Thought.* Berkeley, 1978.

Pfeiffer, Ernst, ed. *Friedrich Nietzsche, Paul Rée, Lou von Salomé: Die Dokumente ihrer Begegnung.* Frankfurt/M., 1970.

Podach, Erich. *Friedrich Nietzsches Werke des Zusammenbruchs.* Heidelberg, 1961.

Podach, Erich, ed. *Der kranke Nietzsche. Briefe seiner Mutter an Franz Overbeck.* Vienna, 1937.

Pütz, Peter. *Friedrich Nietzsche.* Stuttgart, 1967.

Reichert, Herbert W. and Karl Schlechta. *International Nietzsche Bibliography.* Chapel Hill, 1968.

Salin, Edgar. *Vom deutschen Verhängnis: Gespräch an der Zeitenwende: Burckhardt-Nietzsche.* Hamburg, 1959.

Salis-Marschlins, Meta von. *Philosoph und Edelmensch: Ein Beitrag zur Charakteristik Friedrich Nietzsches.* Leipzig, 1897.

Scheuer, O. F. *Friedrich Nietzsche als Student.* Bonn, 1923.

Schieder, Theodor. "Nietzsche und Bismarck." *Historische Zeitschrift* 196 (1963).

Schirnhofer, Resa von. "Vom Menschen Nietzsche." *Zeitschrift für Philosophische Forschung* 22 (1968).

Schmidt, Alfred. *Zur Frage der Dialektik in Nietzsches Erkenntnistheorie.* Frankfurt/M., 1963.

Schoeck, Helmut. *Nietzsches Philosophie des 'Menschlich-Allzumenschlichen': Kritische Darstellung der Aphorismen-Welt der mittleren Schaffenszeit als Versuch einer Neuorientierung des Gesamtbildes.* Tübingen, 1948.

Solomon, Robert, ed. *Nietzsche.* Garden City, 1973.

Stambaugh, Joan. *Nietzsche's Thought of Eternal Return.* Baltimore, 1972.

Steffen, Hans, ed. *Nietzsche, Werk und Wirkungen.* Göttingen, 1974.

Stern, J. P. *A Study of Nietzsche.* Cambridge, 1979.

Stoux, Johannes. *Nietzsches Professur in Basel.* Jena, 1928.

Strong, Tracy. *Friedrich Nietzsche and the Transfiguration of Politics.* Berkeley, 1975.

Thatcher, David S. *Nietzsche in England, 1890–1914.* Toronto, 1970.

Tönnies, Ferdinand. *Der Nietzsche-Kultus.* Leipzig, 1897.

Williams, W. D. *Nietzsche and the French: A Study of the Influence of Nietzsche's French Reading on His Thought and Writing.* Oxford, 1952.

II. NIETZSCHE'S TIME

Adams, Henry. *The Education of Henry Adams.* New York, 1931.

Andernach, Norbert. *Der Einfluss der Parteien auf das Hochschulwesen in Preussen, 1848–1919.* Göttingen, 1972.

Andreas-Salomé, Lou. *Lebensrückblick*, ed. Ernst Pfeiffer. Frankfurt/M., 1974.

Arnold, Matthew. *Culture and Anarchy.* Cambridge, 1957.

————. *Higher Schools and Universities in Germany.* London, 1874.

Die Aufgabe und Stellung der heutigen Burschenschaft. Eine Festgabe zum funfzigjährigen Burschenschaftsjubilaum. Jena, 1865.

Bachofen, Johann Jacob. *Gesammelte Werke.* Vol. 10. *Briefe.* Basel, 1967.

Bahr, Hermann. *Selbstbildnis.* Berlin, 1923.

Barkeley, Richard. *Die Deutsche Friedensbewegung, 1870–1933.* Hamburg, 1948.

Barnikol, Ernst. *Bruno Bauer: Studien und Materialien.* Assen, 1972.

Barth, Karl. *Protestant Theology in the Nineteenth Century.* Valley Forge, 1973.

Bauer, Bruno. *Zur Orientierung über die Bismarck'sche Aera.* Chemnitz, 1880. Repr. Aalen, 1969.

―――. "Die socialpolitische Bilanz d.J. 1881," *Internationale Monatsschrift* 1 (1882).

Baumgarten, Hermann. *Der deutsche Liberalismus: Eine Selbstkritik.* 1st ed., 1866. Repr. ed. Adolf M. Birke. Frankfurt/M., 1974.

Bebel, August. *Ausgewählte Reden und Schriften.* Vol. 1, Berlin, G.D.R., 1970.

Beer, G.R. de, ed. *Travellers in Switzerland.* London, 1949.

Biddiss, Michael D. *Father of Racist Ideology: The Social and Political Thought of Count Gobineau.* New York, 1970.

Biedermann, Karl. *Mein Leben und ein Stück Zeitgeschichte.* 2 vols. Breslau, 1886.

Bigler, Robert M. *The Politics of Protestantism: The Rise of the Protestant Church Elite in Prussia, 1815–1848.* Berkeley, 1972.

Binion, Rudolph. *Frau Lou: Nietzsche's Wayward Disciple.* Princeton, 1968.

Birker, Karl. *Die Deutschen Arbeiterbildungsvereine, 1840–1870.* Berlin, 1973.

Blackmore, John T. *Ernst Mach: His Work, Life and Influence.* Berkeley, 1972.

Blum, Hans. *Lebenserinnerungen.* Vol. 1. Berlin, 1907.

Blunt, Wilfrid. *The Dream King: Ludwig II of Bavaria.* New York, 1970.

Bocke, G. *Vom Niederrhein ins Baltenland: Erlebnisse und Beobachtungen eines deutschen Schulmeisters.* Hannover, 1925.

Bodelschwingh, Friedrich von. *Ausgewählte Schriften.* Bielefeld, 1955.

Bolle, Fritz. "Darwinismus und Zeitgeist." *Zeitschrift für Religions- und Geistesgeschichte* 14 (1962).

Boring, Edwin G. *A History of Experimental Psychology.* 2nd ed. New York, 1950.

Borkowsky, Ernst. *Naumburg a.d. S. Eine Geschichte deutschen Bürgertums, 1028 bis 1928.* Jena, 1928.

Brandes, Georg. "Gletscher (1885)." *Gesammelte Schriften.* Vol. 9, Munich, 1906.

Brazill, William J. *The Young Hegelians.* New Haven, 1970.

Broszat, Martin. *Zweihundert Jahre deutsche Polenpolitik.* Frankfurt/M. 2nd ed., 1972.

Buddensieg, Heinrich Wilh. Rob. *Erinnerungen an Heinrich Wilh. Rob. Buddensieg.* Eckartsberga, 1861.

Bücher, Karl. *Lebenserinnerungen.* Vol. 1, Tübingen, 1919.

Bülow, Bernhard von. *Memoirs of Prince von Bülow.* 4 vols., Boston, 1931–1932.

Burckhardt, Jacob. *Briefe,* ed. Max Burckhardt. Vols. 5–8. Basel, 1963–1974.

―――. *The Civilization of the Renaissance in Italy.* 2 vols. New York, 1958.

―――. *Griechische Kulturgeschichte.* Vol. 3. Stuttgart, 1952.

―――. *The Letters of Jacob Burckhardt,* ed. Alexander Dru. New York, 1955.

―――. *Weltgeschichtliche Betrachtungen.* Pfullingen, 1949.

Burckhardt, Paul. *Geschichte der Stadt Basel.* Basel, 1957.

Bussmann, Walter. *Treitschke, Sein Welt- und Geschichtsbild.* Göttingen, 1952.

―――. "Gustav Freytag, Massstäbe seiner Kulturkritik." *Archiv für Kulturgeschichte* 34 (1952).

Carlson, Andrew R. *Anarchism in Germany.* Vol. 1. Metuchen, N.J., 1972.

Cobet, Christoph. *Der Wortschatz des Antisemitsmus in der Bismarckzeit.* Munich, 1973.

Confino, Michael, ed. *Daughter of a Revolutionary. Natalie Herzen and the Bakunin/Nechayev Circle.* Lasalle, 1973.

Conrad-Martins, Hedwig. *Utopien der Menschenzüchtung: Der Sozialdarwinismus und seine Folgen.* Munich, 1955.

Conradi, Hermann. *Wilhelm II und die junge Generation: Eine zeitpsychologische Betrachtung.* Leipzig, [1889].

Corti, Egon Caesar Conte. *The English Empress: A Study in the Relations between*

Queen Victoria and Her Eldest Daughter, Empress Frederick of Germany. London, 1957.

Crusius, Otto. *Erwin Rohde: Ein biographischer Versuch.* Tübingen, 1902.

Deussen, Paul. *Erinnerungen an Friedrich Nietzsche.* Leipzig, 1901.

———. *Mein Leben.* Leipzig, 1922.

———. "Wie ich zu Schopenhauer kam." *Erstes Jahrbuch der Schopenhauer Gesellschaft.* Kiel, 1912.

Dewey, John. "From Absolutism to Experimentalism." In *On Experience, Nature, and Freedom,* ed. R. J. Bernstein. New York, 1960.

———. *The Influence of Darwin on Philosophy.* Repr. Bloomington, 1965.

Dickmann, Fritz. "Bismarck und Sachsen zur Zeit des Norddeutschen Bundes." *Neues Archiv für Sächsische Geschichte* 49 (1928).

Dietrich, Richard. "Der Kampf um das Schicksal Sachsens in der öffentlichen Meinung 1866/67." *Neues Archiv für Sächsische Geschichte und Altertumskunde* 58 (1937).

Dilthey, Wilhelm. *Gesammelte Schriften.* Vol. 5/11. Stuttgart, 1957/1960; Vol. 17. Göttingen, 1974.

———. *Der junge Dilthey. Ein Lebensbild in Briefen und Tagebüchern,* ed. Clara Misch. Stuttgart, 1960.

Dorpalen, Andreas. "Emperor Frederick III and the German Liberal Movement." *American Historical Review* 54 (1948).

Durr, Emil. *Jacob Burckhardt als Politischer Publizist: Mit seinem Zeitungsberichten aus dem Jahre 1844/5.* Zurich, 1937.

Ebrard, August. *Bericht des Erlanger Vereins für Felddiakonie über seine Tätigkeit im Kriege 1870/71.* Erlangen, 1871.

Eckardt, Julius von. *Lebenserinnerungen.* Vol. 1. Leipzig, 1910.

Eucken, Rudolf. *His Life Work and Travels. By Himself.* London, 1921.

Eulenberg, Franz. *Die Entwicklung der Universität Leipzig in den letzten hundert Jahren.* Leipzig, 1909.

Faber, Karl-Georg. "Realpolitik als Ideologie. Die Bedeutung des Jahres 1866 für das politische Denken in Deutschland." *Historische Zeitschrift* 203 (1966).

Farago, Ladislas and Andrew Sinclair. *Royal Web. The Story of Princess Victoria and Frederick of Prussia.* New York, 1982.

Fehr, Karl. "'Die öffentlichen Verleumder.' Zu einem Altersgedicht Gottfried Kellers." In *Gottfried Keller: Aufschlüsse und Deutungen.* Bern, 1972.

Fehrenbach, Elisabeth. *Wandlungen des deutschen Kaisergedankens 1871–1918.* Munich, 1969.

Feuerbach, Anselm. *Ein Vermächtnis.* Berlin, 1912.

Feuerbach, Ludwig. *Kleine Schriften.* Frankfurt/M., 1966.

Fischer, Fritz. *Moritz August von Bethmann-Hollweg und der Protestantismus.* Berlin, 1937.

Förster, Bernhard. *Parsifal-Nachklänge.* Leipzig, 1883.

Frank, Walter. *Hofprediger Adolf Stöcker und die christsoziale Bewegung.* Hamburg, 1935.

Freeman, Eugene. *The Categories of Charles Peirce.* Chicago, 1934.

Freund, Michael. *Das Drama der 99 Tage: Krankheit und Tod Friedrichs III.* Cologne, 1966.

Freytag, Gustav. *Auf der Höhe der Vogesen: Kriegsberichte von 1870/71.* Leipzig, 1914.

———. *Reminiscences of My Life.* 2 vols. London, 1890.

Froebel, Julius. *Die Gesichtspunkte und Aufgaben der Politik.* Leipzig, 1878. Repr. Aalen, 1971.

———. *Ein Lebenslauf.* 2 vols. Stuttgart, 1890–91.

Ganter, Theo. *Der Festumzug: Ein volkskundlicher Beitrag zum Festwesen des 19. Jahrhunderts in der Schweiz*. Basel, 1970.

Gay, Peter. *The Dilemma of Democratic Socialism: Eduard Bernstein's Challenge to Marx*. New York, 1962.

Gehring, Alex. *Genie und Verehrergemeinde*. Bonn, 1968.

Gersdorff, Carl von. *Die Briefe des Freiherrn Carl von Gersdorff an Friedrich Nietzsche*. Vol. 3, ed. Karl Schlechta. Vol. 4, ed. E. Thierbach. Weimar, 1936/1937.

Gollwitzer, Heinz. "Der Cäsarismus Napoleons III. im Widerhall der öffentlichen Meinung Deutschlands." *Historische Zeitschrift* 173 (1952).

———. *Europabild und Europagedanke*. Munich, 1964.

Griewank, Karl. "Wissenschaft und Kunst in der Politik Kaiser Wilhelms I. und Bismarcks." *Archiv für Kulturgeschichte* 34 (1952).

Grossmann-Vendrey, Susanna, ed. *Bayreuth in der deutschen Presse*. Regensburg, 1977.

Gruner, Erich. *Die Parteien in der Schweiz*. Bern, 1969.

———. "Die Schweiz als Schauplatz internationaler Macht- und Prinzipienkämpfe in der ersten Internationale." *Historische Zeitschrift* 204 (1967).

Grützner, Günter, *Die Pariser Kommune, Macht und Karriere einer politischen Legende: Die Auswirkungen auf das politische Denken in Deutschland*. Cologne, 1963.

Gutman, Robert W. *Richard Wagner*. New York, 1968.

Guyau, J.M. *Sittlichkeit ohne 'Pflicht.'* Leipzig, 1909.

Haffter, Heinz. "Geschichte der klassischen Philologie." In *Das Erbe der Antike,* ed. Fritz Wehrli. Zurich, 1963.

Hamann, Richard. *Die deutsche Malerei im 19. Jahrhundert*. Leipzig, 1914.

Hamann, Richard, and Jost Hermand. *Epochen Deutscher Kultur von 1870 bis zur Gegenwart*. 6 vols. Munich, 1971ff.

Hammer, Karl. *Deutsche Kriegstheologie, 1870–1918*. Munich, 1971.

Hanstein, Adalbert von. *Das jüngste Deutschland*. Leipzig, 1905.

Hart, James Morgan. *German Universities: A Narrative of Personal Experiences*. New York, 1874.

Haupt Hermann, and Paul Wentzcke, eds. *Hundert Jahre Deutscher Burschenschaft*. Heidelberg, 1921.

Hayes, Carlton J. H. *A Generation of Materialism, 1871–1900*. New York, 1941.

Heffter, Heinrich. *Die deutsche Selbstverwaltung im 19. Jahrhundert*. Stuttgart, 1950.

———. "Die Kreuzzeitungspartei und die Kartellpolitik Bismarcks." Dissertation. Leipzig, 1927.

Hege, Fritz, and Kurt Wassermann. *Naumburg: Stadt und Dom*. Dresden, 1952.

Henderson, W. O. *The Rise of German Industrial Power, 1834–1914*. Berkeley, 1975.

Hertel, Johannes. "Nekrolog auf Ernst Windisch." *Berichte über die Verhandlungen der Sächsischen Akademie der Wissenschaften. Philogisch-historische Klasse*. Vol. 73 (1921).

Herzen, Alexander. *My Past and Thoughts: The Memoirs of Alexander Herzen,* ed. Dwight Macdonald. New York, 1973.

Herzfeld, Hans. "Ernst Ludwig von Gerlach." *Mitteldeutscher Lebensbilder*. Vol. 5. Magdeburg, 1926.

Hinrichs, Carl. *Preussentum und Pietismus*. Göttingen, 1971.

His, Eduard. *Basler Gelehrte des 19. Jahrhunderts*. Basel, 1941.

———. *Basler Handelsherren des 19. Jahrhunderts*. Basel, 1929.

Howard, Michael. *The Franco-Prussian War*. New York, 1961.

Höfele, Karl Heinrich. "Sendungsglaube und Epochenbewusstsein in Deutschland." *Zeitschrift für Religions- und Geistesgeschichte* 15 (1963).

Hunziker, Guido. *Die Schweiz und das Nationalitätsprinzip im 19. Jahrhundert.* Basel, 1970.

Hübinger, Paul Egon. "Heinrich v. Sybel und der Bonner Philologenkrieg." *Historisches Jahrbuch* 83 (1964).

Ignotus, Paul. *The Paradox of Maupassant.* New York, 1968.

Irmen, Hans-Josef. "Richard Wagner und die öffentliche Meinung in Munich bis zur Uraufführung des Tristan." Edited by Carl Dahlhaus. *Richard Wagner. Werk und Wirkung.* Regensburg, 1971.

Isenschmid, Heinz. *Wilhelm Klein, 1825–1887: Ein freisinniger Politiker.* Basel, 1972.

James, Henry. *The Princess Casamassima.* Middlesex, 1977. 1st ed. 1886.

Kantzenbach, Friedrich Wilhelm. "Zur geistig-religiösen Situation der christlichen Konfessionen zwischen 1850 und 1860." *Zeitschrift für Religions- und Geistesgeschichte* 18 (1966).

Karbaum, Michael. *Studien zur Geschichte der Bayreuther Festspiele (1876–1976).* Vol. 1. Regensburg, 1976.

Kehr, Eckart. *Der Primat der Innenpolitik,* ed. H.-U. Wehler. Berlin, 1965.

Keller, Gottfried. *Gesammelte Gedichte.* Vol. 1. Stuttgart, 1914.

Kiesselbach, Wilhelm. "Drei Generationen." *Socialpolitische Studien.* Stuttgart, 1862.

Klose, O., E. G. Jacoby, I. Fischer, eds. *Ferdinand Tönnies–Friedrich Paulsen Briefwechsel, 1876–1908.* Kiel, 1961.

Kretzschmar, Hellmut. "Das Sächsische Königtum im 19. Jahrhundert." *Historische Zeitschrift* 170 (1950).

Kropotkin, P. A. *Selected Writings on Anarchism and Revolution.* Cambridge, Mass., 1970.

Kupisch, Karl. *Vom Pietismus zum Kommunismus: Zur Jugendentwicklung von Friedrich Engels.* Berlin, 1953.

Lehmann, Hartmut. "Friedrich von Bodelschwingh und das Sedanfest. Ein Beitrag zum nationalen Denken der politisch aktiven Richtung im deutschen Pietismus des 19 Jahrhunderts." *Historische Zeitschrift* 202 (1966).

Lidtke, Vernon L. *The Outlawed Party: Social Democracy in Germany, 1878–1890.* Princeton, 1966.

Liebeschütz, Hans. *Das Judentum im deutschen Geschichtsbild von Hegel bis Max Weber.* Tübingen, 1967.

Loubére, Leo A. *Radicalism in Mediterranean France: Its Rise and Decline, 1848–1914.* Albany, 1974.

Löhneysen, Wolfgang Frhr. von. "Der Einfluss der Reichsgründung von 1871 auf Kunst und Kunstgeschmack in Deutschland." *Zeitschrift für Religions- und Geistesgeschichte* 12 (1960).

Lukács, Georg. *Deutsche Realisten des 19. Jahrhunderts.* Bern, 1951.

———. "The Zola Centenary." In *Studies in European Realism.* New York, 1964.

Luthi, Walter. "Die Struktur des Basler Grossen Rat von 1875 bis 1914 nach politischer Parteizugehörigkeit und sozialer Schichtung." *Basler Zeitschrift für Geschichte und Altertumkunde* 62 (1962): 63 (1963).

Martini, Fritz. *Deutsche Literatur im bürgerlichen Realismus, 1848–1898.* Stuttgart, 1962.

Massing, Paul W. *Rehearsal for Destruction: A Study of Political Anti-Semitism in Imperial Germany.* New York, 1949.

Mayer, Gustav. *Friedrich Engels: Eine Biographie.* 2 vols. The Hague, 1934.

———. *Johann Baptist von Schweitzer und die Sozialdemokratie.* Jena, 1909.

——— *Radikalismus, Sozialismus und bürgerliche Demokratie,* ed. H.-U. Wehler. Frankfurt/M, 1968.

McGrath, William J. *Dionysian Art and Populist Politics in Austria.* New Haven, 1974.

Meier-Graefe, Julius. *Hans von Marées.* 3 vols. Munich, 1909–1910.

Meinecke, Friedrich. "Drei Generationen deutscher Gelehrtenpolitik." *Historische Zeitschrift* 125 (1922).

———. "Ranke in der Auffassung von Ottokar von Lorenz und die Generationslehre" (1891). In *Zur Geschichte der Geschichtsschribung.* Munich, 1968.

Merton, Robert. Preface to *The Crowd,* by Gustave Le Bon. New York, 1966.

Meyer, Michael. *Ibsen: A Biography.* Garden City, 1971.

Meysenbug, Malwida von. *Briefe von und an Malwida von Meysenbug,* ed. Berta Schleicher. Berlin, 1920.

———. *Im Anfang war die Liebe: Briefe an ihre Pflegetochter.* Munich, 1926.

———. *Der Lebensabend einer Idealisten.* Berlin, 1898.

Mommsen, Wilhelm. "Julius Fröbel: Wirrnis und Weltsicht." *Historische Zeitschrift* 181 (1956).

Müller, Georg Hermann. *Das Stadt-Theater zu Leipzig von 1. Januar 1862 bis 1. September 1887.* Leipzig, 1887.

Müller, Harald. "Die deutsche Arbeiterklasse und die Sedanfeiern: Zum antimilitarischen Kampf der Sozialdemokratischen Arbeiterpartei in den ersten Jahren nach der Reichsgründung." *Zeitschrift für Geschichtswissenschaft* 17 (1969).

Müller, Joachim. "Der Historiker Johann Heinrich Wuttke als Politiker." *Karl-Marx-Universität Leipzig, 1409–1959.* Vol. 1, Leipzig, 1959.

Neubach, Helmut. *Die Ausweisungen von Polen und Juden aus Preussen, 1885/86.* Wiesbaden, 1967.

Niebour, Hermann. "Die Abgeordneten des Provinz Sachsen in der Frankfurter Nationalversammlung." *Thüringisch-Sächsische Zeitschrift für Geschichte und Kunst* 4 (1914).

Nigg, Walter, *Franz Overbeck: Versuch einer Würdigung.* Munich, 1931.

Nipperdey, Thomas. "Nationalidee und Nationaldenkmal im Deutschland im 19. Jahrhundert." *Historische Zeitschrift* 206 (1968), 529–585.

Noyes, George Rapall. *Tolstoy.* New York, 1968. 1st ed., 1918.

Oehler, Adalbert. *Nietzsches Mutter.* Munich, 1941.

Overbeck, Franz. *Christentum und Kultur.* Basel, 1919. Repr. Darmstadt, 1973.

———. *Selbstbekenntnisse,* ed. Jacob Taube. Frankfurt/M., 1966.

———. *Über die Christlichkeit unserer heutigen Theologie.* 2nd ed. Leipzig, 1903. Repr. Darmstadt, 1963.

Pater, Walter. *Greek Studies: A Series of Essays.* London, 1901.

Paterson, R. W. K. *The Nihilistic Egoist Max Stirner.* Hull, 1971.

Patze Hans, and Walter Schlesinger, eds. *Geschichte Thüringens.* Vol. 4. *Kirche und Staat in der Neuzeit.* Cologne, 1971.

Paulsen, Friedrich. *An Autobiography.* New York, 1938.

Perosa, Sergio. *Henry James and the Experimental Novel.* Charlottesville, 1978.

Peter, Hermann. "Peter: Karl Ludwig." *Allgemeine Deutsche Biographie* 53 (1907).

Peters, H. F. *My Sister, My Spouse: A Biography of Lou Andreas-Salomé.* New York, 1974.

———. *Zarathustra's Sister: The Case of Elisabeth and Friedrich Nietzsche.* New York, 1977.

Pflanze, Otto. *Bismarck and the Development of Germany, 1815–1871.* Princeton, 1963.

Philippi, Hans. "Preussisch-sächsische Verstimmungen im Jahrzehnt nach der Reichsgründung." *Jahrbuch für die Geschichte Mittel- und Ostdeutschlands* 15 (1966).

Podach, Erich. *Gestalten um Nietzsche: Mit unveröffentlichten Dokumenten zur Geschichte seines Lebens und seines Werkes.* Weimar, 1932.

Poschinger, Margarethe von. *Diaries of the Emperor Frederick.* London, 1902.

Pulzer, Peter G. J. *The Rise of Political Anti-Semitism in Germany and Austria.* New York, 1964.

Reichle, Walter. *Zwischen Staat und Kirche: Das Leben und Wirken des preussischen Kulturministers Heinrich v. Mühler.* Berlin, 1938.

Rée, Paul. *Philosophie.* Berlin, 1903.

Ribbeck, Otto. *Ein Bild seines Leben aus seinem Briefen, 1846–1898.* Stuttgart, 1901.

———. *Friedrich Wilhelm Ritschl.* 2 vols. Leipzig, 1879/1881.

Ritter, Armgard. "Der Einfluss des Dreissigjahrigen Krieges auf die Stadt Naumburg." *Thüringisch-Sächsische Zeitschrift für Geschichte und Kunst* 15 (1926).

Rochau, Ludwig August von. *Grundsätze der Realpolitik.* Repr. ed. H.-U. Wehler. Frankfurt/M., 1972.

Rodenberg, Julius. *Aus seinem Tagebüchern.* Berlin, 1919.

Rohde, Erwin. *Psyche: Seelenkult und Unsterblichkeitsglaube.* Leipzig, n.d.

Rohr, D. G. *The Origins of Social Liberalism in Germany.* Chicago, 1963.

Rosenberg, Hans. *Grosse Depression und Bismarckzeit.* Berlin, 1967.

———. "Honoratiorenpolitiker und 'Grossdeutsche' Sammlungsbestrebungen im Reichgründungsjahrzehnt." *Jahrbuch für die Geschichte Mittel- und Ostdeutschland* 19 (1970).

———. *Rudolf Haym und die Anfänge des klassischen Liberalismus.* Munich & Berlin. 1933.

Ruskin, John. *The Crown of Wild Olive.* London, 1906.

Rümelin, Gustav. "Über den Begriff und die Dauer einer Generation." *Reden und Aufsätze,* Vol. 1. Freiburg, 1875.

Schaffner, Martin. *Die Basler Arbeiterbevölkerung im 19. Jahrhundert.* Basel, 1972.

Schanze, Helmut. *Drama in Bürgerlichen Realismus.* Frankfurt/M., 1973.

Schieder, Theodor. *Das Deutsche Kaiserreich von 1871 als Nationalstaat.* Cologne, 1961.

Schleich, Carl Ludwig. *Besonnte Vergangenheit: Lebenserinnerungen, 1859–1919.* Leipzig, 1977.

Schmidt, Julian. *Bilder aus dem geistigen Leben unserer Zeit.* 2 vols. Leipzig, 1870/1871.

Schorske, Carl E. "The Quest for the Grail: Wagner and Morris." Edited by K. Wolff and B. Moore. *The Critical Spirit: Essays in Honor of Herbert Marcuse.* Boston, 1967.

Schulze, Friedrich. *Hundert Jahre Leipziger Stadttheater.* Leipzig, 1917.

Schüler, Winfried. *Der Bayreuther Kreis von seiner Entstehung bis zum Ausgang der Wilhelminischen Aera.* Münster, 1971.

Seier, Hellmut. "Sybels Vorlesung über Politik und die Kontinuität des 'staatsbildenden' Liberalismus." *Historische Zeitschrift* 187 (1959).

Seillière, Ernst. *Nietzsches Waffenbruder, Erwin Rohde.* Berlin, 1911.

Siemens-Helmholtz, Ellen von. *Anna von Helmholtz.* Vol. 1. Berlin, 1929.

Silberstein, Adolf. *Im Strome der Zeit.* 4 vols. Budapest, 1894–1895.

Silverman, Dan P. *Reluctant Union. Alsace-Lorraine and Imperial Germany, 1871–1918.* University Park, 1972.

Spitteler, Carl. *Autobiographische Schriften.* Zürich, 1947.

Springer, Anton. *Aus meinem Leben.* Berlin, 1892.

Stackelberg, R. "The Role of H. v. Stein in Nietzsche's Emergence as a Critic of Wagnerian Idealism and Cultural Nationalism." *Nietzsche-Studien* 5 (1976).

Stadler, Peter. "Die Schweiz und die deutsche Reichsgründung." *Geschichte in Wissenschaft und Unterricht.* 25 (1974).

Staehelin, Andreas. *Geschichte der Universität Basel, 1818–1835.* Basel, 1959.

Staehelin, Ernst, ed. *Overbeckiana.* 2 vols. Basel, 1960/1962.

Stein, Heinrich von. *Idee und Welt,* ed. Guenter Ralfs. Stuttgart, 1940.

Stern, Fritz. *The Politics of Cultural Despair.* Berkeley, 1961.

Strauss, David Friedrich. *Ausgewählte Briefe.* Bonn, 1895.

Strindberg, August. *Die Entwicklung einer Seele.* Munich, 1916.

Sybel, Heinrich von. *Vorträge und Aufsätze.* Berlin, 1874.

Taylor, A. J. P. *Germany's First Bid for Colonies, 1884–1885: A Move in Bismarck's European Policy.* London, 1938.

Teichmann, Albert. *Die Universität Basel in den fünfzig Jahren seit ihrer Reorganisation im Jahre 1835.* Basel, 1885.

Tolstoy, Leo. *A Confession: The Gospel in Brief and What I Believe.* London, 1971.

Treitschke, Heinrich von. *Heinrich von Trietschkes Briefe,* ed. Max Cornicelius. Vol. 3. Leipzig, 1920.

———. *Politics,* ed. Hans Kohn. New York, 1963.

Trilling, Lionel. "The Princess Casamassima." In *The Liberal Imagination: Essays on Literature and Society.* New York, 1950.

Van der Kiste, John. *Frederick III.* Gloucester, 1981.

Vaihinger, Hans. *Die Philosophie des Als Ob.* Leipzig, 1922.

Virtanen, Reino. *Claude Bernard and His Place in the History of Ideas.* Lincoln, 1960.

Vischer, Eduard. *Wilhelm Vischer. Gelehrter und Ratsherr, 1808–1874, im Spiegel seiner Korrespondenz mit Rudolf Rauchenstein.* Basel, 1958.

Voss, Richard. *Aus einem phantastischen Leben.* Stuttgart, 1920.

Wagner, Cosima. *Die Briefe Cosima Wagners an Friedrich Nietzsche.* Edited by Erhart Thierbach. 2 vol. Weimar, 1938/1941.

———. *Die Tagebücher, 1869–1877.* Vol. 1. Munich, 1976.

Wagner, Richard. *Mein Leben.* 2 vols. Munich, 1969.

———. *Richard Wagner's Prose Works.* Vol. 6. London, 1897.

Weber, Robert. *Geschichte des klassisch-philogischen Vereines zu Leipzig von 1865–1890.* Leipzig, n.d.

Wehler, H.-U. *Krisenherde des Kaiserreichs.* Göttingen, 1970.

———. *Bismarck und der Imperialismus.* Cologne, 1969.

Wentzcke, Paul, ed. *Im Neuen Reich, 1871–1890: Politische Briefe aus dem Nachlass liberaler Parteiführer.* 2nd ed. Osnabrück, 1970.

Wiener, Philip P. *Evolution and the Founders of Pragmatism.* Philadelphia, 1972.

Wilamowitz-Möllendorff, Ulrich von. *My Recollections, 1848–1914.* London, 1930.

Wilson, R. Jackson. *In Quest of Community: Social Philosophy in the United States, 1860–1920.* London, 1968.

Wolzogen, Hans von. *Lebensbilder.* Regensburg, 1923.

Woodcock, George. *The Anarchist Prince: Peter Kropotkin.* New York, 1971.

Wundt, Wilhelm. *Erlebtes und Erkanntes.* Stuttgart, 1920.

———. "Philosophy in Germany." *Mind* 2 (1877).

Young, E. J. *Gobineau und der Rassismus.* Meisenheim am Glau, 1968.

Zimmermann, G. A. *Kriegs-Erinnerungen.* Milwaukee, 1895.

Zmarzlik, Hans-Günter. "Der Sozialdarwinismus in Deutschland." *Vierteljahrshefte für Zeitgeschichte* 11 (1963).

Zola, Emile. "The Experimental Novel." In *Documents of Modern Literary Realism,* ed. George J. Becker, Princeton, 1963.

III. GENERAL

Arendt, Dieter. "Der Nihilismus—Ursprung und Geschichte im Spiegel der Forschungs-Literatur seit 1945." *Deutsche Vierteljahrsschrift für Literaturwissenschaft und Geistesgeschichte* 43 (1969).

Auerbach, Erich. *Mimesis.* [1st ed., Princeton, 1953] Garden City, 1957.

Bunzel, John H. *Anti-politics in America.* New York, 1967.

Butterfield, Herbert. "The Discontinuities between the Generations in History." *The Rede Lecture 1971.* Cambridge, 1972.

Dehio, Ludwig. *The Precarious Balance: Four Centuries of European Power Struggle.* New York, 1962.

Ellul, Jacques. *The Political Illusion.* New York, 1967.

Engel, Hans. *Musik in Thüringen.* Cologne, 1966.

Feuer, Lewis. *The Conflict of Generations.* New York, 1969.

Heinrich, Klaus. *Parmenides and Jona: Vier Studien über das Verhältnis von Philosophie and Mythologie.* Frankfurt/M, 1966.

Hof, Walter. *Pessimistisch-nihilistische Strömungen in der deutschen Literatur vom Sturm und Drang bis zum Jungen Deutschland.* Tübingen, 1970.

Horowitz, Irving L., ed. *The Anarchists.* New York, 1964.

Joll, James. *The Anarchists.* Boston, 1964.

Jost, Dominik. *Literarischer Jugendstil.* Stuttgart, 1969.

Kaiser, Gerhard. *Pietismus und Patriotismus in literarischen Deutschland.* Wiesbaden, 1961.

Kobler, Franz, ed. *Juden und Judentum in Deutschen Briefen aus Drei Jahrhunderten.* Vienna, 1935.

Kreuzer, Helmut. *Die Boheme.* Stuttgart, 1968.

Kuhlen, R. and U. Schneider. "Experimentalphilosophie." *Historische Wörterbuch der Philosophie.* Vol. 2. Basel, 1972.

Langen, August. *Der Wortschatz des deutschen Pietismus.* Tübingen, 1968.

Lehmann, Hartmut. *Pietismus und weltliche Ordnung in Württemburg.* Stuttgart, 1969.

Leitschuh, Franz Friedrich. *Die Schweizer Landschaft in der deutschen Malerei.* Leipzig, 1924.

Lessing, Theodor. *Untergang der Erde am Geist.* Hannover, 1924.

Lichtheim, George. *Europe in the Twentieth Century.* New York, 1972.

———. *The Concept of Ideology.* New York, 1967.

Lukács, Georg. *Studies in European Realism.* New York, 1964.

Lucas, John, ed. *Literature and Politics in the Nineteenth Century.* London, 1971.

Lübbe, Hermann. *Politische Philosophie in Deutschland.* Basel, 1963.

Mann, Thomas. *Betrachtungen eines Unpolitischen.* Frankfurt/M., 1968. 1st ed. 1918.

Marcuse, Ludwig. *Amerikanisches Philosophieren Pragmatisten Polytheisten, Tragiker.* Hamburg, 1959.

Marias, Juan. *Generations.* University, 1972.

Mosse, George L. *The Nationalization of the Masses: Political Symbolism and Mass Movements in Germany from the Napoleonic Wars through the Third Reich.* New York, 1975.

Nolte, Ernst. *Three Faces of Fascism.* New York, 1966.

Paine, Thomas. *The Rights of Man.* New York, 1961.

Pinson, Koppel Shub. *Pietism as a Factor in the Rise of German Nationalism.* New York, 1934.

Poggioli, Renato. *The Theory of the Avant-Garde.* New York, 1971.

Politzer, Heinz. *Hatte Oedipus einen Oedipus-Komplex?* Munich, 1974.

Riedel, Manfred. *Wandel des Generationsproblems in der modernen Gesellschaft.* Düsseldorf, 1969.

Rocker, Rudolf. *Nationalism and Culture.* New York, 1937.

Rosenberg, Hans. *Politische Denkströmungen im deutschen Vormärz,* Göttingen, 1972.

————. *Probleme der deutschen Sozialgeschichte.* Frankfurt/M, 1969.

Salis, J. R. de. *Switzerland and Europe.* London, 1971.

Sauer, Wolfgang. "Das Problem des deutschen Nationalstaates." In *Moderne deutsche Sozialgeschichte,* ed. H.-U. Wehler. Cologne, 1966.

Schnabel, Franz. "Die Denkmalkunst und der Geist des 19. Jahrhunderts." *Abhandlungen und Vorträge, 1914–1965.* Basel, 1970.

Schoene, Albrecht. *Säkularisation als sprachbildende Kraft: Studien zur Dichtung deutscher Pfarrersöhne.* Göttingen. 1958.

Schopenhauer, Arthur. *The World as Will and Idea.* 2 vols. London, 1957.

Schuhmann, Detlev W. "Cultural Age-Groups in German Thought." *PMLA* (1935).

Schweitzer, Albert. *Geschichte der Leben-Jesu-Forschung.* 2 vols. Munich, 1966.

Stern, J. P. *Re-interpretations.* London, 1964.

Vagts, Alfred. *A History of Militarism.* Rev. ed., New York, 1959.

Valéry, Paul. *The Collected Works of Paul Valéry,* ed. Jackson Matthews. Vol. 9. Princeton, 1968.

Venturi, Franco. *Roots of Revolution.* New York. 1960.

Vierhaus, Rudolf. "Bildung." *Geschichtliche Grundbegriffe,* ed. O. Brunner, W. Conze, & R. Kosselleck. Vol. 1. A–D. Stuttgart, 1972.

Vlastos, Gregory, ed. *Plato. A Collection of Critical Essays.* Vol. 2. Garden City, 1971.

Vogel, Martin. *Apollinisch und Dionysisch: Geschichte eines genialen Irrtums.* Regensburg, 1966.

Walker, Mack. *German Home Towns: Community, State, and General Estate, 1648–1871.* Ithaca, 1971.

Weber, Max. *The Sociology of Religion.* Boston, 1964.

Weil, Hans. *Die Enstehung des deutschen Bildungsprinzip.* Bonn, 1930.

Wellek, René. *The Later Nineteenth Century.* Vol. 4. *A History of Modern Criticism: 1750–1950.* New Haven, 1965.

Weymar, Ernst. *Das Selbstverständnis der Deutschen: Ein Bericht über den Geist des Geschichtsunterrichts des höheren Schulen im 19. Jahrhundert.* Stuttgart, 1961.

Widmann, Wilhelm. *Theater und Revolution.* Berlin, 1920.

Wilson, A. Leslie. *A Mythical Image: The Ideal of India in German Romanticism.* Durham, 1964.

Wolin, Sheldon. *Politics and Vision.* Boston, 1960.

INDEX

Adams, Henry, 165
Adler, Viktor, 92
agonism, 4, 60–64, 75–76, 78, 81, 87, 92, 94, 99, 108–109, 112, 116; anti-motif, 61
Aiken, Henry David, 159, 186
Alexander II, Czar, 145, 147, 171
Alexander of Battenberg, 165
Alexander the Great, 181
Alps, Alpinism, 138, 158–159
Alsace and Lorraine, 75, 80, 83, 85–86, 94–95
America, 27, 148, 150, 153, 164
anarchism, 4, 145, 147, 213
Andreas-Salomé, Lou von, 113, 153, 154, 155, 156, 158, 170
antipolitical, antipolitics, 1–8, 55, 59, 82, 164, 176–177, 183–186, 188–190; Forebel, 2–3, 4, 59; Paine, 2; Weber, 5; Wolin, 5–6, 190; Plato, 190; N.'s interpreters, 1–2, 188–189; religious politics, 9–12, 48; Schopenhauerian, 43, 46–47, 50, 62; academic professionalism, 52; N.'s Wagnerianism, 82; Dionysus, 87; N.'s exegesis of failure, 185
anti-self, 5, 29, 142, 159
anti-Semitism, 1, 43, 66, 114, 121, 142, 155, 157, 163, 170, 202; N.'s youthful prejudice, 43, 77; Schopenhauer & Wagner, 76–78, 98, 102, 122; Dühring, 124–126; politicized, 143–144; 1881 election, 148–150; Bismarckian succession crisis, 171–173; N.'s entanglement in, 142; N. attacks, 176, 179
aphorism, 108, 111, 117, 129–134, 147, 150–151, 159–160
Apollonian, 4–5, 75, 86
Arnim, Harry von, 119
Arnold, Matthew, 3, 19–20
Auber, Daniel, 65
Auden, W. H., 127
Augusta, Empress, 173
Austria, 20, 37, 47, 63, 68, 85
avant-garde, 7, 133, 161, 170, 186

Baader, Franz von, 146
Bach, Johann Sebastian, 18
Bachofen, Johann Jacob, 74, 75, 90, 203
Bacon, Francis, 112
Bahnsen, Julius, 140
Bahr, Hermann, 157
Bakunin, Mikhail, 66, 74, 86, 116, 120, 203
Basel, city and university, 51, 107, 108, 110–112, 117, 120, 125, 128, 151, 156; N.'s first year, 70–75, 81; Franco-Prussian War, 84–

86, 203; internal politics, 88–92, 93, 94; "Basel v. Berlin," 97–100, 106, 205; fall of patriciate, 104–106; pietism, 144, 207; N.'s statelessness, 204; N.'s pension, 215
Baudelaire, Charles, 67
Bauer, Bruno, 11, 52, 129, 149, 150, 161, 169
Baumgarten, Hermann, 68
Baumgartner, Adolf, 95, 128
Baumgartner, Marie, 94, 107
Bavaria, 67–68, 78, 83
Bayreuth, 3, 77; N.'s break with, 108–110, 114–115, 124–129, 143, 155, 156, 176. See Wagner
Bebel, August, 20, 52–53, 57, 74, 121, 122
Becker, Bernhard, 53
Beethoven, Ludwig van, 65, 78
Bellamy, Edward, 148
Berg, Leo, 170
Berlin, 32, 35, 42, 63, 83, 94, 121, 124, 144, 148–149, 156, 177; N.'s polemic against, 98–99, 106–107, 205
Berlioz, Hector, 24
Bernard, Claude, 133, 134
Bernays, Jacob, 75
Bernstein, Eduard, 57, 122
Bethmann-Hollweg, Moritz August von, 23
Bethmann Hollweg, Theobald von, 93
Biedermann, Karl, 47–49, 52, 193
Bildung, 19–23, 35–36, 52–53, 69, 92, 99, 106–107, 122
Binion, Rudolph, 156
Bismarck, Otto von, 57, 165–167, 169; & N., 30–32, 182, 185; ascendancy, 34–37, 39–41; war of 1866, 46–49, 56, 59, 62, 64, 68–69, 85, 88, 90, 95, 100, 102; change of course, 119–120, 122, 125, 128, 147, 148, 149; colonial policy, 162–163; succession crisis, 171–172, 174–175; N.'s Bismarckianism, 46–64; N. repudiates, 177–179
Björnson, Björnsterne, 29
Blanqui, Auguste, 140
Blum, Robert, 22
Bodelschwingh, Pastor Friedrich von, 88, 202
Böcklin, Arnold, 90
Bonn, town and university, 27, 38–44, 52, 65, 93–94
Boulanger, Boulangist agitation, 171, 178, 181
Bourget, Paul, 159
Brahms, Johannes, 57, 73, 104, 158
Brandes, George, 57, 158, 169–170, 173, 176, 177, 182, 217

Peter Bergmann has taught at the University of San
Francisco and Bates College, and is currently on the
history faculty at Wellesley College.

EDITOR: *Roberta L. Diehl*
BOOK DESIGNER: *Matthew Williamson*
JACKET DESIGNER: *Matthew Williamson*
PRODUCTION COORDINATOR: *Harriet Curry*
TYPEFACE: *ITC Garamond with Benguiat Medium*
TYPESETTER: *Modern Typographers, Inc. of Florida*
PRINTER: *Braun-Brumfield, Inc.*
BINDER: *Braun-Brumfield, Inc.*